AVAILABLE ON
DISKETTE

BANK PROFITABILITY
Financial Statements
of Banks
[1979–1991]

The data, provided on either 5 1/4" or 3 1/2" double-sided, double-density diskettes formatted on both sides, suitable for IBM or IBM-compatible microcomputers, are supplied in a compressed format specific to OECD. The diskettes include a simple program for transferring data into DIF, SYLK, or LOTUS WKS formats. Data can therefore be readily used with such software packages as LOTUS 1-2-3, QUATTRO-PRO, EXCEL and the MS-DOS operating system.

Full technical documentation and a detailed section on "Definitions" accompanies each data package.

The price for the 1993 edition of this annual diskette has been fixed at:

FF 1 200   US\$ 215   £ 135   DM 365

with discounts for academic circles and government agencies. Subscribers wishing to redistribute the statistics shall be required to complete a special contract.

Orders or enquiries should be sent to OECD Electronic Editions in Paris, one of OECD's Publication and Information Centres in Bonn, Tokyo or Washington, or the OECD Distributor in your country.

OECD
Electronic Editions
2, rue André-Pascal, 75775 Paris Cedex 16, France
Fax: (33)1-45.24.98.99

RENTABILITÉ DES BANQUES
Comptes des banques [1979–1991]

Les données sont fournies sur des disquettes double face, double densité formatées sur chaque face de format 5 pouces 1/4 ou 3 pouces 1/2 pour les micro-ordinateurs IBM ou compatibles. Les données sont enregistrées dans un format compacté particulier à l'OCDE. Un programme simple est disponible sur les disquettes permettant le transfert des données dans un format DIF, SYLK, ou LOTUS WKS. Les données peuvent ainsi être facilement utilisées avec les logiciels tels que LOTUS 1-2-3, QUATTRO-PRO, EXCEL et le système d'exploitation MS-DOS.

Chaque livraison est accompagnée d'une documentation technique complète et d'une section détaillée sur les « Définitions ».

Le prix pour l'édition 1993 de cette disquette, mise à jour annuellement, a été fixé à :

FF 1 200	US$ 215	£ 135	DM 365

Des remises sont accordées aux universités, au corps enseignant et aux organismes gouvernementaux. Les abonnés désireux d'acquérir les disquettes afin d'assurer une rediffusion des données doivent remplir un contrat spécial.

Pour vous procurer cette disquette ou pour tout renseignement, contacter les Éditions Électroniques de l'OCDE à Paris, l'un des Centres des Publications et d'Information de l'OCDE à Bonn, Tokyo ou Washington, ou le distributeur OCDE dans votre pays.

OCDE
Éditions Électroniques
2, rue André-Pascal, 75775 Paris Cedex 16, France
Fax : (33)1-45.24.98.99

BANK PROFITABILITY

RENTABILITÉ DES BANQUES

STATISTICAL SUPPLEMENT
SUPPLÉMENT STATISTIQUE

FINANCIAL
STATEMENTS OF BANKS
COMPTES DES BANQUES

1982-1991

ORGANISATION FOR ECONOMIC CO-OPERATION AND DEVELOPMENT
ORGANISATION DE COOPÉRATION ET DE DÉVELOPPEMENT ÉCONOMIQUES

ORGANISATION FOR ECONOMIC CO-OPERATION AND DEVELOPMENT

ORGANISATION DE COOPÉRATION ET DE DÉVELOPPEMENT ÉCONOMIQUES

Pursuant to Article 1 of the Convention signed in Paris on 14th December 1960, and which came into force on 30th September 1961, the Organisation for Economic Co-operation and Development (OECD) shall promote policies designed:

— to achieve the highest sustainable economic growth and employment and a rising standard of living in Member countries, while maintaining financial stability, and thus to contribute to the development of the world economy;
— to contribute to sound economic expansion in Member as well as non-member countries in the process of economic development; and
— to contribute to the expansion of world trade on a multilateral, non-discriminatory basis in accordance with international obligations.

The original Member countries of the OECD are Austria, Belgium, Canada, Denmark, France, Germany, Greece, Iceland, Ireland, Italy, Luxembourg, the Netherlands, Norway, Portugal, Spain, Sweden, Switzerland, Turkey, the United Kingdom and the United States. The following countries became Members subsequently through accession at the dates indicated hereafter: Japan (28th April 1964), Finland (28th January 1969), Australia (7th June 1971) and New Zealand (29th May 1973). The Commission of the European Communities takes part in the work of the OECD (Article 13 of the OECD Convention).

En vertu de l'article 1er de la Convention signée le 14 décembre 1960, à Paris, et entrée en vigueur le 30 septembre 1961, l'Organisation de Coopération et de Développement Economiques (OCDE) a pour objectif de promouvoir des politiques visant :

— à réaliser la plus forte expansion de l'économie et de l'emploi et une progression du niveau de vie dans les pays Membres, tout en maintenant la stabilité financière, et à contribuer ainsi au développement de l'économie mondiale ;
— à contribuer à une saine expansion économique dans les pays Membres, ainsi que les pays non membres, en voie de développement économique ;
— à contribuer à l'expansion du commerce mondial sur une base multilatérale et non discriminatoire conformément aux obligations internationales.

Les pays Membres originaires de l'OCDE sont : l'Allemagne, l'Autriche, la Belgique, le Canada, le Danemark, l'Espagne, les Etats-Unis, la France, la Grèce, l'Irlande, l'Islande, l'Italie, le Luxembourg, la Norvège, les Pays-Bas, le Portugal, le Royaume-Uni, la Suède, la Suisse et la Turquie. Les pays suivants sont ultérieurement devenus Membres par adhésion aux dates indiquées ci-après : le Japon (28 avril 1964), la Finlande (28 janvier 1969), l'Australie (7 juin 1971) et la Nouvelle-Zélande (29 mai 1973). La Commission des Communautés européennes participe aux travaux de l'OCDE (article 13 de la Convention de l'OCDE).

FOREWARD

The present statistical supplement includes data on financial statements of banks for the period 1982-1991. It thus updates the data on financial statements of banks published in "Bank Profitability, Statistical Supplement, Financial Statements of Banks 1981-90", OECD, Paris, 1992. The coverage of banks in these statistics is not the same in each country, though the objective is to cover all institutions which conduct ordinary banking business, namely institutions which primarily take deposits from the public at large and provide finance for a wide range of purposes. Some supplementary information on the number of reporting banks, their branches and staff is also included.

The institutional coverage of the tables has been largely dictated by the availability of data on income and expenditure accounts of banks. As a result of the reporting methods which are being used in OECD countries, the tables are not integrated in the system of national accounts and are, therefore, not compatible with the "Financial Accounts of OECD Countries". International comparisons in the field of income and expenditure accounts of banks are particularly difficult due to considerable differences in OECD countries as regards structural and regulatory features of national banking systems, accounting rules and practices, and reporting methods.

The statistical part is updated and published annually while the methodological country notes are issued less frequently. The next version of the methological notes is scheduled for publication in the course of 1993.

The preparation of this publication could not have been accomplished without the assistance of the members of the OECD Group of Financial Statisticians and the national administrations which they represent. It is published, on the Group's recommendation, under the responsibility of the Secretary-General.

AVANT-PROPOS

Le présent supplément statistique contient les données relatives aux comptes de résultats et aux bilans des banques pour la période 1982-91. Ainsi, sont mises à jour et étendues les statistiques publiées dans "Rentabilité des Banques, Supplément Statistique, Comptes des Banques 1981-90", OCDE, Paris, 1992. Les banques sur lesquelles portent ces statistiques ne sont pas les mêmes selon les pays, mais l'objectif est d'englober toutes les institutions qui effectuent des opérations courantes de banque, c'est-à-dire qui reçoivent des dépôts du public et offrent des concours destinés à financer un large éventail de besoins. Figurent en outre des renseignements complémentaires sur le nombre de banques qui communiquent leurs données, celui de leurs succursales et de leurs salariés.

La délimitation du cercle des institutions recensées dans les tableaux a été, en grande partie, dictée par les données existantes sur les comptes de résultats des banques. Du fait des modes de communication des données en vigueur dans les pays de l'OCDE, ces tableaux ne sont pas intégrés dans le Système de comptabilité nationale et ne sont donc pas compatibles avec les "Comptes financiers des pays de l'OCDE". Les comparaisons internationales sont délicates étant donné les différences qui existent entre les pays en ce qui concerne la structure du système bancaire et la réglementation des banques, les règles et pratiques comptables et le système de communication des données.

La partie statistique est mise à jour et publiée annuellement tandis que les notes méthodologiques par pays sont émises moins souvent. La prochaine version des notes méthodologiques est prévue pour courant 1993.

Ces statistiques n'auraient pu être établies sans l'aide des membres du Groupe de statisticiens financiers de l'OCDE ni de celle des administrations nationales qu'ils représentent. Elles sont publiées, sur la recommandation du Groupe, sous la responsabilité du Secrétaire Général.

ÉGALEMENT DISPONIBLES

La Concurrence dans le secteur bancaire *par G. Bröker* . Série Tendances de la structure et de la réglementation des systèmes bancaires dans les pays de l'OCDE (1989)
(21 89 01 2) ISBN 92-64-23197-8   FF195   £23.50   US$41.00   DM80

Nouveaux défis pour les banques (1992)
(21 91 04 2) ISBN 92-64-23631-7   FF140   £19.00   US$35.00   DM56

Risques systémiques dans les marchés des valeurs mobilières (1991)
(21 91 01 2) ISBN 92-64-23454-3   FF100   £12.00   US$21.00   DM39

Statistiques financières de l'OCDE
(20 00 00 3)
Abonnement. Pas vendu au numéro   FF1.450 £174.00   US$300.00   DM560

Tendances des marchés des capitaux
(27 00 00 2)
Au numéro   FF85   £10.50   US$18.00   DM33
Abonnement   FF215   £26.00   US$45.00   DM84

CONTENTS

1. New series. Series on "Large commercial banks" and "Savings banks" are discontinued.
2. New series.
3. Due to methodological changes, as from this issue, data are published under the title "All banks".
4. Series on "Large commercial banks" are not available in this issue.
5. Series on "Savings and loan associations" are not available in this issue.

CONVENTIONAL SIGNS

N.A.   *Not available*
-     *Nil or negligible*
..   *Not applicable or*
        breakdown not available
·   *Decimal point*

TABLE DES MATIERES

1. Nouvelles séries. Celles sur les "Grandes banques commerciales" et les "Caisses d'épargne" sont discontinues.
2. Les séries relatives aux "Grandes banques commerciales" ne sont pas disponibles dans cette livraison.
3. Les séries relatives aux "Associations d'épargne et de prêts" ne sont pas disponibles dans cette livraison.
4. Nouvelles séries.
5. Dû à des changements de méthodologies, les données sont publiées, à compter de cette publication, sous le titre "Ensemble des banques".

SIGNES CONVENTIONNELS

N.A.   *Non disponible*
\-   *Nul ou négligeable*
..   *Non approprié ou ventilation non disponible*
·   *Point decimal (sépare les unités des décimale)*

INTRODUCTION

National data on **income and expenditure accounts of banks** are grouped and, where necessary, re-classified to fit as far as possible into the following standard framework of presentation:

Income statement

1. Interest income

2. Interest expenses

3. Net interest income (item 1 minus item 2)

4. Non-interest income (net)

5. Gross income (item 3 plus item 4)

6. Operating expenses

7. Net income (item 5 minus item 6)

8. Provisions (net)

9. Profit before tax (item 7 minus item 8)

10. Income tax

11. Profit after tax (item 9 minus item 10)

12. Distributed profit

13. Retained profit (item 11 minus item 12)

Memorandum items

14. Staff costs (included in item 6)

15. Net provisions on loans (included in item 8)

16. Net provisions on securities (included in item 8)

Interest income (item 1) generally includes income on interest-bearing assets, fee income related to lending operations, and dividend income on shares and participations. In some cases it may also include income on bonds calculated as the difference between the book value and the redemption value of bonds.

Interest expenses (item 2) generally includes interest paid on liabilities, fee expenses related to borrowing operations and may include in some cases the difference between the issue price on debt instruments and their par value.

Non-interest income (net) (item 4) is generally the net result of a number of different income and expense items (other than those included in items 1 and 2) such as the following: commissions received and paid in connection with payments services, securities transactions and related services (new issues, trading, portfolio management, safe-custody) and foreign exchange transactions in the banks' own name and on behalf of clients. Other income and expenses resulting from special transactions which do not represent ordinary and regular banking business may also be included. Realised losses and gains on foreign-exchange operations and securities transactions are generally included as well.

Operating expenses (item 6) usually include all expenses relating to the ordinary and regular banking business other than those included in items 2 and 4, particularly salaries and other employee benefits, including transfers to pension reserves (staff costs), and expenses for property and equipment and related depreciation expenses. Taxes other than income or corporate taxes are also included.

Provisions (net) (item 8) generally include, in part or in full, charges for value adjustments in respect of loans, credits and securities, book gains from such adjustments, losses on loans and transfers to and from reserves for possible losses on such assets. Realised gains or losses from foreign exchange transactions and securities transactions are, however, generally included under *Non-interest income (net)* (item 4).

Any deviation from this standard presentation and classification of income and expenditure account items is generally indicated in the methodological country notes.

National data on **balance sheets of banks** are grouped and, where necessary, re-classified in order to fit as far as possible into the following standard framework of presentations:

Balance sheet

Assets

17.   Cash and balance with central bank

18.   Interbank deposits

19.   Loans

20.   Securities

21.   Other assets

Liabilities

22.   Capital and reserves

23.   Borrowing from central bank

24.   Interbank deposits

25.   Non-bank deposits

26.   Bonds

27.   Other liabilities

Balance sheet total

28.   End-year total (sum of items 17 to 21 or 22 to 27)

29.   Average total

Memorandum items

30.   Short-term securities (included in item 20)

31.   Bonds (included in item 20)

32.   Shares and participations (included in item 20)

33.   Claims on non-residents (included in items 18 to 21)

34.   Liabilities to non-residents (included in items 24 to 27)

Short-term securities (item 30) are, following the definition used in the European System of Integrated Accounts (paragraph 539), securities with an original maturity of usually up to 12 months, but with a maximum maturity of two years.

Bonds (item 31), are, following the definition of the European System of Integrated Accounts (paragraph 542), fixed or variable-interest rate securities with an original maturity of several years.

In countries in which there is re-discounting of commercial bills with the central bank, the volume of re-discounted bills is usually included on each side of the balance sheet, under *Loans* (item 19) on the assets side and under *Borrowing from central bank* (item 23) on the liabilities side.

The following **supplementary information** is provided:

35.   Number of institutions (covered by the data)

36.   Number of branches (covered by the data)

37.   Number of staff ('000) (of the institutions covered by the data)

In order to facilitate the interpretation and analysis of the data included in the present publication and to enable the user of the data to judge how cautiously the figures should be used for comparative purposes, national administrations have prepared methodological country notes which give detailed information on the following:

- Institutional coverage, and the relative importance of the institutions covered as compared with the whole financial system;

- Geographical coverage and degree of consolidation indicating whether domestic or foreign financial or non-financial subsidiaries of the reporting banks are covered by the data and whether branches and/or subsidiaries of foreign banks are included;

- Summary description of activities of banks indicating in particular whether the banks carry out important service activities producing fee income such as a wide range of securities-related activities and foreign exchange trading;

- Income statement reconciliation table giving detailed information on the way in which the income statement data shown in the present publication are derived from generally more detailed national data;

- Balance sheet reconciliation table giving detailed information on the way in which the balance sheet data shown in the present publication are derived from more detailed national balance sheet data;

- Explanations on some items of the income statement and balance sheet in cases in which national data cannot entirely be fitted into the standard framework. The income statement item *Provisions (net)* (item 8) receives special attention in the commentary;

- Sources of data on income statements and balance sheets of banks with indication of method of compilation.

INTRODUCTION

Les données communiquées par les pays concernant **les comptes de résultats des banques** sont groupées après, le cas échéant, reclassement pour cadrer, autant que possible, avec le modèle de présentation ci-après :

Compte de resultats

1. Produits financiers,

2. Frais financiers

3. Produits financiers nets (poste 1 moins poste 2)

4. Produits non financiers (nets)

5. Résultat brut (poste 3 plus poste 4)

6. Frais d'exploitation

7. Résultat net (poste 5 moins poste 6)

8. Provisions (nettes)

9. Bénéfices avant impôt (poste 7 moins poste 8)

10. Impôt sur le revenu/les sociétés

11. Bénéfices après impôt (poste 9 moins poste 10)

12. Bénéfices distribués

13. Bénéfices mis en réserve (poste 11 moins poste 12)

Pour mémoire

14. Frais de personnel (comptabilisés au poste 6)

15. Provisions nettes sur prêts (comptabilisées au poste 8)

16. Provisions nettes sur titres (comptabilisées au poste 8)

Le poste *Produits financiers,* (poste 1) comprend, en principe, les revenus procurés par les actifs porteurs d'intérêts, les commissions afférentes aux opérations de prêt, ainsi que les dividendes d'actions et titres de participation. Dans certains cas, il peut comprendre aussi les revenus d'obligations considérés comme étant égaux à la différence entre la valeur comptable et la valeur de remboursement des titres.

Le poste *Frais financiers* (poste 2) comprend, en principe, les intérêts versés sur les emprunts et les commissions versées sur les opérations d'emprunt. Il peut comprendre aussi la différence entre la valeur d'émission des instruments de dette et leur valeur nominale.

Le poste *Produits non financiers (nets)* (poste 4) est normalement le résultat net d'un certain nombre de produits et frais différents (autres que ceux repris aux postes 1 et 2) comme les commissions perçues et versées à l'occasion de diverses opérations -- paiements, opérations sur titres (placement d'émissions, contrepartie, gestion de portefeuille, garde de titres), opérations de change -- effectuées par les banques tant pour leur propre compte que pour celui de leurs clients. Figurent aussi à ce poste, les produits et les charges résultant d'opérations exceptionnelles et non des activités courantes des banques. Les gains et pertes de change et les plus-values et moins-values sur la réalisation de titres de placement y figurent également.

Le poste *Frais d'exploitation* (poste 6) comprend, normalement, toutes les charges afférentes aux activités courantes des banques (à l'exclusion de celles reprises aux postes 2 et 4), en particulier les salaires et autres avantages perçus par les salariés, y compris les dotations au fonds de pension (frais de personnel) et les charges afférentes aux terrains et immeubles et aux matériels, mobilier et installations ainsi que les amortissements. Sont aussi comptabilisés à ce poste les impôts autres que l'impôt sur le revenu ou les sociétés.

Le poste *Provisions (nettes)* (poste 8) comprend, en principe, en partie ou en totalité, les charges pour ajustement de la valeur comptable des prêts, crédits et titres de placement, les plus-values comptables découlant de cet ajustement, les pertes sur prêts, les dotations aux provisions pour pertes sur ces éléments d'actif et les reprises de provisions. En revanche, les gains ou pertes de change et les plus-values ou moins-values sur la réalisation de titres de placement figurent normalement au poste *Produits non financiers (nets)* (poste 4).

Toute différence de présentation avec le présent modèle des éléments du compte de résultats est en principe indiquée dans les notes méthodologiques par pays.

Les données communiquées par les pays concernant **les bilans des banques** sont groupées après, le cas échéant, reclassement pour cadrer, autant que possible, avec le modèle de présentation ci-après :

Bilan

Actif

17. Caisse et soldes auprès de la Banque centrale

18. Dépôts interbancaires

19. Prêts

20.	Valeurs mobilières

21.	Autres actifs

Passif

22.	Capital et réserves

23.	Emprunts auprès de la Banque centrale

24.	Dépôts interbancaires

25.	Dépôts non bancaires

26.	Obligations

27.	Autres engagements

Total du bilan

28.	Total en fin d'exercice (somme des postes 17 à 21 ou 22 à 27)

29.	Total moyen

Pour mémoire

30.	Titres à court terme (comptabilisés au poste 20)

31.	Obligations (comptabilisées au poste 20)

32.	Actions et participations (comptabilisées au poste 20)

33.	Créances sur des non résidents (comptabilisées aux postes 18 à 21)

34.	Engagements envers des non résidents (comptabilisés aux postes 24 à 27)

Le poste *Titres à court terme* (poste 30) comprend, selon la définition du Système européen de comptes économiques intégrés (paragraphe 539), les titres dont l'échéance initiale est normalement de 12 mois, deux ans maximum.

Le poste *Obligations* (poste 31) comprend, selon la définition du Système européen de comptes économiques intégrés (paragraphe 542), les titres à revenu fixe ou variable initialement à plusieurs années d'échéance.

Dans les pays où existe la possibilité de réescompter des effets de commerce auprès de la Banque centrale, le montant des effets réescomptés figure habituellement à la fois à l'actif du bilan poste *Prêts* (poste 19) et au passif poste *Emprunts auprès de la Banque centrale* (poste 23).

On trouvera également les **renseignements complémentaires** suivants:

35.   Nombre d'institutions (prises en compte)

36.   Nombre de succursales (prises en compte)

37.   Nombre de salariés (en milliers) (des institutions prises en compte)

Pour faciliter l'interprétation et l'analyse des données reprises dans la présente publication et pour inciter l'utilisateur à être prudent dans l'utilisation des statistiques à des fins de comparaisons internationales, les administrations nationales ont rédigé des notes par pays qui apportent des précisions sur les points suivants :

- Les institutions sur lesquelles portent les statistiques et leur importance par rapport à l'ensemble du système financier.

- Le champ géographique et le degré de consolidation des opérations de ces institutions. Il sera précisé si sont comprises dans les données les filiales financières ou non financières, domestiques ou étrangères, des banques déclarantes ainsi que les succursales/filiales des banques étrangères.

- Une description succincte des activités des banques . Il sera indiqué, en particulier, si les banques se livrent à des activités de service génératrices de commissions, telles que des activités se rapportant aux valeurs mobilières et au commerce de devises.

- Un tableau de concordance des comptes de résultats qui donne des renseignements précis sur la façon dont les informations relatives aux comptes de résultats publiées dans cette publication ont été obtenues à partir de sources nationales, en général plus détaillées.

- Un tableau de concordance des bilans qui donne des renseignements précis sur la façon dont les bilans reproduits dans cette publication ont été construits à partir des bilans, plus détaillés, publiés dans le pays.

- Des explications sur certains postes des comptes de résultats et des bilans des banques, lorsqu'il n'est pas possible de faire parfaitement cadrer les données nationales avec la présentation type retenue. Le poste du compte de résultats *Provisions (nettes)* (poste 8), notamment, donne lieu à des commentaires.

- Les sources des données concernant les comptes de résultats et les bilans des banques ainsi que le mode de collecte.

STATISTICS ON FINANCIAL STATEMENTS OF BANKS 1982-91

STATISTIQUES SUR LES COMPTES DES BANQUES 1982-91

AUSTRALIA / AUSTRALIE

All banks / Ensemble des banques

Million Australian dollars / Millions de dollars australiens

	1986	1987	1988	1989	1990	1991	
INCOME STATEMENT							**COMPTE DE RESULTATS**
1. Interest income	21114	25061	27384	37341	48101	42744	1. Produits financiers
2. Interest expenses	15770	18869	19173	27691	37442	31712	2. Frais financiers
3. Net interest income	5344	6192	8211	9650	10659	11032	3. Produits financiers nets
4. Non-interest income (net)	3420	4658	5327	5948	7129	10075	4. Produits non financiers (nets)
5. Gross income	8764	10850	13538	15598	17788	21107	5. Résultat brut
6. Operating expenses	6430	7238	8770	10144	11748	12672	6. Frais d'exploitation
7. Net income	2334	3612	4768	5454	6040	8435	7. Résultat net
8. Provisions (net)	461	803	1052	1709	3402	5117	8. Provisions (nettes)
9. Profit before tax	1873	2809	3716	3745	2638	3318	9. Bénéfices avant impôt
10. Income tax	658	1198	1703	1446	1079	1500	10. Impôt
11. Profit after tax	1215	1611	2013	2299	1559	1818	11. Bénéfices après impôt
12. Distributed profit	571	579	1220	2102	1742	1390	12. Bénéfices distribués
13. Retained profit	644	1032	793	197	-183	428	13. Bénéfices mis en réserve
Memoranda							*Pour mémoire*
14. Staff costs	..	..	..	..	..	..	14. Frais de personnel
15. Provisions on loans	..	..	..	..	..	..	15. Provisions sur prêts
16. Provisions on securities	..	..	..	..	..	..	16. Provisions sur titres
BALANCE SHEET							**BILAN**
Assets							**Actif**
17. Cash & balance with Central bank	4639	4633	4714	4376	4197	3919	17. Caisse & solde auprès de la Banque centrale
18. Interbank deposits	18751	18121	19191	31833	34483	32884	18. Dépôts interbancaires
19. Loans (1)	116315	137164	161963	206300	239334	249425	19. Prêts (1)
20. Securities (1)	33487	37877	46875	49597	31009	35460	20. Valeurs mobilières (1)
21. Other assets (1)	37892	49876	68955	82233	109299	111918	21. Autres actifs (1)
Liabilities							**Passif**
22. Capital & reserves	12766	15796	22953	28363	39300	43289	22. Capital et réserves
23. Borrowing from Central bank							23. Emprunts auprès de la Banque centrale
24. Interbank deposits	24152	25528	26175	38352	36263	36914	24. Dépôts interbancaires
25. Non-bank deposits (1)					228711	232934	25. Dépôts non bancaires (1)
26. Bonds							26. Obligations
27. Other liabilities (1)	174166	206348	252568	307624	114046	120471	27. Autres engagements (1)
Balance sheet total							**Total du bilan**
28. End-year total	211085	247673	301697	374339	418322	433608	28. En fin d'exercice
29. Average total	184463	229379	274685	338018	396331	425965	29. Moyen
Memoranda							*Pour mémoire*
30. Short-term securities	2874	6405	7712	8958	5919	10780	30. Titres à court terme
31. Bonds	18288	18802	19443	14369	17160	14159	31. Obligations
32. Shares and participations (1)	8047	8929	13508	14219	..	..	32. Actions et participations (1)
33. Claims on non-residents	..	..	..	..	..	..	33. Créances sur des non résidents
34. Liabilities to non-residents	..	..	..	..	..	..	34. Engagements envers des non résidents
SUPPLEMENTARY INFORMATION							**RENSEIGNEMENTS COMPLEMENTAIRES**
35. Number of institutions	31	32	32	32	32	29	35. Nombre d'institutions
36. Number of branches	15462	14981	14381	15009	14617	14203	36. Nombre de succursales
37. Number of employees (x 1000)	NA	NA	NA	NA	NA	NA	37. Nombre de salariés (x 1000)

AUSTRALIA

All banks

AUSTRALIE

Ensemble des banques

Per cent — *Pourcentage*

INCOME STATEMENT ANALYSIS — **ANALYSE DU COMPTE DE RESULTATS**

	1986	1987	1988	1989	1990	1991		
% of average balance sheet total								**% du total moyen du bilan**
38. Interest income	11.45	10.93	9.97	11.05	12.14	10.03	38.	Produits financiers
39. Interest expenses	8.55	8.23	6.98	8.19	9.45	7.44	39.	Frais financiers
40. Net interest income	2.90	2.70	2.99	2.85	2.69	2.59	40.	Produits financiers nets
41. Non-interest income (net)	1.85	2.03	1.94	1.76	1.80	2.37	41.	Produits non financiers (nets)
42. Gross income	4.75	4.73	4.93	4.61	4.49	4.96	42.	Résultat brut
43. Operating expenses	3.49	3.16	3.19	3.00	2.96	2.97	43.	Frais d'exploitation
44. Net income	1.27	1.57	1.74	1.61	1.52	1.98	44.	Résultat net
45. Provisions (net)	0.25	0.35	0.38	0.51	0.86	1.20	45.	Provisions (nettes)
46. Profit before tax	1.02	1.22	1.35	1.11	0.67	0.78	46.	Bénéfices avant impôt
47. Income tax	0.36	0.52	0.62	0.43	0.27	0.35	47.	Impôt
48. Profit after tax	0.66	0.70	0.73	0.68	0.39	0.43	48.	Bénéfices après impôt
49. Distributed profit	0.31	0.25	0.44	0.62	0.44	0.33	49.	Bénéfices distribués
50. Retained profit	0.35	0.45	0.29	0.06	-0.05	0.10	50.	Bénéfices mis en réserve
51. Staff costs	..	..	..	..	..	..	51.	Frais de personnel
52. Provisions on loans	..	..	..	..	..	..	52.	Provisions sur prêts
53. Provisions on securities	..	..	..	..	..	..	53.	Provisions sur titres
% of gross income								**% du total du résultat brut**
54. Net interest income	60.98	57.07	60.65	61.87	59.92	52.27	54.	Produits financiers nets
55. Non-interest income (net)	39.02	42.93	39.35	38.13	40.08	47.73	55.	Produits non financiers (nets)
56. Operating expenses	73.37	66.71	64.78	65.03	66.04	60.04	56.	Frais d'exploitation
57. Net income	26.63	33.29	35.22	34.97	33.96	39.96	57.	Résultat net
58. Provisions (net)	5.26	7.40	7.77	10.96	19.13	24.24	58.	Provisions (nettes)
59. Profit before tax	21.37	25.89	27.45	24.01	14.83	15.72	59.	Bénéfices avant impôt
60. Income tax	7.51	11.04	12.58	9.27	6.07	7.11	60.	Impôt
61. Profit after tax	13.86	14.85	14.87	14.74	8.76	8.61	61.	Bénéfices après impôt
62. Staff costs	..	..	..	..	..	..	62.	Frais de personnel
% of net income								**% du total du résultat net**
63. Provisions (net)	19.75	22.23	22.06	31.33	56.32	60.66	63.	Provisions (nettes)
64. Profit before tax	80.25	77.77	77.94	68.67	43.68	39.34	64.	Bénéfices avant impôt
65. Income tax	28.19	33.17	35.72	26.51	17.86	17.78	65.	Impôt
66. Profit after tax	52.06	44.60	42.22	42.15	25.81	21.55	66.	Bénéfices après impôt

AUSTRALIA

All banks

Per cent

BALANCE SHEET ANALYSIS

% of year-end balance sheet total

	1986	1987	1988	1989	1990	1991
Assets						
67. Cash & balance with Central bank	2.20	1.87	1.56	1.17	1.00	0.90
68. Interbank deposits	8.88	7.32	6.36	8.50	8.24	7.58
69. Loans (1)	55.10	55.38	53.68	55.11	57.21	57.52
70. Securities (1)	15.86	15.29	15.54	13.25	7.41	8.18
71. Other assets (1)	17.95	20.14	22.86	21.97	26.13	25.81
Liabilities						
72. Capital & reserves	6.05	6.38	7.61	7.58	9.39	9.98
73. Borrowing from Central bank						
74. Interbank deposits	11.44	10.31	8.68	10.25	8.67	8.51
75. Non-bank deposits (1)						
76. Bonds						
77. Other liabilities (1)	82.51	83.31	83.72	82.18	27.26	27.78
Memoranda						
78. Short-term securities	*1.36*	*2.59*	*2.56*	*2.39*	*1.41*	*2.49*
79. Bonds	*8.66*	*7.59*	*6.44*	*3.84*	*4.10*	*3.27*
80. Shares and participations (1)	*3.81*	*3.61*	*4.48*	*3.80*	*..*	*..*
81. Claims on non-residents	*..*	*..*	*..*	*..*	*..*	*..*
82. Liabilities to non-residents	*..*	*..*	*..*	*..*	*..*	*..*

1. Change in methodology.

Change in methodology:

- Introduction of revised statistical collection in 1990 resulted in reclassification of shares and participations from "Securities" (item 20 or item 70) to "Loans" (item 19 or item 69) and "Other assets" (item 21 or item 71).

- As from 1990, "Shares and participations" (item 32 or item 80) are not separately available following the introduction of revised statistical collection.

- Until 1990, "Non-bank deposits" (item 25 or item 75) were included under "Other liabilities" (item 27 or item 77). This item includes a small proportion of deposits from other banks.

- Historical data were recalculated and therefore not comparable with the series published earlier under the same title.

AUSTRALIE

Ensemble des banques

Pourcentage

ANALYSE DU BILAN

% du total du bilan en fin d'exercice

Actif
67. Caisse & solde auprès de la Banque centrale
68. Dépôts interbancaires
69. Prêts (1)
70. Valeurs mobilières (1)
71. Autres actifs (1)

Passif
72. Capital et réserves
73. Emprunts auprès de la Banque centrale
74. Dépôts interbancaires
75. Dépôts non bancaires (1)
76. Obligations
77. Autres engagements (1)

Pour mémoire
78. Titres à court terme
79. Obligations
80. Actions et participations (1)
81. Créances sur des non résidents
82. Engagements envers des non résidents

1. Changement méthodologique.

Changement méthodologique :

- La reclassification des actions et participations du poste 20 (ou poste 70) "Titres" au poste 19 (ou poste 69) "Prêts" et 21 (ou poste 71) "Autres actifs" est consécutive à l'introduction en 1990 d'une révision de la collecte statistique.

- A partir de 1990, les "Actions et participations" (poste 32 ou poste 80) ne sont plus disponibles séparément suite à l'introduction d'une révision de la collecte statistique.

- Jusqu'en 1990, les "Dépôts non bancaires" (poste 25 ou poste 75) étaient inclus sous "Autres engagements" (poste 27 ou poste 77). Ce poste inclut une petite partie des dépôts des autres banques.

- Les données rétrospectives ont été recalculées et en conséquence ne sont pas comparables avec les séries publiées antérieurement sous le même titre.

AUSTRIA
All banks

AUTRICHE
Ensemble des banques

Million schillings / *Millions de schillings*

	1987	1988	1989	1990	1991	
INCOME STATEMENT						**COMPTE DE RESULTATS**
1. Interest income	215539	229896	275916	327360	347980	1. Produits financiers
2. Interest expenses	156960	166908	210562	256357	271594	2. Frais financiers
3. Net interest income	58579	62988	65354	71003	76386	3. Produits financiers nets
4. Non-interest income (net)	14353	17415	25226	31767	36158	4. Produits non financiers (nets)
5. Gross income	72932	80403	90580	102770	112544	5. Résultat brut
6. Operating expenses	51111	55047	59340	66661	73061	6. Frais d'exploitation
7. Net income	21821	25356	31240	36109	39483	7. Résultat net
8. Provisions (net)		..	14813	20032	22077	8. Provisions (nettes)
9. Profit before tax	21821	25356	16427	16077	17406	9. Bénéfices avant impôt
10. Income tax	2934	3103	3157	3032	2911	10. Impôt
11. Profit after tax	18887	22253	13270	13045	14495	11. Bénéfices après impôt
12. Distributed profit	..	..	..	..	..	12. Bénéfices distribués
13. Retained profit	..	..	..	..	..	13. Bénéfices mis en réserve
Memoranda						*Pour mémoire*
14. Staff costs	*30098*	*32181*	*34696*	*39547*	*43379*	*14. Frais de personnel*
15. Provisions on loans	*..*	*..*	*6566*	*8050*	*11875*	*15. Provisions sur prêts*
16. Provisions on securities	*..*	*..*	*5789*	*7348*	*3206*	*16. Provisions sur titres*
BALANCE SHEET						**BILAN**
Assets						**Actif**
17. Cash & balance with Central bank	63737	67199	76883	73166	68441	17. Caisse & solde auprès de la Banque centrale
18. Interbank deposits	1220499	1231639	1223461	1235092	1242533	18. Dépôts interbancaires
19. Loans	1561331	1710902	1884902	2048063	2213849	19. Prêts
20. Securities	388599	424417	445993	468099	492964	20. Valeurs mobilières
21. Other assets	184965	183171	199619	216056	258405	21. Autres actifs
Liabilities						**Passif**
22. Capital & reserves	119054	141636	163595	186199	202114	22. Capital et réserves
23. Borrowing from Central bank	2298	2792	1144	1533	1103	23. Emprunts auprès de la Banque centrale
24. Interbank deposits	1254249	1287885	1286495	1280553	1315567	24. Dépôts interbancaires
25. Non-bank deposits	1373945	1452911	1569986	1725712	1876343	25. Dépôts non bancaires
26. Bonds	517067	593320	659477	692662	705669	26. Obligations
27. Other liabilities	152517	138785	150162	153816	175396	27. Autres engagements
Balance sheet total						**Total du bilan**
28. End-year total	3419130	3617329	3830858	4040476	4276192	28. En fin d'exercice
29. Average total	3334251	3543249	3769759	4012331	4228420	29. Moyen
Memoranda						*Pour mémoire*
30. Short-term securities	*10145*	*8439*	*5951*	*6807*	*6088*	*30. Titres à court terme*
31. Bonds	*305492*	*334051*	*348443*	*352728*	*366784*	*31. Obligations*
32. Shares and participations	*51819*	*62326*	*76772*	*93973*	*112789*	*32. Actions et participations*
33. Claims on non-residents	*751664*	*816929*	*842040*	*843875*	*846806*	*33. Créances sur des non résidents*
34. Liabilities to non-residents	*790712*	*877311*	*926274*	*932278*	*958893*	*34. Engagements envers des non résidents*
SUPPLEMENTARY INFORMATION						**RENSEIGNEMENTS COMPLEMENTAIRES**
35. Number of institutions	1252	1250	1240	1210	1165	35. Nombre d'institutions
36. Number of branches	4203	4295	4373	4497	4594	36. Nombre de succursales
37. Number of employees (x 1000)	67.6	70.2	71.5	74.6	76.0	37. Nombre de salariés (x 1000)

AUSTRIA

All banks

Per cent

INCOME STATEMENT ANALYSIS

AUTRICHE

Ensemble des banques

Pourcentage

ANALYSE DU COMPTE DE RESULTATS

		1987	1988	1989	1990	1991		
	% of average balance sheet total							**% du total moyen du bilan**
38.	Interest income	6.46	6.49	7.32	8.16	8.23	38.	Produits financiers
39.	Interest expenses	4.71	4.71	5.59	6.39	6.42	39.	Frais financiers
40.	Net interest income	1.76	1.78	1.73	1.77	1.81	40.	Produits financiers nets
41.	Non-interest income (net)	0.43	0.49	0.67	0.79	0.86	41.	Produits non financiers (nets)
42.	Gross income	2.19	2.27	2.40	2.56	2.66	42.	Résultat brut
43.	Operating expenses	1.53	1.55	1.57	1.66	1.73	43.	Frais d'exploitation
44.	Net income	0.65	0.72	0.83	0.90	0.93	44.	Résultat net
45.	Provisions (net)	..	..	0.39	0.50	0.52	45.	Provisions (nettes)
46.	Profit before tax	0.65	0.72	0.44	0.40	0.41	46.	Bénéfices avant impôt
47.	Income tax	0.09	0.09	0.08	0.08	0.07	47.	Impôt
48.	Profit after tax	0.57	0.63	0.35	0.33	0.34	48.	Bénéfices après impôt
49.	Distributed profit	..	..	..	..	..	49.	Bénéfices distribués
50.	Retained profit	..	..	..	..	..	50.	Bénéfices mis en réserve
51.	Staff costs	0.90	0.91	0.92	0.99	1.03	51.	Frais de personnel
52.	Provisions on loans	..	..	0.17	0.20	0.28	52.	Provisions sur prêts
53.	Provisions on securities	..	..	0.15	0.18	0.08	53.	Provisions sur titres
	% of gross income							**% du total du résultat brut**
54.	Net interest income	80.32	78.34	72.15	69.09	67.87	54.	Produits financiers nets
55.	Non-interest income (net)	19.68	21.66	27.85	30.91	32.13	55.	Produits non financiers (nets)
56.	Operating expenses	70.08	68.46	65.51	64.86	64.92	56.	Frais d'exploitation
57.	Net income	29.92	31.54	34.49	35.14	35.08	57.	Résultat net
58.	Provisions (net)	..	..	16.35	19.49	19.62	58.	Provisions (nettes)
59.	Profit before tax	29.92	31.54	18.14	15.64	15.47	59.	Bénéfices avant impôt
60.	Income tax	4.02	3.86	3.49	2.95	2.59	60.	Impôt
61.	Profit after tax	25.90	27.68	14.65	12.69	12.88	61.	Bénéfices après impôt
62.	Staff costs	41.27	40.02	38.30	38.48	38.54	62.	Frais de personnel
	% of net income							**% du total du résultat net**
63.	Provisions (net)	..	..	47.42	55.48	55.92	63.	Provisions (nettes)
64.	Profit before tax	100.00	100.00	52.58	44.52	44.08	64.	Bénéfices avant impôt
65.	Income tax	13.45	12.24	10.11	8.40	7.37	65.	Impôt
66.	Profit after tax	86.55	87.76	42.48	36.13	36.71	66.	Bénéfices après impôt

AUSTRIA

All banks

Per cent

BALANCE SHEET ANALYSIS

% of year-end balance sheet total

AUTRICHE

Ensemble des banques

Pourcentage

ANALYSE DU BILAN

% du total du bilan en fin d'exercice

		1987	1988	1989	1990	1991		
	Assets						**Actif**	
67.	Cash & balance with Central bank	1.86	1.86	2.01	1.81	1.60	67.	Caisse & solde auprès de la Banque centrale
68.	Interbank deposits	35.70	34.05	31.94	30.57	29.06	68.	Dépôts interbancaires
69.	Loans	45.66	47.30	49.20	50.69	51.77	69.	Prêts
70.	Securities	11.37	11.73	11.64	11.59	11.53	70.	Valeurs mobilières
71.	Other assets	5.41	5.06	5.21	5.35	6.04	71.	Autres actifs
	Liabilities						**Passif**	
72.	Capital & reserves	3.48	3.92	4.27	4.61	4.73	72.	Capital et réserves
73.	Borrowing from Central bank	0.07	0.08	0.03	0.04	0.03	73.	Emprunts auprès de la Banque centrale
74.	Interbank deposits	36.68	35.60	33.58	31.69	30.76	74.	Dépôts interbancaires
75.	Non-bank deposits	40.18	40.17	40.98	42.71	43.88	75.	Dépôts non bancaires
76.	Bonds	15.12	16.40	17.21	17.14	16.50	76.	Obligations
77.	Other liabilities	4.46	3.84	3.92	3.81	4.10	77.	Autres engagements
	Memoranda						***Pour mémoire***	
78.	*Short-term securities*	*0.30*	*0.23*	*0.16*	*0.17*	*0.14*	*78.*	*Titres à court terme*
79.	*Bonds*	*8.93*	*9.23*	*9.10*	*8.73*	*8.58*	*79.*	*Obligations*
80.	*Shares and participations*	*1.52*	*1.72*	*2.00*	*2.33*	*2.64*	*80.*	*Actions et participations*
81.	*Claims on non-residents*	*21.98*	*22.58*	*21.98*	*20.89*	*19.80*	*81.*	*Créances sur des non résidents*
82.	*Liabilities to non-residents*	*23.13*	*24.25*	*24.18*	*23.07*	*22.42*	*82.*	*Engagements envers des non résidents*

Notes

- Average balance sheet totals (item 29) are based on twelve end-month data.

Notes

- La moyenne du total des actifs/passifs (poste 29) est basée sur douze données de fin de mois.

BELGIUM
Commercial banks

BELGIQUE
Banques commerciales

Million Belgian francs / *Millions de francs belges*

		1982	1983	1984	1985	1986	1987	1988	1989	1990	1991		
INCOME STATEMENT												**COMPTE DE RESULTATS**	
1.	Interest income	749156	669100	806059	828268	737264	746312	881211	1181729	1340128	1348800	Produits financiers	1.
2.	Interest expenses	647701	563717	682959	691999	592534	603087	734640	1024583	1175443	1174587	Frais financiers	2.
3.	Net interest income	101455	105383	123100	136269	144730	143225	146571	157146	164685	174213	Produits financiers nets	3.
4.	Non-interest income (net)	27249	34159	32245	42207	50376	52677	62690	59356	49298	57555	Produits non financiers (nets)	4.
5.	Gross income	128704	139542	155345	178476	195106	195902	209261	216502	213983	231768	Résultat brut	5.
6.	Operating expenses	90117	97114	107112	118868	127114	133471	129875	142420	148349	152371	Frais d'exploitation	6.
7.	Net income	38587	42428	48233	59608	67992	62431	79386	74082	65634	79397	Résultat net	7.
8.	Provisions (net)	18353	19985	22202	26691	27674	27283	42820	51126	24684	39710	Provisions (nettes)	8.
9.	Profit before tax	20234	22443	26031	32917	40318	35148	36566	22956	40950	39687	Bénéfices avant impôt	9.
10.	Income tax	8353	9817	10497	13178	16452	14019	10574	10757	7999	10132	Impôt	10.
11.	Profit after tax	11881	12626	15534	19739	23866	21129	25992	12199	32951	29555	Bénéfices après impôt	11.
12.	Distributed profit	..	..	..	..	..	..	..	..	..	..	Bénéfices distribués	12.
13.	Retained profit	..	..	..	..	..	..	..	..	..	..	Bénéfices mis en réserve	13.
	Memoranda											*Pour mémoire*	
14.	Staff costs	67093	70216	76799	81949	87027	89840	92900	99174	104217	106548	Frais de personnel	14.
15.	Provisions on loans	..	..	..	..	..	..	..	..	..	..	Provisions sur prêts	15.
16.	Provisions on securities	..	..	..	..	..	..	..	..	..	..	Provisions sur titres	16.
BALANCE SHEET												**BILAN**	
Assets												**Actif**	
17.	Cash & balance with Central bank	14017	14193	18457	16192	15868	16176	16746	21245	21497	20942	Caisse & solde auprès de la Banque centrale	17.
18.	Interbank deposits	2649023	3159291	3741946	4034081	4082213	4451386	4955770	5143367	5420716	5351044	Dépôts interbancaires	18.
19.	Loans	2014749	2198088	2455976	2365024	2360343	2457869	2830155	3382345	3504562	3681628	Prêts	19.
20.	Securities	1159624	1524243	1743217	2104831	2452736	2584660	2679435	2765878	2947941	2855554	Valeurs mobilières	20.
21.	Other assets	241127	255945	349158	336801	335413	343897	472092	538690	596691	584472	Autres actifs	21.
Liabilities												**Passif**	
22.	Capital & reserves	144983	179699	209130	222335	265151	289072	334754	401677	424618	483618	Capital et réserves	22.
23.	Borrowing from Central bank (1)	..	..	..	..	..	..	..	..	..	..	Emprunts auprès de la Banque centrale (1)	23.
24.	Interbank deposits	3727766	4472755	5332728	5626035	5738639	6024254	6658012	6866565	7104733	6636136	Dépôts interbancaires	24.
25.	Non-bank deposits	1620759	1845512	2015844	2164325	2399149	2647782	2983769	3410030	3628596	3922770	Dépôts non bancaires	25.
26.	Bonds	293916	352256	390843	443984	450272	461609	470744	533357	690846	809709	Obligations	26.
27.	Other liabilities	291116	301538	360209	400250	393362	431271	506919	639894	642609	641405	Autres engagements	27.
Balance sheet total												**Total du bilan**	
28.	End-year total	6078540	7151760	8308754	8856929	9246573	9853988	10954198	11851524	12491405	12493639	En fin d'exercice	28.
29.	Average total	5959419	6556728	7717112	8931514	8939174	9622585	10652680	11942592	12228867	12983213	Moyen	29.
	Memoranda											*Pour mémoire*	
30.	Short-term securities	408388	562871	569664	644492	843583	901385	838423	917605	980824	718797	Titres à court terme	30.
31.	Bonds	715042	916353	1123848	1424718	1569827	1618476	1752486	1742043	1871557	2028855	Obligations	31.
32.	Shares and participations	36194	45019	45705	35621	39327	64799	88525	106230	95560	107902	Actions et participations	32.
33.	Claims on non-residents	3110528	3728352	4479931	4758378	4856012	5036791	5740857	6015304	6069778	6173962	Créances sur des non résidents	33.
34.	Liabilities to non-residents	3660891	4432503	5400433	5645082	5802900	6023515	6894915	7277340	7356089	7113229	Engagements envers des non résidents	34.
SUPPLEMENTARY INFORMATION												**RENSEIGNEMENTS COMPLEMENTAIRES**	
35.	Number of institutions	84	84	84	85	86	86	85	85	87	91	Nombre d'institutions	35.
36.	Number of branches	3678	3680	3654	3656	3646	3631	3617	3618	3592	3547	Nombre de succursales	36.
37.	Number of employees (x 1000)	46.7	47.4	48.4	48.4	49.2	50.0	50.2	51.6	50.7	49.6	Nombre de salariés (x 1000)	37.

26

Per cent — *Pourcentage*

INCOME STATEMENT ANALYSIS — ANALYSE DU COMPTE DE RESULTATS

	1982	1983	1984	1985	1986	1987	1988	1989	1990	1991		
% of average balance sheet total												**% du total moyen du bilan**
38. Interest income	12.57	10.20	10.45	9.27	8.25	7.76	8.27	9.90	10.96	10.39	38.	Produits financiers
39. Interest expenses	10.87	8.60	8.85	7.75	6.63	6.27	6.90	8.58	9.61	9.05	39.	Frais financiers
40. Net interest income	1.70	1.61	1.60	1.53	1.62	1.49	1.38	1.32	1.35	1.34	40.	Produits financiers nets
41. Non-interest income (net)	0.46	0.52	0.42	0.47	0.56	0.55	0.59	0.50	0.40	0.44	41.	Produits non financiers (nets)
42. Gross income	2.16	2.13	2.01	2.00	2.18	2.04	1.96	1.81	1.75	1.79	42.	Résultat brut
43. Operating expenses	1.51	1.48	1.39	1.33	1.42	1.39	1.22	1.19	1.21	1.17	43.	Frais d'exploitation
44. Net income	0.65	0.65	0.63	0.67	0.76	0.65	0.75	0.62	0.54	0.61	44.	Résultat net
45. Provisions (net)	0.31	0.30	0.29	0.30	0.31	0.28	0.40	0.43	0.20	0.31	45.	Provisions (nettes)
46. Profit before tax	0.34	0.34	0.34	0.37	0.45	0.37	0.34	0.19	0.33	0.31	46.	Bénéfices avant impôt
47. Income tax	0.14	0.15	0.14	0.15	0.18	0.15	0.10	0.09	0.07	0.08	47.	Impôt
48. Profit after tax	0.20	0.19	0.20	0.22	0.27	0.22	0.24	0.10	0.27	0.23	48.	Bénéfices après impôt
49. Distributed profit	::	::	::	::	::	::	::	::	::	::	49.	Bénéfices distribués
50. Retained profit	::	::	::	::	::	::	::	::	::	::	50.	Bénéfices mis en réserve
51. Staff costs	1.13	1.07	1.00	0.92	0.97	0.93	0.87	0.83	0.85	0.82	51.	Frais de personnel
52. Provisions on loans	::	::	::	::	::	::	::	::	::	::	52.	Provisions sur prêts
53. Provisions on securities	::	::	::	::	::	::	::	::	::	::	53.	Provisions sur titres
% of gross income												**% du total du résultat brut**
54. Net interest income	78.83	75.52	79.24	76.35	74.18	73.11	70.04	72.58	76.96	75.17	54.	Produits financiers nets
55. Non-interest income (net)	21.17	24.48	20.76	23.65	25.82	26.89	29.96	27.42	23.04	24.83	55.	Produits non financiers (nets)
56. Operating expenses	70.02	69.59	68.95	66.60	65.15	68.13	62.06	65.78	69.33	65.74	56.	Frais d'exploitation
57. Net income	29.98	30.41	31.05	33.40	34.85	31.87	37.94	34.22	30.67	34.26	57.	Résultat net
58. Provisions (net)	14.26	14.32	14.29	14.95	14.18	13.93	20.46	23.61	11.54	17.13	58.	Provisions (nettes)
59. Profit before tax	15.72	16.08	16.76	18.44	20.66	17.94	17.47	10.60	19.14	17.12	59.	Bénéfices avant impôt
60. Income tax	6.49	7.04	6.76	7.38	8.43	7.16	5.05	4.97	3.74	4.37	60.	Impôt
61. Profit after tax	9.23	9.05	10.00	11.06	12.23	10.79	12.42	5.63	15.40	12.75	61.	Bénéfices après impôt
62. Staff costs	52.13	50.32	49.44	45.92	44.60	45.86	44.39	45.81	48.70	45.97	62.	Frais de personnel
% of net income												**% du total du résultat net**
63. Provisions (net)	47.56	47.10	46.03	44.78	40.70	43.70	53.94	69.01	37.61	50.01	63.	Provisions (nettes)
64. Profit before tax	52.44	52.90	53.97	55.22	59.30	56.30	46.06	30.99	62.39	49.99	64.	Bénéfices avant impôt
65. Income tax	21.65	23.14	21.76	22.11	24.20	22.46	13.32	14.52	12.19	12.76	65.	Impôt
66. Profit after tax	30.79	29.76	32.21	33.11	35.10	33.84	32.74	16.47	50.20	37.22	66.	Bénéfices après impôt

BELGIUM

Commercial banks

Per cent

BALANCE SHEET ANALYSIS

% of year-end balance sheet total

BELGIQUE

Banques commerciales

Pourcentage

ANALYSE DU BILAN

% du total du bilan en fin d'exercice

	1982	1983	1984	1985	1986	1987	1988	1989	1990	1991		
Assets												**Actif**
67. Cash & balance with Central bank	0.23	0.20	0.22	0.18	0.17	0.16	0.15	0.18	0.17	0.17	67.	Caisse & solde auprès de la Banque centrale
68. Interbank deposits	43.58	44.18	45.04	45.55	44.15	45.17	45.24	43.40	43.40	42.83	68.	Dépôts interbancaires
69. Loans	33.15	30.73	29.56	26.70	25.53	24.94	25.84	28.54	28.06	29.47	69.	Prêts
70. Securities	19.08	21.31	20.98	23.76	26.53	26.23	24.46	23.34	23.60	22.86	70.	Valeurs mobilières
71. Other assets	3.97	3.58	4.20	3.80	3.63	3.49	4.31	4.55	4.78	4.68	71.	Autres actifs
Liabilities												**Passif**
72. Capital & reserves	2.39	2.51	2.52	2.51	2.87	2.93	3.06	3.39	3.40	3.87	72.	Capital et réserves
73. Borrowing from Central bank (1)	..	..	..	..	..	..	..	..	..	..	73.	Emprunts auprès de la Banque centrale (1)
74. Interbank deposits	61.33	62.54	64.18	63.52	62.06	61.14	60.78	57.94	56.88	53.12	74.	Dépôts interbancaires
75. Non-bank deposits	26.66	25.81	24.26	24.44	25.95	26.87	27.24	28.77	29.05	31.40	75.	Dépôts non bancaires
76. Bonds	4.84	4.93	4.70	5.01	4.87	4.68	4.30	4.50	5.53	6.48	76.	Obligations
77. Other liabilities	4.79	4.22	4.34	4.52	4.25	4.38	4.63	5.40	5.14	5.13	77.	Autres engagements
Memoranda												*Pour mémoire*
78. Short-term securities	*6.72*	*7.87*	*6.86*	*7.28*	*9.12*	*9.15*	*7.65*	*7.74*	*7.85*	*5.75*	*78.*	*Titres à court terme*
79. Bonds	*11.76*	*12.81*	*13.53*	*16.09*	*16.98*	*16.42*	*16.00*	*14.70*	*14.98*	*16.24*	*79.*	*Obligations*
80. Shares and participations	*0.60*	*0.63*	*0.60*	*0.40*	*0.43*	*0.66*	*0.81*	*0.90*	*0.77*	*0.86*	*80.*	*Actions et participations*
81. Claims on non-residents	*51.17*	*52.13*	*53.92*	*53.72*	*52.52*	*51.11*	*52.41*	*50.76*	*48.59*	*49.42*	*81.*	*Créances sur des non résidents*
82. Liabilities to non-residents	*60.23*	*61.98*	*65.00*	*63.74*	*62.76*	*61.13*	*62.94*	*61.40*	*58.89*	*56.93*	*82.*	*Engagements envers des non résidents*

1. Included under "Interbank deposits" (item 24 or item 74).

Notes

• Average balance sheet totals (item 29) are based on twelve end-month data.

1. Inclus sous "Dépôts interbancaires" (poste 24 ou poste 74).

Notes

• La moyenne du total des actifs/passifs (poste 29) est basée sur douze données de fin de mois.

Savings banks

BELGIQUE

Caisses d'épargne

Million Belgian francs / *Millions de francs belges*

	Item / Poste	1982	1983	1984	1985	1986	1987	1988	1989	1990	1991
	INCOME STATEMENT / COMPTE DE RESULTATS										
1.	Interest income / Produits financiers	72819	83843	102559	113277	121355	125968	133363	146022	169453	190572
2.	Interest expenses / Frais financiers	54168	62578	75754	83382	84970	86716	91504	104267	129473	147603
3.	Net interest income / Produits financiers nets	18651	21265	26805	29895	36385	39252	41859	41755	39980	42969
4.	Non-interest income (net) / Produits non financiers (nets)	1534	1130	434	973	2037	4408	5295	5025	5613	6296
5.	Gross income / Résultat brut	20185	22395	27239	30868	38422	43660	47154	46780	45593	49265
6.	Operating expenses / Frais d'exploitation	14874	16272	19532	22576	28172	31431	34072	35431	38480	39945
7.	Net income / Résultat net	5311	6123	7707	8292	10250	12229	13082	11349	7113	9320
8.	Provisions (net) / Provisions (nettes)	2873	3115	3338	3692	3622	4991	5892	4800	2065	3319
9.	Profit before tax / Bénéfices avant impôt	2438	3008	4369	4600	6628	7238	7190	6549	5048	6001
10.	Income tax / Impôt	1327	1150	1755	1638	2709	2489	1796	1161	1157	1562
11.	Profit after tax / Bénéfices après impôt	1111	1858	2614	2962	3919	4749	5394	5388	3891	4439
12.	Distributed profit / Bénéfices distribués	:	:	:	:	:	:	:	:	:	:
13.	Retained profit / Bénéfices mis en réserve	:	:	:	:	:	:	:	:	:	:
	Memoranda / Pour mémoire										
14.	*Staff costs / Frais de personnel*	7473	8270	9881	11188	12352	13925	14966	15617	17723	18833
15.	*Provisions on loans (1) / Provisions sur prêts (1)*	:	:	:	:	:	:	:	:	:	:
16.	*Provisions on securities / Provisions sur titres*	507	620	603	700	527	1033	1398	1720	656	1086
	BALANCE SHEET / BILAN										
	Assets / Actif										
17.	Cash & balance with Central bank / Caisse & solde auprès de la Banque centrale	2858	2512	3019	3063	3049	3330	3560	4038	4103	4384
18.	Interbank deposits / Dépôts interbancaires	32660	38625	48209	44251	68512	105515	147927	145792	235831	282915
19.	Loans / Prêts	333493	361105	371076	395434	447263	495642	563040	613483	717609	793969
20.	Securities / Valeurs mobilières	340682	442835	518349	608364	683574	744773	849684	891046	934398	999841
21.	Other assets / Autres actifs	45250	54754	64266	74165	78135	87532	90307	105564	118727	125592
	Liabilities / Passif										
22.	Capital & reserves / Capital et réserves	29700	34774	41554	50894	61190	73769	93754	104312	107794	114062
23.	Borrowing from Central bank / Emprunts auprès de la Banque centrale	150	123	–	–	–	–	–	500	3000	4703
24.	Interbank deposits / Dépôts interbancaires	2899	4191	4396	110181	133636	161371	254573	333522	418620	419914
25.	Non-bank deposits / Dépôts non bancaires	508262	594413	678992	655064	762471	888076	1022818	1070494	1212979	1361841
26.	Bonds / Obligations	174557	216829	228833	250354	251190	232040	210703	162488	167968	181141
27.	Other liabilities / Autres engagements	39375	49501	51144	58784	72046	81537	72670	88606	100308	125039
	Balance sheet total / Total du bilan										
28.	End-year total / En fin d'exercice	754943	899831	1004919	1125277	1280533	1436792	1654518	1759922	2010668	2206700
29.	Average total / Moyen	705483	808293	948693	1065807	1201908	1351237	1548762	1712194	1870927	2105510
	Memoranda / Pour mémoire										
30.	*Short-term securities / Titres à court terme*	33782	48282	71246	66620	71608	75504	73426	96203	92783	131500
31.	*Bonds / Obligations*	301051	381924	435011	528849	597747	654131	760088	778413	822355	847594
32.	*Shares and participations / Actions et participations*	5850	12629	12092	12895	14219	15138	16169	16430	19260	20747
33.	*Claims on non-residents / Créances sur des non résidents*	23532	39164	56627	84465	118630	143276	221209	301080	384462	433860
34.	*Liabilities to non-residents / Engagements envers des non résidents*	9169	24645	33663	51387	81185	106354	172459	268177	352223	393697
	SUPPLEMENTARY INFORMATION / RENSEIGNEMENTS COMPLEMENTAIRES										
35.	Number of institutions / Nombre d'institutions	30	31	28	29	31	32	31	29	28	28
36.	Number of branches / Nombre de succursales	21414	20659	19849	21281	20810	19804	18614	15593	14797	13531
37.	Number of employees (x 1000) / Nombre de salariés (x 1000)	6.6	7.0	8.7	9.2	9.8	10.7	11.4	11.3	11.6	11.8

BELGIUM

Savings banks

BELGIQUE

Caisses d'épargne

Per cent / *Pourcentage*

INCOME STATEMENT ANALYSIS / ANALYSE DU COMPTE DE RESULTATS

		1982	1983	1984	1985	1986	1987	1988	1989	1990	1991		
% of average balance sheet total													**% du total moyen du bilan**
38.	Interest income	10.32	10.37	10.81	10.63	10.10	9.32	8.61	8.53	9.06	9.05	38.	Produits financiers
39.	Interest expenses	7.68	7.74	7.99	7.82	7.07	6.42	5.91	6.09	6.92	7.01	39.	Frais financiers
40.	Net interest income	2.64	2.63	2.83	2.80	3.03	2.90	2.70	2.44	2.14	2.04	40.	Produits financiers nets
41.	Non-interest income (net)	0.22	0.14	0.05	0.09	0.17	0.33	0.34	0.29	0.30	0.30	41.	Produits non financiers (nets)
42.	Gross income	2.86	2.77	2.87	2.90	3.20	3.23	3.04	2.73	2.44	2.34	42.	Résultat brut
43.	Operating expenses	2.11	2.01	2.06	2.12	2.34	2.33	2.20	2.07	2.06	1.90	43.	Frais d'exploitation
44.	Net income	0.75	0.76	0.81	0.78	0.85	0.91	0.84	0.66	0.38	0.44	44.	Résultat net
45.	Provisions (net)	0.41	0.39	0.35	0.35	0.30	0.37	0.38	0.28	0.11	0.16	45.	Provisions (nettes)
46.	Profit before tax	0.35	0.37	0.46	0.43	0.55	0.54	0.46	0.38	0.27	0.29	46.	Bénéfices avant impôt
47.	Income tax	0.19	0.14	0.18	0.15	0.23	0.18	0.12	0.07	0.06	0.07	47.	Impôt
48.	Profit after tax	0.16	0.23	0.28	0.28	0.33	0.35	0.35	0.31	0.21	0.21	48.	Bénéfices après impôt
49.	Distributed profit	..	..	..	..	..	..	..	..	..	..	49.	Bénéfices distribués
50.	Retained profit	..	..	..	..	..	..	..	..	..	..	50.	Bénéfices mis en réserve
51.	Staff costs	1.06	1.02	1.04	1.05	1.03	1.03	0.97	0.91	0.95	0.89	51.	Frais de personnel
52.	Provisions on loans (1)	..	..	..	..	..	..	..	..	..	..	52.	Provisions sur prêts (1)
53.	Provisions on securities	0.07	0.08	0.06	0.07	0.04	0.08	0.09	0.10	0.04	0.05	53.	Provisions sur titres
% of gross income													**% du total du résultat brut**
54.	Net interest income	92.40	94.95	98.41	96.85	94.70	89.90	88.77	89.26	87.69	87.22	54.	Produits financiers nets
55.	Non-interest income (net)	7.60	5.05	1.59	3.15	5.30	10.10	11.23	10.74	12.31	12.78	55.	Produits non financiers (nets)
56.	Operating expenses	73.69	72.66	71.71	73.14	73.32	71.99	72.26	75.74	84.40	81.08	56.	Frais d'exploitation
57.	Net income	26.31	27.34	28.29	26.86	26.68	28.01	27.74	24.26	15.60	18.92	57.	Résultat net
58.	Provisions (net)	14.23	13.91	12.25	11.96	9.43	11.43	12.50	10.26	4.53	6.74	58.	Provisions (nettes)
59.	Profit before tax	12.08	13.43	16.04	14.90	17.25	16.58	15.25	14.00	11.07	12.18	59.	Bénéfices avant impôt
60.	Income tax	6.57	5.14	6.44	5.31	7.05	5.70	3.81	2.48	2.54	3.17	60.	Impôt
61.	Profit after tax	5.50	8.30	9.60	9.60	10.20	10.88	11.44	11.52	8.53	9.01	61.	Bénéfices après impôt
62.	Staff costs	37.02	36.93	36.28	36.24	32.15	31.89	31.74	33.38	38.87	38.23	62.	Frais de personnel
% of net income													**% du total du résultat net**
63.	Provisions (net)	54.10	50.87	43.31	44.52	35.34	40.81	45.04	42.29	29.03	35.61	63.	Provisions (nettes)
64.	Profit before tax	45.90	49.13	56.69	55.48	64.66	59.19	54.96	57.71	70.97	64.39	64.	Bénéfices avant impôt
65.	Income tax	24.99	18.78	22.77	19.75	26.43	20.35	13.73	10.23	16.27	16.76	65.	Impôt
66.	Profit after tax	20.92	30.34	33.92	35.72	38.23	38.83	41.23	47.48	54.70	47.63	66.	Bénéfices après impôt

BELGIUM

Savings banks

Per cent

BALANCE SHEET ANALYSIS

% of year-end balance sheet total

	1982	1983	1984	1985	1986	1987	1988	1989	1990	1991
Assets										
67. Cash & balance with Central bank	0.38	0.28	0.30	0.27	0.24	0.23	0.22	0.23	0.20	0.20
68. Interbank deposits	4.33	4.29	4.80	3.93	5.35	7.34	8.94	8.28	11.73	12.82
69. Loans	44.17	40.13	36.93	35.14	34.93	34.50	34.03	34.86	35.69	35.98
70. Securities	45.13	49.21	51.58	54.06	53.38	51.84	51.36	50.63	46.47	45.31
71. Other assets	5.99	6.08	6.40	6.59	6.10	6.09	5.46	6.00	5.90	5.69
Liabilities										
72. Capital & reserves	3.93	3.86	4.14	4.52	4.78	5.13	5.67	5.93	5.36	5.17
73. Borrowing from Central bank	0.02	0.01	-	-	-	-	-	0.03	0.15	0.21
74. Interbank deposits	0.38	0.47	0.44	9.79	10.44	11.23	15.39	18.95	20.82	19.03
75. Non-bank deposits	67.32	66.06	67.57	58.21	59.54	61.81	61.82	60.83	60.33	61.71
76. Bonds	23.12	24.10	22.77	22.25	19.62	16.15	12.74	9.23	8.35	8.21
77. Other liabilities	5.22	5.50	5.09	5.22	5.63	5.67	4.39	5.03	4.99	5.67
Memoranda										
78. Short-term securities	*4.47*	*5.37*	*7.09*	*5.92*	*5.59*	*5.26*	*4.44*	*5.47*	*4.61*	*5.96*
79. Bonds	*39.88*	*42.44*	*43.29*	*47.00*	*46.68*	*45.53*	*45.94*	*44.23*	*40.90*	*38.41*
80. Shares and participations	*0.77*	*1.40*	*1.20*	*1.15*	*1.11*	*1.05*	*0.98*	*0.93*	*0.96*	*0.94*
81. Claims on non-residents	*3.12*	*4.35*	*5.63*	*7.51*	*9.26*	*9.97*	*13.37*	*17.11*	*19.12*	*19.66*
82. Liabilities to non-residents	*1.21*	*2.74*	*3.35*	*4.57*	*6.34*	*7.40*	*10.42*	*15.24*	*17.52*	*17.84*

1. Included under "Provisions on securities" (item 16 or item 53).

Notes

• Private independent persons acting as savings bank agents are included in the number of branches.

• Average balance sheet totals (item 29) are based on twelve end-month data.

BELGIQUE

Caisses d'épargne

Pourcentage

ANALYSE DU BILAN

% du total du bilan en fin d'exercice

Actif
67. Caisse & solde auprès de la Banque centrale
68. Dépôts interbancaires
69. Prêts
70. Valeurs mobilières
71. Autres actifs

Passif
72. Capital et réserves
73. Emprunts auprès de la Banque centrale
74. Dépôts interbancaires
75. Dépôts non bancaires
76. Obligations
77. Autres engagements

Pour mémoire
78. Titres à court terme
79. Obligations
80. Actions et participations
81. Créances sur des non résidents
82. Engagements envers des non résidents

1. Inclus sous "Provisions sur titres" (poste 16 ou poste 53).

Notes

• Les agents indépendants sont compris dans le total des succursales.

• La moyenne du total des actifs/passifs (poste 29) est basée sur douze données de fin de mois.

CANADA

Commercial banks (consolidated world-wide)
Banques commerciales (consolidées sur une base mondiale)

Million Canadian dollars / *Millions de dollars canadiens*

	1982	1983	1984	1985	1986	1987	1988	1989	1990	1991	
INCOME STATEMENT											**COMPTE DE RESULTATS**
1. Interest income	48696	36528	38368	38809	37719	35560	40482	49671	54109	51530	1. Produits financiers
2. Interest expenses	41198	27671	29446	28719	26758	24210	27110	35516	40006	35688	2. Frais financiers
3. Net interest income	7498	8857	8922	10090	10961	11350	13372	14155	14103	15842	3. Produits financiers nets
4. Non-interest income (net)	2067	2364	2617	3135	3601	4491	5044	5831	6321	6821	4. Produits non financiers (nets)
5. Gross income	9565	11221	11539	13225	14562	15841	18416	19986	20424	22663	5. Résultat brut
6. Operating expenses	6550	6764	7120	7915	8576	9108	10362	11798	12996	14063	6. Frais d'exploitation
7. Net income	3015	4457	4419	5310	5986	6733	8054	8188	7428	8600	7. Résultat net
8. Provisions (net)	1397	1710	2003	2340	2996	2771	2520	5108	1692	2704	8. Provisions (nettes)
9. Profit before tax	1618	2747	2416	2970	2990	3962	5534	3080	5736	5896	9. Bénéfices avant impôt
10. Income tax	105	813	630	861	854	1440	2230	1106	2127	2086	10. Impôt
11. Profit after tax	1513	1934	1786	2109	2136	2522	3304	1974	3609	3810	11. Bénéfices après impôt
12. Distributed profit	..	..	..	..	..	..	..	..	..	..	12. Bénéfices distribués
13. Retained profit	..	..	..	..	..	..	..	..	..	..	13. Bénéfices mis en réserve
Memoranda											***Pour mémoire***
14. Staff costs	*4041*	*4123*	*4323*	*4761*	*4942*	*5186*	*5980*	*6785*	*7433*	*7970*	*14. Frais de personnel*
15. Provisions on loans	*1397*	*1710*	*2003*	*2340*	*2996*	*2771*	*2520*	*5108*	*1692*	*2704*	*15. Provisions sur prêts*
16. Provisions on securities	*..*	*..*	*..*	*..*	*..*	*..*	*..*	*..*	*..*	*..*	*16. Provisions sur titres*
BALANCE SHEET											**BILAN**
Assets											**Actif**
17. Cash & balance with Central bank	7331	6260	6080	5928	6419	6913	6834	6446	5653	6113	17. Caisse & solde auprès de la Banque centrale
18. Interbank deposits	38698	40668	46865	47183	50221	42233	34129	33346	32947	33609	18. Dépôts interbancaires
19. Loans	251051	241208	265778	289770	289762	307519	320722	351748	375601	393693	19. Prêts
20. Securities	27830	33011	35151	40212	43867	38711	43971	46347	49147	68855	20. Valeurs mobilières
21. Other assets	10862	9638	11459	11857	12772	15329	17093	18914	20289	19457	21. Autres actifs
Liabilities											**Passif**
22. Capital & reserves	12372	13618	16389	18383	20966	20648	22830	24926	27326	31066	22. Capital et réserves
23. Borrowing from Central bank	143	25	50	2368	71	376	342	261	38	53	23. Emprunts auprès de la Banque centrale
24. Interbank deposits	79924	79283	85719	89920	80609	73953	56068	54211	60214	60955	24. Dépôts interbancaires
25. Non-bank deposits	223951	224261	247453	265050	280380	292328	311483	339626	354773	381258	25. Dépôts non bancaires
26. Bonds	4173	4146	4692	5921	6986	5579	7862	8270	9212	10817	26. Obligations
27. Other liabilities	15209	9452	11030	13308	14029	17821	24164	29507	32074	37578	27. Autres engagements
Balance sheet total											**Total du bilan**
28. End-year total	335772	330785	365333	394950	403041	410705	422749	456801	483637	521727	28. En fin d'exercice
29. Average total	334289	333279	348059	380142	398996	406873	416727	439775	470219	502682	29. Moyen
Memoranda											***Pour mémoire***
30. Short-term securities	*..*	*..*	*..*	*..*	*..*	*..*	*..*	*..*	*..*	*..*	*30. Titres à court terme*
31. Bonds	*..*	*..*	*..*	*..*	*..*	*..*	*..*	*..*	*..*	*..*	*31. Obligations*
32. Shares and participations	*..*	*..*	*..*	*..*	*..*	*..*	*..*	*..*	*..*	*..*	*32. Actions et participations*
33. Claims on non-residents	*..*	*..*	*..*	*..*	*..*	*..*	*..*	*..*	*..*	*..*	*33. Créances sur des non résidents*
34. Liabilities to non-residents	*..*	*..*	*..*	*..*	*..*	*..*	*..*	*..*	*..*	*..*	*34. Engagements envers des non résidents*
SUPPLEMENTARY INFORMATION											**RENSEIGNEMENTS COMPLEMENTAIRES**
35. Number of institutions	NA	NA	NA	NA	NA	11	10	10	10	10	35. Nombre d'institutions
36. Number of branches	NA	NA	NA	NA	NA	NA	NA	NA	NA	NA	36. Nombre de succursales
37. Number of employees (x 1000)	NA	NA	NA	NA	NA	NA	NA	NA	NA	NA	37. Nombre de salariés (x 1000)

CANADA

Commercial banks (consolidated world-wide)

CANADA

Banques commerciales (consolidées sur une base mondiale)

Per cent — *Pourcentage*

INCOME STATEMENT ANALYSIS — ANALYSE DU COMPTE DE RESULTATS

	1982	1983	1984	1985	1986	1987	1988	1989	1990	1991		
% of average balance sheet total												**% du total moyen du bilan**
38. Interest income	14.57	10.96	11.02	10.21	9.45	8.74	9.71	11.29	11.51	10.25	38.	Produits financiers
39. Interest expenses	12.32	8.30	8.46	7.55	6.71	5.95	6.51	8.08	8.51	7.10	39.	Frais financiers
40. Net interest income	2.24	2.66	2.56	2.65	2.75	2.79	3.21	3.22	3.00	3.15	40.	Produits financiers nets
41. Non-interest income (net)	0.62	0.71	0.75	0.82	0.90	1.10	1.21	1.33	1.34	1.36	41.	Produits non financiers (nets)
42. Gross income	2.86	3.37	3.32	3.48	3.65	3.89	4.42	4.54	4.34	4.51	42.	Résultat brut
43. Operating expenses	1.96	2.03	2.05	2.08	2.15	2.24	2.49	2.68	2.76	2.80	43.	Frais d'exploitation
44. Net income	0.90	1.34	1.27	1.40	1.50	1.65	1.93	1.86	1.58	1.71	44.	Résultat net
45. Provisions (net)	0.42	0.51	0.58	0.62	0.75	0.68	0.60	1.16	0.36	0.54	45.	Provisions (nettes)
46. Profit before tax	0.48	0.82	0.69	0.78	0.75	0.97	1.33	0.70	1.22	1.17	46.	Bénéfices avant impôt
47. Income tax	0.03	0.24	0.18	0.23	0.21	0.35	0.54	0.25	0.45	0.41	47.	Impôt
48. Profit after tax	0.45	0.58	0.51	0.55	0.54	0.62	0.79	0.45	0.77	0.76	48.	Bénéfices après impôt
49. Distributed profit	::	::	::	::	::	::	::	::	::	::	49.	Bénéfices distribués
50. Retained profit	::	::	::	::	::	::	::	::	::	::	50.	Bénéfices mis en réserve
51. Staff costs	1.21	1.24	1.24	1.25	1.24	1.27	1.43	1.54	1.58	1.59	51.	Frais de personnel
52. Provisions on loans	0.42	0.51	0.58	0.62	0.75	0.68	0.60	1.16	0.36	0.54	52.	Provisions sur prêts
53. Provisions on securities	::	::	::	::	::	::	::	::	::	::	53.	Provisions sur titres
% of gross income												**% du total du résultat brut**
54. Net interest income	78.39	78.93	77.32	76.29	75.27	71.65	72.61	70.82	69.05	69.90	54.	Produits financiers nets
55. Non-interest income (net)	21.61	21.07	22.68	23.71	24.73	28.35	27.39	29.18	30.95	30.10	55.	Produits non financiers (nets)
56. Operating expenses	68.48	60.28	61.70	59.85	58.89	57.50	56.27	59.03	63.63	62.05	56.	Frais d'exploitation
57. Net income	31.52	39.72	38.30	40.15	41.11	42.50	43.73	40.97	36.37	37.95	57.	Résultat net
58. Provisions (net)	14.61	15.24	17.36	17.69	20.57	17.49	13.68	25.56	8.28	11.93	58.	Provisions (nettes)
59. Profit before tax	16.92	24.48	20.94	22.46	20.53	25.01	30.05	15.41	28.08	26.02	59.	Bénéfices avant impôt
60. Income tax	1.10	7.25	5.46	6.51	5.86	9.09	12.11	5.53	10.41	9.20	60.	Impôt
61. Profit after tax	15.82	17.24	15.48	15.95	14.67	15.92	17.94	9.88	17.67	16.81	61.	Bénéfices après impôt
62. Staff costs	42.25	36.74	37.46	36.00	33.94	32.74	32.47	33.95	36.39	35.17	62.	Frais de personnel
% of net income												**% du total du résultat net**
63. Provisions (net)	46.33	38.37	45.33	44.07	50.05	41.16	31.29	62.38	22.78	31.44	63.	Provisions (nettes)
64. Profit before tax	53.67	61.63	54.67	55.93	49.95	58.84	68.71	37.62	77.22	68.56	64.	Bénéfices avant impôt
65. Income tax	3.48	18.24	14.26	16.21	14.27	21.39	27.69	13.51	28.63	24.26	65.	Impôt
66. Profit after tax	50.18	43.39	40.42	39.72	35.68	37.46	41.02	24.11	48.59	44.30	66.	Bénéfices après impôt

CANADA

Commercial banks (consolidated world-wide)

Per cent

BALANCE SHEET ANALYSIS

% of year-end balance sheet total

	1982	1983	1984	1985	1986	1987	1988	1989	1990	1991
Assets										
67. Cash & balance with Central bank	2.18	1.89	1.66	1.50	1.59	1.68	1.62	1.41	1.17	1.17
68. Interbank deposits	11.53	12.29	12.83	11.95	12.46	10.28	8.07	7.30	6.81	6.44
69. Loans	74.77	72.92	72.75	73.37	71.89	74.88	75.87	77.00	77.66	75.46
70. Securities	8.29	9.98	9.62	10.18	10.88	9.43	10.40	10.15	10.16	13.20
71. Other assets	3.23	2.91	3.14	3.00	3.17	3.73	4.04	4.14	4.20	3.73
Liabilities										
72. Capital & reserves	3.68	4.12	4.49	4.65	5.20	5.03	5.40	5.46	5.65	5.95
73. Borrowing from Central bank	0.04	0.01	0.01	0.60	0.02	0.09	0.08	0.06	0.01	0.01
74. Interbank deposits	23.80	23.97	23.46	22.77	20.00	18.01	13.26	11.87	12.45	11.68
75. Non-bank deposits	66.70	67.80	67.73	67.11	69.57	71.18	73.68	74.35	73.36	73.08
76. Bonds	1.24	1.25	1.28	1.50	1.73	1.36	1.86	1.81	1.90	2.07
77. Other liabilities	4.53	2.86	3.02	3.37	3.48	4.34	5.72	6.46	6.63	7.20
Memoranda										
78. Short-term securities	..	..	..	..	..	..	..	..	..	..
79. Bonds	..	..	..	..	..	..	..	..	..	..
80. Shares and participations	..	..	..	..	..	..	..	..	..	..
81. Claims on non-residents	..	..	..	..	..	..	..	..	..	..
82. Liabilities to non-residents	..	..	..	..	..	..	..	..	..	..

Notes

- Data relate to Canadian bank groups reporting on a consolidated world-wide basis.
- The reporting period is the fiscal year ending 31st October.

CANADA

Banques commerciales (consolidées sur une base mondiale)

Pourcentage

ANALYSE DU BILAN

% du total du bilan en fin d'exercice

	1987	1988	1989	1990	1991
Actif					
67. Caisse & solde auprès de la Banque centrale	1.68	1.62	1.41	1.17	1.17
68. Dépôts interbancaires	10.28	8.07	7.30	6.81	6.44
69. Prêts	74.88	75.87	77.00	77.66	75.46
70. Valeurs mobilières	9.43	10.40	10.15	10.16	13.20
71. Autres actifs	3.73	4.04	4.14	4.20	3.73
Passif					
72. Capital et réserves	5.03	5.40	5.46	5.65	5.95
73. Emprunts auprès de la Banque centrale	0.09	0.08	0.06	0.01	0.01
74. Dépôts interbancaires	18.01	13.26	11.87	12.45	11.68
75. Dépôts non bancaires	71.18	73.68	74.35	73.36	73.08
76. Obligations	1.36	1.86	1.81	1.90	2.07
77. Autres engagements	4.34	5.72	6.46	6.63	7.20
Pour mémoire					
78. Titres à court terme	..	..	..	..	..
79. Obligations	..	..	..	..	..
80. Actions et participations	..	..	..	..	..
81. Créances sur des non résidents	..	..	..	..	..
82. Engagements envers des non résidents	..	..	..	..	..

Notes

- Les données se rapportent au groupe de banques canadiennes qui consolident leurs comptes à l'échelle mondiale.
- La période couverte est l'exercice financier qui se termine le 31 octobre.

CANADA

Foreign commercial banks

Million Canadian dollars

CANADA

Banques commerciales étrangères

Millions de dollars canadiens

		1982	1983	1984	1985	1986	1987	1988	1989	1990	1991		
INCOME STATEMENT													**COMPTE DE RESULTATS**
1.	Interest income	2149	2050	2421	2416	2366	2845	3391	4003	4945	4669	1.	Produits financiers
2.	Interest expenses	1896	1685	2038	1985	1911	2247	2671	3250	4030	3664	2.	Frais financiers
3.	Net interest income	253	365	383	431	455	598	720	753	915	1005	3.	Produits financiers nets
4.	Non-interest income (net)	58	80	117	163	223	278	331	378	511	775	4.	Produits non financiers (nets)
5.	Gross income	311	445	500	594	678	876	1051	1131	1426	1780	5.	Résultat brut
6.	Operating expenses	206	259	304	346	402	590	657	626	865	1143	6.	Frais d'exploitation
7.	Net income	105	186	196	248	276	286	394	505	561	637	7.	Résultat net
8.	Provisions (net)	33	73	40	50	146	216	95	106	288	524	8.	Provisions (nettes)
9.	Profit before tax	72	113	156	198	130	70	299	399	273	113	9.	Bénéfices avant impôt
10.	Income tax	37	58	72	92	60	78	140	164	112	53	10.	Impôt
11.	Profit after tax	35	55	84	106	70	-8	159	235	161	60	11.	Bénéfices après impôt
12.	Distributed profit	..	..	..	..	..	..	..	..	..	..	12.	Bénéfices distribués
13.	Retained profit	..	..	..	..	..	..	..	..	..	..	13.	Bénéfices mis en réserve
Memoranda													***Pour mémoire***
14.	*Staff costs*	*93*	*121*	*145*	*163*	*185*	*289*	*320*	*308*	*376*	*426*	*14.*	*Frais de personnel*
15.	*Provisions on loans*	*33*	*73*	*40*	*50*	*146*	*216*	*95*	*106*	*288*	*524*	*15.*	*Provisions sur prêts*
16.	*Provisions on securities*	*..*	*..*	*..*	*..*	*..*	*..*	*..*	*..*	*..*	*..*	*16.*	*Provisions sur titres*
BALANCE SHEET													**BILAN**
Assets													**Actif**
17.	Cash & balance with Central bank	5	8	14	21	117	185	234	267	123	146	17.	Caisse & solde auprès de la Banque centrale
18.	Interbank deposits	3381	4863	4903	5074	6053	7050	6134	7221	6177	7427	18.	Dépôts interbancaires
19.	Loans	13124	13616	15224	17085	24098	25327	28207	31037	33987	34140	19.	Prêts
20.	Securities	668	1329	1363	2168	2850	4442	4920	4664	5932	7071	20.	Valeurs mobilières
21.	Other assets	381	424	610	724	914	1008	1029	1167	1507	1303	21.	Autres actifs
Liabilities													**Passif**
22.	Capital & reserves	1220	1448	1643	1857	2586	2816	3107	3416	3973	3952	22.	Capital et réserves
23.	Borrowing from Central bank	-	-	-	-	6	60	-	-	-	-	23.	Emprunts auprès de la Banque centrale
24.	Interbank deposits	5035	5782	5845	7491	8966	10940	12185	13080	15281	15530	24.	Dépôts interbancaires
25.	Non-bank deposits	10949	12371	13917	14713	20730	22219	22752	24545	23863	24857	25.	Dépôts non bancaires
26.	Bonds	10	38	43	44	91	99	192	292	557	873	26.	Obligations
27.	Other liabilities	345	602	666	967	1653	1878	2288	3023	4052	4875	27.	Autres engagements
Balance sheet total													**Total du bilan**
28.	End-year total	17559	20240	22114	25072	34032	38012	40524	44356	47726	50087	28.	En fin d'exercice
29.	Average total	12098	18900	21177	23593	29552	36022	39268	42440	46041	48906	29.	Moyen
Memoranda													***Pour mémoire***
30.	*Short-term securities*	*..*	*..*	*..*	*..*	*..*	*..*	*..*	*..*	*..*	*..*	*30.*	*Titres à court terme*
31.	*Bonds*	*..*	*..*	*..*	*..*	*..*	*..*	*..*	*..*	*..*	*..*	*31.*	*Obligations*
32.	*Shares and participations*	*..*	*..*	*..*	*..*	*..*	*..*	*..*	*..*	*..*	*..*	*32.*	*Actions et participations*
33.	*Claims on non-residents*	*..*	*..*	*..*	*..*	*..*	*..*	*..*	*..*	*..*	*..*	*33.*	*Créances sur des non résidents*
34.	*Liabilities to non-residents*	*..*	*..*	*..*	*..*	*..*	*..*	*..*	*..*	*..*	*..*	*34.*	*Engagements envers des non résidents*
SUPPLEMENTARY INFORMATION													**RENSEIGNEMENTS COMPLEMENTAIRES**
35.	Number of institutions	NA	NA	NA	NA	NA	58	57	57	56	56	35.	Nombre d'institutions
36.	Number of branches	NA	NA	NA	NA	NA	NA	NA	NA	NA	NA	36.	Nombre de succursales
37.	Number of employees (x 1000)	NA	NA	NA	NA	NA	NA	NA	NA	NA	NA	37.	Nombre de salariés (x 1000)

CANADA

Foreign commercial banks

CANADA

Banques commerciales étrangères

Per cent — *Pourcentage*

INCOME STATEMENT ANALYSIS — **ANALYSE DU COMPTE DE RESULTATS**

		1982	1983	1984	1985	1986	1987	1988	1989	1990	1991		
	% of average balance sheet total												**% du total moyen du bilan**
38.	Interest income	17.76	10.85	11.43	10.24	8.01	7.90	8.64	9.43	10.74	9.55	38.	Produits financiers
39.	Interest expenses	15.67	8.92	9.62	8.41	6.47	6.24	6.80	7.66	8.75	7.49	39.	Frais financiers
40.	Net interest income	2.09	1.93	1.81	1.83	1.54	1.66	1.83	1.77	1.99	2.05	40.	Produits financiers nets
41.	Non-interest income (net)	0.48	0.42	0.55	0.69	0.75	0.77	0.84	0.89	1.11	1.58	41.	Produits non financiers (nets)
42.	Gross income	2.57	2.35	2.36	2.52	2.29	2.43	2.68	2.66	3.10	3.64	42.	Résultat brut
43.	Operating expenses	1.70	1.37	1.44	1.47	1.36	1.64	1.67	1.48	1.88	2.34	43.	Frais d'exploitation
44.	Net income	0.87	0.98	0.93	1.05	0.93	0.79	1.00	1.19	1.22	1.30	44.	Résultat net
45.	Provisions (net)	0.27	0.39	0.19	0.21	0.49	0.60	0.24	0.25	0.63	1.07	45.	Provisions (nettes)
46.	Profit before tax	0.60	0.60	0.74	0.84	0.44	0.19	0.76	0.94	0.59	0.23	46.	Bénéfices avant impôt
47.	Income tax	0.31	0.31	0.34	0.39	0.20	0.22	0.36	0.39	0.24	0.11	47.	Impôt
48.	Profit after tax	0.29	0.29	0.40	0.45	0.24	-0.02	0.40	0.55	0.35	0.12	48.	Bénéfices après impôt
49.	Distributed profit	..	..	..	..	..	..	..	..	..	..	49.	Bénéfices distribués
50.	Retained profit	..	..	..	..	..	..	..	..	..	..	50.	Bénéfices mis en réserve
51.	Staff costs	0.77	0.64	0.68	0.69	0.63	0.80	0.81	0.73	0.82	0.87	51.	Frais de personnel
52.	Provisions on loans	0.27	0.39	0.19	0.21	0.49	0.60	0.24	0.25	0.63	1.07	52.	Provisions sur prêts
53.	Provisions on securities	..	..	..	..	..	..	..	..	..	..	53.	Provisions sur titres
	% of gross income												**% du total du résultat brut**
54.	Net interest income	81.35	82.02	76.60	72.56	67.11	68.26	68.51	66.58	64.17	56.46	54.	Produits financiers nets
55.	Non-interest income (net)	18.65	17.98	23.40	27.44	32.89	31.74	31.49	33.42	35.83	43.54	55.	Produits non financiers (nets)
56.	Operating expenses	66.24	58.20	60.80	58.25	59.29	67.35	62.51	55.35	60.66	64.21	56.	Frais d'exploitation
57.	Net income	33.76	41.80	39.20	41.75	40.71	32.65	37.49	44.65	39.34	35.79	57.	Résultat net
58.	Provisions (net)	10.61	16.40	8.00	8.42	21.53	24.66	9.04	9.37	20.20	29.44	58.	Provisions (nettes)
59.	Profit before tax	23.15	25.39	31.20	33.33	19.17	7.99	28.45	35.28	19.14	6.35	59.	Bénéfices avant impôt
60.	Income tax	11.90	13.03	14.40	15.49	8.85	8.90	13.32	14.50	7.85	2.98	60.	Impôt
61.	Profit after tax	11.25	12.36	16.80	17.85	10.32	-0.91	15.13	20.78	11.29	3.37	61.	Bénéfices après impôt
62.	Staff costs	29.90	27.19	29.00	27.44	27.29	32.99	30.45	27.23	26.37	23.93	62.	Frais de personnel
	% of net income												**% du total du résultat net**
63.	Provisions (net)	31.43	39.25	20.41	20.16	52.90	75.52	24.11	20.99	51.34	82.26	63.	Provisions (nettes)
64.	Profit before tax	68.57	60.75	79.59	79.84	47.10	24.48	75.89	79.01	48.66	17.74	64.	Bénéfices avant impôt
65.	Income tax	35.24	31.18	36.73	37.10	21.74	27.27	35.53	32.48	19.96	8.32	65.	Impôt
66.	Profit after tax	33.33	29.57	42.86	42.74	25.36	-2.80	40.36	46.53	28.70	9.42	66.	Bénéfices après impôt

CANADA

Foreign commercial banks

Per cent

BALANCE SHEET ANALYSIS

% of year-end balance sheet total

	1982	1983	1984	1985	1986	1987	1988	1989	1990	1991
Assets										
67. Cash & balance with Central bank	0.03	0.04	0.06	0.08	0.34	0.49	0.58	0.60	0.26	0.29
68. Interbank deposits	19.26	24.03	22.17	20.24	17.79	18.55	15.14	16.28	12.94	14.83
69. Loans	74.74	67.27	68.84	68.14	70.81	66.63	69.61	69.97	71.21	68.16
70. Securities	3.80	6.57	6.16	8.65	8.37	11.69	12.14	10.51	12.43	14.12
71. Other assets	2.17	2.09	2.76	2.89	2.69	2.65	2.54	2.63	3.16	2.60
Liabilities										
72. Capital & reserves	6.95	7.15	7.43	7.41	7.60	7.41	7.67	7.70	8.32	7.89
73. Borrowing from Central bank	-	-	-	-	0.02	0.16	-	-	-	-
74. Interbank deposits	28.67	28.57	26.43	29.88	26.35	28.78	30.07	29.49	32.02	31.01
75. Non-bank deposits	62.36	61.12	62.93	58.68	60.91	58.45	56.14	55.34	50.00	49.63
76. Bonds	0.06	0.19	0.19	0.18	0.27	0.26	0.47	0.66	1.17	1.74
77. Other liabilities	1.96	2.97	3.01	3.86	4.86	4.94	5.65	6.82	8.49	9.73
Memoranda										
78. Short-term securities	:	:	:	:	:	:	:	:	:	:
79. Bonds	:	:	:	:	:	:	:	:	:	:
80. Shares and participations	:	:	:	:	:	:	:	:	:	:
81. Claims on non-residents	:	:	:	:	:	:	:	:	:	:
82. Liabilities to non-residents	:	:	:	:	:	:	:	:	:	:

Notes

- The reporting period is the fiscal year ending 31st October.

CANADA

Banques commerciales étrangères

Pourcentage

ANALYSE DU BILAN

% du total du bilan en fin d'exercice

Actif
67. Caisse & solde auprès de la Banque centrale
68. Dépôts interbancaires
69. Prêts
70. Valeurs mobilières
71. Autres actifs

Passif
72. Capital et réserves
73. Emprunts auprès de la Banque centrale
74. Dépôts interbancaires
75. Dépôts non bancaires
76. Obligations
77. Autres engagements

Pour mémoire
78. Titres à court terme
79. Obligations
80. Actions et participations
81. Créances sur des non résidents
82. Engagements envers des non résidents

Notes

- La période couverte est l'exercice financier qui se termine le 31 octobre.

DENMARK

Commercial banks and savings banks

DANEMARK

Banques commerciales et caisses d'épargne

Million Danish kroner / *Millions de couronnes danoises*

		1982	1983	1984	1985	1986	1987	1988	1989	1990	1991 (1)	
INCOME STATEMENT												**COMPTE DE RESULTATS**
1.	Interest income	41062	41563	49736	57628	60547	66452	68776	87280	103599	100453	Produits financiers
2.	Interest expenses	28344	28177	34551	39956	40002	43458	44703	61504	75254	66050	Frais financiers
3.	Net interest income	12718	13386	15185	18472	20545	22994	24073	25776	28345	34403	Produits financiers nets
4.	Non-interest income (net)	7753	24559	2780	25248	-3668	4205	13784	7170	4016	5728	Produits non financiers (nets)
5.	Gross income	20471	37945	17965	43720	16877	27199	37857	32946	32361	40131	Résultat brut
6.	Operating expenses	11078	12424	13586	15106	16686	18686	20135	21383	22200	25112	Frais d'exploitation
7.	Net income	9393	25521	4379	28614	191	8513	17722	11563	10161	15019	Résultat net
8.	Provisions (net)	5337	5535	3904	5928	3084	5662	9416	8777	13111	15113	Provisions (nettes)
9.	Profit before tax	4056	19986	475	22686	-2893	2851	8306	2786	-2950	-94	Bénéfices avant impôt
10.	Income tax	1124	7697	414	10657	-251	1067	2572	522	-238	331	Impôt
11.	Profit after tax	2932	12289	61	12029	-2642	1784	5734	2264	-2712	-425	Bénéfices après impôt
12.	Distributed profit	723	882	882	1150	1242	1245	1274	1666	1320	1861	Bénéfices distribués
13.	Retained profit	2209	11407	-821	10879	-3884	539	4460	598	-4032	-2286	Bénéfices mis en réserve
Memoranda												***Pour mémoire***
14.	Staff costs	7394	8142	8772	9593	10446	11776	12682	13340	13814	15165	Frais de personnel
15.	Provisions on loans	4645	4409	3065	3985	2019	4303	8043	7388	11408	13592	Provisions sur prêts
16.	Provisions on securities	..	..	..	..	..	..	..	..	..	..	Provisions sur titres
BALANCE SHEET												**BILAN**
Assets												**Actif**
17.	Cash & balance with Central bank	8107	8876	11800	38627	21640	11618	16180	17005	14341	19979	Caisse & solde auprès de la Banque centrale
18.	Interbank deposits	56855	76050	104302	123235	107838	141350	169575	171700	170112	189185	Dépôts interbancaires
19.	Loans	149426	173395	208851	269248	341748	390488	410545	456793	495821	508427	Prêts
20.	Securities	82639	144564	162240	210632	207587	171418	200753	230152	212276	244309	Valeurs mobilières
21.	Other assets	65776	80141	99446	123818	142785	155521	175828	184476	228538	47885	Autres actifs
Liabilities												**Passif**
22.	Capital & reserves	33759	47963	49991	66424	70790	74779	87933	92470	88199	67564	Capital et réserves
23.	Borrowing from Central bank	6491	6129	10327	23177	45170	18178	3513	19844	4880	19339	Emprunts auprès de la Banque centrale
24.	Interbank deposits	59338	89159	129091	177718	162959	201379	233807	271829	292874	313462	Dépôts interbancaires
25.	Non-bank deposits	200612	259300	305316	369105	406369	424496	471360	496049	526552	503260	Dépôts non bancaires
26.	Bonds	-	-	-	-	-	-	-	-	-	42821	Obligations
27.	Other liabilities	62603	80475	91914	129136	136310	151563	176268	179934	209083	63339	Autres engagements
Balance sheet total												**Total du bilan**
28.	End-year total	362803	483026	586639	765560	821598	870395	972881	1060126	1121588	1009785	En fin d'exercice
29.	Average total	336690	393261	504813	609853	781707	805018	867164	1010504	1084007	NA	Moyen
Memoranda												***Pour mémoire***
30.	Short-term securities	..	17909	15315	12394	11712	21118	34208	21240	23713	48935	Titres à court terme
31.	Bonds	..	110257	129605	173747	165718	121559	132322	165343	147593	159252	Obligations
32.	Shares and participations	7259	12574	13740	19525	22633	21721	27553	36782	34341	36122	Actions et participations
33.	Claims on non-residents	59461	81314	117785	166477	167628	209273	276874	324297	365812	..	Créances sur des non résidents
34.	Liabilities to non-residents	84374	109534	150931	208806	212624	251325	329555	386679	420807	..	Engagements envers des non résidents
SUPPLEMENTARY INFORMATION												**RENSEIGNEMENTS COMPLEMENTAIRES**
35.	Number of institutions	224	224	219	217	216	214	206	199	189	119	Nombre d'institutions
36.	Number of branches	3559	3502	3480	3331	3302	3264	3159	3059	2884	2652	Nombre de succursales
37.	Number of employees (x 1000)	48	49	50	52	55	57	56	56	55	56	Nombre de salariés (x 1000)

DENMARK

Commercial banks and savings banks

DANEMARK

Banques commerciales et caisses d'épargne

Per cent — *Pourcentage*

	1982	1983	1984	1985	1986	1987	1988	1989	1990	1991 (1)		
INCOME STATEMENT ANALYSIS												**ANALYSE DU COMPTE DE RESULTATS**
% of average balance sheet total												**% du total moyen du bilan**
38. Interest income	12.20	10.57	9.85	9.45	7.75	8.25	7.93	8.64	9.56	NA	38.	Produits financiers
39. Interest expenses	8.42	7.16	6.84	6.42	5.12	5.40	5.16	6.09	6.94	NA	39.	Frais financiers
40. Net interest income	3.78	3.40	3.01	3.03	2.63	2.86	2.78	2.55	2.61	NA	40.	Produits financiers nets
41. Non-interest income (net)	2.30	6.24	0.55	4.14	-0.47	0.52	1.59	0.71	0.37	NA	41.	Produits non financiers (nets)
42. Gross income	6.08	9.65	3.56	7.17	2.16	3.38	4.37	3.26	2.99	NA	42.	Résultat brut
43. Operating expenses	3.29	3.16	2.69	2.48	2.13	2.32	2.32	2.12	2.05	NA	43.	Frais d'exploitation
44. Net income	2.79	6.49	0.87	4.69	0.02	1.06	2.04	1.14	0.94	NA	44.	Résultat net
45. Provisions (net)	1.59	1.41	0.77	0.97	0.39	0.70	1.09	0.87	1.21	NA	45.	Provisions (nettes)
46. Profit before tax	1.20	5.08	0.09	3.72	-0.37	0.35	0.96	0.28	-0.27	NA	46.	Bénéfices avant impôt
47. Income tax	0.33	1.96	0.08	1.75	-0.03	0.13	0.30	0.05	-0.02	NA	47.	Impôt
48. Profit after tax	0.87	3.12	0.01	1.97	-0.34	0.22	0.66	0.22	-0.25	NA	48.	Bénéfices après impôt
49. Distributed profit	0.21	0.22	0.17	0.19	0.16	0.15	0.15	0.16	0.12	NA	49.	Bénéfices distribués
50. Retained profit	0.66	2.90	-0.16	1.78	-0.50	0.07	0.51	0.06	-0.37	NA	50.	Bénéfices mis en réserve
51. Staff costs	2.20	2.07	1.74	1.57	1.34	1.46	1.46	1.32	1.27	NA	51.	Frais de personnel
52. Provisions on loans	1.38	1.12	0.61	0.65	0.26	0.53	0.93	0.73	1.05	NA	52.	Provisions sur prêts
53. Provisions on securities	..	..	..	..	..	..	..	..	..	..	53.	Provisions sur titres
% of gross income												**% du total du résultat brut**
54. Net interest income	62.13	35.28	84.53	42.25	121.73	84.54	63.59	78.24	87.59	85.73	54.	Produits financiers nets
55. Non-interest income (net)	37.87	64.72	15.47	57.75	-21.73	15.46	36.41	21.76	12.41	14.27	55.	Produits non financiers (nets)
56. Operating expenses	54.12	32.74	75.62	34.55	98.87	68.70	53.19	64.90	68.60	62.58	56.	Frais d'exploitation
57. Net income	45.88	67.26	24.38	65.45	1.13	31.30	46.81	35.10	31.40	37.42	57.	Résultat net
58. Provisions (net)	26.07	14.59	21.73	13.56	18.27	20.82	24.87	26.64	40.51	37.66	58.	Provisions (nettes)
59. Profit before tax	19.81	52.67	2.64	51.89	-17.14	10.48	21.94	8.46	-9.12	-0.23	59.	Bénéfices avant impôt
60. Income tax	5.49	20.28	2.30	24.38	-1.49	3.92	6.79	1.58	-0.74	0.82	60.	Impôt
61. Profit after tax	14.32	32.39	0.34	27.51	-15.65	6.56	15.15	6.87	-8.38	-1.06	61.	Bénéfices après impôt
62. Staff costs	36.12	21.46	48.83	21.94	61.89	43.30	33.50	40.49	42.69	37.79	62.	Frais de personnel
% of net income												**% du total du résultat net**
63. Provisions (net)	56.82	21.69	89.15	20.72	..	66.51	53.13	75.91	129.03	100.63	63.	Provisions (nettes)
64. Profit before tax	43.18	78.31	10.85	79.28	..	33.49	46.87	24.09	-29.03	-0.63	64.	Bénéfices avant impôt
65. Income tax	11.97	30.16	9.45	37.24	..	12.53	14.51	4.51	-2.34	2.20	65.	Impôt
66. Profit after tax	31.21	48.15	1.39	42.04	..	20.96	32.36	19.58	-26.69	-2.83	66.	Bénéfices après impôt

DENMARK

Commercial banks and savings banks

DANEMARK

Banques commerciales et caisses d'épargne

Per cent — *Pourcentage*

BALANCE SHEET ANALYSIS — ANALYSE DU BILAN

% of year-end balance sheet total — **% du total du bilan en fin d'exercice**

	1982	1983	1984	1985	1986	1987	1988	1989	1990	1991 (1)	
Assets											**Actif**
67. Cash & balance with Central bank	2.23	1.84	2.01	5.05	2.63	1.33	1.66	1.60	1.28	1.98	67. Caisse & solde auprès de la Banque centrale
68. Interbank deposits	15.67	15.74	17.78	16.10	13.13	16.24	17.43	16.20	15.17	18.74	68. Dépôts interbancaires
69. Loans	41.19	35.90	35.60	35.17	41.60	44.86	42.20	43.09	44.21	50.35	69. Prêts
70. Securities	22.78	29.93	27.66	27.51	25.27	19.69	20.63	21.71	18.97	24.19	70. Valeurs mobilières
71. Other assets	18.13	16.59	16.95	16.17	17.38	17.87	18.07	17.40	20.38	4.74	71. Autres actifs
Liabilities											**Passif**
72. Capital & reserves	9.31	9.93	8.52	8.68	8.62	8.59	9.04	8.72	7.86	6.69	72. Capital et réserves
73. Borrowing from Central bank	1.79	1.27	1.76	3.03	5.50	2.09	0.36	1.87	0.44	1.92	73. Emprunts auprès de la Banque centrale
74. Interbank deposits	16.36	18.46	22.01	23.21	19.83	23.14	24.03	25.64	26.11	31.04	74. Dépôts interbancaires
75. Non-bank deposits	55.30	53.68	52.04	48.21	49.46	48.77	48.45	46.79	46.95	49.84	75. Dépôts non bancaires
76. Bonds	-	-	-	-	-	-	-	-	-	4.24	76. Obligations
77. Other liabilities	17.26	16.66	15.67	16.87	16.59	17.41	18.12	16.97	18.64	6.27	77. Autres engagements
Memoranda											*Pour mémoire*
78. Short-term securities	..	*3.71*	*2.61*	*1.62*	*1.43*	*2.43*	*3.52*	*2.00*	*2.11*	*4.85*	*78. Titres à court terme*
79. Bonds	..	*22.83*	*22.09*	*22.70*	*20.17*	*13.97*	*13.60*	*15.60*	*13.16*	*15.77*	*79. Obligations*
80. Shares and participations	*2.00*	*2.60*	*2.34*	*2.55*	*2.75*	*2.50*	*2.83*	*3.47*	*3.06*	*3.58*	*80. Actions et participations*
81. Claims on non-residents	*16.39*	*16.83*	*20.08*	*21.75*	*20.40*	*24.04*	*28.46*	*30.59*	*32.62*	..	*81. Créances sur des non résidents*
82. Liabilities to non-residents	*23.26*	*22.68*	*25.73*	*27.27*	*25.88*	*28.87*	*33.87*	*36.47*	*37.52*	..	*82. Engagements envers des non résidents*

1. Break in series.

1. Rupture dans les séries.

Notes

- "Non-interest income (net)" (item 4) includes value adjustments on foreign currency assets and liabilities and on securities.

- Average balance sheet totals (item 29) are based on twelve end-month data.

Notes

- Les "Produits non financiers (net)" (poste 4) contiennent des ajustements en valeurs concernant les actifs/passifs en monnaies étrangères et les valeurs mobilières.

- La moyenne du total des actifs/passifs (poste 29) est basée sur douze données de fin de mois.

FINLAND
All banks
Million markkaa

FINLANDE
Ensemble des banques
Millions de markkaa

#	Item / Poste	1982	1983	1984	1985	1986	1987	1988	1989	1990	1991
INCOME STATEMENT / COMPTE DE RESULTATS											
1.	Interest income / Produits financiers	14549	17385	22975	26513	26760	32567	43193	60507	74459	77567
2.	Interest expenses / Frais financiers	9848	12324	17087	19483	19540	23530	32492	48838	65052	65331
3.	Net interest income / Produits financiers nets	4701	5061	5888	7030	7220	9037	10701	11669	9407	12236
4.	Non-interest income (net) / Produits non financiers (nets)	3057	3505	4485	5835	6603	8018	12112	10977	16126	10810
5.	Gross income / Résultat brut	7758	8566	10373	12865	13823	17055	22813	22646	25533	23046
6.	Operating expenses / Frais d'exploitation	6301	7060	8712	10177	11314	13712	16790	19199	20807	28954
7.	Net income / Résultat net	1457	1506	1661	2688	2509	3343	6023	3447	4726	-5908
8.	Provisions (net) / Provisions (nettes)	902	914	832	1558	1116	1922	2980	1618	1890	-53
9.	Profit before tax / Bénéfices avant impôt	555	592	829	1130	1393	1421	3043	1829	2836	-5855
10.	Income tax / Impôt	251	225	260	359	316	332	457	602	961	475
11.	Profit after tax / Bénéfices après impôt	304	367	569	771	1077	1089	2586	1227	1875	-6330
12.	Distributed profit / Bénéfices distribués	273	330	515	677	835	896	1052	1177	727	273
13.	Retained profit / Bénéfices mis en réserve	31	37	54	94	242	193	1534	50	1148	-6603
Memoranda / Pour mémoire											
14.	*Staff costs / Frais de personnel*	*2598*	*2965*	*3412*	*3941*	*4281*	*4828*	*5416*	*6029*	*6075*	*6277*
15.	*Provisions on loans / Provisions sur prêts*	*665*	*653*	*688*	*1023*	*1106*	*1546*	*2084*	*2231*	*2192*	*-10*
16.	*Provisions on securities / Provisions sur titres*	*..*	*..*	*..*	*..*	*..*	*376*	*675*	*-623*	*-973*	*-43*
BALANCE SHEET / BILAN											
Assets / Actif											
17.	Cash & balance with Central bank / Caisse & solde auprès de la Banque centrale	6317	7307	13700	14257	12367	15567	24465	32085	24491	19090
18.	Interbank deposits / Dépôts interbancaires	6761	8185	10633	13562	19865	17692	22749	24534	24072	22011
19.	Loans / Prêts	123070	143840	167219	199393	232398	277749	367326	444797	483139	490581
20.	Securities / Valeurs mobilières	11433	17580	24414	30104	45230	62843	77809	89223	95149	126973
21.	Other assets / Autres actifs	34085	40978	52863	54745	72137	78623	91617	91812	107152	111736
Liabilities / Passif											
22.	Capital & reserves / Capital et réserves	10553	12940	16304	20059	23075	27045	39098	45677	50563	53350
23.	Borrowing from Central bank / Emprunts auprès de la Banque centrale	4216	7280	7131	7144	11477	2711	4813	3871	3918	5804
24.	Interbank deposits / Dépôts interbancaires	6869	7668	9437	11527	16293	13656	16480	18075	17363	18828
25.	Non-bank deposits / Dépôts non bancaires	126335	147922	175352	200859	222640	264361	328332	347022	378838	390247
26.	Bonds / Obligations	1983	2390	5765	7164	12731	17404	29922	44580	62675	78444
27.	Other liabilities / Autres engagements	31710	39690	54840	65308	95781	127297	165321	223226	220646	223718
Balance sheet total / Total du bilan											
28.	End-year total / En fin d'exercice	181666	217890	268829	312061	381997	452474	583966	682451	734003	770391
29.	Average total / Moyen	165341	200186	243361	290447	347030	417236	518221	633209	708228	752198
Memoranda / Pour mémoire											
30.	*Short-term securities (1) / Titres à court terme (1)*	*9256*	*14796*	*20569*	*25165*	*2688*	*18505*	*28582*	*30029*	*36176*	*46860*
31.	*Bonds / Obligations*	*2177*	*2784*	*3845*	*4939*	*36457*	*36675*	*36546*	*42763*	*42423*	*55802*
32.	*Shares and participations / Actions et participations*	*..*	*..*	*..*	*..*	*6085*	*7663*	*10681*	*16431*	*16550*	*24311*
33.	*Claims on non-residents / Créances sur des non résidents*	*21100*	*27335*	*42947*	*42239*	*69528*	*76255*	*88306*	*94136*	*102036*	*103688*
34.	*Liabilities to non-residents / Engagements envers des non résidents*	*32628*	*41917*	*61653*	*71030*	*98424*	*130202*	*156315*	*176339*	*218019*	*221916*
SUPPLEMENTARY INFORMATION / RENSEIGNEMENTS COMPLEMENTAIRES											
35.	Number of institutions / Nombre d'institutions	651	652	644	635	621	610	589	553	523	438
36.	Number of branches / Nombre de succursales	2784	2838	2886	2934	2924	2938	2956	2977	2821	2662
37.	Number of employees (x 1000) / Nombre de salariés (x 1000)	39.6	40.4	41.5	42.9	44.4	45.5	47.4	48.6	46.1	42.8

FINLAND

All banks

FINLANDE

Ensemble des banques

Per cent — *Pourcentage*

INCOME STATEMENT ANALYSIS — ANALYSE DU COMPTE DE RESULTATS

		1982	1983	1984	1985	1986	1987	1988	1989	1990	1991		
	% of average balance sheet total											**% du total moyen du bilan**	
38.	Interest income	8.80	8.68	9.44	9.13	7.71	7.81	8.33	9.56	10.51	10.31	Produits financiers	38.
39.	Interest expenses	5.96	6.16	7.02	6.71	5.63	5.64	6.27	7.71	9.19	8.69	Frais financiers	39.
40.	Net interest income	2.84	2.53	2.42	2.42	2.08	2.17	2.06	1.84	1.33	1.63	Produits financiers nets	40.
41.	Non-interest income (net)	1.85	1.75	1.84	2.01	1.90	1.92	2.34	1.73	2.28	1.44	Produits non financiers (nets)	41.
42.	Gross income	4.69	4.28	4.26	4.43	3.98	4.09	4.40	3.58	3.61	3.06	Résultat brut	42.
43.	Operating expenses	3.81	3.53	3.58	3.50	3.26	3.29	3.24	3.03	2.94	3.85	Frais d'exploitation	43.
44.	Net income	0.88	0.75	0.68	0.93	0.72	0.80	1.16	0.54	0.67	-0.79	Résultat net	44.
45.	Provisions (net)	0.55	0.46	0.34	0.54	0.32	0.46	0.58	0.26	0.27	-0.01	Provisions (nettes)	45.
46.	Profit before tax	0.34	0.30	0.34	0.39	0.40	0.34	0.59	0.29	0.40	-0.78	Bénéfices avant impôt	46.
47.	Income tax	0.15	0.11	0.11	0.12	0.09	0.08	0.09	0.10	0.14	0.06	Impôt	47.
48.	Profit after tax	0.18	0.18	0.23	0.27	0.31	0.26	0.50	0.19	0.26	-0.84	Bénéfices après impôt	48.
49.	Distributed profit	0.17	0.16	0.21	0.23	0.24	0.21	0.20	0.19	0.10	0.04	Bénéfices distribués	49.
50.	Retained profit	0.02	0.02	0.02	0.03	0.07	0.05	0.30	0.01	0.16	-0.88	Bénéfices mis en réserve	50.
51.	Staff costs	1.57	1.48	1.40	1.36	1.23	1.16	1.05	0.95	0.86	0.83	Frais de personnel	51.
52.	Provisions on loans	0.40	0.33	0.28	0.35	0.32	0.37	0.40	0.35	0.31	0.00	Provisions sur prêts	52.
53.	Provisions on securities	::	::	::	::	::	0.09	0.13	-0.10	-0.14	-0.01	Provisions sur titres	53.
	% of gross income											**% du total du résultat brut**	
54.	Net interest income	60.60	59.08	56.76	54.64	52.23	52.99	46.91	51.53	36.84	53.09	Produits financiers nets	54.
55.	Non-interest income (net)	39.40	40.92	43.24	45.36	47.77	47.01	53.09	48.47	63.16	46.91	Produits non financiers (nets)	55.
56.	Operating expenses	81.22	82.42	83.99	79.11	81.85	80.40	73.60	84.78	81.49	125.64	Frais d'exploitation	56.
57.	Net income	18.78	17.58	16.01	20.89	18.15	19.60	26.40	15.22	18.51	-25.64	Résultat net	57.
58.	Provisions (net)	11.63	10.67	8.02	12.11	8.07	11.27	13.06	7.14	7.40	-0.23	Provisions (nettes)	58.
59.	Profit before tax	7.15	6.91	7.99	8.78	10.08	8.33	13.34	8.08	11.11	-25.41	Bénéfices avant impôt	59.
60.	Income tax	3.24	2.63	2.51	2.79	2.29	1.95	2.00	2.66	3.76	2.06	Impôt	60.
61.	Profit after tax	3.92	4.28	5.49	5.99	7.79	6.39	11.34	5.42	7.34	-27.47	Bénéfices après impôt	61.
62.	Staff costs	33.49	34.61	32.89	30.63	30.97	28.31	23.74	26.62	23.79	27.24	Frais de personnel	62.
	% of net income											**% du total du résultat net**	
63.	Provisions (net)	61.91	60.69	50.09	57.96	44.48	57.49	49.48	46.94	39.99	::	Provisions (nettes)	63.
64.	Profit before tax	38.09	39.31	49.91	42.04	55.52	42.51	50.52	53.06	60.01	::	Bénéfices avant impôt	64.
65.	Income tax	17.23	14.94	15.65	13.36	12.59	9.93	7.59	17.46	20.33	::	Impôt	65.
66.	Profit after tax	20.86	24.37	34.26	28.68	42.93	32.58	42.94	35.60	39.67	::	Bénéfices après impôt	66.

FINLAND

All banks

Per cent

BALANCE SHEET ANALYSIS

% of year-end balance sheet total

	1982	1983	1984	1985	1986	1987	1988	1989	1990	1991		
Assets												**Actif**
67. Cash & balance with Central bank	3.48	3.35	5.10	4.57	3.24	3.44	4.19	4.70	3.34	2.48	67.	Caisse & solde auprès de la Banque centrale
68. Interbank deposits	3.72	3.76	3.96	4.35	5.20	3.91	3.90	3.59	3.28	2.86	68.	Dépôts interbancaires
69. Loans	67.75	66.01	62.20	63.90	60.84	61.38	62.90	65.18	65.82	63.68	69.	Prêts
70. Securities	6.29	8.07	9.08	9.65	11.84	13.89	13.32	13.07	12.96	16.48	70.	Valeurs mobilières
71. Other assets	18.76	18.81	19.66	17.54	18.88	17.38	15.69	13.45	14.60	14.50	71.	Autres actifs
Liabilities												**Passif**
72. Capital & reserves	5.81	5.94	6.06	6.43	6.04	5.98	6.70	6.69	6.89	6.93	72.	Capital et réserves
73. Borrowing from Central bank	2.32	3.34	2.65	2.29	3.00	0.60	0.82	0.57	0.53	0.75	73.	Emprunts auprès de la Banque centrale
74. Interbank deposits	3.78	3.52	3.51	3.69	4.27	3.02	2.82	2.65	2.37	2.44	74.	Dépôts interbancaires
75. Non-bank deposits	69.54	67.89	65.23	64.37	58.28	58.43	56.22	50.85	51.61	50.66	75.	Dépôts non bancaires
76. Bonds	1.09	1.10	2.14	2.30	3.33	3.85	5.12	6.53	8.54	10.18	76.	Obligations
77. Other liabilities	17.46	18.22	20.40	20.93	25.07	28.13	28.31	32.71	30.06	29.04	77.	Autres engagements
Memoranda												*Pour mémoire*
78. Short-term securities (1)	..	..	..	..	*0.70*	*4.09*	*4.89*	*4.40*	*4.93*	*6.08*	*78.*	*Titres à court terme (1)*
79. Bonds	*5.10*	*6.79*	*7.65*	*8.06*	*9.54*	*8.11*	*6.60*	*6.27*	*5.78*	*7.24*	*79.*	*Obligations*
80. Shares and participations	*1.20*	*1.28*	*1.43*	*1.58*	*1.59*	*1.69*	*1.83*	*2.41*	*2.25*	*3.16*	*80.*	*Actions et participations*
81. Claims on non-residents	*11.61*	*12.55*	*15.98*	*13.54*	*18.20*	*16.85*	*15.12*	*13.79*	*13.90*	*13.46*	*81.*	*Créances sur des non résidents*
82. Liabilities to non-residents	*17.96*	*19.24*	*22.93*	*22.76*	*25.77*	*28.78*	*27.11*	*25.84*	*29.70*	*28.81*	*82.*	*Engagements envers des non résidents*

1. Until 1986, included under "Bonds" (item 31 or item 79).

Notes

- All banks include Commercial banks, Post office banks, Foreign commercial banks (since 1983), Savings banks and Co-operative banks.

Change in methodology:

- As from 1984, foreign branches of Finnish commercial banks are also included in the data.

FINLANDE

Ensemble des banques

Pourcentage

ANALYSE DU BILAN

% du total du bilan en fin d'exercice

1. Jusqu'à 1986, inclus sous "Obligations" (poste 31 ou poste 79).

Notes

- L'Ensemble des banques comprend les Banques commerciales, la Banque postale, les Banques commerciales étrangères (depuis 1983), les Caisses d'épargne et les Banques mutualistes.

Changement méthodologique :

- Depuis 1984, les données comprennent les chiffres relatifs aux succursales étrangères des banques commerciales finlandaises.

FINLAND
Commercial banks

Million markkaa

FINLANDE
Banques commerciales

Millions de markkaa

	1982	1983	1984	1985	1986	1987	1988	1989	1990	1991	
INCOME STATEMENT											**COMPTE DE RESULTATS**
1. Interest income	7400	8801	12156	14335	14165	18048	28941	41113	51091	52508	1. Produits financiers
2. Interest expenses	5628	7047	9990	11605	11682	14349	23252	35004	43382	46022	2. Frais financiers
3. Net interest income	1772	1754	2166	2730	2483	3699	5689	6109	7709	6486	3. Produits financiers nets
4. Non-interest income (net)	1751	2018	2661	3719	4053	4589	5703	7679	8060	6425	4. Produits non financiers (nets)
5. Gross income	3523	3772	4827	6449	6536	8288	13392	13788	15769	12911	5. Résultat brut
6. Operating expenses	2699	3036	3767	4638	5055	6103	9951	11300	12589	18584	6. Frais d'exploitation
7. Net income	824	736	1060	1811	1481	2185	3441	2488	3180	-5673	7. Résultat net
8. Provisions (net)	388	290	417	939	401	1131	1407	1024	924	-54	8. Provisions (nettes)
9. Profit before tax	436	446	643	872	1080	1054	2034	1464	2256	-5619	9. Bénéfices avant impôt
10. Income tax	177	143	166	250	182	189	326	421	735	272	10. Impôt
11. Profit after tax	259	303	477	622	898	865	1708	1043	1521	-5891	11. Bénéfices après impôt
12. Distributed profit	255	298	474	616	761	812	991	1111	665	223	12. Bénéfices distribués
13. Retained profit	4	5	3	6	137	53	717	-68	856	-6114	13. Bénéfices mis en réserve
Memoranda											*Pour mémoire*
14. Staff costs	1141	1281	1504	1759	1852	2159	3135	3503	3685	3693	14. Frais de personnel
15. Provisions on loans	319	278	304	546	487	871	1354	1355	1225	-465	15. Provisions sur prêts
16. Provisions on securities	..	..	..	..	..	258	52	-330	-950	411	16. Provisions sur titres
BALANCE SHEET											**BILAN**
Assets											**Actif**
17. Cash & balance with Central bank	1801	2530	5414	6216	5397	7147	13457	16228	12485	10489	17. Caisse & solde auprès de la Banque centrale
18. Interbank deposits	523	688	1981	1565	2292	4255	7586	8034	6464	3232	18. Dépôts interbancaires
19. Loans	58636	69501	83730	103700	121845	149775	235294	289508	321154	327169	19. Prêts
20. Securities	8019	12834	18030	22119	33069	37963	64450	72232	77896	107596	20. Valeurs mobilières
21. Other assets	25982	30072	38318	40456	53995	56944	74991	74888	85839	83810	21. Autres actifs
Liabilities											**Passif**
22. Capital & reserves	6626	7980	10517	13257	15072	17490	28065	32255	36206	39140	22. Capital et réserves
23. Borrowing from Central bank	3582	6548	5987	5769	9511	856	3283	2001	2292	4013	23. Emprunts auprès de la Banque centrale
24. Interbank deposits	6493	7358	9043	11364	15929	12744	16142	17207	17139	18706	24. Dépôts interbancaires
25. Non-bank deposits	58253	68537	83354	98347	111246	137585	204387	212448	241785	245535	25. Dépôts non bancaires
26. Bonds	1726	1966	4817	5128	7007	8784	25529	37690	54424	63503	26. Obligations
27. Other liabilities	18281	23236	33755	40191	57833	78625	118372	159289	151992	161599	27. Autres engagements
Balance sheet total											**Total du bilan**
28. End-year total	94961	115625	147473	174056	216598	256084	395778	460890	503838	532296	28. En fin d'exercice
29. Average total	85305	105293	131549	160765	195327	236341	353724	428334	482364	518067	29. Moyen
Memoranda											*Pour mémoire*
30. Short-term securities (1)	..	..	..	..	954	7227	24184	25650	31939	39914	30. Titres à court terme (1)
31. Bonds	6711	11198	15431	18677	28261	25810	32844	36928	35860	50301	31. Obligations
32. Shares and participations	1308	1636	2599	3442	3854	4926	7422	9654	10097	17981	32. Actions et participations
33. Claims on non-residents	18935	22893	35168	35588	61473	66516	87112	92621	101667	102735	33. Créances sur des non résidents
34. Liabilities to non-residents	29408	35649	52098	58491	84898	111453	154544	172104	215469	218400	34. Engagements envers des non résidents
SUPPLEMENTARY INFORMATION											**RENSEIGNEMENTS COMPLEMENTAIRES**
35. Number of institutions	7	7	7	7	6	6	7	10	10	12	35. Nombre d'institutions
36. Number of branches	900	924	942	959	930	937	1004	1010	1037	948	36. Nombre de succursales
37. Number of employees (x 1000)	15.7	16.0	16.6	17.5	18.5	18.8	26.2	26.9	26.5	24.2	37. Nombre de salariés (x 1000)

FINLAND

Commercial banks

Per cent — *Pourcentage*

INCOME STATEMENT ANALYSIS — ANALYSE DU COMPTE DE RESULTATS

		1982	1983	1984	1985	1986	1987	1988	1989	1990	1991		
% of average balance sheet total													**% du total moyen du bilan**
38.	Interest income	8.67	8.36	9.24	8.92	7.25	7.64	8.18	9.60	10.59	10.14	38.	Produits financiers
39.	Interest expenses	6.60	6.69	7.59	7.22	5.98	6.07	6.57	8.17	8.99	8.88	39.	Frais financiers
40.	Net interest income	2.08	1.67	1.65	1.70	1.27	1.57	1.61	1.43	1.60	1.25	40.	Produits financiers nets
41.	Non-interest income (net)	2.05	1.92	2.02	2.31	2.07	1.94	2.18	1.79	1.67	1.24	41.	Produits non financiers (nets)
42.	Gross income	4.13	3.58	3.67	4.01	3.35	3.51	3.79	3.22	3.27	2.49	42.	Résultat brut
43.	Operating expenses	3.16	2.88	2.86	2.88	2.59	2.58	2.81	2.64	2.61	3.59	43.	Frais d'exploitation
44.	Net income	0.97	0.70	0.81	1.13	0.76	0.92	0.97	0.58	0.66	-1.10	44.	Résultat net
45.	Provisions (net)	0.45	0.28	0.32	0.58	0.21	0.48	0.40	0.24	0.19	-0.01	45.	Provisions (nettes)
46.	Profit before tax	0.51	0.42	0.49	0.54	0.55	0.45	0.58	0.34	0.47	-1.08	46.	Bénéfices avant impôt
47.	Income tax	0.21	0.14	0.13	0.16	0.09	0.08	0.09	0.10	0.15	0.05	47.	Impôt
48.	Profit after tax	0.30	0.29	0.36	0.39	0.46	0.37	0.48	0.24	0.32	-1.14	48.	Bénéfices après impôt
49.	Distributed profit	0.30	0.28	0.36	0.38	0.39	0.34	0.28	0.26	0.14	0.04	49.	Bénéfices distribués
50.	Retained profit	0.00	0.00	0.00	0.00	0.07	0.02	0.20	-0.02	0.18	-1.18	50.	Bénéfices mis en réserve
51.	Staff costs	1.34	1.22	1.14	1.09	0.95	0.91	0.89	0.82	0.76	0.71	51.	Frais de personnel
52.	Provisions on loans	0.37	0.26	0.23	0.34	0.25	0.37	0.38	0.32	0.25	-0.09	52.	Provisions sur prêts
53.	Provisions on securities	..	..	..	..	..	0.11	0.01	-0.08	-0.20	0.08	53.	Provisions sur titres
% of gross income													**% du total du résultat brut**
54.	Net interest income	50.30	46.50	44.87	42.33	37.99	44.63	42.48	44.31	48.89	50.24	54.	Produits financiers nets
55.	Non-interest income (net)	49.70	53.50	55.13	57.67	62.01	55.37	57.52	55.69	51.11	49.76	55.	Produits non financiers (nets)
56.	Operating expenses	76.61	80.49	78.04	71.92	77.34	73.64	74.31	81.96	79.83	143.94	56.	Frais d'exploitation
57.	Net income	23.39	19.51	21.96	28.08	22.66	26.36	25.69	18.04	20.17	-43.94	57.	Résultat net
58.	Provisions (net)	11.01	7.69	8.64	14.56	6.14	13.65	10.51	7.43	5.86	-0.42	58.	Provisions (nettes)
59.	Profit before tax	12.38	11.82	13.32	13.52	16.52	12.72	15.19	10.62	14.31	-43.52	59.	Bénéfices avant impôt
60.	Income tax	5.02	3.79	3.44	3.88	2.78	2.28	2.43	3.05	4.66	2.11	60.	Impôt
61.	Profit after tax	7.35	8.03	9.88	9.64	13.74	10.44	12.75	7.56	9.65	-45.63	61.	Bénéfices après impôt
62.	Staff costs	32.39	33.96	31.16	27.28	28.34	26.05	23.41	25.41	23.37	28.60	62.	Frais de personnel
% of net income													**% du total du résultat net**
63.	Provisions (net)	47.09	39.40	39.34	51.85	27.08	51.76	40.89	41.16	29.06	..	63.	Provisions (nettes)
64.	Profit before tax	52.91	60.60	60.66	48.15	72.92	48.24	59.11	58.84	70.94	..	64.	Bénéfices avant impôt
65.	Income tax	21.48	19.43	15.66	13.80	12.29	8.65	9.47	16.92	23.11	..	65.	Impôt
66.	Profit after tax	31.43	41.17	45.00	34.35	60.63	39.59	49.64	41.92	47.83	..	66.	Bénéfices après impôt

FINLAND

Commercial banks

Per cent

BALANCE SHEET ANALYSIS

% of year-end balance sheet total

FINLANDE

Banques commerciales

Pourcentage

ANALYSE DU BILAN

% du total du bilan en fin d'exercice

		1982	1983	1984	1985	1986	1987	1988	1989	1990	1991	
Assets												**Actif**
67.	Cash & balance with Central bank	1.90	2.19	3.67	3.57	2.49	2.79	3.40	3.52	2.48	1.97	Caisse & solde auprès de la Banque centrale
68.	Interbank deposits	0.55	0.60	1.34	0.90	1.06	1.66	1.92	1.74	1.28	0.61	Dépôts interbancaires
69.	Loans	61.75	60.11	56.78	59.58	56.25	58.49	59.45	62.81	63.74	61.46	Prêts
70.	Securities	8.44	11.10	12.23	12.71	15.27	14.82	16.28	15.67	15.46	20.21	Valeurs mobilières
71.	Other assets	27.36	26.01	25.98	23.24	24.93	22.24	18.95	16.25	17.04	15.74	Autres actifs
Liabilities												**Passif**
72.	Capital & reserves	6.98	6.90	7.13	7.62	6.96	6.83	7.09	7.00	7.19	7.35	Capital et réserves
73.	Borrowing from Central bank	3.77	5.66	4.06	3.31	4.39	0.33	0.83	0.43	0.45	0.75	Emprunts auprès de la Banque centrale
74.	Interbank deposits	6.84	6.36	6.13	6.53	7.35	4.98	4.08	3.73	3.40	3.51	Dépôts interbancaires
75.	Non-bank deposits	61.34	59.28	56.52	56.50	51.36	53.73	51.64	46.10	47.99	46.09	Dépôts non bancaires
76.	Bonds	1.82	1.70	3.27	2.95	3.24	3.43	6.45	8.18	10.80	11.93	Obligations
77.	Other liabilities	19.25	20.10	22.89	23.09	26.70	30.70	29.91	34.56	30.17	30.36	Autres engagements
Memoranda												***Pour mémoire***
78.	*Short-term securities (1)*	..	..	..	..	*0.44*	*2.82*	*6.11*	*5.57*	*6.34*	*7.39*	*Titres à court terme (1)*
79.	*Bonds*	*7.07*	*9.68*	*10.46*	*10.73*	*13.05*	*10.08*	*8.30*	*8.01*	*7.12*	*9.45*	*Obligations*
80.	*Shares and participations*	*1.38*	*1.41*	*1.76*	*1.98*	*1.78*	*1.92*	*1.88*	*2.09*	*2.00*	*3.38*	*Actions et participations*
81.	*Claims on non-residents*	*19.94*	*19.80*	*23.85*	*20.45*	*28.38*	*25.97*	*22.01*	*20.10*	*20.18*	*19.30*	*Créances sur des non résidents*
82.	*Liabilities to non-residents*	*30.97*	*30.83*	*35.33*	*33.60*	*39.20*	*43.52*	*39.05*	*37.34*	*42.77*	*41.03*	*Engagements envers des non résidents*

1. Until 1986, included under "Bonds" (item 31 or item 79).

Change in methodology:

• As from 1984, foreign branches of Finnish commercial banks are also included in the data.

• As from 1988, data include the Post office bank (Postipankki) classified thereafter under Commercial banks.

1. Jusqu'à 1986, inclus sous "Obligations" (poste 31 ou poste 79).

Changement méthodologique :

• Depuis 1984, les données comprennent les chiffres relatifs aux succursales étrangères des banques commerciales finlandaises.

• Depuis 1988, la Banque postale (Postipankki) est classée dans les données concernant les Banques commerciales.

FINLAND
Post office bank
Million markkaa

FINLANDE
Banque postale
Millions de markkas

	1982	1983	1984	1985	1986	1987	
INCOME STATEMENT							**COMPTE DE RESULTATS**
1. Interest income	1798	2128	2921	3434	3715	4151	1. Produits financiers
2. Interest expenses	1047	1216	1830	2256	2468	2942	2. Frais financiers
3. Net interest income	751	912	1091	1178	1247	1209	3. Produits financiers nets
4. Non-interest income (net)	372	407	498	549	630	1030	4. Produits non financiers (nets)
5. Gross income	1123	1319	1589	1727	1877	2239	5. Résultat brut
6. Operating expenses	912	965	1420	1493	1554	1993	6. Frais d'exploitation
7. Net income	211	354	169	234	323	246	7. Résultat net
8. Provisions (net)	180	311	110	152	217	129	8. Provisions (nettes)
9. Profit before tax	31	43	59	82	106	117	9. Bénéfices avant impôt
10. Income tax	21	22	29	32	46	47	10. Impôt
11. Profit after tax	10	21	30	50	60	70	11. Bénéfices après impôt
12. Distributed profit	5	10	15	25	30	35	12. Bénéfices distribués
13. Retained profit	5	11	15	25	30	35	13. Bénéfices mis en réserve
Memoranda							*Pour mémoire*
14. Staff costs	*329*	*376*	*412*	*502*	*576*	*635*	*14. Frais de personnel*
15. Provisions on loans	*91*	*99*	*110*	*126*	*203*	*183*	*15. Provisions sur prêts*
16. Provisions on securities	*..*	*..*	*..*	*..*	*..*	*-42*	*16. Provisions sur titres*
BALANCE SHEET							**BILAN**
Assets							**Actif**
17. Cash & balance with Central bank	2551	1557	3129	2143	1536	1992	17. Caisse & solde auprès de la Banque centrale
18. Interbank deposits	6	24	60	2072	6308	1321	18. Dépôts interbancaires
19. Loans	15115	16983	19143	22319	26606	27829	19. Prêts
20. Securities	1314	2117	3262	4168	6705	15077	20. Valeurs mobilières
21. Other assets	2826	3414	6147	5274	7774	9366	21. Autres actifs
Liabilities							**Passif**
22. Capital & reserves	1030	1367	1526	1716	1980	2154	22. Capital et réserves
23. Borrowing from Central bank	85	82	254	337	755	472	23. Emprunts auprès de la Banque centrale
24. Interbank deposits	374	217	322	148	109	106	24. Dépôts interbancaires
25. Non-bank deposits	17241	19019	23263	24434	24935	27030	25. Dépôts non bancaires
26. Bonds	167	270	652	1209	4360	6714	26. Obligations
27. Other liabilities	2915	3140	5724	8132	16790	19109	27. Autres engagements
Balance sheet total							**Total du bilan**
28. End-year total	21812	24095	31741	35976	48929	55585	28. En fin d'exercice
29. Average total	19923	22954	27918	33859	42453	52257	29. Moyen
Memoranda							*Pour mémoire*
30. Short-term securities (1)	*..*	*..*	*..*	*..*	*1504*	*7990*	*30. Titres à court terme (1)*
31. Bonds	*1125*	*1920*	*3061*	*3865*	*4687*	*6548*	*31. Obligations*
32. Shares and participations	*188*	*197*	*201*	*303*	*514*	*539*	*32. Actions et participations*
33. Claims on non-residents	*2112*	*3001*	*6667*	*5812*	*7295*	*8994*	*33. Créances sur des non résidents*
34. Liabilities to non-residents	*3220*	*4188*	*7710*	*9281*	*12194*	*15790*	*34. Engagements envers des non résidents*
SUPPLEMENTARY INFORMATION							**RENSEIGNEMENTS COMPLEMENTAIRES**
35. Number of institutions	1	1	1	1	1	1	35. Nombre d'institutions
36. Number of branches	35	39	39	47	49	56	36. Nombre de succursales
37. Number of employees (x 1000)	5.5	5.5	5.7	5.9	6.0	6.1	37. Nombre de salariés (x 1000)

FINLAND

Post office bank

FINLANDE

Banque postale

Per cent

Pourcentage

INCOME STATEMENT ANALYSIS

ANALYSE DU COMPTE DE RESULTATS

		1982	1983	1984	1985	1986	1987		
% of average balance sheet total									**% du total moyen du bilan**
38.	Interest income	9.02	9.27	10.46	10.14	8.75	7.94	38.	Produits financiers
39.	Interest expenses	5.26	5.30	6.55	6.66	5.81	5.63	39.	Frais financiers
40.	Net interest income	3.77	3.97	3.91	3.48	2.94	2.31	40.	Produits financiers nets
41.	Non-interest income (net)	1.87	1.77	1.78	1.62	1.48	1.97	41.	Produits non financiers (nets)
42.	Gross income	5.64	5.75	5.69	5.10	4.42	4.28	42.	Résultat brut
43.	Operating expenses	4.58	4.20	5.09	4.41	3.66	3.81	43.	Frais d'exploitation
44.	Net income	1.06	1.54	0.61	0.69	0.76	0.47	44.	Résultat net
45.	Provisions (net)	0.90	1.35	0.39	0.45	0.51	0.25	45.	Provisions (nettes)
46.	Profit before tax	0.16	0.19	0.21	0.24	0.25	0.22	46.	Bénéfices avant impôt
47.	Income tax	0.11	0.10	0.10	0.09	0.11	0.09	47.	Impôt
48.	Profit after tax	0.05	0.09	0.11	0.15	0.14	0.13	48.	Bénéfices après impôt
49.	Distributed profit	0.03	0.04	0.05	0.07	0.07	0.07	49.	Bénéfices distribués
50.	Retained profit	0.03	0.05	0.05	0.07	0.07	0.07	50.	Bénéfices mis en réserve
51.	Staff costs	1.65	1.64	1.48	1.48	1.36	1.22	51.	Frais de personnel
52.	Provisions on loans	0.46	0.43	0.39	0.37	0.48	0.35	52.	Provisions sur prêts
53.	Provisions on securities	..	..	..	..	..	-0.08	53.	Provisions sur titres
% of gross income									**% du total du résultat brut**
54.	Net interest income	66.87	69.14	68.66	68.21	66.44	54.00	54.	Produits financiers nets
55.	Non-interest income (net)	33.13	30.86	31.34	31.79	33.56	46.00	55.	Produits non financiers (nets)
56.	Operating expenses	81.21	73.16	89.36	86.45	82.79	89.01	56.	Frais d'exploitation
57.	Net income	18.79	26.84	10.64	13.55	17.21	10.99	57.	Résultat net
58.	Provisions (net)	16.03	23.58	6.92	8.80	11.56	5.76	58.	Provisions (nettes)
59.	Profit before tax	2.76	3.26	3.71	4.75	5.65	5.23	59.	Bénéfices avant impôt
60.	Income tax	1.87	1.67	1.83	1.85	2.45	2.10	60.	Impôt
61.	Profit after tax	0.89	1.59	1.89	2.90	3.20	3.13	61.	Bénéfices après impôt
62.	Staff costs	29.30	28.51	25.93	29.07	30.69	28.36	62.	Frais de personnel
% of net income									**% du total du résultat net**
63.	Provisions (net)	85.31	87.85	65.09	64.96	67.18	52.44	63.	Provisions (nettes)
64.	Profit before tax	14.69	12.15	34.91	35.04	32.82	47.56	64.	Bénéfices avant impôt
65.	Income tax	9.95	6.21	17.16	13.68	14.24	19.11	65.	Impôt
66.	Profit after tax	4.74	5.93	17.75	21.37	18.58	28.46	66.	Bénéfices après impôt

FINLAND

Post office bank

FINLANDE

Banque postale

Per cent

Pourcentage

BALANCE SHEET ANALYSIS

ANALYSE DU BILAN

% of year-end balance sheet total

% du total du bilan en fin d'exercice

	1982	1983	1984	1985	1986	1987		
Assets							**Actif**	
67. Cash & balance with Central bank	11.70	6.46	9.86	5.96	3.14	3.58	67.	Caisse & solde auprès de la Banque centrale
68. Interbank deposits	0.03	0.10	0.19	5.76	12.89	2.38	68.	Dépôts interbancaires
69. Loans	69.30	70.48	60.31	62.04	54.38	50.07	69.	Prêts
70. Securities	6.02	8.79	10.28	11.59	13.70	27.12	70.	Valeurs mobilières
71. Other assets	12.96	14.17	19.37	14.66	15.89	16.85	71.	Autres actifs
Liabilities							**Passif**	
72. Capital & reserves	4.72	5.67	4.81	4.77	4.05	3.88	72.	Capital et réserves
73. Borrowing from Central bank	0.39	0.34	0.80	0.94	1.54	0.85	73.	Emprunts auprès de la Banque centrale
74. Interbank deposits	1.71	0.90	1.01	0.41	0.22	0.19	74.	Dépôts interbancaires
75. Non-bank deposits	79.04	78.93	73.29	67.92	50.96	48.63	75.	Dépôts non bancaires
76. Bonds	0.77	1.12	2.05	3.36	8.91	12.08	76.	Obligations
77. Other liabilities	13.36	13.03	18.03	22.60	34.32	34.38	77.	Autres engagements
Memoranda							***Pour mémoire***	
78. Short-term securities (1)	*..*	*..*	*..*	*..*	*3.07*	*14.37*	*78.*	*Titres à court terme (1)*
79. Bonds	*5.16*	*7.97*	*9.64*	*10.74*	*9.58*	*11.78*	*79.*	*Obligations*
80. Shares and participations	*0.86*	*0.82*	*0.63*	*0.84*	*1.05*	*0.97*	*80.*	*Actions et participations*
81. Claims on non-residents	*9.68*	*12.45*	*21.00*	*16.16*	*14.91*	*16.18*	*81.*	*Créances sur des non résidents*
82. Liabilities to non-residents	*14.76*	*17.38*	*24.29*	*25.80*	*24.92*	*28.41*	*82.*	*Engagements envers des non résidents*

1. Until 1986, included under "Bonds" (item 31 or item 79).

1. Jusqu'à 1986, inclus sous "Obligations" (poste 31 ou poste 79).

Change in methodology:

- As from 1988, the Post office bank (Postipankki) is included under Commercial banks.

Changement méthodologique :

- Depuis 1988, la Banque postale (Postipankki) est classée dans les données concernant les Banques commerciales.

FINLAND
Foreign commercial banks

FINLANDE
Banques commerciales étrangères

Million markkaa / *Millions de markkaa*

		1983	1984	1985	1986	1987	1988	1989	1990	1991	
INCOME STATEMENT											**COMPTE DE RESULTATS**
1.	Interest income	138	262	196	182	488	744	1121	984	1526	Produits financiers
2.	Interest expenses	128	242	175	163	459	715	1086	923	1507	Frais financiers
3.	Net interest income	10	20	21	19	29	29	35	61	19	Produits financiers nets
4.	Non-interest income (net)	14	26	30	27	37	37	40	38	36	Produits non financiers (nets)
5.	Gross income	24	46	51	46	66	66	75	99	55	Résultat brut
6.	Operating expenses	24	30	33	37	63	70	126	95	133	Frais d'exploitation
7.	Net income	-	16	18	9	3	-4	-51	4	-78	Résultat net
8.	Provisions (net)	2	8	5	4	11	-3	3	-	5	Provisions (nettes)
9.	Profit before tax	-2	8	13	5	-8	-1	-54	-	-83	Bénéfices avant impôt
10.	Income tax	-	-	4	2	-	3	2	4	-	Impôt
11.	Profit after tax	-2	8	9	3	-8	-4	-56	-	-84	Bénéfices après impôt
12.	Distributed profit	-	-	4	6	-	-	-	-	-	Bénéfices distribués
13.	Retained profit	-2	8	5	-3	-8	-4	-56	-	-84	Bénéfices mis en réserve
Memoranda											*Pour mémoire*
14.	*Staff costs*	*11*	*12*	*14*	*15*	*26*	*28*	*27*	*30*	*34*	*Frais de personnel*
15.	*Provisions on loans*	*2*	*2*	*3*	*3*	*3*	*1*	*1*	*2*	*5*	*Provisions sur prêts*
16.	*Provisions on securities*	*..*	*..*	*..*	*..*	*8*	*3*	*2*	*-2*	*..*	*Provisions sur titres*
BALANCE SHEET											**BILAN**
Assets											**Actif**
17.	Cash & balance with Central bank	1	375	358	21	126	176	154	36	108	Caisse & solde auprès de la Banque centrale
18.	Interbank deposits	574	465	309	528	171	323	81	297	314	Dépôts interbancaires
19.	Loans	628	410	579	887	586	447	1458	792	1771	Prêts
20.	Securities	5	21	20	305	3292	3315	2637	2896	4528	Valeurs mobilières
21.	Other assets	1408	1314	768	423	803	950	488	356	463	Autres actifs
Liabilities											**Passif**
22.	Capital & reserves	53	69	122	122	211	243	240	186	254	Capital et réserves
23.	Borrowing from Central bank	-	52	38	21	-	1	-	-	99	Emprunts auprès de la Banque centrale
24.	Interbank deposits	92	68	3	183	794	244	608	51	50	Dépôts interbancaires
25.	Non-bank deposits	2286	2149	1664	1380	2542	2910	1966	2267	2642	Dépôts non bancaires
26.	Bonds	-	-	-	-	-	-	-	-	-	Obligations
27.	Other liabilities	185	247	207	458	1431	1813	2004	1873	4139	Autres engagements
Balance sheet total											**Total du bilan**
28.	End-year total	2616	2585	2034	2164	4978	5211	4818	4377	7184	En fin d'exercice
29.	Average total	1715	2601	2310	2099	3571	5095	5015	4598	5781	Moyen
Memoranda											*Pour mémoire*
30.	*Short-term securities (1)*	*..*	*..*	*..*	*230*	*3094*	*3152*	*2304*	*2747*	*4298*	*Titres à court terme (1)*
31.	*Bonds*	*-*	*16*	*15*	*70*	*186*	*150*	*319*	*136*	*216*	*Obligations*
32.	*Shares and participations*	*5*	*5*	*5*	*5*	*12*	*13*	*14*	*13*	*14*	*Actions et participations*
33.	*Claims on non-residents*	*1372*	*1040*	*757*	*680*	*604*	*745*	*714*	*237*	*918*	*Créances sur des non résidents*
34.	*Liabilities to non-residents*	*2080*	*1845*	*1629*	*1332*	*2828*	*2860*	*1917*	*2229*	*2517*	*Engagements envers des non résidents*
SUPPLEMENTARY INFORMATION											**RENSEIGNEMENTS COMPLEMENTAIRES**
35.	Number of institutions	3	3	3	3	4	4	4	4	5	Nombre d'institutions
36.	Number of branches	-	-	-	-	-	-	-	-	-	Nombre de succursales
37.	Number of employees	84	93	103	98	169	156	154	137	144	Nombre de salariés

FINLAND

Foreign commercial banks

Per cent

INCOME STATEMENT ANALYSIS

	1983	1984	1985	1986	1987	1988	1989	1990	1991
% of average balance sheet total									
38. Interest income	8.05	10.07	8.48	8.67	13.67	14.60	22.35	21.40	26.40
39. Interest expenses	7.46	9.30	7.58	7.77	12.85	14.03	21.66	20.07	26.07
40. Net interest income	0.58	0.77	0.91	0.91	0.81	0.57	0.70	1.33	0.33
41. Non-interest income (net)	0.82	1.00	1.30	1.29	1.04	0.73	0.80	0.83	0.62
42. Gross income	1.40	1.77	2.21	2.19	1.85	1.30	1.50	2.15	0.95
43. Operating expenses	1.40	1.15	1.43	1.76	1.76	1.37	2.51	2.07	2.30
44. Net income	-	0.62	0.78	0.43	0.08	-0.08	-1.02	0.09	-1.35
45. Provisions (net)	0.12	0.31	0.22	0.19	0.31	-0.06	-0.06	-	0.09
46. Profit before tax	-0.12	0.31	0.56	0.24	-0.22	-0.02	-1.08	0.09	-1.44
47. Income tax	-	-	0.17	0.10	-	0.06	0.04	0.09	0.02
48. Profit after tax	-0.12	0.31	0.39	0.14	-0.22	-0.08	-1.12	-	-1.45
49. Distributed profit	-	-	0.17	0.29	-	-	-	-	-
50. Retained profit	-0.12	0.31	0.22	-0.14	-0.22	-0.08	-1.12	-	-1.45
51. Staff costs	0.64	0.46	0.61	0.71	0.73	0.55	0.54	0.65	0.59
52. Provisions on loans	0.12	0.08	0.13	0.14	0.08	0.02	0.02	0.04	0.09
53. Provisions on securities	..	..	..	..	0.22	0.06	0.04	-0.04	..
% of gross income									
54. Net interest income	41.67	43.48	41.18	41.30	43.94	43.94	46.67	61.62	34.55
55. Non-interest income (net)	58.33	56.52	58.82	58.70	56.06	56.06	53.33	38.38	65.45
56. Operating expenses	100.00	65.22	64.71	80.43	95.45	106.06	168.00	95.96	241.82
57. Net income	-	34.78	35.29	19.57	4.55	-6.06	-68.00	4.04	-141.82
58. Provisions (net)	8.33	17.39	9.80	8.70	16.67	-4.55	4.00	-	9.09
59. Profit before tax	-8.33	17.39	25.49	10.87	-12.12	-1.52	-72.00	4.04	-150.91
60. Income tax	-	-	7.84	4.35	-	4.55	2.67	4.04	1.82
61. Profit after tax	-8.33	17.39	17.65	6.52	-12.12	-6.06	-74.67	-	-152.73
62. Staff costs	45.83	26.09	27.45	32.61	39.39	42.42	36.00	30.30	61.82
% of net income									
63. Provisions (net)	..	50.00	27.78	44.44	..	..	..	..	..
64. Profit before tax	..	50.00	72.22	55.56	..	..	..	..	..
65. Income tax	-	-	22.22	22.22	..	..	..	..	..
66. Profit after tax	..	50.00	50.00	33.33	..	..	..	..	..

FINLANDE

Banques commerciales étrangères

Pourcentage

ANALYSE DU COMPTE DE RESULTATS

% du total moyen du bilan
- 38. Produits financiers
- 39. Frais financiers
- 40. Produits financiers nets
- 41. Produits non financiers (nets)
- 42. Résultat brut
- 43. Frais d'exploitation
- 44. Résultat net
- 45. Provisions (nettes)
- 46. Bénéfices avant impôt
- 47. Impôt
- 48. Bénéfices après impôt
- 49. Bénéfices distribués
- 50. Bénéfices mis en réserve
- 51. Frais de personnel
- 52. Provisions sur prêts
- 53. Provisions sur titres

% du total du résultat brut
- 54. Produits financiers nets
- 55. Produits non financiers (nets)
- 56. Frais d'exploitation
- 57. Résultat net
- 58. Provisions (nettes)
- 59. Bénéfices avant impôt
- 60. Impôt
- 61. Bénéfices après impôt
- 62. Frais de personnel

% du total du résultat net
- 63. Provisions (nettes)
- 64. Bénéfices avant impôt
- 65. Impôt
- 66. Bénéfices après impôt

FINLAND

Foreign commercial banks

Per cent

BALANCE SHEET ANALYSIS

% of year-end balance sheet total

	1983	1984	1985	1986	1987	1988	1989	1990	1991
Assets									
67. Cash & balance with Central bank	0.04	14.51	17.60	0.97	2.53	3.38	3.20	0.82	1.50
68. Interbank deposits	21.94	17.99	15.19	24.40	3.44	6.20	1.68	6.79	4.37
69. Loans	24.01	15.86	28.47	40.99	11.77	8.58	30.26	18.09	24.65
70. Securities	0.19	0.81	0.98	14.09	66.13	63.62	54.73	66.16	63.03
71. Other assets	53.82	50.83	37.76	19.55	16.13	18.23	10.13	8.13	6.44
Liabilities									
72. Capital & reserves	2.03	2.67	6.00	5.64	4.24	4.66	4.98	4.25	3.54
73. Borrowing from Central bank	-	2.01	1.87	0.97	-	0.02	-	-	1.38
74. Interbank deposits	3.52	2.63	0.15	8.46	15.95	4.68	12.62	1.17	0.70
75. Non-bank deposits	87.39	83.13	81.81	63.77	51.06	55.84	40.81	51.79	36.78
76. Bonds	-	-	-	-	-	-	-	-	-
77. Other liabilities	7.07	9.56	10.18	21.16	28.75	34.79	41.59	42.79	57.61
Memoranda									
78. Short-term securities (1)	..	..	..	*10.63*	*62.15*	*60.49*	*47.82*	*62.76*	*59.83*
79. Bonds	-	..	..	*3.23*	*3.74*	*2.88*	*6.62*	*3.11*	*3.01*
80. Shares and participations	*0.19*	*0.62*	*0.74*	*0.23*	*0.24*	*0.25*	*0.29*	*0.30*	*0.19*
81. Claims on non-residents	*52.45*	*40.23*	*37.22*	*31.42*	*12.13*	*14.30*	*14.82*	*5.41*	*12.78*
82. Liabilities to non-residents	*79.51*	*71.37*	*80.09*	*61.55*	*56.81*	*54.88*	*39.79*	*50.93*	*35.04*

1. Until 1986, included under "Bonds" (item 31 or item 79).

FINLANDE

Banques commerciales étrangères

Pourcentage

ANALYSE DU BILAN

% du total du bilan en fin d'exercice

Actif
67. Caisse & solde auprès de la Banque centrale
68. Dépôts interbancaires
69. Prêts
70. Valeurs mobilières
71. Autres actifs

Passif
72. Capital et réserves
73. Emprunts auprès de la Banque centrale
74. Dépôts interbancaires
75. Dépôts non bancaires
76. Obligations
77. Autres engagements

Pour mémoire
78. Titres à court terme (1)
79. Obligations
80. Actions et participations
81. Créances sur des non résidents
82. Engagements envers des non résidents

1. Jusqu'à 1986, inclus sous "Obligations" (poste 31 ou poste 79).

FINLAND

Savings banks

Million markkaa

FINLANDE

Caisses d'épargne

Millions de markkas

	1982	1983	1984	1985	1986	1987	1988	1989	1990	1991	
INCOME STATEMENT											**COMPTE DE RESULTATS**
1. Interest income	2868	3381	4036	4498	4575	5171	7171	9967	12042	12413	1. Produits financiers
2. Interest expenses	1717	2145	2703	2886	2739	3022	4572	7041	11130	9888	2. Frais financiers
3. Net interest income	1151	1236	1333	1612	1836	2149	2599	2926	912	2525	3. Produits financiers nets
4. Non-interest income (net)	550	638	772	902	1098	1412	3051	1865	4139	2231	4. Produits non financiers (nets)
5. Gross income	1701	1874	2105	2514	2934	3561	5650	4791	5051	4756	5. Résultat brut
6. Operating expenses	1495	1685	1933	2220	2579	3087	3777	4337	4298	5590	6. Frais d'exploitation
7. Net income	206	189	172	294	355	474	1873	454	753	-834	7. Résultat net
8. Provisions (net)	166	142	121	211	248	332	1028	234	508	-319	8. Provisions (nettes)
9. Profit before tax	40	47	51	83	107	142	845	220	245	-515	9. Bénéfices avant impôt
10. Income tax	27	29	33	38	47	51	68	100	97	50	10. Impôt
11. Profit after tax	13	18	18	45	60	91	777	120	148	-565	11. Bénéfices après impôt
12. Distributed profit	-	-	-	-	-	-	-	-	-	-	12. Bénéfices distribués
13. Retained profit	13	18	18	45	60	91	777	120	148	-565	13. Bénéfices mis en réserve
Memoranda											*Pour mémoire*
14. Staff costs	631	729	834	930	1020	1116	1257	1390	1234	1315	14. Frais de personnel
15. Provisions on loans	129	135	120	172	210	253	399	494	523	94	15. Provisions sur prêts
16. Provisions on securities	..	..	..	..	..	77	425	-263	-23	-413	16. Provisions sur titres
BALANCE SHEET											**BILAN**
Assets											**Actif**
17. Cash & balance with Central bank	1203	1783	2583	3025	2930	3486	5960	9169	6279	4459	17. Caisse & solde auprès de la Banque centrale
18. Interbank deposits	3273	3684	4449	5160	5519	6020	8182	8564	9134	9109	18. Dépôts interbancaires
19. Loans	25699	29367	32743	37006	42263	51152	69181	83957	85554	82047	19. Prêts
20. Securities	1302	1503	1815	2083	2579	3650	5603	9777	8780	8228	20. Valeurs mobilières
21. Other assets	3128	3772	4474	5124	6184	7077	10031	9786	12072	16181	21. Autres actifs
Liabilities											**Passif**
22. Capital & reserves	1519	1817	2167	2546	2980	3706	6317	8144	7891	7227	22. Capital et réserves
23. Borrowing from Central bank	317	376	503	599	736	855	1028	1178	1107	1150	23. Emprunts auprès de la Banque centrale
24. Interbank deposits	2	1	4	2	2	-	84	250	173	72	24. Dépôts interbancaires
25. Non-bank deposits	27990	31757	36266	41562	45933	52440	65717	71340	68107	70422	25. Dépôts non bancaires
26. Bonds	40	73	155	612	709	835	1891	3238	2229	5516	26. Obligations
27. Other liabilities	4737	6085	6969	7077	9115	13547	23920	37103	42312	35637	27. Autres engagements
Balance sheet total											**Total du bilan**
28. End-year total	34605	40109	46064	52398	59475	71385	98957	121253	121819	120024	28. En fin d'exercice
29. Average total	32055	37357	43087	49231	55937	65430	85171	110105	121536	120922	29. Moyen
Memoranda											*Pour mémoire*
30. Short-term securities (1)	..	..	..	..	..	169	953	1946	1329	1810	30. Titres à court terme (1)
31. Bonds	848	968	1203	1394	1725	2210	2661	2611	2420	1742	31. Obligations
32. Shares and participations	454	535	612	689	854	1271	1789	5220	5031	4676	32. Actions et participations
33. Claims on non-residents	-	-	-	2	6	92	394	742	54	28	33. Créances sur des non résidents
34. Liabilities to non-residents	-	-	-	1629	-	129	911	2318	321	4	34. Engagements envers des non résidents
SUPPLEMENTARY INFORMATION											**RENSEIGNEMENTS COMPLEMENTAIRES**
35. Number of institutions	273	270	263	254	241	230	211	178	150	86	35. Nombre d'institutions
36. Number of branches	1022	1035	1056	1076	1091	1093	1102	1130	984	967	36. Nombre de succursales
37. Number of employees (x 1000)	10.2	10.5	10.7	10.7	10.9	11.2	11.7	11.9	10.1	9.5	37. Nombre de salariés (x 1000)

FINLAND

Savings banks

Per cent / *Pourcentage*

INCOME STATEMENT ANALYSIS / **ANALYSE DU COMPTE DE RESULTATS**

	1982	1983	1984	1985	1986	1987	1988	1989	1990	1991		
% of average balance sheet total												**% du total moyen du bilan**
38. Interest income	8.95	9.05	9.37	9.14	8.18	7.90	8.42	9.05	9.91	10.27	38.	Produits financiers
39. Interest expenses	5.36	5.74	6.27	5.86	4.90	4.62	5.37	6.39	9.16	8.18	39.	Frais financiers
40. Net interest income	3.59	3.31	3.09	3.27	3.28	3.28	3.05	2.66	0.75	2.09	40.	Produits financiers nets
41. Non-interest income (net)	1.72	1.71	1.79	1.83	1.96	2.16	3.58	1.69	3.41	1.84	41.	Produits non financiers (nets)
42. Gross income	5.31	5.02	4.89	5.11	5.25	5.44	6.63	4.35	4.16	3.93	42.	Résultat brut
43. Operating expenses	4.66	4.51	4.49	4.51	4.61	4.72	4.43	3.94	3.54	4.62	43.	Frais d'exploitation
44. Net income	0.64	0.51	0.40	0.60	0.63	0.72	2.20	0.41	0.62	-0.69	44.	Résultat net
45. Provisions (net)	0.52	0.38	0.28	0.43	0.44	0.51	1.21	0.21	0.42	-0.26	45.	Provisions (nettes)
46. Profit before tax	0.12	0.13	0.12	0.17	0.19	0.22	0.99	0.20	0.20	-0.43	46.	Bénéfices avant impôt
47. Income tax	0.08	0.08	0.08	0.08	0.08	0.08	0.08	0.09	0.08	0.04	47.	Impôt
48. Profit after tax	0.04	0.05	0.04	0.09	0.11	0.14	0.91	0.11	0.12	-0.47	48.	Bénéfices après impôt
49. Distributed profit	-	-	-	-	-	-	-	-	-	-	49.	Bénéfices distribués
50. Retained profit	0.04	0.05	0.04	0.09	0.11	0.14	0.91	0.11	0.12	-0.47	50.	Bénéfices mis en réserve
51. Staff costs	1.97	1.95	1.94	1.89	1.82	1.71	1.48	1.26	1.02	1.09	51.	Frais de personnel
52. Provisions on loans	0.40	0.36	0.28	0.35	0.38	0.39	0.47	0.45	0.43	0.08	52.	Provisions sur prêts
53. Provisions on securities	..	..	..	..	..	0.12	0.50	-0.24	-0.02	-0.34	53.	Provisions sur titres
% of gross income												**% du total du résultat brut**
54. Net interest income	67.67	65.96	63.33	64.12	62.58	60.35	46.00	61.07	18.06	53.09	54.	Produits financiers nets
55. Non-interest income (net)	32.33	34.04	36.67	35.88	37.42	39.65	54.00	38.93	81.94	46.91	55.	Produits non financiers (nets)
56. Operating expenses	87.89	89.91	91.83	88.31	87.90	86.69	66.85	90.52	85.09	117.54	56.	Frais d'exploitation
57. Net income	12.11	10.09	8.17	11.69	12.10	13.31	33.15	9.48	14.91	-17.54	57.	Résultat net
58. Provisions (net)	9.76	7.58	5.75	8.39	8.45	9.32	18.19	4.88	10.06	-6.71	58.	Provisions (nettes)
59. Profit before tax	2.35	2.51	2.42	3.30	3.65	3.99	14.96	4.59	4.85	-10.83	59.	Bénéfices avant impôt
60. Income tax	1.59	1.55	1.57	1.51	1.60	1.43	1.20	2.09	1.92	1.05	60.	Impôt
61. Profit after tax	0.76	0.96	0.86	1.79	2.04	2.56	13.75	2.50	2.93	-11.88	61.	Bénéfices après impôt
62. Staff costs	37.10	38.90	39.62	36.99	34.76	31.34	22.25	29.01	24.43	27.65	62.	Frais de personnel
% of net income												**% du total du résultat net**
63. Provisions (net)	80.58	75.13	70.35	71.77	69.86	70.04	54.89	51.54	67.46	..	63.	Provisions (nettes)
64. Profit before tax	19.42	24.87	29.65	28.23	30.14	29.96	45.11	48.46	32.54	..	64.	Bénéfices avant impôt
65. Income tax	13.11	15.34	19.19	12.93	13.24	10.76	3.63	22.03	12.88	..	65.	Impôt
66. Profit after tax	6.31	9.52	10.47	15.31	16.90	19.20	41.48	26.43	19.65	..	66.	Bénéfices après impôt

FINLAND

Savings banks

Per cent

BALANCE SHEET ANALYSIS

% of year-end balance sheet total

	1982	1983	1984	1985	1986	1987	1988	1989	1990	1991
Assets										
67. Cash & balance with Central bank	3.48	4.45	5.61	5.77	4.93	4.88	6.02	7.56	5.15	3.72
68. Interbank deposits	9.46	9.18	9.66	9.85	9.28	8.43	8.27	7.06	7.50	7.59
69. Loans	74.26	73.22	71.08	70.62	71.06	71.66	69.91	69.24	70.23	68.36
70. Securities	3.76	3.75	3.94	3.98	4.34	5.11	5.66	8.06	7.21	6.86
71. Other assets	9.04	9.40	9.71	9.78	10.40	9.91	10.14	8.07	9.91	13.48
Liabilities										
72. Capital & reserves	4.39	4.53	4.70	4.86	5.01	5.19	6.38	6.72	6.48	6.02
73. Borrowing from Central bank	0.92	0.94	1.09	1.14	1.24	1.20	1.04	0.97	0.91	0.96
74. Interbank deposits	0.01	0.00	0.01	0.00	0.00	0.00	0.08	0.21	0.14	0.06
75. Non-bank deposits	80.88	79.18	78.73	79.32	77.23	73.46	66.41	58.84	55.91	58.67
76. Bonds	0.12	0.18	0.34	1.17	1.19	1.17	1.91	2.67	1.83	4.60
77. Other liabilities	13.69	15.17	15.13	13.51	15.33	18.98	24.17	30.60	34.73	29.69
Memoranda										
78. Short-term securities (1)	*..*	*..*	*..*	*..*	*..*	*0.24*	*0.96*	*1.60*	*1.09*	*1.51*
79. Bonds	*2.45*	*2.41*	*2.61*	*2.66*	*2.90*	*3.10*	*2.89*	*2.15*	*1.99*	*1.45*
80. Shares and participations	*1.31*	*1.33*	*1.33*	*1.31*	*1.44*	*1.78*	*1.81*	*4.31*	*4.13*	*3.90*
81. Claims on non-residents	*-*	*-*	*-*	*0.00*	*0.01*	*0.13*	*0.40*	*0.61*	*0.04*	*0.02*
82. Liabilities to non-residents	*-*	*-*	*-*	*3.11*	*-*	*0.18*	*0.92*	*1.91*	*0.26*	*0.00*

1. Until 1987, included under "Bonds" (item 31 or item 79).

FINLANDE

Caisses d'épargne

Pourcentage

ANALYSE DU BILAN

% du total du bilan en fin d'exercice

Actif
67. Caisse & solde auprès de la Banque centrale
68. Dépôts interbancaires
69. Prêts
70. Valeurs mobilières
71. Autres actifs

Passif
72. Capital et réserves
73. Emprunts auprès de la Banque centrale
74. Dépôts interbancaires
75. Dépôts non bancaires
76. Obligations
77. Autres engagements

Pour mémoire
78. Titres à court terme (1)
79. Obligations
80. Actions et participations
81. Créances sur des non résidents
82. Engagements envers des non résidents

1. Jusqu'à 1987, inclus sous "Obligations" (poste 31 ou poste 79).

FINLAND

Co-operative banks

Million markkaa

FINLANDE

Banques mutualistes

Millions de markkaa

#	Item (EN)	Poste (FR)	1982	1983	1984	1985	1986	1987	1988	1989	1990	1991
	INCOME STATEMENT	**COMPTE DE RESULTATS**										
1.	Interest income	Produits financiers	2483	2937	3600	4050	4123	4709	6337	8306	10342	11120
2.	Interest expenses	Frais financiers	1456	1788	2322	2561	2488	2758	3953	5707	9617	7914
3.	Net interest income	Produits financiers nets	1027	1149	1278	1489	1635	1951	2384	2599	725	3206
4.	Non-interest income (net)	Produits non financiers (nets)	384	428	528	635	795	950	1321	1393	3889	2118
5.	Gross income	Résultat brut	1411	1577	1806	2124	2430	2901	3705	3992	4614	5324
6.	Operating expenses	Frais d'exploitation	1195	1350	1562	1793	2089	2466	2992	3436	3825	4647
7.	Net income	Résultat net	216	227	244	331	341	435	713	556	789	677
8.	Provisions (net)	Provisions (nettes)	168	169	176	251	246	319	548	357	458	315
9.	Profit before tax	Bénéfices avant impôt	48	58	68	80	95	116	165	199	331	362
10.	Income tax	Impôt	26	31	32	35	39	45	60	79	125	152
11.	Profit after tax	Bénéfices après impôt	22	27	36	45	56	71	105	120	206	210
12.	Distributed profit	Bénéfices distribués	13	22	26	32	38	49	61	66	62	50
13.	Retained profit	Bénéfices mis en réserve	9	5	10	13	18	22	44	54	144	160
	Memoranda	*Pour mémoire*										
14.	Staff costs	Frais de personnel	497	568	650	736	818	892	996	1109	1126	1235
15.	Provisions on loans	Provisions sur prêts	126	139	152	176	203	236	330	381	442	356
16.	Provisions on securities	Provisions sur titres	..	..	..	..	..	75	195	-32	2	-41
	BALANCE SHEET	**BILAN**										
	Assets	**Actif**										
17.	Cash & balance with Central bank	Caisse & solde auprès de la Banque centrale	762	1436	2199	2515	2483	2816	4872	6534	5691	4034
18.	Interbank deposits	Dépôts interbancaires	2959	3215	3678	4456	5218	5925	6658	7855	8177	9356
19.	Loans	Prêts	23620	27361	31193	35789	40797	48407	62404	69874	75639	79594
20.	Securities	Valeurs mobilières	798	1121	1286	1714	2572	2861	4441	4577	5577	6621
21.	Other assets	Autres actifs	2149	2312	2610	3123	3761	4433	5645	6650	8885	11282
	Liabilities	**Passif**										
22.	Capital & reserves	Capital et réserves	1378	1723	2025	2418	2921	3484	4473	5038	6280	6729
23.	Borrowing from Central bank	Emprunts auprès de la Banque centrale	232	274	335	401	454	528	501	692	519	542
24.	Interbank deposits	Dépôts interbancaires	-	-	-	10	70	10	10	10	-	-
25.	Non-bank deposits	Dépôts non bancaires	22851	26323	30320	34852	39146	44764	55318	61268	66679	71848
26.	Bonds	Obligations	50	81	141	215	655	1071	2502	3652	6022	9425
27.	Other liabilities	Autres engagements	5777	7044	8145	9701	11585	14585	21216	24830	24469	22343
	Balance sheet total	**Total du bilan**										
28.	End-year total	En fin d'exercice	30288	35445	40966	47597	54831	64442	84020	95490	103969	110887
29.	Average total	Moyen	28058	32867	38206	44282	51214	59637	74231	89755	99730	107428
	Memoranda	*Pour mémoire*										
30.	Short-term securities (1)	Titres à court terme (1)	..	..	..	..	..	25	293	129	161	1438
31.	Bonds	Obligations	572	710	858	1214	1714	1921	2691	2905	4007	3543
32.	Shares and participations	Actions et participations	226	411	428	500	858	915	1457	1543	1409	1640
33.	Claims on non-residents	Créances sur des non résidents	53	69	72	80	74	49	55	59	78	7
34.	Liabilities to non-residents	Engagements envers des non résidents	-	-	-	-	-	2	-	-	-	995
	SUPPLEMENTARY INFORMATION	**RENSEIGNEMENTS COMPLEMENTAIRES**										
35.	Number of institutions	Nombre d'institutions	370	371	370	370	370	369	367	361	359	335
36.	Number of branches	Nombre de succursales	827	840	849	852	854	852	850	837	800	747
37.	Number of employees (x 1000)	Nombre de salariés (x 1000)	8.2	8.3	8.5	8.7	9.0	9.2	9.4	9.6	9.3	9.0

FINLAND

Co-operative banks

FINLANDE

Banques mutualistes

Per cent / *Pourcentage*

INCOME STATEMENT ANALYSIS / ANALYSE DU COMPTE DE RESULTATS

		1982	1983	1984	1985	1986	1987	1988	1989	1990	1991		
% of average balance sheet total												**% du total moyen du bilan**	
38.	Interest income	8.85	8.94	9.42	9.15	8.05	7.90	8.54	9.25	10.37	10.35	Produits financiers	38.
39.	Interest expenses	5.19	5.44	6.08	5.78	4.86	4.62	5.33	6.36	9.64	7.37	Frais financiers	39.
40.	Net interest income	3.66	3.50	3.35	3.36	3.19	3.27	3.21	2.90	0.73	2.98	Produits financiers nets	40.
41.	Non-interest income (net)	1.37	1.30	1.38	1.43	1.55	1.59	1.78	1.55	3.90	1.97	Produits non financiers (nets)	41.
42.	Gross income	5.03	4.80	4.73	4.80	4.74	4.86	4.99	4.45	4.63	4.96	Résultat brut	42.
43.	Operating expenses	4.26	4.11	4.09	4.05	4.08	4.14	4.03	3.83	3.84	4.33	Frais d'exploitation	43.
44.	Net income	0.77	0.69	0.64	0.75	0.67	0.73	0.96	0.62	0.79	0.63	Résultat net	44.
45.	Provisions (net)	0.60	0.51	0.46	0.57	0.48	0.53	0.74	0.40	0.46	0.29	Provisions (nettes)	45.
46.	Profit before tax	0.17	0.18	0.18	0.18	0.19	0.19	0.22	0.22	0.33	0.34	Bénéfices avant impôt	46.
47.	Income tax	0.09	0.09	0.08	0.08	0.08	0.08	0.08	0.09	0.13	0.14	Impôt	47.
48.	Profit after tax	0.08	0.08	0.09	0.10	0.11	0.12	0.14	0.13	0.21	0.20	Bénéfices après impôt	48.
49.	Distributed profit	0.05	0.07	0.07	0.07	0.07	0.08	0.08	0.07	0.06	0.05	Bénéfices distribués	49.
50.	Retained profit	0.03	0.02	0.03	0.03	0.04	0.04	0.06	0.06	0.14	0.15	Bénéfices mis en réserve	50.
51.	Staff costs	1.77	1.73	1.70	1.66	1.60	1.50	1.34	1.24	1.13	1.15	Frais de personnel	51.
52.	Provisions on loans	0.45	0.42	0.40	0.40	0.40	0.40	0.44	0.42	0.44	0.33	Provisions sur prêts	52.
53.	Provisions on securities	..	..	..	..	..	0.13	0.26	-0.04	0.00	-0.04	Provisions sur titres	53.
% of gross income												**% du total du résultat brut**	
54.	Net interest income	72.79	72.86	70.76	70.10	67.28	67.25	64.35	65.11	15.71	60.22	Produits financiers nets	54.
55.	Non-interest income (net)	27.21	27.14	29.24	29.90	32.72	32.75	35.65	34.89	84.29	39.78	Produits non financiers (nets)	55.
56.	Operating expenses	84.69	85.61	86.49	84.42	85.97	85.01	80.76	86.07	82.90	87.28	Frais d'exploitation	56.
57.	Net income	15.31	14.39	13.51	15.58	14.03	14.99	19.24	13.93	17.10	12.72	Résultat net	57.
58.	Provisions (net)	11.91	10.72	9.75	11.82	10.12	11.00	14.79	8.94	9.93	5.92	Provisions (nettes)	58.
59.	Profit before tax	3.40	3.68	3.77	3.77	3.91	4.00	4.45	4.98	7.17	6.80	Bénéfices avant impôt	59.
60.	Income tax	1.84	1.97	1.77	1.65	1.60	1.55	1.62	1.98	2.71	2.85	Impôt	60.
61.	Profit after tax	1.56	1.71	1.99	2.12	2.30	2.45	2.83	3.01	4.46	3.94	Bénéfices après impôt	61.
62.	Staff costs	35.22	36.02	35.99	34.65	33.66	30.75	26.88	27.78	24.40	23.20	Frais de personnel	62.
% of net income												**% du total du résultat net**	
63.	Provisions (net)	77.78	74.45	72.13	75.83	72.14	73.33	76.86	64.21	58.05	46.53	Provisions (nettes)	63.
64.	Profit before tax	22.22	25.55	27.87	24.17	27.86	26.67	23.14	35.79	41.95	53.47	Bénéfices avant impôt	64.
65.	Income tax	12.04	13.66	13.11	10.57	11.44	10.34	8.42	14.21	15.84	22.45	Impôt	65.
66.	Profit after tax	10.19	11.89	14.75	13.60	16.42	16.32	14.73	21.58	26.11	31.02	Bénéfices après impôt	66.

FINLAND

Co-operative banks

Per cent

BALANCE SHEET ANALYSIS

% of year-end balance sheet total

	1982	1983	1984	1985	1986	1987	1988	1989	1990	1991
Assets										
67. Cash & balance with Central bank	2.52	4.05	5.37	5.28	4.53	4.37	5.80	6.84	5.47	3.64
68. Interbank deposits	9.77	9.07	8.98	9.36	9.52	9.19	7.92	8.23	7.86	8.44
69. Loans	77.98	77.19	76.14	75.19	74.40	75.12	74.27	73.17	72.75	71.78
70. Securities	2.63	3.16	3.14	3.60	4.69	4.44	5.29	4.79	5.36	5.97
71. Other assets	7.10	6.52	6.37	6.56	6.86	6.88	6.72	6.96	8.55	10.17
Liabilities										
72. Capital & reserves	4.55	4.86	4.94	5.08	5.33	5.41	5.32	5.28	6.04	6.07
73. Borrowing from Central bank	0.77	0.77	0.82	0.84	0.83	0.82	0.60	0.72	0.50	0.49
74. Interbank deposits	-	-	-	0.02	0.13	0.02	0.01	0.01	-	-
75. Non-bank deposits	75.45	74.26	74.01	73.22	71.39	69.46	65.84	64.16	64.13	64.79
76. Bonds	0.17	0.23	0.34	0.45	1.19	1.66	2.98	3.82	5.79	8.50
77. Other liabilities	19.07	19.87	19.88	20.38	21.13	22.63	25.25	26.00	23.53	20.15
Memoranda										
78. Short-term securities (1)	*..*	*..*	*..*	*..*	*..*	*0.04*	*0.35*	*0.14*	*0.15*	*1.30*
79. Bonds	*1.89*	*2.00*	*2.09*	*2.55*	*3.13*	*2.98*	*3.20*	*3.04*	*3.85*	*3.20*
80. Shares and participations	*0.75*	*1.16*	*1.04*	*1.05*	*1.56*	*1.42*	*1.73*	*1.62*	*1.36*	*1.48*
81. Claims on non-residents	*0.17*	*0.19*	*0.18*	*0.17*	*0.13*	*0.08*	*0.07*	*0.06*	*0.08*	*0.01*
82. Liabilities to non-residents	*-*	*-*	*-*	*-*	*-*	*0.00*	*-*	*-*	*-*	*0.90*

1. Until 1986, included under "Bonds" (item 31 or item 79).

FINLANDE

Banques mutualistes

Pourcentage

ANALYSE DU BILAN

% du total du bilan en fin d'exercice

Actif
67. Caisse & solde auprès de la Banque centrale
68. Dépôts interbancaires
69. Prêts
70. Valeurs mobilières
71. Autres actifs

Passif
72. Capital et réserves
73. Emprunts auprès de la Banque centrale
74. Dépôts interbancaires
75. Dépôts non bancaires
76. Obligations
77. Autres engagements

Pour mémoire
78. Titres à court terme (1)
79. Obligations
80. Actions et participations
81. Créances sur des non résidents
82. Engagements envers des non résidents

1. Jusqu'à 1986, inclus sous "Obligations" (poste 31 ou poste 79).

Commercial banks and credit co-operatives

Million French francs

	1982	1983	1984	1985	1986 (2)	1987	1988	1989	1990	1991		
INCOME STATEMENT												**COMPTE DE RESULTATS**
1. Interest income	522115	538151	628469	562425	579965	601939	695263	853155	965053	973966	1.	Produits financiers
2. Interest expenses	407569	408770	482132	409493	408865	426755	503338	658953	765556	773421	2.	Frais financiers
3. Net interest income	114546	129381	146337	152932	171100	175184	191925	194202	199497	200545	3.	Produits financiers nets
4. Non-interest income (net)	22119	26069	22230	25052	28835	31863	33452	45182	48403	69851	4.	Produits non financiers (nets)
5. Gross income	136665	155450	168567	177984	199935	207047	225377	239384	247900	270396	5.	Résultat brut
6. Operating expenses	92321	105174	116971	124648	133227	141543	150377	159652	169324	177241	6.	Frais d'exploitation
7. Net income	44344	50276	51596	53336	66708	65504	75000	79732	78576	93155	7.	Résultat net
8. Provisions (net)	28553	33549	34394	34412	42482	39397	43516	51630	52180	59916	8.	Provisions (nettes)
9. Profit before tax	15791	16727	17202	18924	24226	26107	31484	28102	26396	33239	9.	Bénéfices avant impôt
10. Income tax	7556	7404	6927	8432	9324	9172	10333	9393	7647	9658	10.	Impôt
11. Profit after tax	8235	9323	10275	10492	14902	16935	21151	18709	18749	23581	11.	Bénéfices après impôt
12. Distributed profit	..	..	..	..	5645	6362	8348	9478	9587	10677	12.	Bénéfices distribués
13. Retained profit	..	..	..	..	9257	10573	12803	9231	9162	12904	13.	Bénéfices mis en réserve
Memoranda												**Pour mémoire**
14. Staff costs	61789	69600	76134	80437	84740	88278	92415	97157	102094	105482	14.	Frais de personnel
15. Provisions on loans	..	..	..	..	22645	15968	26139	30159	32923	42595	15.	Provisions sur prêts
16. Provisions on securities	..	..	..	..	2691	6027	-2764	2254	6644	292	16.	Provisions sur titres
BALANCE SHEET												**BILAN**
Assets												**Actif**
17. Cash & balance with Central bank	104015	112866	130010	152714	186978	143610	158030	158977	116272	103291	17.	Caisse & solde auprès de la Banque centrale
18. Interbank deposits	1862752	2216412	2623425	2571559	3204683	3490402	3901829	4274116	4639338	4419924	18.	Dépôts interbancaires
19. Loans	1987353	2269879	2526317	2417469	2491881	2785380	3274425	3746651	4193607	4413169	19.	Prêts
20. Securities	112414	157104	196659	243633	500447	636019	690656	797998	893069	1330776	20.	Valeurs mobilières
21. Other assets	489390	509408	619171	602699	743625	761527	921162	1116835	1340114	1153924	21.	Autres actifs
Liabilities												**Passif**
22. Capital & reserves	114794	125890	143247	145038	173221	199629	244488	285828	338487	389370	22.	Capital et réserves
23. Borrowing from Central bank (1)	..	..	..	..	..	..	..	..	..	..	23.	Emprunts auprès de la Banque centrale (1)
24. Interbank deposits	2172114	2571799	2957347	2717110	3464918	3818201	4277345	4757650	4913847	4629260	24.	Dépôts interbancaires
25. Non-bank deposits	1612879	1836298	2033452	2138051	2264839	2512900	2876815	3289459	3896984	4025008	25.	Dépôts non bancaires
26. Bonds	213107	274940	388368	402609	507441	539396	676504	733507	772866	853375	26.	Obligations
27. Other liabilities	443030	456742	573168	585266	717195	746813	870950	1028133	1260415	1523772	27.	Autres engagements
Balance sheet total												**Total du bilan**
28. End-year total	4555924	5265669	6095582	5988074	7127614	7816939	8946102	10094577	11182400	11420785	28.	En fin d'exercice
29. Average total	4182764	4910797	5680626	6041828	6934649	7450417	8369027	9658989	10521007	11522443	29.	Moyen
Memoranda												**Pour mémoire**
30. Short-term securities	..	..	..	..	..	..	..	..	..	..	30.	Titres à court terme
31. Bonds	..	..	..	..	..	..	..	..	..	..	31.	Obligations
32. Shares and participations	..	..	..	..	..	..	..	..	..	..	32.	Actions et participations
33. Claims on non-residents	1776284	2160039	2575183	2277469	2230900	2368657	2878458	3179968	3645239	3632368	33.	Créances sur des non résidents
34. Liabilities to non-residents	1670918	2075894	2449924	2112122	2143305	2249641	2827614	3213276	3739650	3817369	34.	Engagements envers des non résidents
SUPPLEMENTARY INFORMATION												**RENSEIGNEMENTS COMPLEMENTAIRES**
35. Number of institutions	427	429	435	390	389	399	411	424	427	431	35.	Nombre d'institutions
36. Number of branches	21314	21395	21323	21030	21025	21362	20943	21119	20771	20680	36.	Nombre de succursales
37. Number of employees (x 1000)	365.5	368.0	375.6	372.9	373.3	371.7	370.2	369.9	365.5	358.6	37.	Nombre de salariés (x 1000)

FRANCE

Commercial banks and credit co-operatives

Banques commerciales et mutualistes

Per cent	1982	1983	1984	1985	1986 (2)	1987	1988	1989	1990	1991		*Pourcentage*
INCOME STATEMENT ANALYSIS												**ANALYSE DU COMPTE DE RESULTATS**
% of average balance sheet total												**% du total moyen du bilan**
38. Interest income	12.48	10.96	11.06	9.31	8.36	8.08	8.31	8.83	9.17	8.45	38.	Produits financiers
39. Interest expenses	9.74	8.32	8.49	6.78	5.90	5.73	6.01	6.82	7.28	6.71	39.	Frais financiers
40. Net interest income	2.74	2.63	2.58	2.53	2.47	2.35	2.29	2.01	1.90	1.74	40.	Produits financiers nets
41. Non-interest income (net)	0.53	0.53	0.39	0.41	0.42	0.43	0.40	0.47	0.46	0.61	41.	Produits non financiers (nets)
42. Gross income	3.27	3.17	2.97	2.95	2.88	2.78	2.69	2.48	2.36	2.35	42.	Résultat brut
43. Operating expenses	2.21	2.14	2.06	2.06	1.92	1.90	1.80	1.65	1.61	1.54	43.	Frais d'exploitation
44. Net income	1.06	1.02	0.91	0.88	0.96	0.88	0.90	0.83	0.75	0.81	44.	Résultat net
45. Provisions (net)	0.68	0.68	0.61	0.57	0.61	0.53	0.52	0.53	0.50	0.52	45.	Provisions (nettes)
46. Profit before tax	0.38	0.34	0.30	0.31	0.35	0.35	0.38	0.29	0.25	0.29	46.	Bénéfices avant impôt
47. Income tax	0.18	0.15	0.12	0.14	0.13	0.12	0.12	0.10	0.07	0.08	47.	Impôt
48. Profit after tax	0.20	0.19	0.18	0.17	0.21	0.23	0.25	0.19	0.18	0.20	48.	Bénéfices après impôt
49. Distributed profit	::	::	::	::	0.08	0.09	0.10	0.10	0.09	0.09	49.	Bénéfices distribués
50. Retained profit	::	::	::	::	0.13	0.14	0.15	0.10	0.09	0.11	50.	Bénéfices mis en réserve
51. Staff costs	1.48	1.42	1.34	1.33	1.22	1.18	1.10	1.01	0.97	0.92	51.	Frais de personnel
52. Provisions on loans	::	::	::	::	0.33	0.21	0.31	0.31	0.31	0.37	52.	Provisions sur prêts
53. Provisions on securities	::	::	::	::	0.04	0.08	-0.03	0.02	0.06	0.00	53.	Provisions sur titres
% of gross income												**% du total du résultat brut**
54. Net interest income	83.82	83.23	86.81	85.92	85.58	84.61	85.16	81.13	80.47	74.17	54.	Produits financiers nets
55. Non-interest income (net)	16.18	16.77	13.19	14.08	14.42	15.39	14.84	18.87	19.53	25.83	55.	Produits non financiers (nets)
56. Operating expenses	67.55	67.66	69.39	70.03	66.64	68.36	66.72	66.69	68.30	65.55	56.	Frais d'exploitation
57. Net income	32.45	32.34	30.61	29.97	33.36	31.64	33.28	33.31	31.70	34.45	57.	Résultat net
58. Provisions (net)	20.89	21.58	20.40	19.33	21.25	19.03	19.31	21.57	21.05	22.16	58.	Provisions (nettes)
59. Profit before tax	11.55	10.76	10.20	10.63	12.12	12.61	13.97	11.74	10.65	12.29	59.	Bénéfices avant impôt
60. Income tax	5.53	4.76	4.11	4.74	4.66	4.43	4.58	3.92	3.08	3.57	60.	Impôt
61. Profit after tax	6.03	6.00	6.10	5.89	7.45	8.18	9.38	7.82	7.56	8.72	61.	Bénéfices après impôt
62. Staff costs	45.21	44.77	45.17	45.19	42.38	42.64	41.00	40.59	41.18	39.01	62.	Frais de personnel
% of net income												**% du total du résultat net**
63. Provisions (net)	64.39	66.73	66.66	64.52	63.68	60.14	58.02	64.75	66.41	64.32	63.	Provisions (nettes)
64. Profit before tax	35.61	33.27	33.34	35.48	36.32	39.86	41.98	35.25	33.59	35.68	64.	Bénéfices avant impôt
65. Income tax	17.04	14.73	13.43	15.81	13.98	14.00	13.78	11.78	9.73	10.37	65.	Impôt
66. Profit after tax	18.57	18.54	19.91	19.67	22.34	25.85	28.20	23.46	23.86	25.31	66.	Bénéfices après impôt

FRANCE

Commercial banks and credit co-operatives

FRANCE

Banques commerciales et mutualistes

Per cent / *Pourcentage*

BALANCE SHEET ANALYSIS / ANALYSE DU BILAN

% of year-end balance sheet total / % du total du bilan en fin d'exercice

	1982	1983	1984	1985	1986 (2)	1987	1988	1989	1990	1991		
Assets												**Actif**
67. Cash & balance with Central bank	2.28	2.14	2.13	2.55	2.62	1.84	1.77	1.57	1.04	0.90	67.	Caisse & solde auprès de la Banque centrale
68. Interbank deposits	40.89	42.09	43.04	42.94	44.96	44.65	43.61	42.34	41.49	38.70	68.	Dépôts interbancaires
69. Loans	43.62	43.11	41.45	40.37	34.96	35.63	36.60	37.12	37.50	38.64	69.	Prêts
70. Securities	2.47	2.98	3.23	4.07	7.02	8.14	7.72	7.91	7.99	11.65	70.	Valeurs mobilières
71. Other assets	10.74	9.67	10.16	10.06	10.43	9.74	10.30	11.06	11.98	10.10	71.	Autres actifs
Liabilities												**Passif**
72. Capital & reserves	2.52	2.39	2.35	2.42	2.43	2.55	2.73	2.83	3.03	3.41	72.	Capital et réserves
73. Borrowing from Central bank (1)	..	..	..	..	..	..	..	..	..	..	73.	Emprunts auprès de la Banque centrale (1)
74. Interbank deposits	47.68	48.84	48.52	45.38	48.61	48.85	47.81	47.13	43.94	40.53	74.	Dépôts interbancaires
75. Non-bank deposits	35.40	34.87	33.36	35.71	31.78	32.15	32.16	32.59	34.85	35.24	75.	Dépôts non bancaires
76. Bonds	4.68	5.22	6.37	6.72	7.12	6.90	7.56	7.27	6.91	7.47	76.	Obligations
77. Other liabilities	9.72	8.67	9.40	9.77	10.06	9.55	9.74	10.19	11.27	13.34	77.	Autres engagements
Memoranda												***Pour mémoire***
78. Short-term securities	..	..	..	..	..	..	..	..	..	..	*78.*	*Titres à court terme*
79. Bonds	..	..	..	..	..	..	..	..	..	..	*79.*	*Obligations*
80. Shares and participations	..	..	..	..	..	..	..	..	..	..	*80.*	*Actions et participations*
81. Claims on non-residents	*38.99*	*41.02*	*42.25*	*38.03*	*31.30*	*30.30*	*32.18*	*31.50*	*32.60*	*31.80*	*81.*	*Créances sur des non résidents*
82. Liabilities to non-residents	*36.68*	*39.42*	*40.19*	*35.27*	*30.07*	*28.78*	*31.61*	*31.83*	*33.44*	*33.42*	*82.*	*Engagements envers des non résidents*

1. Included under "Interbank deposits" (item 24 or item 74).
2. Change in methodology as from 1986.

Change in methodology:

- Following the accounting reform of 1991, the presentation of "Securities" items in the balance sheet and income statement was modified. Data, as from 1986, were recalculated on the basis of these modifications.

- As from 1986, average balance sheet totals (item 29) are based on the average of quarterly totals.

1. Inclus sous "Dépôts interbancaires" (poste 24 ou poste 74).
2. Changement méthodologique à partir de 1986.

Changement méthodologique :

- Une réforme comptable intervenue en 1991 a entraîné des modifications dans la présentation des opérations sur titres dans le bilan et le compte de résultat. Les données, à partir de 1986, ont été recalculées selon ces modifications.

- A partir de 1986 la moyenne du total des actifs/passifs (poste 29) est basée sur la moyenne des totaux des situations trimestrielles.

Million French francs / *Millions de francs français*

			1982	1983	1984	1985	1986 (2)	1987	1988	1989	1990	1991
INCOME STATEMENT		**COMPTE DE RESULTATS**										
1.	Interest income	Produits financiers	319973	333528	391406	345399	351130	356026	401540	490370	555315	561510
2.	Interest expenses	Frais financiers	249750	254343	302348	251589	252016	255096	293382	377307	440707	446446
3.	Net interest income	Produits financiers nets	70223	79185	89058	93810	99114	100930	108158	113063	114608	115064
4.	Non-interest income (net)	Produits non financiers (nets)	13142	16237	13263	17460	20424	24225	25285	30732	32065	46273
5.	Gross income	Résultat brut	83365	95422	102321	111270	119538	125155	133443	143795	146673	161337
6.	Operating expenses	Frais d'exploitation	56024	65130	72065	77694	80104	84024	88434	93711	99388	104081
7.	Net income	Résultat net	26441	30292	30256	33576	39434	41131	45009	50084	47285	57256
8.	Provisions (net)	Provisions (nettes)	19786	23120	23339	25379	30046	26763	30652	34841	34073	36155
9.	Profit before tax	Bénéfices avant impôt	6655	7172	6917	8197	9388	14368	14357	15243	13212	21101
10.	Income tax	Impôt	3820	3950	3807	4551	4531	5016	5280	5072	3570	5605
11.	Profit after tax	Bénéfices après impôt	2835	3222	3110	3646	4857	9352	9077	10171	9642	15496
12.	Distributed profit	Bénéfices distribués	..	..	..	..	2198	2590	3627	4393	4150	4785
13.	Retained profit	Bénéfices mis en réserve	..	..	..	..	2659	6762	5450	5778	5492	10711
Memoranda		*Pour mémoire*										
14.	*Staff costs*	*Frais de personnel*	*38868*	*44120*	*47822*	*51057*	*52316*	*54068*	*56219*	*59099*	*62068*	*64434*
15.	*Provisions on loans*	*Provisions sur prêts*	*..*	*..*	*..*	*..*	*16132*	*9964*	*18661*	*20591*	*21226*	*24575*
16.	*Provisions on securities*	*Provisions sur titres*	*..*	*..*	*..*	*..*	*2011*	*4238*	*-1975*	*776*	*4214*	*-784*
BALANCE SHEET		**BILAN**										
Assets		**Actif**										
17.	Cash & balance with Central bank	Caisse & solde auprès de la Banque centrale	69677	71034	84021	105693	103408	86041	101200	93336	77326	71870
18.	Interbank deposits	Dépôts interbancaires	1138723	1346855	1598632	1545198	1905147	2018331	2272590	2456510	2735222	2547642
19.	Loans	Prêts	1285368	1481751	1663103	1661410	1652581	1810929	2113731	2403158	2673198	2812344
20.	Securities	Valeurs mobilières	55269	77845	90453	105333	253128	305635	323492	384174	427499	728643
21.	Other assets	Autres actifs	307344	298971	419666	418192	487633	488265	575967	716147	908076	747557
Liabilities		**Passif**										
22.	Capital & reserves	Capital et réserves	56784	61105	66205	73183	81077	89728	116334	131226	172624	192201
23.	Borrowing from Central bank (1)	Emprunts auprès de la Banque centrale (1)	..	..	..	..	..	..	..	..	..	..
24.	Interbank deposits	Dépôts interbancaires	1262226	1477802	1726155	1585187	2003491	2146014	2442461	2724819	2887902	2710582
25.	Non-bank deposits	Dépôts non bancaires	1107541	1267005	1425156	1496823	1557540	1674689	1897973	2129064	2512440	2557516
26.	Bonds	Obligations	132750	169610	232187	266552	277859	293689	368874	392809	411924	462954
27.	Other liabilities	Autres engagements	297080	300934	406172	414081	481931	505080	561337	675408	836430	984802
Balance sheet total		**Total du bilan**										
28.	End-year total	En fin d'exercice	2856381	3276456	3855875	3835826	4401897	4709201	5386980	6053326	6821321	6908056
29.	Average total	Moyen	2606176	3066419	3566166	3845851	4324061	4527626	5033297	5751364	6316663	6969143
Memoranda		*Pour mémoire*										
30.	*Short-term securities*	*Titres à court terme*	*..*	*..*	*..*	*..*	*..*	*..*	*..*	*..*	*..*	*..*
31.	*Bonds*	*Obligations*	*..*	*..*	*..*	*..*	*..*	*..*	*..*	*..*	*..*	*..*
32.	*Shares and participations*	*Actions et participations*	*..*	*..*	*..*	*..*	*..*	*..*	*..*	*..*	*..*	*..*
33.	*Claims on non-residents*	*Créances sur des non résidents*	*1316515*	*1606047*	*1939830*	*1701130*	*1592649*	*1611696*	*1971750*	*2138301*	*2492038*	*2475228*
34.	*Liabilities to non-residents*	*Engagements envers des non résidents*	*1236543*	*1535807*	*1829965*	*1552763*	*1524045*	*1510481*	*1907909*	*2133156*	*2555351*	*2637372*
SUPPLEMENTARY INFORMATION		**RENSEIGNEMENTS COMPLEMENTAIRES**										
35.	Number of institutions	Nombre d'institutions	8	8	8	8	8	8	8	8	8	8
36.	Number of branches	Nombre de succursales	12187	12272	12276	12300	12412	12357	12305	12365	12233	12202
37.	Number of employees (x 1000)	Nombre de salariés (x 1000)	228.6	231.5	236.2	236.4	232.5	230.9	229.6	228.3	224.9	222.2

Large commercial banks

FRANCE

Grandes banques commerciales

Per cent

Pourcentage

INCOME STATEMENT ANALYSIS

ANALYSE DU COMPTE DE RESULTATS

	1982	1983	1984	1985	1986 (2)	1987	1988	1989	1990	1991		
% of average balance sheet total												**% du total moyen du bilan**
38. Interest income	12.28	10.88	10.98	8.98	8.12	7.86	7.98	8.53	8.79	8.06	38.	Produits financiers
39. Interest expenses	9.58	8.29	8.48	6.54	5.83	5.63	5.83	6.56	6.98	6.41	39.	Frais financiers
40. Net interest income	2.69	2.58	2.50	2.44	2.29	2.23	2.15	1.97	1.81	1.65	40.	Produits financiers nets
41. Non-interest income (net)	0.50	0.53	0.37	0.45	0.47	0.54	0.50	0.53	0.51	0.66	41.	Produits non financiers (nets)
42. Gross income	3.20	3.11	2.87	2.89	2.76	2.76	2.65	2.50	2.32	2.32	42.	Résultat brut
43. Operating expenses	2.18	2.12	2.02	2.02	1.85	1.86	1.76	1.63	1.57	1.49	43.	Frais d'exploitation
44. Net income	1.01	0.99	0.85	0.87	0.91	0.91	0.89	0.87	0.75	0.82	44.	Résultat net
45. Provisions (net)	0.76	0.75	0.65	0.66	0.69	0.59	0.61	0.61	0.54	0.52	45.	Provisions (nettes)
46. Profit before tax	0.26	0.23	0.19	0.21	0.22	0.32	0.29	0.27	0.21	0.30	46.	Bénéfices avant impôt
47. Income tax	0.15	0.13	0.11	0.12	0.10	0.11	0.10	0.09	0.06	0.08	47.	Impôt
48. Profit after tax	0.11	0.11	0.09	0.09	0.11	0.21	0.18	0.18	0.15	0.22	48.	Bénéfices après impôt
49. Distributed profit	:	:	:	:	0.05	0.06	0.07	0.08	0.07	0.07	49.	Bénéfices distribués
50. Retained profit	:	:	:	:	0.06	0.15	0.11	0.10	0.09	0.15	50.	Bénéfices mis en réserve
51. Staff costs	1.49	1.44	1.34	1.33	1.21	1.19	1.12	1.03	0.98	0.92	51.	Frais de personnel
52. Provisions on loans	:	:	:	:	0.37	0.22	0.37	0.36	0.34	0.35	52.	Provisions sur prêts
53. Provisions on securities	:	:	:	:	0.05	0.09	-0.04	0.01	0.07	-0.01	53.	Provisions sur titres
% of gross income												**% du total du résultat brut**
54. Net interest income	84.24	82.98	87.04	84.31	82.91	80.64	81.05	78.63	78.14	71.32	54.	Produits financiers nets
55. Non-interest income (net)	15.76	17.02	12.96	15.69	17.09	19.36	18.95	21.37	21.86	28.68	55.	Produits non financiers (nets)
56. Operating expenses	68.28	68.25	70.43	69.82	67.01	67.14	66.27	65.17	67.76	64.51	56.	Frais d'exploitation
57. Net income	31.72	31.75	29.57	30.18	32.99	32.86	33.73	34.83	32.24	35.49	57.	Résultat net
58. Provisions (net)	23.73	24.23	22.81	22.81	25.14	21.38	22.97	24.23	23.23	22.41	58.	Provisions (nettes)
59. Profit before tax	7.98	7.52	6.76	7.37	7.85	11.48	10.76	10.60	9.01	13.08	59.	Bénéfices avant impôt
60. Income tax	4.58	4.14	3.72	4.09	3.79	4.01	3.96	3.53	2.43	3.47	60.	Impôt
61. Profit after tax	3.40	3.38	3.04	3.28	4.06	7.47	6.80	7.07	6.57	9.60	61.	Bénéfices après impôt
62. Staff costs	46.62	46.24	46.74	45.89	43.77	43.20	42.13	41.10	42.32	39.94	62.	Frais de personnel
% of net income												**% du total du résultat net**
63. Provisions (net)	74.83	76.32	77.14	75.59	76.19	65.07	68.10	69.57	72.06	63.15	63.	Provisions (nettes)
64. Profit before tax	25.17	23.68	22.86	24.41	23.81	34.93	31.90	30.43	27.94	36.85	64.	Bénéfices avant impôt
65. Income tax	14.45	13.04	12.58	13.55	11.49	12.20	11.73	10.13	7.55	9.79	65.	Impôt
66. Profit after tax	10.72	10.64	10.28	10.86	12.32	22.74	20.17	20.31	20.39	27.06	66.	Bénéfices après impôt

FRANCE

Large commercial banks

Per cent

BALANCE SHEET ANALYSIS

% of year-end balance sheet total

	1982	1983	1984	1985	1986 (2)	1987	1988	1989	1990	1991
Assets										
67. Cash & balance with Central bank	2.44	2.17	2.18	2.76	2.35	1.83	1.88	1.54	1.13	1.04
68. Interbank deposits	39.87	41.11	41.46	40.28	43.28	42.86	42.19	40.58	40.10	36.88
69. Loans	45.00	45.22	43.13	43.31	37.54	38.46	39.24	39.70	39.19	40.71
70. Securities	1.93	2.38	2.35	2.75	5.75	6.49	6.01	6.35	6.27	10.55
71. Other assets	10.76	9.12	10.88	10.90	11.08	10.37	10.69	11.83	13.31	10.82
Liabilities										
72. Capital & reserves	1.99	1.86	1.72	1.91	1.84	1.91	2.16	2.17	2.53	2.78
73. Borrowing from Central bank (1)	..	..	..	..	..	..	..	..	..	..
74. Interbank deposits	44.19	45.10	44.77	41.33	45.51	45.57	45.34	45.01	42.34	39.24
75. Non-bank deposits	38.77	38.67	36.96	39.02	35.38	35.56	35.23	35.17	36.83	37.02
76. Bonds	4.65	5.18	6.02	6.95	6.31	6.24	6.85	6.49	6.04	6.70
77. Other liabilities	10.40	9.18	10.53	10.80	10.95	10.73	10.42	11.16	12.26	14.26
Memoranda										
78. Short-term securities	..	..	..	..	..	..	..	..	..	..
79. Bonds	..	..	..	..	..	..	..	..	..	..
80. Shares and participations	..	..	..	..	..	..	..	..	..	..
81. Claims on non-residents	46.09	49.02	50.31	44.35	36.18	34.22	36.60	35.32	36.53	35.83
82. Liabilities to non-residents	43.29	46.87	47.46	40.48	34.62	32.08	35.42	35.24	37.46	38.18

1. Included under "Interbank deposits" (item 24 or item 74).
2. Change in methodology as from 1986.

Notes

- Large commercial banks are a subgroup of Commercial banks and credit co-operatives.

Change in methodology:

- Following the accounting reform of 1991, the presentation of "Securities" items in the balance sheet and income statement was modified. Data, as from 1986, were recalculated on the basis of these modifications.

- As from 1986, average balance sheet totals (item 29) are based on the average of quarterly totals.

FRANCE

Grandes banques commerciales

Pourcentage

ANALYSE DU BILAN

% du total du bilan en fin d'exercice

Actif
67. Caisse & solde auprès de la Banque centrale
68. Dépôts interbancaires
69. Prêts
70. Valeurs mobilières
71. Autres actifs

Passif
72. Capital et réserves
73. Emprunts auprès de la Banque centrale (1)
74. Dépôts interbancaires
75. Dépôts non bancaires
76. Obligations
77. Autres engagements

Pour mémoire
78. Titres à court terme
79. Obligations
80. Actions et participations
81. Créances sur des non résidents
82. Engagements envers des non résidents

1. Inclus sous "Dépôts interbancaires" (poste 24 ou poste 74).
2. Changement méthodologique à partir de 1986.

Notes

- Les Grandes banques commerciales sont un sous-groupe des Banques commerciales et mutualistes.

Changement méthodologique :

- Une réforme comptable intervenue en 1991 a entraîné des modifications dans la présentation des opérations sur titres dans le bilan et le compte de résultat. Les données, à partir de 1986, ont été recalculées selon ces modifications.

- A partir de 1986 la moyenne du total des actifs/passifs (poste 29) est basée sur la moyenne des totaux des situations trimestrielles.

GERMANY

All banks

Million DM

ALLEMAGNE

Ensemble des banques

Millions de DM

	1982	1983	1984	1985	1986	1987	1988	1989	1990	1991	
INCOME STATEMENT											**COMPTE DE RESULTATS**
1. Interest income	181861	166935	175343	180527	181159	182155	191817	224774	272413	317946	1. Produits financiers
2. Interest expenses	131669	110129	118350	120692	116811	117875	125596	157915	201200	236652	2. Frais financiers
3. Net interest income	50192	56806	56993	59835	64348	64280	66221	66859	71213	81294	3. Produits financiers nets
4. Non-interest income (net)	10906	11366	12541	15515	16335	16131	15442	22957	26055	25789	4. Produits non financiers (nets)
5. Gross income	61098	68172	69534	75350	80683	80411	81663	89816	97268	107083	5. Résultat brut
6. Operating expenses	35868	38803	41230	45627	50530	53176	55598	57993	62987	69979	6. Frais d'exploitation
7. Net income	25230	29369	28304	29723	30153	27235	26065	31823	34281	37304	7. Résultat net
8. Provisions (net)	11075	12849	10938	11958	11488	10477	6808	15294	16807	14008	8. Provisions (nettes)
9. Profit before tax	14155	16520	17366	17765	18665	16758	19257	16529	17474	23296	9. Bénéfices avant impôt
10. Income tax	9176	11009	11060	11393	11595	10316	11965	9275	9408	13585	10. Impôt
11. Profit after tax	4979	5511	6306	6372	7070	6442	7292	7254	8066	9711	11. Bénéfices après impôt
12. Distributed profit	3292	3321	4150	4417	5063	4844	5088	5506	5828	6192	12. Bénéfices distribués
13. Retained profit	1687	2190	2156	1955	2007	1598	2204	1748	2238	3519	13. Bénéfices mis en réserve
Memoranda											***Pour mémoire***
14. Staff costs	23814	25575	26819	29379	32328	34180	35770	36971	40178	44264	14. Frais de personnel
15. Provisions on loans	10856	12597	10707	11661	11142	10218	6736	15093	16295	13680	15. Provisions sur prêts
16. Provisions on securities (1)	..	..	..	..	..	..	..	..	..	..	16. Provisions sur titres (1)
BALANCE SHEET											**BILAN**
Assets											**Actif**
17. Cash & balance with Central bank	61182	62643	67390	69835	71528	75478	76127	85858	92447	93037	17. Caisse & solde auprès de la Banque centrale
18. Interbank deposits	432616	446230	498412	541786	641874	703121	773067	855091	942832	957065	18. Dépôts interbancaires
19. Loans	1272560	1358061	1438759	1525921	1616444	1684653	1802314	1923523	2103045	2369128	19. Prêts
20. Securities	293424	328544	356306	398718	433365	476356	511376	535369	627941	667975	20. Valeurs mobilières
21. Other assets	56932	61964	66464	73062	80010	81740	84842	90902	95027	114465	21. Autres actifs
Liabilities											**Passif**
22. Capital & reserves	70609	75815	82239	92823	105015	113259	119755	133480	146444	161711	22. Capital et réserves
23. Borrowing from Central bank	62812	70444	79332	87133	81888	71563	125163	153961	164043	186258	23. Emprunts auprès de la Banque centrale
24. Interbank deposits	490018	505793	548764	568000	640764	694531	758172	798405	914820	964156	24. Dépôts interbancaires
25. Non-bank deposits	1134856	1202849	1294839	1408483	1532971	1632736	1735511	1843035	2010213	2197757	25. Dépôts non bancaires
26. Bonds	289200	324161	338999	358217	374807	397643	392924	434797	480036	526137	26. Obligations
27. Other liabilities	69219	78380	83158	94666	107776	111616	118201	127065	145736	165651	27. Autres engagements
Balance sheet total											**Total du bilan**
28. End-year total	2116714	2257442	2427331	2609322	2843221	3021348	3247726	3490743	3861292	4201670	28. En fin d'exercice
29. Average total	2023461	2154333	2281097	2481800	2695352	2901013	3101033	3318573	3625716	3993346	29. Moyen
Memoranda											***Pour mémoire***
30. Short-term securities	64291	69538	68562	69639	64291	67080	58176	51859	104948	132657	30. Titres à court terme
31. Bonds	198732	225426	251071	287412	318939	353433	394145	412249	431455	432428	31. Obligations
32. Shares and participations	30401	33580	36673	41667	50135	55843	59055	71261	91538	102890	32. Actions et participations
33. Claims on non-residents	222130	233429	269861	299645	374699	413771	494438	572825	745902	687097	33. Créances sur des non résidents
34. Liabilities to non-residents	209893	222982	255675	249585	251922	275524	326618	337417	440078	423857	34. Engagements envers des non résidents
SUPPLEMENTARY INFORMATION											**RENSEIGNEMENTS COMPLEMENTAIRES**
35. Number of institutions	3061	3039	3025	4439	4465	4340	4223	4089	3913	3716	35. Nombre d'institutions
36. Number of branches	35499	35611	35752	38867	39812	39744	39679	39651	39576	39395	36. Nombre de succursales
37. Number of employees (x 1000)	NA	NA	NA	NA	NA	NA	NA	NA	NA	NA	37. Nombre de salariés (x 1000)

GERMANY
All banks

Per cent

INCOME STATEMENT ANALYSIS

	1982	1983	1984	1985	1986	1987	1988	1989	1990	1991		
% of average balance sheet total												**% du total moyen du bilan**
38. Interest income	8.99	7.75	7.69	7.27	6.72	6.28	6.19	6.77	7.51	7.96	38.	Produits financiers
39. Interest expenses	6.51	5.11	5.19	4.86	4.33	4.06	4.05	4.76	5.55	5.93	39.	Frais financiers
40. Net interest income	2.48	2.64	2.50	2.41	2.39	2.22	2.14	2.01	1.96	2.04	40.	Produits financiers nets
41. Non-interest income (net)	0.54	0.53	0.55	0.63	0.61	0.56	0.50	0.69	0.72	0.65	41.	Produits non financiers (nets)
42. Gross income	3.02	3.16	3.05	3.04	2.99	2.77	2.63	2.71	2.68	2.68	42.	Résultat brut
43. Operating expenses	1.77	1.80	1.81	1.84	1.87	1.83	1.79	1.75	1.74	1.75	43.	Frais d'exploitation
44. Net income	1.25	1.36	1.24	1.20	1.12	0.94	0.84	0.96	0.95	0.93	44.	Résultat net
45. Provisions (net)	0.55	0.60	0.48	0.48	0.43	0.36	0.22	0.46	0.46	0.35	45.	Provisions (nettes)
46. Profit before tax	0.70	0.77	0.76	0.72	0.69	0.58	0.62	0.50	0.48	0.58	46.	Bénéfices avant impôt
47. Income tax	0.45	0.51	0.48	0.46	0.43	0.36	0.39	0.28	0.26	0.34	47.	Impôt
48. Profit after tax	0.25	0.26	0.28	0.26	0.26	0.22	0.24	0.22	0.22	0.24	48.	Bénéfices après impôt
49. Distributed profit	0.16	0.15	0.18	0.18	0.19	0.17	0.16	0.17	0.16	0.16	49.	Bénéfices distribués
50. Retained profit	0.08	0.10	0.09	0.08	0.07	0.06	0.07	0.05	0.06	0.09	50.	Bénéfices mis en réserve
51. Staff costs	1.18	1.19	1.18	1.18	1.20	1.18	1.15	1.11	1.11	1.11	51.	Frais de personnel
52. Provisions on loans	0.54	0.58	0.47	0.47	0.41	0.35	0.22	0.45	0.45	0.34	52.	Provisions sur prêts
53. Provisions on securities (1)	:	:	:	:	:	:	:	:	:	:	53.	Provisions sur titres (1)
% of gross income												**% du total du résultat brut**
54. Net interest income	82.15	83.33	81.96	79.41	79.75	79.94	81.09	74.44	73.21	75.92	54.	Produits financiers nets
55. Non-interest income (net)	17.85	16.67	18.04	20.59	20.25	20.06	18.91	25.56	26.79	24.08	55.	Produits non financiers (nets)
56. Operating expenses	58.71	56.92	59.29	60.55	62.63	66.13	68.08	64.57	64.76	65.16	56.	Frais d'exploitation
57. Net income	41.29	43.08	40.71	39.45	37.37	33.87	31.92	35.43	35.24	34.84	57.	Résultat net
58. Provisions (net)	18.13	18.85	15.73	15.87	14.24	13.03	8.34	17.03	17.28	13.08	58.	Provisions (nettes)
59. Profit before tax	23.17	24.23	24.97	23.58	23.13	20.84	23.58	18.40	17.96	21.76	59.	Bénéfices avant impôt
60. Income tax	15.02	16.15	15.91	15.12	14.37	12.83	14.65	10.33	9.67	12.69	60.	Impôt
61. Profit after tax	8.15	8.08	9.07	8.46	8.76	8.01	8.93	8.08	8.29	9.07	61.	Bénéfices après impôt
62. Staff costs	38.98	37.52	38.57	38.99	40.07	42.51	43.80	41.16	41.31	41.34	62.	Frais de personnel
% of net income												**% du total du résultat net**
63. Provisions (net)	43.90	43.75	38.64	40.23	38.10	38.47	26.12	48.06	49.03	37.55	63.	Provisions (nettes)
64. Profit before tax	56.10	56.25	61.36	59.77	61.90	61.53	73.88	51.94	50.97	62.45	64.	Bénéfices avant impôt
65. Income tax	36.37	37.49	39.08	38.33	38.45	37.88	45.90	29.15	27.44	36.42	65.	Impôt
66. Profit after tax	19.73	18.76	22.28	21.44	23.45	23.65	27.98	22.79	23.53	26.03	66.	Bénéfices après impôt

GERMANY

All banks

ALLEMAGNE

Ensemble des banques

Per cent / *Pourcentage*

BALANCE SHEET ANALYSIS / ANALYSE DU BILAN

% of year-end balance sheet total / **% du total du bilan en fin d'exercice**

	1982	1983	1984	1985	1986	1987	1988	1989	1990	1991	
Assets											**Actif**
67. Cash & balance with Central bank	2.89	2.77	2.78	2.68	2.52	2.50	2.34	2.46	2.39	2.21	67. Caisse & solde auprès de la Banque centrale
68. Interbank deposits	20.44	19.77	20.53	20.76	22.58	23.27	23.80	24.50	24.42	22.78	68. Dépôts interbancaires
69. Loans	60.12	60.16	59.27	58.48	56.85	55.76	55.49	55.10	54.46	56.39	69. Prêts
70. Securities	13.86	14.55	14.68	15.28	15.24	15.77	15.75	15.34	16.26	15.90	70. Valeurs mobilières
71. Other assets	2.69	2.74	2.74	2.80	2.81	2.71	2.61	2.60	2.46	2.72	71. Autres actifs
Liabilities											**Passif**
72. Capital & reserves	3.34	3.36	3.39	3.56	3.69	3.75	3.69	3.82	3.79	3.85	72. Capital et réserves
73. Borrowing from Central bank	2.97	3.12	3.27	3.34	2.88	2.37	3.85	4.41	4.25	4.43	73. Emprunts auprès de la Banque centrale
74. Interbank deposits	23.15	22.41	22.61	21.77	22.54	22.99	23.34	22.87	23.69	22.95	74. Dépôts interbancaires
75. Non-bank deposits	53.61	53.28	53.34	53.98	53.92	54.04	53.38	52.80	52.06	52.31	75. Dépôts non bancaires
76. Bonds	13.66	14.36	13.97	13.73	13.18	13.16	12.10	12.46	12.43	12.52	76. Obligations
77. Other liabilities	3.27	3.47	3.43	3.63	3.79	3.69	3.64	3.64	3.77	3.94	77. Autres engagements
Memoranda											*Pour mémoire*
78. Short-term securities	*3.04*	*3.08*	*2.82*	*2.67*	*2.26*	*2.22*	*1.79*	*1.49*	*2.72*	*3.16*	*78. Titres à court terme*
79. Bonds	*9.39*	*9.99*	*10.34*	*11.01*	*11.22*	*11.70*	*12.14*	*11.81*	*11.17*	*10.29*	*79. Obligations*
80. Shares and participations	*1.44*	*1.49*	*1.51*	*1.60*	*1.76*	*1.85*	*1.82*	*2.04*	*2.37*	*2.45*	*80. Actions et participations*
81. Claims on non-residents	*10.49*	*10.34*	*11.12*	*11.45*	*13.18*	*13.69*	*15.22*	*16.41*	*19.32*	*16.35*	*81. Créances sur des non résidents*
82. Liabilities to non-residents	*9.92*	*9.88*	*10.53*	*9.57*	*8.86*	*9.12*	*10.12*	*9.67*	*11.40*	*10.09*	*82. Engagements envers des non résidents*

1. Included under "Provisions on loans" (item 15 or item 52).

1. Inclus sous "Provisions sur prêts" (poste 15 ou poste 52).

Notes

- All banks include Commercial banks, Regional giro institutions, Savings banks, Regional institutions of co-operative banks and Co-operative banks.

- Average balance sheet totals (item 29) are based on twelve end-month data.

- Data for banks domiciled in the new Länder of the Federal Republic of Germany are not included.

Change in methodology:

- As from 1985, all credit co-operatives are included in the data.

- As from 1986, the so-called Instalment sales financing institutions are included in the data.

Notes

- L'Ensemble des banques comprend les Banques commerciales, les Organismes régionaux de compensation, les Caisses d'épargne, les Institutions régionales des banques mutualistes et les Banques mutualistes.

- La moyenne du total des actifs/passifs (poste 29) est basée sur douze données de fin de mois.

- Les données portant sur les banques domiciliées dans les nouveaux Länder de la République fédérale d'Allemagne ne sont pas incluses.

Changement méthodologique :

- Depuis 1985, l'ensemble des banques mutualistes est compris dans les données.

- Depuis 1986, les Etablissements de financement des ventes à crédit sont compris dans les données.

GERMANY

Commercial banks

Million DM

ALLEMAGNE

Banques commerciales

Millions de DM

		1982	1983	1984	1985	1986	1987	1988	1989	1990	1991	
INCOME STATEMENT												**COMPTE DE RESULTATS**
1.	Interest income	56746	48735	51953	51916	54708	55057	60714	75952	93502	109785	1. Produits financiers
2.	Interest expenses	41954	31745	35062	34339	33552	34574	39455	54081	68910	80576	2. Frais financiers
3.	Net interest income	14792	16990	16891	17577	21156	20483	21259	21871	24592	29209	3. Produits financiers nets
4.	Non-interest income (net)	5429	5608	5915	7551	8872	8709	9283	12315	13742	12825	4. Produits non financiers (nets)
5.	Gross income	20221	22598	22806	25128	30028	29192	30542	34186	38834	42034	5. Résultat brut
6.	Operating expenses	12589	13738	14552	15799	18911	19976	21137	22245	24427	27834	6. Frais d'exploitation
7.	Net income	7632	8860	8254	9329	11117	9216	9405	11941	13907	14200	7. Résultat net
8.	Provisions (net)	4427	5104	3487	3377	4518	3872	2374	4467	6328	6317	8. Provisions (nettes)
9.	Profit before tax	3205	3756	4767	5952	6599	5344	7031	7474	7579	7883	9. Bénéfices avant impôt
10.	Income tax	1856	2320	2561	3234	3481	2737	3839	3994	3434	3883	10. Impôt
11.	Profit after tax	1349	1436	2206	2718	3118	2607	3192	3480	4145	4000	11. Bénéfices après impôt
12.	Distributed profit	1149	868	1635	1889	2329	2202	2309	2584	3041	2840	12. Bénéfices distribués
13.	Retained profit	200	568	571	829	789	405	883	896	1104	1160	13. Bénéfices mis en réserve
Memoranda												*Pour mémoire*
14.	*Staff costs*	*8673*	*9401*	*9790*	*10465*	*12336*	*12985*	*13729*	*14259*	*15555*	*17477*	14. *Frais de personnel*
15.	*Provisions on loans*	*4326*	*5004*	*3368*	*3183*	*4304*	*3697*	*2353*	*4314*	*5983*	*6157*	15. *Provisions sur prêts*
16.	*Provisions on securities (1)*	*..*	*..*	*..*	*..*	*..*	*..*	*..*	*..*	*..*	*..*	16. *Provisions sur titres (1)*
BALANCE SHEET												**BILAN**
Assets												**Actif**
17.	Cash & balance with Central bank	24374	24798	27297	29095	29491	30940	28116	32043	35665	37627	17. Caisse & solde auprès de la Banque centrale
18.	Interbank deposits	162542	157380	177389	187019	213482	230538	254751	283241	311569	314516	18. Dépôts interbancaires
19.	Loans	363369	383289	413529	438301	506244	537300	602864	664124	757560	865039	19. Prêts
20.	Securities	70593	79358	90627	100452	108981	111209	117005	132739	156499	177995	20. Valeurs mobilières
21.	Other assets	13153	14517	14586	15655	21459	22180	24399	26549	25353	26307	21. Autres actifs
Liabilities												**Passif**
22.	Capital & reserves	25605	26533	28456	32633	40298	44399	47034	55417	64922	72356	22. Capital et réserves
23.	Borrowing from Central bank	24484	27120	31725	34776	41126	34090	50803	60371	57210	60178	23. Emprunts auprès de la Banque centrale
24.	Interbank deposits	192341	189075	205990	211301	247319	266114	293506	314931	348978	362607	24. Dépôts interbancaires
25.	Non-bank deposits	310577	325662	356513	377964	423698	454523	501012	551267	634532	727241	25. Dépôts non bancaires
26.	Bonds	57127	63991	71419	77443	81095	84686	84760	101409	115170	125817	26. Obligations
27.	Other liabilities	23897	26961	29325	36405	46121	48355	50020	55301	65834	73285	27. Autres engagements
Balance sheet total												**Total du bilan**
28.	End-year total	634031	659342	723428	770522	879657	932167	1027135	1138696	1286646	1421484	28. En fin d'exercice
29.	Average total	606839	626162	665005	719619	818825	889239	968536	1072589	1203377	1350934	29. Moyen
Memoranda												*Pour mémoire*
30.	*Short-term securities*	*19418*	*23687*	*25603*	*22960*	*18210*	*17037*	*16986*	*13915*	*23196*	*38361*	30. *Titres à court terme*
31.	*Bonds*	*32672*	*35326*	*42681*	*52792*	*60112*	*61295*	*65546*	*75707*	*76814*	*79766*	31. *Obligations*
32.	*Shares and participations*	*18503*	*20345*	*22143*	*24700*	*30659*	*32877*	*34473*	*43117*	*56489*	*59868*	32. *Actions et participations*
33.	*Claims on non-residents*	*142991*	*147927*	*174079*	*185372*	*227950*	*246090*	*298773*	*330289*	*397119*	*405332*	33. *Créances sur des non résidents*
34.	*Liabilities to non-residents*	*154569*	*162699*	*191273*	*190391*	*195971*	*211822*	*252393*	*260075*	*306926*	*319405*	34. *Engagements envers des non résidents*
SUPPLEMENTARY INFORMATION												**RENSEIGNEMENTS COMPLEMENTAIRES**
35.	Number of institutions	182	176	174	173	252	255	259	264	274	281	35. Nombre d'institutions
36.	Number of branches	5471	5433	5430	5449	6346	6260	6242	6252	6255	6181	36. Nombre de succursales
37.	Number of employees (x 1000)	NA	NA	NA	NA	NA	NA	NA	NA	NA	NA	37. Nombre de salariés (x 1000)

GERMANY

Commercial banks

Per cent

INCOME STATEMENT ANALYSIS

ALLEMAGNE

Banques commerciales

Pourcentage

ANALYSE DU COMPTE DE RESULTATS

		1982	1983	1984	1985	1986	1987	1988	1989	1990	1991		
	% of average balance sheet total												**% du total moyen du bilan**
38.	Interest income	9.35	7.78	7.81	7.21	6.68	6.19	6.27	7.08	7.77	8.13	38.	Produits financiers
39.	Interest expenses	6.91	5.07	5.27	4.77	4.10	3.89	4.07	5.04	5.73	5.96	39.	Frais financiers
40.	Net interest income	2.44	2.71	2.54	2.44	2.58	2.30	2.19	2.04	2.04	2.16	40.	Produits financiers nets
41.	Non-interest income (net)	0.89	0.90	0.89	1.05	1.08	0.98	0.96	1.15	1.14	0.95	41.	Produits non financiers (nets)
42.	Gross income	3.33	3.61	3.43	3.49	3.67	3.28	3.15	3.19	3.19	3.11	42.	Résultat brut
43.	Operating expenses	2.07	2.19	2.19	2.20	2.31	2.25	2.18	2.07	2.03	2.06	43.	Frais d'exploitation
44.	Net income	1.26	1.41	1.24	1.30	1.36	1.04	0.97	1.11	1.16	1.05	44.	Résultat net
45.	Provisions (net)	0.73	0.82	0.52	0.47	0.55	0.44	0.25	0.42	0.53	0.47	45.	Provisions (nettes)
46.	Profit before tax	0.53	0.60	0.72	0.83	0.81	0.60	0.73	0.70	0.63	0.58	46.	Bénéfices avant impôt
47.	Income tax	0.31	0.37	0.39	0.45	0.43	0.31	0.40	0.37	0.29	0.29	47.	Impôt
48.	Profit after tax	0.22	0.23	0.33	0.38	0.38	0.29	0.33	0.32	0.34	0.30	48.	Bénéfices après impôt
49.	Distributed profit	0.19	0.14	0.25	0.26	0.28	0.25	0.24	0.24	0.25	0.21	49.	Bénéfices distribués
50.	Retained profit	0.03	0.09	0.09	0.12	0.10	0.05	0.09	0.08	0.09	0.09	50.	Bénéfices mis en réserve
51.	Staff costs	1.43	1.50	1.47	1.45	1.51	1.46	1.42	1.33	1.29	1.29	51.	Frais de personnel
52.	Provisions on loans	0.71	0.80	0.51	0.44	0.53	0.42	0.24	0.40	0.50	0.46	52.	Provisions sur prêts
53.	Provisions on securities (1)	..	..	..	..	..	..	..	..	..	..	53.	Provisions sur titres (1)
	% of gross income												**% du total du résultat brut**
54.	Net interest income	73.15	75.18	74.06	69.95	70.45	70.17	69.61	63.98	64.15	69.49	54.	Produits financiers nets
55.	Non-interest income (net)	26.85	24.82	25.94	30.05	29.55	29.83	30.39	36.02	35.85	30.51	55.	Produits non financiers (nets)
56.	Operating expenses	62.26	60.79	63.81	62.87	62.98	68.43	69.21	65.07	63.72	66.22	56.	Frais d'exploitation
57.	Net income	37.74	39.21	36.19	37.13	37.02	31.57	30.79	34.93	36.28	33.78	57.	Résultat net
58.	Provisions (net)	21.89	22.59	15.29	13.44	15.05	13.26	7.77	13.07	16.51	15.03	58.	Provisions (nettes)
59.	Profit before tax	15.85	16.62	20.90	23.69	21.98	18.31	23.02	21.86	19.77	18.75	59.	Bénéfices avant impôt
60.	Income tax	9.18	10.27	11.23	12.87	11.59	9.38	12.57	11.68	8.96	9.24	60.	Impôt
61.	Profit after tax	6.67	6.35	9.67	10.82	10.38	8.93	10.45	10.18	10.81	9.52	61.	Bénéfices après impôt
62.	Staff costs	42.89	41.60	42.93	41.65	41.08	44.48	44.95	41.71	40.58	41.58	62.	Frais de personnel
	% of net income												**% du total du résultat net**
63.	Provisions (net)	58.01	57.61	42.25	36.20	40.64	42.01	25.24	37.41	45.50	44.49	63.	Provisions (nettes)
64.	Profit before tax	41.99	42.39	57.75	63.80	59.36	57.99	74.76	62.59	54.50	55.51	64.	Bénéfices avant impôt
65.	Income tax	24.32	26.19	31.03	34.67	31.31	29.70	40.82	33.45	24.69	27.35	65.	Impôt
66.	Profit after tax	17.68	16.21	26.73	29.13	28.05	28.29	33.94	29.14	29.81	28.17	66.	Bénéfices après impôt

GERMANY

Commercial banks

ALLEMAGNE

Banques commerciales

Per cent — *Pourcentage*

BALANCE SHEET ANALYSIS — ANALYSE DU BILAN

% of year-end balance sheet total — **% du total du bilan en fin d'exercice**

	1982	1983	1984	1985	1986	1987	1988	1989	1990	1991		
Assets											**Actif**	
67. Cash & balance with Central bank	3.84	3.76	3.77	3.78	3.35	3.32	2.74	2.81	2.77	2.65	67.	Caisse & solde auprès de la Banque centrale
68. Interbank deposits	25.64	23.87	24.52	24.27	24.27	24.73	24.80	24.87	24.22	22.13	68.	Dépôts interbancaires
69. Loans	57.31	58.13	57.16	56.88	57.55	57.64	58.69	58.32	58.88	60.85	69.	Prêts
70. Securities	11.13	12.04	12.53	13.04	12.39	11.93	11.39	11.66	12.16	12.52	70.	Valeurs mobilières
71. Other assets	2.07	2.20	2.02	2.03	2.44	2.38	2.38	2.33	1.97	1.85	71.	Autres actifs
Liabilities											**Passif**	
72. Capital & reserves	4.04	4.02	3.93	4.24	4.58	4.76	4.58	4.87	5.05	5.09	72.	Capital et réserves
73. Borrowing from Central bank	3.86	4.11	4.39	4.51	4.68	3.66	4.95	5.30	4.45	4.23	73.	Emprunts auprès de la Banque centrale
74. Interbank deposits	30.34	28.68	28.47	27.42	28.12	28.55	28.58	27.66	27.12	25.51	74.	Dépôts interbancaires
75. Non-bank deposits	48.98	49.39	49.28	49.05	48.17	48.76	48.78	48.41	49.32	51.16	75.	Dépôts non bancaires
76. Bonds	9.01	9.71	9.87	10.05	9.22	9.08	8.25	8.91	8.95	8.85	76.	Obligations
77. Other liabilities	3.77	4.09	4.05	4.72	5.24	5.19	4.87	4.86	5.12	5.16	77.	Autres engagements
Memoranda											*Pour mémoire*	
78. Short-term securities	*3.06*	*3.59*	*3.57*	*2.98*	*2.07*	*1.83*	*1.65*	*1.22*	*1.80*	*2.70*	*78.*	*Titres à court terme*
79. Bonds	*5.15*	*5.36*	*5.90*	*6.85*	*6.83*	*6.58*	*6.38*	*6.65*	*5.97*	*5.61*	*79.*	*Obligations*
80. Shares and participations	*2.92*	*3.09*	*3.06*	*3.21*	*3.49*	*3.53*	*3.36*	*3.79*	*4.39*	*4.21*	*80.*	*Actions et participations*
81. Claims on non-residents	*22.55*	*22.44*	*24.06*	*24.06*	*25.91*	*26.40*	*29.09*	*29.01*	*30.86*	*28.51*	*81.*	*Créances sur des non résidents*
82. Liabilities to non-residents	*24.38*	*24.68*	*26.44*	*24.71*	*22.28*	*22.72*	*24.57*	*22.84*	*23.85*	*22.47*	*82.*	*Engagements envers des non résidents*

1. Included under "Provisions on loans" (item 15 or item 52).

Notes

• Average balance sheet totals (item 29) are based on twelve end-month data.

Change in methodology:

• As from 1986, the so called Instalment sales financing institutions are included in the data.

1. Inclus sous "Provisions sur prêts" (poste 15 ou poste 52).

Notes

• La moyenne du total des actifs/passifs (poste 29) est basée sur douze données de fin de mois.

Changement méthodologique :

• Depuis 1986, les Etablissements de financement des ventes à crédit sont compris dans les données.

GERMANY

Large commercial banks

Million DM

ALLEMAGNE

Grandes banques commerciales

Millions de DM

	1982	1983	1984	1985	1986	1987	1988	1989	1990	1991	
INCOME STATEMENT											**COMPTE DE RESULTATS**
1. Interest income	26610	22863	24389	24185	24338	24256	28090	35221	43650	50489	1. Produits financiers
2. Interest expenses	18857	13853	15294	14769	13370	14257	17400	23823	30612	34827	2. Frais financiers
3. Net interest income	7753	9010	9095	9416	10968	9999	10690	11398	13038	15662	3. Produits financiers nets
4. Non-interest income (net)	3368	3279	3392	4261	4169	4313	4901	5773	6997	6315	4. Produits non financiers (nets)
5. Gross income	11121	12289	12487	13677	15137	14312	15591	17171	20035	21977	5. Résultat brut
6. Operating expenses	7172	7858	8290	9063	10056	10442	11105	11571	12657	14795	6. Frais d'exploitation
7. Net income	3949	4431	4197	4614	5081	3870	4486	5600	7378	7182	7. Résultat net
8. Provisions (net)	2286	1998	1554	1095	1443	1452	517	1053	2708	2395	8. Provisions (nettes)
9. Profit before tax	1663	2433	2643	3519	3638	2418	3969	4547	4670	4787	9. Bénéfices avant impôt
10. Income tax	1102	1470	1576	2017	1987	1201	2245	2493	1915	2320	10. Impôt
11. Profit after tax	561	963	1067	1502	1651	1217	1724	2054	2755	2467	11. Bénéfices après impôt
12. Distributed profit	459	606	675	862	1114	1003	1037	1304	1962	1543	12. Bénéfices distribués
13. Retained profit	102	357	392	640	537	214	687	750	793	924	13. Bénéfices mis en réserve
Memoranda											*Pour mémoire*
14. Staff costs	*5108*	*5509*	*5702*	*6104*	*6770*	*7012*	*7457*	*7702*	*8348*	*9671*	14. Frais de personnel
15. Provisions on loans	*2256*	*1980*	*1465*	*933*	*1296*	*1329*	*504*	*1035*	*2491*	*2327*	15. Provisions sur prêts
16. Provisions on securities (1)	*..*	*..*	*..*	*..*	*..*	*..*	*..*	*..*	*..*	*..*	16. Provisions sur titres (1)
BALANCE SHEET											**BILAN**
Assets											**Actif**
17. Cash & balance with Central bank	12093	11990	14215	15575	15771	17090	14265	17006	20034	22041	17. Caisse & solde auprès de la Banque centrale
18. Interbank deposits	82663	75274	88775	93352	101248	110062	126057	135759	155820	151688	18. Dépôts interbancaires
19. Loans	159816	166805	179551	191921	212505	227226	267545	296500	345721	405306	19. Prêts
20. Securities	32607	39366	43492	50246	55225	53877	55507	63955	74472	83023	20. Valeurs mobilières
21. Other assets	7583	7939	7312	6983	7391	7735	8133	8385	8254	8240	21. Autres actifs
Liabilities											**Passif**
22. Capital & reserves	11960	12166	13240	15839	18766	20761	22133	26944	31303	34258	22. Capital et réserves
23. Borrowing from Central bank	8835	10652	12984	15539	16388	13552	17319	23045	17203	24044	23. Emprunts auprès de la Banque centrale
24. Interbank deposits	85736	83431	88724	91277	99229	105502	123272	127905	151037	148965	24. Dépôts interbancaires
25. Non-bank deposits	164246	169307	189729	200721	217879	233581	264367	291839	343846	402067	25. Dépôts non bancaires
26. Bonds	10432	10392	11434	13948	16008	17005	17585	23021	26870	26312	26. Obligations
27. Other liabilities	13573	15426	16734	20753	23870	25589	26831	28851	34042	34652	27. Autres engagements
Balance sheet total											**Total du bilan**
28. End-year total	294782	301374	332845	358077	392140	415990	471507	521605	604301	670298	28. En fin d'exercice
29. Average total	283694	288832	306864	335269	365894	399553	446084	494426	563239	641255	29. Moyen
Memoranda											*Pour mémoire*
30. Short-term securities	*9356*	*12566*	*13119*	*12216*	*9151*	*7653*	*8334*	*8291*	*10071*	*14800*	30. Titres à court terme
31. Bonds	*11947*	*14039*	*16323*	*22016*	*24818*	*23050*	*24103*	*26290*	*25355*	*28915*	31. Obligations
32. Shares and participations	*11304*	*12761*	*14050*	*16014*	*21256*	*23174*	*23070*	*29374*	*39046*	*39308*	32. Actions et participations
33. Claims on non-residents	*88653*	*90535*	*108495*	*114577*	*138091*	*147374*	*183131*	*194585*	*233940*	*235265*	33. Créances sur des non résidents
34. Liabilities to non-residents	*96264*	*100111*	*119268*	*119745*	*124004*	*131661*	*163674*	*166807*	*197384*	*202878*	34. Engagements envers des non résidents
SUPPLEMENTARY INFORMATION											**RENSEIGNEMENTS COMPLEMENTAIRES**
35. Number of institutions	6	6	6	6	6	6	6	6	6	4	35. Nombre d'institutions
36. Number of branches	3115	3113	3119	3115	3118	3120	3108	3110	3105	3141	36. Nombre de succursales
37. Number of employees (x 1000)	NA	NA	NA	NA	NA	NA	NA	NA	NA	NA	37. Nombre de salariés (x 1000)

Per cent — *Pourcentage*

INCOME STATEMENT ANALYSIS — ANALYSE DU COMPTE DE RESULTATS

		1982	1983	1984	1985	1986	1987	1988	1989	1990	1991		
% of average balance sheet total													**% du total moyen du bilan**
38.	Interest income	9.38	7.92	7.95	7.21	6.65	6.07	6.30	7.12	7.75	7.87	38.	Produits financiers
39.	Interest expenses	6.65	4.80	4.98	4.41	3.65	3.57	3.90	4.82	5.43	5.43	39.	Frais financiers
40.	Net interest income	2.73	3.12	2.96	2.81	3.00	2.50	2.40	2.31	2.31	2.44	40.	Produits financiers nets
41.	Non-interest income (net)	1.19	1.14	1.11	1.27	1.14	1.08	1.10	1.17	1.24	0.98	41.	Produits non financiers (nets)
42.	Gross income	3.92	4.25	4.07	4.08	4.14	3.58	3.50	3.47	3.56	3.43	42.	Résultat brut
43.	Operating expenses	2.53	2.72	2.70	2.70	2.75	2.61	2.49	2.34	2.25	2.31	43.	Frais d'exploitation
44.	Net income	1.39	1.53	1.37	1.38	1.39	0.97	1.01	1.13	1.31	1.12	44.	Résultat net
45.	Provisions (net)	0.81	0.69	0.51	0.33	0.39	0.36	0.12	0.21	0.48	0.37	45.	Provisions (nettes)
46.	Profit before tax	0.59	0.84	0.86	1.05	0.99	0.61	0.89	0.92	0.83	0.75	46.	Bénéfices avant impôt
47.	Income tax	0.39	0.51	0.51	0.60	0.54	0.30	0.50	0.50	0.34	0.36	47.	Impôt
48.	Profit after tax	0.20	0.33	0.35	0.45	0.45	0.30	0.39	0.42	0.49	0.38	48.	Bénéfices après impôt
49.	Distributed profit	0.16	0.21	0.22	0.26	0.30	0.25	0.23	0.26	0.35	0.24	49.	Bénéfices distribués
50.	Retained profit	0.04	0.12	0.13	0.19	0.15	0.05	0.15	0.15	0.14	0.14	50.	Bénéfices mis en réserve
51.	Staff costs	1.80	1.91	1.86	1.82	1.85	1.75	1.67	1.56	1.48	1.51	51.	Frais de personnel
52.	Provisions on loans	0.80	0.69	0.48	0.28	0.35	0.33	0.11	0.21	0.44	0.36	52.	Provisions sur prêts
53.	Provisions on securities (1)	..	..	..	..	..	..	..	..	..	..	53.	Provisions sur titres (1)
% of gross income													**% du total du résultat brut**
54.	Net interest income	69.71	73.32	72.84	68.85	72.46	69.86	68.57	66.38	65.08	71.27	54.	Produits financiers nets
55.	Non-interest income (net)	30.29	26.68	27.16	31.15	27.54	30.14	31.43	33.62	34.92	28.73	55.	Produits non financiers (nets)
56.	Operating expenses	64.49	63.94	66.39	66.26	66.43	72.96	71.23	67.39	63.17	67.32	56.	Frais d'exploitation
57.	Net income	35.51	36.06	33.61	33.74	33.57	27.04	28.77	32.61	36.83	32.68	57.	Résultat net
58.	Provisions (net)	20.56	16.26	12.44	8.01	9.53	10.15	3.32	6.13	13.52	10.90	58.	Provisions (nettes)
59.	Profit before tax	14.95	19.80	21.17	25.73	24.03	16.89	25.46	26.48	23.31	21.78	59.	Bénéfices avant impôt
60.	Income tax	9.91	11.96	12.62	14.75	13.13	8.39	14.40	14.52	9.56	10.56	60.	Impôt
61.	Profit after tax	5.04	7.84	8.54	10.98	10.91	8.50	11.06	11.96	13.75	11.23	61.	Bénéfices après impôt
62.	Staff costs	45.93	44.83	45.66	44.63	44.72	48.99	47.83	44.85	41.67	44.01	62.	Frais de personnel
% of net income													**% du total du résultat net**
63.	Provisions (net)	57.89	45.09	37.03	23.73	28.40	37.52	11.52	18.80	36.70	33.35	63.	Provisions (nettes)
64.	Profit before tax	42.11	54.91	62.97	76.27	71.60	62.48	88.48	81.20	63.30	66.65	64.	Bénéfices avant impôt
65.	Income tax	27.91	33.18	37.55	43.71	39.11	31.03	50.04	44.52	25.96	32.30	65.	Impôt
66.	Profit after tax	14.21	21.73	25.42	32.55	32.49	31.45	38.43	36.68	37.34	34.35	66.	Bénéfices après impôt

GERMANY

Large commercial banks

ALLEMAGNE

Grandes banques commerciales

Per cent	1982	1983	1984	1985	1986	1987	1988	1989	1990	1991	
											Pourcentage
BALANCE SHEET ANALYSIS											**ANALYSE DU BILAN**
% of year-end balance sheet total											**% du total du bilan en fin d'exercice**
Assets											**Actif**
67. Cash & balance with Central bank	4.10	3.98	4.27	4.35	4.02	4.11	3.03	3.26	3.32	3.29	67. Caisse & solde auprès de la Banque centrale
68. Interbank deposits	28.05	24.98	26.52	26.07	25.82	26.46	26.73	26.03	25.79	22.63	68. Dépôts interbancaires
69. Loans	54.21	55.35	53.94	53.60	54.19	54.62	56.74	56.84	57.21	60.47	69. Prêts
70. Securities	11.06	13.06	13.07	14.03	14.08	12.95	11.77	12.26	12.32	12.39	70. Valeurs mobilières
71. Other assets	2.57	2.63	2.20	1.95	1.88	1.86	1.72	1.61	1.37	1.23	71. Autres actifs
Liabilities											**Passif**
72. Capital & reserves	4.06	4.04	3.98	4.42	4.79	4.99	4.69	5.17	5.18	5.11	72. Capital et réserves
73. Borrowing from Central bank	3.00	3.53	3.90	4.34	4.18	3.26	3.67	4.42	2.85	3.59	73. Emprunts auprès de la Banque centrale
74. Interbank deposits	29.08	27.68	26.66	25.49	25.30	25.36	26.14	24.52	24.99	22.22	74. Dépôts interbancaires
75. Non-bank deposits	55.72	56.18	57.00	56.06	55.56	56.15	56.07	55.95	56.90	59.98	75. Dépôts non bancaires
76. Bonds	3.54	3.45	3.44	3.90	4.08	4.09	3.73	4.41	4.45	3.93	76. Obligations
77. Other liabilities	4.60	5.12	5.03	5.80	6.09	6.15	5.69	5.53	5.63	5.17	77. Autres engagements
Memoranda											***Pour mémoire***
78. Short-term securities	*3.17*	*4.17*	*3.94*	*3.41*	*2.33*	*1.84*	*1.77*	*1.59*	*1.67*	*2.21*	*78. Titres à court terme*
79. Bonds	*4.05*	*4.66*	*4.90*	*6.15*	*6.33*	*5.54*	*5.11*	*5.04*	*4.20*	*4.31*	*79. Obligations*
80. Shares and participations	*3.83*	*4.23*	*4.22*	*4.47*	*5.42*	*5.57*	*4.89*	*5.63*	*6.46*	*5.86*	*80. Actions et participations*
81. Claims on non-residents	*30.07*	*30.04*	*32.60*	*32.00*	*35.21*	*35.43*	*38.84*	*37.31*	*38.71*	*35.10*	*81. Créances sur des non résidents*
82. Liabilities to non-residents	*32.66*	*33.22*	*35.83*	*33.44*	*31.62*	*31.65*	*34.71*	*31.98*	*32.66*	*30.27*	*82. Engagements envers des non résidents*

1. Included under "Provisions on loans" (item 15 or item 52).

Notes

• Large commercial banks are a sub-group of Commercial banks.

• Average balance sheet totals (item 29) are based on twelve end-month data.

1. Inclus sous "Provisions sur prêts" (poste 15 ou poste 52).

Notes

• Les Grandes banques commerciales sont un sous-groupe des Banques commerciales.

• La moyenne du total des actifs/passifs (poste 29) est basée sur douze données de fin de mois.

GERMANY

Regional giro institutions

ALLEMAGNE

Organismes régionaux de compensation

Million DM / *Millions de DM*

	1982	1983	1984	1985	1986	1987	1988	1989	1990	1991	
INCOME STATEMENT											**COMPTE DE RESULTATS**
1. Interest income	37094	36771	38271	38132	37898	38471	40388	46856	56817	67101	1. Produits financiers
2. Interest expenses	33874	32306	33652	33348	33068	33756	35646	42153	52078	61750	2. Frais financiers
3. Net interest income	3220	4465	4619	4784	4830	4715	4742	4703	4739	5351	3. Produits financiers nets
4. Non-interest income (net)	1548	1259	1118	1797	1389	1287	1188	1473	1349	1857	4. Produits non financiers (nets)
5. Gross income	4768	5724	5737	6581	6219	6002	5930	6176	6088	7208	5. Résultat brut
6. Operating expenses	2087	2265	2427	2576	2776	2919	3117	3308	3604	3873	6. Frais d'exploitation
7. Net income	2681	3459	3310	4005	3443	3083	2813	2868	2484	3335	7. Résultat net
8. Provisions (net)	2005	2389	2217	2788	2104	1839	1200	1122	1579	1899	8. Provisions (nettes)
9. Profit before tax	676	1070	1093	1217	1339	1244	1613	1746	905	1436	9. Bénéfices avant impôt
10. Income tax	408	693	738	796	880	747	1089	1016	433	766	10. Impôt
11. Profit after tax	268	377	355	421	459	497	524	730	472	670	11. Bénéfices après impôt
12. Distributed profit	147	237	219	283	321	350	359	374	336	327	12. Bénéfices distribués
13. Retained profit	121	140	136	138	138	147	165	356	136	343	13. Bénéfices mis en réserve
Memoranda											*Pour mémoire*
14. Staff costs	1394	1499	1616	1738	1842	1942	2069	2171	2393	2468	14. Frais de personnel
15. Provisions on loans	1904	2250	2156	2740	2005	1787	1174	1090	1551	1825	15. Provisions sur prêts
16. Provisions on securities (1)	:	:	:	:	:	:	:	:	:	:	16. Provisions sur titres (1)
BALANCE SHEET											**BILAN**
Assets											**Actif**
17. Cash & balance with Central bank	4913	4871	4350	4543	4590	3708	4030	5325	7106	4334	17. Caisse & solde auprès de la Banque centrale
18. Interbank deposits	115924	125732	141016	154205	187446	218430	254734	286439	317729	329932	18. Dépôts interbancaires
19. Loans	291331	315685	321595	328885	333939	342577	349487	354110	382774	444196	19. Prêts
20. Securities	46887	50735	55469	59383	59305	60068	62549	69504	116932	124858	20. Valeurs mobilières
21. Other assets	7631	8289	9247	9215	9595	11052	12591	13529	14559	16378	21. Autres actifs
Liabilities											**Passif**
22. Capital & reserves	10507	11283	11741	12160	13341	13930	14624	16331	17442	20265	22. Capital et réserves
23. Borrowing from Central bank	7744	8970	9688	13920	7879	6816	21939	25183	32448	43979	23. Emprunts auprès de la Banque centrale
24. Interbank deposits	133829	136285	142568	141307	158442	171508	198227	213735	280076	305577	24. Dépôts interbancaires
25. Non-bank deposits	81433	92567	103655	112754	130238	149124	165298	178316	191566	211546	25. Dépôts non bancaires
26. Bonds	221322	242915	250456	260911	268873	279056	266228	277285	295797	312236	26. Obligations
27. Other liabilities	11851	13292	13569	15179	16102	15401	17075	18057	21771	26095	27. Autres engagements
Balance sheet total											**Total du bilan**
28. End-year total	466686	505312	531677	556231	594875	635835	683391	728907	839100	919698	28. En fin d'exercice
29. Average total	449750	488702	503875	533905	573933	617561	655600	699495	774961	872439	29. Moyen
Memoranda											*Pour mémoire*
30. Short-term securities	13443	14611	14667	15398	12062	10605	7331	7514	40637	44911	30. Titres à court terme
31. Bonds	28809	30996	35445	37879	40633	42226	47644	52600	63689	65609	31. Obligations
32. Shares and participations	4635	5128	5357	6106	6610	7237	7574	9390	12606	14138	32. Actions et participations
33. Claims on non-residents	68186	74741	83481	94562	118012	130839	155053	184436	272157	222613	33. Créances sur des non résidents
34. Liabilities to non-residents	47563	51477	53272	46261	43867	50691	61614	61469	104877	87723	34. Engagements envers des non résidents
SUPPLEMENTARY INFORMATION											**RENSEIGNEMENTS COMPLEMENTAIRES**
35. Number of institutions	12	12	12	12	12	12	12	11	11	11	35. Nombre d'institutions
36. Number of branches	261	257	245	239	235	231	226	219	309	329	36. Nombre de succursales
37. Number of employees (x 1000)	NA	NA	NA	NA	NA	NA	NA	NA	NA	NA	37. Nombre de salariés (x 1000)

Regional giro institutions — **Organismes régionaux de compensation**

Per cent — *Pourcentage*

INCOME STATEMENT ANALYSIS — ANALYSE DU COMPTE DE RESULTATS

		1982	1983	1984	1985	1986	1987	1988	1989	1990	1991		
	% of average balance sheet total											**% du total moyen du bilan**	
38.	Interest income	8.25	7.52	7.60	7.14	6.60	6.23	6.16	6.70	7.33	7.69	Produits financiers	38.
39.	Interest expenses	7.53	6.61	6.68	6.25	5.76	5.47	5.44	6.03	6.72	7.08	Frais financiers	39.
40.	Net interest income	0.72	0.91	0.92	0.90	0.84	0.76	0.72	0.67	0.61	0.61	Produits financiers nets	40.
41.	Non-interest income (net)	0.34	0.26	0.22	0.34	0.24	0.21	0.18	0.21	0.17	0.21	Produits non financiers (nets)	41.
42.	Gross income	1.06	1.17	1.14	1.23	1.08	0.97	0.90	0.88	0.79	0.83	Résultat brut	42.
43.	Operating expenses	0.46	0.46	0.48	0.48	0.48	0.47	0.48	0.47	0.47	0.44	Frais d'exploitation	43.
44.	Net income	0.60	0.71	0.66	0.75	0.60	0.50	0.43	0.41	0.32	0.38	Résultat net	44.
45.	Provisions (net)	0.45	0.49	0.44	0.52	0.37	0.30	0.18	0.16	0.20	0.22	Provisions (nettes)	45.
46.	Profit before tax	0.15	0.22	0.22	0.23	0.23	0.20	0.25	0.25	0.12	0.16	Bénéfices avant impôt	46.
47.	Income tax	0.09	0.14	0.15	0.15	0.15	0.12	0.17	0.15	0.06	0.09	Impôt	47.
48.	Profit after tax	0.06	0.08	0.07	0.08	0.08	0.08	0.08	0.10	0.06	0.08	Bénéfices après impôt	48.
49.	Distributed profit	0.03	0.05	0.04	0.05	0.06	0.06	0.05	0.05	0.04	0.04	Bénéfices distribués	49.
50.	Retained profit	0.03	0.03	0.03	0.03	0.02	0.02	0.03	0.05	0.02	0.04	Bénéfices mis en réserve	50.
51.	Staff costs	0.31	0.31	0.32	0.33	0.32	0.31	0.32	0.31	0.31	0.28	Frais de personnel	51.
52.	Provisions on loans	0.42	0.46	0.43	0.51	0.35	0.29	0.18	0.16	0.20	0.21	Provisions sur prêts	52.
53.	Provisions on securities (1)	..	..	..	..	..	..	..	..	..	..	Provisions sur titres (1)	53.
	% of gross income											**% du total du résultat brut**	
54.	Net interest income	67.53	78.00	80.51	72.69	77.67	78.56	79.97	76.15	77.84	74.24	Produits financiers nets	54.
55.	Non-interest income (net)	32.47	22.00	19.49	27.31	22.33	21.44	20.03	23.85	22.16	25.76	Produits non financiers (nets)	55.
56.	Operating expenses	43.77	39.57	42.30	39.14	44.64	48.63	52.56	53.56	59.20	53.73	Frais d'exploitation	56.
57.	Net income	56.23	60.43	57.70	60.86	55.36	51.37	47.44	46.44	40.80	46.27	Résultat net	57.
58.	Provisions (net)	42.05	41.74	38.64	42.36	33.83	30.64	20.24	18.17	25.94	26.35	Provisions (nettes)	58.
59.	Profit before tax	14.18	18.69	19.05	18.49	21.53	20.73	27.20	28.27	14.87	19.92	Bénéfices avant impôt	59.
60.	Income tax	8.56	12.11	12.86	12.10	14.15	12.45	18.36	16.45	7.11	10.63	Impôt	60.
61.	Profit after tax	5.62	6.59	6.19	6.40	7.38	8.28	8.84	11.82	7.75	9.30	Bénéfices après impôt	61.
62.	Staff costs	29.24	26.19	28.17	26.41	29.62	32.36	34.89	35.15	39.31	34.24	Frais de personnel	62.
	% of net income											**% du total du résultat net**	
63.	Provisions (net)	74.79	69.07	66.98	69.61	61.11	59.65	42.66	39.12	63.57	56.94	Provisions (nettes)	63.
64.	Profit before tax	25.21	30.93	33.02	30.39	38.89	40.35	57.34	60.88	36.43	43.06	Bénéfices avant impôt	64.
65.	Income tax	15.22	20.03	22.30	19.88	25.56	24.23	38.71	35.43	17.43	22.97	Impôt	65.
66.	Profit after tax	10.00	10.90	10.73	10.51	13.33	16.12	18.63	25.45	19.00	20.09	Bénéfices après impôt	66.

GERMANY

Regional giro institutions

Per cent

BALANCE SHEET ANALYSIS

% of year-end balance sheet total

ALLEMAGNE

Organismes régionaux de compensation

Pourcentage

ANALYSE DU BILAN

% du total du bilan en fin d'exercice

	1982	1983	1984	1985	1986	1987	1988	1989	1990	1991		
Assets												**Actif**
67. Cash & balance with Central bank	1.05	0.96	0.82	0.82	0.77	0.58	0.59	0.73	0.85	0.47	67.	Caisse & solde auprès de la Banque centrale
68. Interbank deposits	24.84	24.88	26.52	27.72	31.51	34.35	37.28	39.30	37.87	35.87	68.	Dépôts interbancaires
69. Loans	62.43	62.47	60.49	59.13	56.14	53.88	51.14	48.58	45.62	48.30	69.	Prêts
70. Securities	10.05	10.04	10.43	10.68	9.97	9.45	9.15	9.54	13.94	13.58	70.	Valeurs mobilières
71. Other assets	1.64	1.64	1.74	1.66	1.61	1.74	1.84	1.86	1.74	1.78	71.	Autres actifs
Liabilities												**Passif**
72. Capital & reserves	2.25	2.23	2.21	2.19	2.24	2.19	2.14	2.24	2.08	2.20	72.	Capital et réserves
73. Borrowing from Central bank	1.66	1.78	1.82	2.50	1.32	1.07	3.21	3.45	3.87	4.78	73.	Emprunts auprès de la Banque centrale
74. Interbank deposits	28.68	26.97	26.81	25.40	26.63	26.97	29.01	29.32	33.38	33.23	74.	Dépôts interbancaires
75. Non-bank deposits	17.45	18.32	19.50	20.27	21.89	23.45	24.19	24.46	22.83	23.00	75.	Dépôts non bancaires
76. Bonds	47.42	48.07	47.11	46.91	45.20	43.89	38.96	38.04	35.25	33.95	76.	Obligations
77. Other liabilities	2.54	2.63	2.55	2.73	2.71	2.42	2.50	2.48	2.59	2.84	77.	Autres engagements
Memoranda												*Pour mémoire*
78. Short-term securities	*2.88*	*2.89*	*2.76*	*2.77*	*2.03*	*1.67*	*1.07*	*1.03*	*4.84*	*4.88*	*78.*	*Titres à court terme*
79. Bonds	*6.17*	*6.13*	*6.67*	*6.81*	*6.83*	*6.64*	*6.97*	*7.22*	*7.59*	*7.16*	*79.*	*Obligations*
80. Shares and participations	*0.99*	*1.01*	*1.01*	*1.10*	*1.11*	*1.14*	*1.11*	*1.29*	*1.50*	*1.54*	*80.*	*Actions et participations*
81. Claims on non-residents	*14.61*	*14.79*	*15.70*	*17.00*	*19.84*	*20.58*	*22.69*	*25.30*	*32.43*	*24.21*	*81.*	*Créances sur des non résidents*
82. Liabilities to non-residents	*10.19*	*10.19*	*10.02*	*8.32*	*7.37*	*7.97*	*9.02*	*8.43*	*12.50*	*9.54*	*82.*	*Engagements envers des non résidents*

1. Included under "Provisions on loans" (item 15 or item 52).

Notes

- Average balance sheet totals (item 29) are based on twelve end-month data.

1. Inclus sous "Provisions sur prêts" (poste 15 ou poste 52).

Notes

- La moyenne du total des actifs/passifs (poste 29) est basée sur douze données de fin de mois.

GERMANY / ALLEMAGNE

Savings banks / Caisses d'épargne

Million DM / Millions de DM

	1982	1983	1984	1985	1986	1987	1988	1989	1990	1991
INCOME STATEMENT / COMPTE DE RESULTATS										
1. Interest income / Produits financiers	50489	47262	49295	50911	50338	50450	51762	57466	67561	78362
2. Interest expenses / Frais financiers	30684	25269	27019	28055	26984	26864	27319	33152	42593	50204
3. Net interest income / Produits financiers nets	19805	21993	22276	22856	23354	23586	24443	24314	24968	28158
4. Non-interest income (net) / Produits non financiers (nets)	2026	2292	2425	2390	2588	2728	1837	4097	5387	5633
5. Gross income / Résultat brut	21831	24285	24701	25246	25942	26314	26280	28411	30355	33791
6. Operating expenses / Frais d'exploitation	12620	13392	14054	14946	15881	16876	17680	18409	19731	21782
7. Net income / Résultat net	9211	10893	10647	10300	10061	9438	8600	10002	10624	12009
8. Provisions (net) / Provisions (nettes)	2905	3475	3057	3202	3160	3216	2425	5859	5681	3573
9. Profit before tax / Bénéfices avant impôt	6306	7418	7590	7098	6901	6222	6175	4143	4943	8436
10. Income tax / Impôt	4337	5196	5256	4900	4762	4224	4095	2466	3133	5612
11. Profit after tax / Bénéfices après impôt	1969	2222	2334	2198	2139	1998	2080	1677	1810	2824
12. Distributed profit / Bénéfices distribués	1132	1316	1397	1379	1377	1317	1345	1159	1240	1614
13. Retained profit / Bénéfices mis en réserve	837	906	937	819	762	681	735	518	570	1210
Memoranda / Pour mémoire										
14. Staff costs / Frais de personnel	8339	8830	9152	9677	10283	11045	11542	11864	12776	14231
15. Provisions on loans / Provisions sur prêts	2898	3470	3038	3181	3142	3205	2420	5850	5671	3550
16. Provisions on securities (1) / Provisions sur titres (1)	..	..	..	..	..	..	..	..	..	..
BALANCE SHEET / BILAN										
Assets / Actif										
17. Cash & balance with Central bank / Caisse & solde auprès de la Banque centrale	20106	20751	21641	21726	22576	25753	27440	29921	30259	29835
18. Interbank deposits / Dépôts interbancaires	48652	46771	55310	59931	73203	70015	76311	95999	107769	112186
19. Loans / Prêts	393658	419180	446785	466780	482066	501094	528417	561165	595639	652219
20. Securities / Valeurs mobilières	110056	122534	128945	141064	160719	186938	203826	200023	213906	220649
21. Other assets / Autres actifs	22618	23952	26056	27331	27950	28136	28016	28700	31408	36684
Liabilities / Passif										
22. Capital & reserves / Capital et réserves	20326	22209	24332	26540	28541	30564	32526	34655	36411	38902
23. Borrowing from Central bank / Emprunts auprès de la Banque centrale	15339	17601	19828	19853	17492	15744	27825	38355	42747	48466
24. Interbank deposits / Dépôts interbancaires	51494	56650	63892	68608	77549	86147	91503	94993	100577	110026
25. Non-bank deposits / Dépôts non bancaires	484242	508843	540313	569248	606075	636267	660439	684637	721904	760427
26. Bonds / Obligations	1453	2330	3051	4000	6783	11589	18246	28102	40537	52477
27. Other liabilities / Autres engagements	22236	25555	27321	28583	30074	31625	33471	35066	36805	41275
Balance sheet total / Total du bilan										
28. End-year total / En fin d'exercice	595090	633188	678737	716832	766514	811936	864010	915808	978981	1051573
29. Average total / Moyen	570029	606704	645764	689295	733290	783133	831211	875042	934259	999930
Memoranda / Pour mémoire										
30. Short-term securities / Titres à court terme	15926	14947	12649	13683	17580	20792	18534	16671	20248	23108
31. Bonds / Obligations	90882	104015	112319	122644	137562	159219	177850	174336	181083	180271
32. Shares and participations / Actions et participations	3248	3572	3977	4737	5577	6927	7442	9016	12575	17270
33. Claims on non-residents / Créances sur des non résidents	3032	2747	3413	4253	7521	8416	11326	21563	27051	24094
34. Liabilities to non-residents / Engagements envers des non résidents	3029	3712	4722	5097	5116	5863	6864	7637	12385	7891
SUPPLEMENTARY INFORMATION / RENSEIGNEMENTS COMPLEMENTAIRES										
35. Number of institutions / Nombre d'institutions	595	592	591	590	589	586	585	583	575	558
36. Number of branches / Nombre de succursales	17021	17076	17131	17204	17248	17307	17355	17359	17212	17033
37. Number of employees (x 1000) / Nombre de salariés (x 1000)	NA	NA	NA	NA	NA	NA	NA	NA	NA	NA

GERMANY

Savings banks

ALLEMAGNE

Caisses d'épargne

Per cent	1982	1983	1984	1985	1986	1987	1988	1989	1990	1991		Pourcentage
INCOME STATEMENT ANALYSIS												**ANALYSE DU COMPTE DE RESULTATS**
% of average balance sheet total												**% du total moyen du bilan**
38. Interest income	8.86	7.79	7.63	7.39	6.86	6.44	6.23	6.57	7.23	7.84	38.	Produits financiers
39. Interest expenses	5.38	4.16	4.18	4.07	3.68	3.43	3.29	3.79	4.56	5.02	39.	Frais financiers
40. Net interest income	3.47	3.62	3.45	3.32	3.18	3.01	2.94	2.78	2.67	2.82	40.	Produits financiers nets
41. Non-interest income (net)	0.36	0.38	0.38	0.35	0.35	0.35	0.22	0.47	0.58	0.56	41.	Produits non financiers (nets)
42. Gross income	3.83	4.00	3.83	3.66	3.54	3.36	3.16	3.25	3.25	3.38	42.	Résultat brut
43. Operating expenses	2.21	2.21	2.18	2.17	2.17	2.15	2.13	2.10	2.11	2.18	43.	Frais d'exploitation
44. Net income	1.62	1.80	1.65	1.49	1.37	1.21	1.03	1.14	1.14	1.20	44.	Résultat net
45. Provisions (net)	0.51	0.57	0.47	0.46	0.43	0.41	0.29	0.67	0.61	0.36	45.	Provisions (nettes)
46. Profit before tax	1.11	1.22	1.18	1.03	0.94	0.79	0.74	0.47	0.53	0.84	46.	Bénéfices avant impôt
47. Income tax	0.76	0.86	0.81	0.71	0.65	0.54	0.49	0.28	0.34	0.56	47.	Impôt
48. Profit after tax	0.35	0.37	0.36	0.32	0.29	0.26	0.25	0.19	0.19	0.28	48.	Bénéfices après impôt
49. Distributed profit	0.20	0.22	0.22	0.20	0.19	0.17	0.16	0.13	0.13	0.16	49.	Bénéfices distribués
50. Retained profit	0.15	0.15	0.15	0.12	0.10	0.09	0.09	0.06	0.06	0.12	50.	Bénéfices mis en réserve
51. Staff costs	1.46	1.46	1.42	1.40	1.40	1.41	1.39	1.36	1.37	1.42	51.	Frais de personnel
52. Provisions on loans	0.51	0.57	0.47	0.46	0.43	0.41	0.29	0.67	0.61	0.36	52.	Provisions sur prêts
53. Provisions on securities (1)	:	:	:	:	:	:	:	:	:	:	53.	Provisions sur titres (1)
% of gross income												**% du total du résultat brut**
54. Net interest income	90.72	90.56	90.18	90.53	90.02	89.63	93.01	85.58	82.25	83.33	54.	Produits financiers nets
55. Non-interest income (net)	9.28	9.44	9.82	9.47	9.98	10.37	6.99	14.42	17.75	16.67	55.	Produits non financiers (nets)
56. Operating expenses	57.81	55.15	56.90	59.20	61.22	64.13	67.28	64.80	65.00	64.46	56.	Frais d'exploitation
57. Net income	42.19	44.85	43.10	40.80	38.78	35.87	32.72	35.20	35.00	35.54	57.	Résultat net
58. Provisions (net)	13.31	14.31	12.38	12.68	12.18	12.22	9.23	20.62	18.72	10.57	58.	Provisions (nettes)
59. Profit before tax	28.89	30.55	30.73	28.12	26.60	23.65	23.50	14.58	16.28	24.97	59.	Bénéfices avant impôt
60. Income tax	19.87	21.40	21.28	19.41	18.36	16.05	15.58	8.68	10.32	16.61	60.	Impôt
61. Profit after tax	9.02	9.15	9.45	8.71	8.25	7.59	7.91	5.90	5.96	8.36	61.	Bénéfices après impôt
62. Staff costs	38.20	36.36	37.05	38.33	39.64	41.97	43.92	41.76	42.09	42.11	62.	Frais de personnel
% of net income												**% du total du résultat net**
63. Provisions (net)	31.54	31.90	28.71	31.09	31.41	34.08	28.20	58.58	53.47	29.75	63.	Provisions (nettes)
64. Profit before tax	68.46	68.10	71.29	68.91	68.59	65.92	71.80	41.42	46.53	70.25	64.	Bénéfices avant impôt
65. Income tax	47.09	47.70	49.37	47.57	47.33	44.76	47.62	24.66	29.49	46.73	65.	Impôt
66. Profit after tax	21.38	20.40	21.92	21.34	21.26	21.17	24.19	16.77	17.04	23.52	66.	Bénéfices après impôt

GERMANY
Savings banks

ALLEMAGNE
Caisses d'épargne

Per cent — *Pourcentage*

BALANCE SHEET ANALYSIS — **ANALYSE DU BILAN**

% of year-end balance sheet total — **% du total du bilan en fin d'exercice**

	1982	1983	1984	1985	1986	1987	1988	1989	1990	1991		
Assets												**Actif**
67. Cash & balance with Central bank	3.38	3.28	3.19	3.03	2.95	3.17	3.18	3.27	3.09	2.84	67.	Caisse & solde auprès de la Banque centrale
68. Interbank deposits	8.18	7.39	8.15	8.36	9.55	8.62	8.83	10.48	11.01	10.67	68.	Dépôts interbancaires
69. Loans	66.15	66.20	65.83	65.12	62.89	61.72	61.16	61.28	60.84	62.02	69.	Prêts
70. Securities	18.49	19.35	19.00	19.68	20.97	23.02	23.59	21.84	21.85	20.98	70.	Valeurs mobilières
71. Other assets	3.80	3.78	3.84	3.81	3.65	3.47	3.24	3.13	3.21	3.49	71.	Autres actifs
Liabilities												**Passif**
72. Capital & reserves	3.42	3.51	3.58	3.70	3.72	3.76	3.76	3.78	3.72	3.70	72.	Capital et réserves
73. Borrowing from Central bank	2.58	2.78	2.92	2.77	2.28	1.94	3.22	4.19	4.37	4.61	73.	Emprunts auprès de la Banque centrale
74. Interbank deposits	8.65	8.95	9.41	9.57	10.12	10.61	10.59	10.37	10.27	10.46	74.	Dépôts interbancaires
75. Non-bank deposits	81.37	80.36	79.61	79.41	79.07	78.36	76.44	74.76	73.74	72.31	75.	Dépôts non bancaires
76. Bonds	0.24	0.37	0.45	0.56	0.88	1.43	2.11	3.07	4.14	4.99	76.	Obligations
77. Other liabilities	3.74	4.04	4.03	3.99	3.92	3.90	3.87	3.83	3.76	3.93	77.	Autres engagements
Memoranda												***Pour mémoire***
78. Short-term securities	*2.68*	*2.36*	*1.86*	*1.91*	*2.29*	*2.56*	*2.15*	*1.82*	*2.07*	*2.20*	*78.*	*Titres à court terme*
79. Bonds	*15.27*	*16.43*	*16.55*	*17.11*	*17.95*	*19.61*	*20.58*	*19.04*	*18.50*	*17.14*	*79.*	*Obligations*
80. Shares and participations	*0.55*	*0.56*	*0.59*	*0.66*	*0.73*	*0.85*	*0.86*	*0.98*	*1.28*	*1.64*	*80.*	*Actions et participations*
81. Claims on non-residents	*0.51*	*0.43*	*0.50*	*0.59*	*0.98*	*1.04*	*1.31*	*2.35*	*2.76*	*2.29*	*81.*	*Créances sur des non résidents*
82. Liabilities to non-residents	*0.51*	*0.59*	*0.70*	*0.71*	*0.67*	*0.72*	*0.79*	*0.83*	*1.27*	*0.75*	*82.*	*Engagements envers des non résidents*

1. Included under "Provisions on loans" (item 15 or item 52).

1. Inclus sous "Provisions sur prêts" (poste 15 ou poste 52).

Notes

• Average balance sheet totals (item 29) are based on twelve end-month data.

Notes

• La moyenne du total des actifs/passifs (poste 29) est basée sur douze données de fin de mois.

GERMANY

Regional institutions of co-operative banks

ALLEMAGNE

Institutions régionales des banques mutualistes

Million DM	1982	1983	1984	1985	1986	1987	1988	1989	1990	1991	Millions de DM
INCOME STATEMENT											**COMPTE DE RESULTATS**
1. Interest income	9857	9228	9644	9675	9036	9216	9630	11113	14172	15773	1. Produits financiers
2. Interest expenses	8421	7375	7940	8098	7329	7413	7898	9891	12999	14684	2. Frais financiers
3. Net interest income	1436	1853	1704	1577	1707	1803	1732	1222	1173	1089	3. Produits financiers nets
4. Non-interest income (net)	267	311	341	1160	578	433	358	938	1307	1271	4. Produits non financiers (nets)
5. Gross income	1703	2164	2045	2737	2285	2236	2090	2160	2480	2360	5. Résultat brut
6. Operating expenses	690	773	796	906	1032	1053	1029	1055	1175	1222	6. Frais d'exploitation
7. Net income	1013	1391	1249	1831	1253	1183	1061	1105	1305	1138	7. Résultat net
8. Provisions (net)	171	417	245	1206	290	245	47	623	844	728	8. Provisions (nettes)
9. Profit before tax	842	974	1004	625	963	938	1014	482	461	410	9. Bénéfices avant impôt
10. Income tax	461	532	537	506	529	542	585	93	177	228	10. Impôt
11. Profit after tax	381	442	467	119	434	396	429	389	284	182	11. Bénéfices après impôt
12. Distributed profit	149	185	226	148	276	200	219	559	219	119	12. Bénéfices distribués
13. Retained profit	232	257	241	-29	158	196	210	-170	65	63	13. Bénéfices mis en réserve
Memoranda											*Pour mémoire*
14. Staff costs	413	447	471	524	536	572	554	577	647	660	14. Frais de personnel
15. Provisions on loans	163	414	241	1198	283	234	34	623	725	670	15. Provisions sur prêts
16. Provisions on securities (1)	..	..	..	..	..	..	..	..	..	..	16. Provisions sur titres (1)
BALANCE SHEET											**BILAN**
Assets											**Actif**
17. Cash & balance with Central bank	2575	2335	3456	3029	3319	2351	2389	2739	2247	2924	17. Caisse & solde auprès de la Banque centrale
18. Interbank deposits	58410	70397	74892	78937	90268	103468	106397	102158	107746	98731	18. Dépôts interbancaires
19. Loans	25036	24903	27530	29305	28722	31166	35220	36028	38412	46924	19. Prêts
20. Securities	24562	26789	28967	32501	31844	33460	35375	39995	40883	38500	20. Valeurs mobilières
21. Other assets	2186	2513	2206	2904	2707	2596	2167	4217	4258	14264	21. Autres actifs
Liabilities											**Passif**
22. Capital & reserves	3279	3796	4561	5394	5556	6013	6218	6725	6446	7180	22. Capital et réserves
23. Borrowing from Central bank	6874	6962	6689	7069	4842	4802	10001	11529	11993	15690	23. Emprunts auprès de la Banque centrale
24. Interbank deposits	80944	87862	98453	106247	116949	129249	131965	130758	139772	140237	24. Dépôts interbancaires
25. Non-bank deposits	11545	12472	13002	12603	12734	12874	12595	12563	14712	13325	25. Dépôts non bancaires
26. Bonds	8501	13447	11694	12477	13676	16677	16654	18525	15454	18330	26. Obligations
27. Other liabilities	1626	2398	2652	2886	3103	3426	4115	4037	5169	6581	27. Autres engagements
Balance sheet total											**Total du bilan**
28. End-year total	112769	126937	137051	146676	158860	173041	181548	184137	193546	201343	28. En fin d'exercice
29. Average total	105403	118133	128336	136874	144403	159944	171195	173658	178846	194435	29. Moyen
Memoranda											*Pour mémoire*
30. Short-term securities	8500	8193	8003	9033	7351	7352	3575	2446	7982	10448	30. Titres à court terme
31. Bonds	13528	15541	17402	19406	19908	20656	25849	30436	27049	21054	31. Obligations
32. Shares and participations	2534	3055	3562	4062	4585	5452	5951	6113	5852	6998	32. Actions et participations
33. Claims on non-residents	7032	7105	7775	12952	19246	25807	25893	31136	42780	26804	33. Créances sur des non résidents
34. Liabilities to non-residents	2342	2106	2923	3979	3128	3150	3530	3745	10054	3865	34. Engagements envers des non résidents
SUPPLEMENTARY INFORMATION											**RENSEIGNEMENTS COMPLEMENTAIRES**
35. Number of institutions	9	9	9	9	8	7	6	6	4	4	35. Nombre d'institutions
36. Number of branches	46	45	46	46	48	36	32	32	31	37	36. Nombre de succursales
37. Number of employees (x 1000)	NA	NA	NA	NA	NA	NA	NA	NA	NA	NA	37. Nombre de salariés (x 1000)

GERMANY

Regional institutions of co-operative banks

Institutions régionales des banques mutualistes

Per cent / *Pourcentage*

	1982	1983	1984	1985	1986	1987	1988	1989	1990	1991		
INCOME STATEMENT ANALYSIS												**ANALYSE DU COMPTE DE RESULTATS**
% of average balance sheet total												**% du total moyen du bilan**
38. Interest income	9.35	7.81	7.51	7.07	6.26	5.76	5.63	6.40	7.92	8.11	38.	Produits financiers
39. Interest expenses	7.99	6.24	6.19	5.92	5.08	4.63	4.61	5.70	7.27	7.55	39.	Frais financiers
40. Net interest income	1.36	1.57	1.33	1.15	1.18	1.13	1.01	0.70	0.66	0.56	40.	Produits financiers nets
41. Non-interest income (net)	0.25	0.26	0.27	0.85	0.40	0.27	0.21	0.54	0.73	0.65	41.	Produits non financiers (nets)
42. Gross income	1.62	1.83	1.59	2.00	1.58	1.40	1.22	1.24	1.39	1.21	42.	Résultat brut
43. Operating expenses	0.65	0.65	0.62	0.66	0.71	0.66	0.60	0.61	0.66	0.63	43.	Frais d'exploitation
44. Net income	0.96	1.18	0.97	1.34	0.87	0.74	0.62	0.64	0.73	0.59	44.	Résultat net
45. Provisions (net)	0.16	0.35	0.19	0.88	0.20	0.15	0.03	0.36	0.47	0.37	45.	Provisions (nettes)
46. Profit before tax	0.80	0.82	0.78	0.46	0.67	0.59	0.59	0.28	0.26	0.21	46.	Bénéfices avant impôt
47. Income tax	0.44	0.45	0.42	0.37	0.37	0.34	0.34	0.05	0.10	0.12	47.	Impôt
48. Profit after tax	0.36	0.37	0.36	0.09	0.30	0.25	0.25	0.22	0.16	0.09	48.	Bénéfices après impôt
49. Distributed profit	0.14	0.16	0.18	0.11	0.19	0.13	0.13	0.32	0.12	0.06	49.	Bénéfices distribués
50. Retained profit	0.22	0.22	0.19	-0.02	0.11	0.12	0.12	-0.10	0.04	0.03	50.	Bénéfices mis en réserve
51. Staff costs	0.39	0.38	0.37	0.38	0.37	0.36	0.32	0.33	0.36	0.34	51.	Frais de personnel
52. Provisions on loans	0.15	0.35	0.19	0.88	0.20	0.15	0.02	0.36	0.41	0.34	52.	Provisions sur prêts
53. Provisions on securities (1)	..	..	..	..	..	..	..	..	..	..	53.	Provisions sur titres (1)
% of gross income												**% du total du résultat brut**
54. Net interest income	84.32	85.63	83.33	57.62	74.70	80.64	82.87	56.57	47.30	46.14	54.	Produits financiers nets
55. Non-interest income (net)	15.68	14.37	16.67	42.38	25.30	19.36	17.13	43.43	52.70	53.86	55.	Produits non financiers (nets)
56. Operating expenses	40.52	35.72	38.92	33.10	45.16	47.09	49.23	48.84	47.38	51.78	56.	Frais d'exploitation
57. Net income	59.48	64.28	61.08	66.90	54.84	52.91	50.77	51.16	52.62	48.22	57.	Résultat net
58. Provisions (net)	10.04	19.27	11.98	44.06	12.69	10.96	2.25	28.84	34.03	30.85	58.	Provisions (nettes)
59. Profit before tax	49.44	45.01	49.10	22.84	42.14	41.95	48.52	22.31	18.59	17.37	59.	Bénéfices avant impôt
60. Income tax	27.07	24.58	26.26	18.49	23.15	24.24	27.99	4.31	7.14	9.66	60.	Impôt
61. Profit after tax	22.37	20.43	22.84	4.35	18.99	17.71	20.53	18.01	11.45	7.71	61.	Bénéfices après impôt
62. Staff costs	24.25	20.66	23.03	19.15	23.46	25.58	26.51	26.71	26.09	27.97	62.	Frais de personnel
% of net income												**% du total du résultat net**
63. Provisions (net)	16.88	29.98	19.62	65.87	23.14	20.71	4.43	56.38	64.67	63.97	63.	Provisions (nettes)
64. Profit before tax	83.12	70.02	80.38	34.13	76.86	79.29	95.57	43.62	35.33	36.03	64.	Bénéfices avant impôt
65. Income tax	45.51	38.25	42.99	27.64	42.22	45.82	55.14	8.42	13.56	20.04	65.	Impôt
66. Profit after tax	37.61	31.78	37.39	6.50	34.64	33.47	40.43	35.20	21.76	15.99	66.	Bénéfices après impôt

GERMANY

Regional institutions of co-operative banks

Per cent

BALANCE SHEET ANALYSIS

% of year-end balance sheet total

ALLEMAGNE

Institutions régionales des banques mutualistes

Pourcentage

ANALYSE DU BILAN

% du total du bilan en fin d'exercice

	1982	1983	1984	1985	1986	1987	1988	1989	1990	1991		
Assets												**Actif**
67. Cash & balance with Central bank	2.28	1.84	2.52	2.07	2.12	1.36	1.32	1.49	1.16	1.45	67.	Caisse & solde auprès de la Banque centrale
68. Interbank deposits	51.80	55.46	54.65	53.82	57.55	59.79	58.61	55.48	55.67	49.04	68.	Dépôts interbancaires
69. Loans	22.20	19.62	20.09	19.98	18.31	18.01	19.40	19.57	19.85	23.31	69.	Prêts
70. Securities	21.78	21.10	21.14	22.16	20.30	19.34	19.49	21.18	21.12	19.12	70.	Valeurs mobilières
71. Other assets	1.94	1.98	1.61	1.98	1.73	1.50	1.19	2.29	2.20	7.08	71.	Autres actifs
Liabilities												**Passif**
72. Capital & reserves	2.91	2.99	3.33	3.68	3.54	3.47	3.42	3.65	3.33	3.57	72.	Capital et réserves
73. Borrowing from Central bank	6.10	5.48	4.88	4.82	3.09	2.78	5.51	6.26	6.20	7.79	73.	Emprunts auprès de la Banque centrale
74. Interbank deposits	71.78	69.22	71.84	72.44	74.56	74.69	72.69	71.01	72.22	69.65	74.	Dépôts interbancaires
75. Non-bank deposits	10.24	9.83	9.49	8.59	8.12	7.44	6.94	6.82	7.60	6.62	75.	Dépôts non bancaires
76. Bonds	7.54	10.59	8.53	8.51	8.72	9.64	9.17	10.06	7.98	9.10	76.	Obligations
77. Other liabilities	1.44	1.89	1.94	1.97	1.98	1.98	2.27	2.19	2.67	3.27	77.	Autres engagements
Memoranda												*Pour mémoire*
78. Short-term securities	*7.54*	*6.45*	*5.84*	*6.16*	*4.69*	*4.25*	*1.97*	*1.33*	*4.12*	*5.19*	*78.*	*Titres à court terme*
79. Bonds	*12.00*	*12.24*	*12.70*	*13.23*	*12.69*	*11.94*	*14.24*	*16.53*	*13.98*	*10.46*	*79.*	*Obligations*
80. Shares and participations	*2.25*	*2.41*	*2.60*	*2.77*	*2.92*	*3.15*	*3.28*	*3.32*	*3.02*	*3.48*	*80.*	*Actions et participations*
81. Claims on non-residents	*6.24*	*5.60*	*5.67*	*8.83*	*12.27*	*14.91*	*14.26*	*16.91*	*22.10*	*13.31*	*81.*	*Créances sur des non résidents*
82. Liabilities to non-residents	*2.08*	*1.66*	*2.13*	*2.71*	*1.99*	*1.82*	*1.94*	*2.03*	*5.19*	*1.92*	*82.*	*Engagements envers des non résidents*

1. Included under "Provisions on loans" (item 15 or item 52).

Notes

• Average balance sheet totals (item 29) are based on twelve end-month data.

1. Inclus sous "Provisions sur prêts" (poste 15 ou poste 52).

Notes

• La moyenne du total des actifs/passifs (poste 29) est basée sur douze données de fin de mois.

GERMANY
Co-operative banks

ALLEMAGNE
Banques mutualistes

Million DM / *Millions de DM*

	1982	1983	1984	1985	1986	1987	1988	1989	1990	1991	
INCOME STATEMENT											**COMPTE DE RESULTATS**
1. Interest income	27675	24939	26180	29893	29179	28961	29323	33387	40361	46925	1. Produits financiers
2. Interest expenses	16736	13434	14677	16852	15878	15268	15278	18638	24620	29438	2. Frais financiers
3. Net interest income	10939	11505	11503	13041	13301	13693	14045	14749	15741	17487	3. Produits financiers nets
4. Non-interest income (net)	1636	1896	2742	2617	2908	2974	2776	4134	4270	4203	4. Produits non financiers (nets)
5. Gross income	12575	13401	14245	15658	16209	16667	16821	18883	20011	21690	5. Résultat brut
6. Operating expenses	7882	8643	9401	11400	11930	12352	12635	12976	14050	15068	6. Frais d'exploitation
7. Net income	4693	4758	4844	4258	4279	4315	4186	5907	5961	6622	7. Résultat net
8. Provisions (net)	1567	1464	1932	1385	1416	1305	762	3223	2375	1491	8. Provisions (nettes)
9. Profit before tax	3126	3294	2912	2873	2863	3010	3424	2684	3586	5131	9. Bénéfices avant impôt
10. Income tax	2114	2268	1968	1957	1943	2066	2357	1706	2231	3096	10. Impôt
11. Profit after tax	1012	1026	944	916	920	944	1067	978	1355	2035	11. Bénéfices après impôt
12. Distributed profit	715	715	673	718	760	775	856	830	992	1292	12. Bénéfices distribués
13. Retained profit	297	311	271	198	160	169	211	148	363	743	13. Bénéfices mis en réserve
Memoranda											*Pour mémoire*
14. *Staff costs*	*4995*	*5398*	*5790*	*6975*	*7331*	*7636*	*7876*	*8100*	*8807*	*9428*	14. *Frais de personnel*
15. *Provisions on loans*	*1565*	*1459*	*1904*	*1359*	*1408*	*1295*	*755*	*3216*	*2365*	*1478*	15. *Provisions sur prêts*
16. *Provisions on securities (1)*	*..*	*..*	*..*	*..*	*..*	*..*	*..*	*..*	*..*	*..*	16. *Provisions sur titres (1)*
BALANCE SHEET											**BILAN**
Assets											**Actif**
17. Cash & balance with Central bank	9214	9888	10646	11442	11552	12726	14152	15830	17170	18317	17. Caisse & solde auprès de la Banque centrale
18. Interbank deposits	47088	45950	49805	61694	77475	80670	80874	87254	98019	101700	18. Dépôts interbancaires
19. Loans	199166	215004	229320	262650	265473	272516	286326	308096	328660	360750	19. Prêts
20. Securities	41326	49128	52298	65318	72516	84681	92621	94108	99721	105973	20. Valeurs mobilières
21. Other assets	11344	12693	14369	17957	18299	17776	17669	17907	19449	20832	21. Autres actifs
Liabilities											**Passif**
22. Capital & reserves	10892	11994	13149	16096	17279	18353	19353	20352	21223	23008	22. Capital et réserves
23. Borrowing from Central bank	8371	9791	11402	11515	10549	10111	14595	18523	19645	17945	23. Emprunts auprès de la Banque centrale
24. Interbank deposits	31410	35921	37861	40537	40505	41513	42971	43988	45417	45709	24. Dépôts interbancaires
25. Non-bank deposits	247059	263305	281356	335914	360226	379948	394167	416252	447499	485218	25. Dépôts non bancaires
26. Bonds	797	1478	2379	3386	4380	5635	7036	9476	13078	17277	26. Obligations
27. Other liabilities	9609	10174	10291	11613	12376	12809	13520	14604	16157	18415	27. Autres engagements
Balance sheet total											**Total du bilan**
28. End-year total	308138	332663	356438	419061	445315	468369	491642	523195	563019	607572	28. En fin d'exercice
29. Average total	291440	314632	338117	402107	424901	451136	474491	497789	534273	575708	29. Moyen
Memoranda											*Pour mémoire*
30. *Short-term securities*	*7004*	*8100*	*7440*	*8565*	*9088*	*11294*	*11750*	*11313*	*12885*	*15829*	30. *Titres à court terme*
31. *Bonds*	*32841*	*39548*	*43234*	*54691*	*60724*	*70037*	*77256*	*79170*	*82820*	*85528*	31. *Obligations*
32. *Shares and participations*	*1481*	*1480*	*1634*	*2062*	*2704*	*3350*	*3615*	*3625*	*4016*	*4616*	32. *Actions et participations*
33. *Claims on non-residents*	*889*	*909*	*1113*	*1506*	*1970*	*2619*	*3393*	*5401*	*6795*	*8254*	33. *Créances sur des non résidents*
34. *Liabilities to non-residents*	*2390*	*2988*	*3485*	*3857*	*3840*	*3998*	*4217*	*4491*	*5836*	*4973*	34. *Engagements envers des non résidents*
SUPPLEMENTARY INFORMATION											**RENSEIGNEMENTS COMPLEMENTAIRES**
35. Number of institutions	2263	2250	2239	3655	3604	3480	3361	3225	3049	2862	35. Nombre d'institutions
36. Number of branches	12700	12800	12900	15929	15935	15910	15824	15789	15769	15815	36. Nombre de succursales
37. Number of employees (x 1000)	NA	NA	NA	NA	NA	NA	NA	NA	NA	NA	37. Nombre de salariés (x 1000)

GERMANY
Co-operative banks

ALLEMAGNE
Banques mutualistes

Per cent / *Pourcentage*

INCOME STATEMENT ANALYSIS / **ANALYSE DU COMPTE DE RESULTATS**

	1982	1983	1984	1985	1986	1987	1988	1989	1990	1991		
% of average balance sheet total												**% du total moyen du bilan**
38. Interest income	9.50	7.93	7.74	7.43	6.87	6.42	6.18	6.71	7.55	8.15	38.	Produits financiers
39. Interest expenses	5.74	4.27	4.34	4.19	3.74	3.38	3.22	3.74	4.61	5.11	39.	Frais financiers
40. Net interest income	3.75	3.66	3.40	3.24	3.13	3.04	2.96	2.96	2.95	3.04	40.	Produits financiers nets
41. Non-interest income (net)	0.56	0.60	0.81	0.65	0.68	0.66	0.59	0.83	0.80	0.73	41.	Produits non financiers (nets)
42. Gross income	4.31	4.26	4.21	3.89	3.81	3.69	3.55	3.79	3.75	3.77	42.	Résultat brut
43. Operating expenses	2.70	2.75	2.78	2.84	2.81	2.74	2.66	2.61	2.63	2.62	43.	Frais d'exploitation
44. Net income	1.61	1.51	1.43	1.06	1.01	0.96	0.88	1.19	1.12	1.15	44.	Résultat net
45. Provisions (net)	0.54	0.47	0.57	0.34	0.33	0.29	0.16	0.65	0.44	0.26	45.	Provisions (nettes)
46. Profit before tax	1.07	1.05	0.86	0.71	0.67	0.67	0.72	0.54	0.67	0.89	46.	Bénéfices avant impôt
47. Income tax	0.73	0.72	0.58	0.49	0.46	0.46	0.50	0.34	0.42	0.54	47.	Impôt
48. Profit after tax	0.35	0.33	0.28	0.23	0.22	0.21	0.22	0.20	0.25	0.35	48.	Bénéfices après impôt
49. Distributed profit	0.25	0.23	0.20	0.18	0.18	0.17	0.18	0.17	0.19	0.22	49.	Bénéfices distribués
50. Retained profit	0.10	0.10	0.08	0.05	0.04	0.04	0.04	0.03	0.07	0.13	50.	Bénéfices mis en réserve
51. Staff costs	1.71	1.72	1.71	1.73	1.73	1.69	1.66	1.63	1.65	1.64	51.	Frais de personnel
52. Provisions on loans	0.54	0.46	0.56	0.34	0.33	0.29	0.16	0.65	0.44	0.26	52.	Provisions sur prêts
53. Provisions on securities (1)	..	..	..	..	..	..	..	..	..	..	53.	Provisions sur titres (1)
% of gross income												**% du total du résultat brut**
54. Net interest income	86.99	85.85	80.75	83.29	82.06	82.16	83.50	78.11	78.66	80.62	54.	Produits financiers nets
55. Non-interest income (net)	13.01	14.15	19.25	16.71	17.94	17.84	16.50	21.89	21.34	19.38	55.	Produits non financiers (nets)
56. Operating expenses	62.68	64.50	66.00	72.81	73.60	74.11	75.11	68.72	70.21	69.47	56.	Frais d'exploitation
57. Net income	37.32	35.50	34.00	27.19	26.40	25.89	24.89	31.28	29.79	30.53	57.	Résultat net
58. Provisions (net)	12.46	10.92	13.56	8.85	8.74	7.83	4.53	17.07	11.87	6.87	58.	Provisions (nettes)
59. Profit before tax	24.86	24.58	20.44	18.35	17.66	18.06	20.36	14.21	17.92	23.66	59.	Bénéfices avant impôt
60. Income tax	16.81	16.92	13.82	12.50	11.99	12.40	14.01	9.03	11.15	14.27	60.	Impôt
61. Profit after tax	8.05	7.66	6.63	5.85	5.68	5.66	6.34	5.18	6.77	9.38	61.	Bénéfices après impôt
62. Staff costs	39.72	40.28	40.65	44.55	45.23	45.82	46.82	42.90	44.01	43.47	62.	Frais de personnel
% of net income												**% du total du résultat net**
63. Provisions (net)	33.39	30.77	39.88	32.53	33.09	30.24	18.20	54.56	39.84	22.52	63.	Provisions (nettes)
64. Profit before tax	66.61	69.23	60.12	67.47	66.91	69.76	81.80	45.44	60.16	77.48	64.	Bénéfices avant impôt
65. Income tax	45.05	47.67	40.63	45.96	45.41	47.88	56.31	28.88	37.43	46.75	65.	Impôt
66. Profit after tax	21.56	21.56	19.49	21.51	21.50	21.88	25.49	16.56	22.73	30.73	66.	Bénéfices après impôt

GERMANY

Co-operative banks

ALLEMAGNE

Banques mutualistes

Per cent — *Pourcentage*

BALANCE SHEET ANALYSIS — ANALYSE DU BILAN

% of year-end balance sheet total — **% du total du bilan en fin d'exercice**

	1982	1983	1984	1985	1986	1987	1988	1989	1990	1991		
Assets												**Actif**
67. Cash & balance with Central bank	2.99	2.97	2.99	2.73	2.59	2.72	2.88	3.03	3.05	3.01	67.	Caisse & solde auprès de la Banque centrale
68. Interbank deposits	15.28	13.81	13.97	14.72	17.40	17.22	16.45	16.68	17.41	16.74	68.	Dépôts interbancaires
69. Loans	64.64	64.63	64.34	62.68	59.61	58.18	58.24	58.89	58.37	59.38	69.	Prêts
70. Securities	13.41	14.77	14.67	15.59	16.28	18.08	18.84	17.99	17.71	17.44	70.	Valeurs mobilières
71. Other assets	3.68	3.82	4.03	4.29	4.11	3.80	3.59	3.42	3.45	3.43	71.	Autres actifs
Liabilities												**Passif**
72. Capital & reserves	3.53	3.61	3.69	3.84	3.88	3.92	3.94	3.89	3.77	3.79	72.	Capital et réserves
73. Borrowing from Central bank	2.72	2.94	3.20	2.75	2.37	2.16	2.97	3.54	3.49	2.95	73.	Emprunts auprès de la Banque centrale
74. Interbank deposits	10.19	10.80	10.62	9.67	9.10	8.86	8.74	8.41	8.07	7.52	74.	Dépôts interbancaires
75. Non-bank deposits	80.18	79.15	78.94	80.16	80.89	81.12	80.17	79.56	79.48	79.86	75.	Dépôts non bancaires
76. Bonds	0.26	0.44	0.67	0.81	0.98	1.20	1.43	1.81	2.32	2.84	76.	Obligations
77. Other liabilities	3.12	3.06	2.89	2.77	2.78	2.73	2.75	2.79	2.87	3.03	77.	Autres engagements
Memoranda												*Pour mémoire*
78. Short-term securities	*2.27*	*2.43*	*2.09*	*2.04*	*2.04*	*2.41*	*2.39*	*2.16*	*2.29*	*2.61*	*78.*	*Titres à court terme*
79. Bonds	*10.66*	*11.89*	*12.13*	*13.05*	*13.64*	*14.95*	*15.71*	*15.13*	*14.71*	*14.08*	*79.*	*Obligations*
80. Shares and participations	*0.48*	*0.44*	*0.46*	*0.49*	*0.61*	*0.72*	*0.74*	*0.69*	*0.71*	*0.76*	*80.*	*Actions et participations*
81. Claims on non-residents	*0.29*	*0.27*	*0.31*	*0.36*	*0.44*	*0.56*	*0.69*	*1.03*	*1.21*	*1.36*	*81.*	*Créances sur des non résidents*
82. Liabilities to non-residents	*0.78*	*0.90*	*0.98*	*0.92*	*0.86*	*0.85*	*0.86*	*0.86*	*1.04*	*0.82*	*82.*	*Engagements envers des non résidents*

1. Included under "Provisions on loans" (item 15 or item 52).

1. Inclus sous "Provisions sur prêts" (poste 15 ou poste 52).

Notes

- Average balance sheet totals (item 29) are based on twelve end-month data.

Change in methodology:

- As from 1985, all credit co-operatives are included in the data.

Notes

- La moyenne du total des actifs/passifs (poste 29) est basée sur douze données de fin de mois.

Changement méthodologique :

- Depuis 1985, l'ensemble des banques mutualistes est compris dans les données.

GREECE

Commercial banks

Million drachmas

GRECE

Banques commerciales

Millions de drachmes

		1989	1990	1991		
INCOME STATEMENT						**COMPTE DE RESULTATS**
1.	Interest income	809952	1035190	1261913	1.	Produits financiers
2.	Interest expenses	725805	906422	1057989	2.	Frais financiers
3.	Net interest income	84147	128768	203924	3.	Produits financiers nets
4.	Non-interest income (net)	124662	162719	233960	4.	Produits non financiers (nets)
5.	Gross income	208809	291487	437884	5.	Résultat brut
6.	Operating expenses	156098	186857	224721	6.	Frais d'exploitation
7.	Net income	52711	104630	213163	7.	Résultat net
8.	Provisions (net)	22034	35758	63983	8.	Provisions (nettes)
9.	Profit before tax	30677	68872	149180	9.	Bénéfices avant impôt
10.	Income tax	3847	14296	24108	10.	Impôt
11.	Profit after tax	26830	54576	125072	11.	Bénéfices après impôt
12.	Distributed profit	15572	32859	59333	12.	Bénéfices distribués
13.	Retained profit	11258	21717	65739	13.	Bénéfices mis en réserve
Memoranda						*Pour mémoire*
14.	Staff costs	*119660*	*143565*	*170332*	14.	*Frais de personnel*
15.	Provisions on loans	*18589*	*32052*	*60506*	15.	*Provisions sur prêts*
16.	Provisions on securities	*..*	*..*	*..*	16.	*Provisions sur titres*
BALANCE SHEET						**BILAN**
Assets						**Actif**
17.	Cash & balance with Central bank	955274	1055865	1244087	17.	Caisse & solde auprès de la Banque centrale
18.	Interbank deposits	400934	459030	572950	18.	Dépôts interbancaires
19.	Loans	2291176	2418951	2605460	19.	Prêts
20.	Securities	2694370	3290618	3870488	20.	Valeurs mobilières
21.	Other assets	386183	463230	920229	21.	Autres actifs
Liabilities						**Passif**
22.	Capital & reserves	230484	340331	479424	22.	Capital et réserves
23.	Borrowing from Central bank	29734	37482	30198	23.	Emprunts auprès de la Banque centrale
24.	Interbank deposits	71987	77288	153731	24.	Dépôts interbancaires
25.	Non-bank deposits	6035693	6884194	7996031	25.	Dépôts non bancaires
26.	Bonds	-	-	119125	26.	Obligations
27.	Other liabilities	360039	348399	434705	27.	Autres engagements
Balance sheet total						**Total du bilan**
28.	End-year total	6727937	7687694	9213214	28.	En fin d'exercice
29.	Average total	6173791	7207815	8450454	29.	Moyen
Memoranda						*Pour mémoire*
30.	Short-term securities	*2287331*	*2609630*	*1332128*	30.	*Titres à court terme*
31.	Bonds	*156967*	*382999*	*2166431*	31.	*Obligations*
32.	Shares and participations	*250072*	*297989*	*371929*	32.	*Actions et participations*
33.	Claims on non-residents	*..*	*..*	*..*	33.	*Créances sur des non résidents*
34.	Liabilities to non-residents	*..*	*..*	*..*	34.	*Engagements envers des non résidents*
SUPPLEMENTARY INFORMATION						**RENSEIGNEMENTS COMPLEMENTAIRES**
35.	Number of institutions	15	18	20	35.	Nombre d'institutions
36.	Number of branches	1065	1062	1121	36.	Nombre de succursales
37.	Number of employees (x 1000)	37.2	36.5	37.3	37.	Nombre de salariés (x 1000)

GREECE

Commercial banks

Per cent

INCOME STATEMENT ANALYSIS

GRECE

Banques commerciales

Pourcentage

ANALYSE DU COMPTE DE RESULTATS

			1989	1990	1991
% of average balance sheet total		**% du total moyen du bilan**			
38. Interest income	38.	Produits financiers	13.12	14.36	14.93
39. Interest expenses	39.	Frais financiers	11.76	12.58	12.52
40. Net interest income	40.	Produits financiers nets	1.36	1.79	2.41
41. Non-interest income (net)	41.	Produits non financiers (nets)	2.02	2.26	2.77
42. Gross income	42.	Résultat brut	3.38	4.04	5.18
43. Operating expenses	43.	Frais d'exploitation	2.53	2.59	2.66
44. Net income	44.	Résultat net	0.85	1.45	2.52
45. Provisions (net)	45.	Provisions (nettes)	0.36	0.50	0.76
46. Profit before tax	46.	Bénéfices avant impôt	0.50	0.96	1.77
47. Income tax	47.	Impôt	0.06	0.20	0.29
48. Profit after tax	48.	Bénéfices après impôt	0.43	0.76	1.48
49. Distributed profit	49.	Bénéfices distribués	0.25	0.46	0.70
50. Retained profit	50.	Bénéfices mis en réserve	0.18	0.30	0.78
51. Staff costs	51.	Frais de personnel	1.94	1.99	2.02
52. Provisions on loans	52.	Provisions sur prêts	0.30	0.44	0.72
53. Provisions on securities	53.	Provisions sur titres	..	..	..
% of gross income		**% du total du résultat brut**			
54. Net interest income	54.	Produits financiers nets	40.30	44.18	46.57
55. Non-interest income (net)	55.	Produits non financiers (nets)	59.70	55.82	53.43
56. Operating expenses	56.	Frais d'exploitation	74.76	64.10	51.32
57. Net income	57.	Résultat net	25.24	35.90	48.68
58. Provisions (net)	58.	Provisions (nettes)	10.55	12.27	14.61
59. Profit before tax	59.	Bénéfices avant impôt	14.69	23.63	34.07
60. Income tax	60.	Impôt	1.84	4.90	5.51
61. Profit after tax	61.	Bénéfices après impôt	12.85	18.72	28.56
62. Staff costs	62.	Frais de personnel	57.31	49.25	38.90
% of net income		**% du total du résultat net**			
63. Provisions (net)	63.	Provisions (nettes)	41.80	34.18	30.02
64. Profit before tax	64.	Bénéfices avant impôt	58.20	65.82	69.98
65. Income tax	65.	Impôt	7.30	13.66	11.31
66. Profit after tax	66.	Bénéfices après impôt	50.90	52.16	58.67

GREECE

Commercial banks

GRECE

Banques commerciales

Per cent

Pourcentage

BALANCE SHEET ANALYSIS

ANALYSE DU BILAN

% of year-end balance sheet total

% du total du bilan en fin d'exercice

		1989	1990	1991		
	Assets					**Actif**
67.	Cash & balance with Central bank	14.20	13.73	13.50	67.	Caisse & solde auprès de la Banque centrale
68.	Interbank deposits	5.96	5.97	6.22	68.	Dépôts interbancaires
69.	Loans	34.05	31.47	28.28	69.	Prêts
70.	Securities	40.05	42.80	42.01	70.	Valeurs mobilières
71.	Other assets	5.74	6.03	9.99	71.	Autres actifs
	Liabilities					**Passif**
72.	Capital & reserves	3.43	4.43	5.20	72.	Capital et réserves
73.	Borrowing from Central bank	0.44	0.49	0.33	73.	Emprunts auprès de la Banque centrale
74.	Interbank deposits	1.07	1.01	1.67	74.	Dépôts interbancaires
75.	Non-bank deposits	89.71	89.55	86.79	75.	Dépôts non bancaires
76.	Bonds	-	-	1.29	76.	Obligations
77.	Other liabilities	5.35	4.53	4.72	77.	Autres engagements
	Memoranda					*Pour mémoire*
78.	*Short-term securities*	*34.00*	*33.95*	*14.46*	78.	*Titres à court terme*
79.	*Bonds*	*2.33*	*4.98*	*23.51*	79.	*Obligations*
80.	*Shares and participations*	*3.72*	*3.88*	*4.04*	80.	*Actions et participations*
81.	*Claims on non-residents*	..	..	..	81.	*Créances sur des non résidents*
82.	*Liabilities to non-residents*	..	..	..	82.	*Engagements envers des non résidents*

GREECE

Large commercial banks

Million drachmas

GREECE

Grandes banques commerciales

Millions de drachmes

	1982	1983	1984	1985	1986	1987	1988	1989	1990	1991
INCOME STATEMENT / COMPTE DE RESULTATS										
1. Interest income / Produits financiers	174193	211197	283474	362938	421524	470044	575166	708956	890880	1068795
2. Interest expenses / Frais financiers	148868	179691	248519	327762	380934	444522	538274	644999	798348	912049
3. Net interest income / Produits financiers nets	25325	31506	34955	35176	40590	25522	36892	63957	92532	156746
4. Non-interest income (net) / Produits non financiers (nets)	17421	20640	32912	46042	56926	80966	96544	103671	135770	196760
5. Gross income / Résultat brut	42746	52146	67867	81218	97516	106488	133436	167628	228302	353506
6. Operating expenses / Frais d'exploitation	31636	39914	51568	63849	73121	83179	108286	128358	151969	178455
7. Net income / Résultat net	11110	12232	16299	17369	24395	23309	25150	39270	76333	175051
8. Provisions (net) / Provisions (nettes)	5657	5679	7590	8598	10344	9491	10760	19350	31240	59044
9. Profit before tax / Bénéfices avant impôt	5453	6553	8709	8771	14051	13818	14390	19920	45093	116007
10. Income tax / Impôt	885	971	932	990	1243	2288	2244	2714	9498	17547
11. Profit after tax / Bénéfices après impôt	4568	5582	7777	7781	12808	11530	12146	17206	35595	98460
12. Distributed profit / Bénéfices distribués	3101	4502	5170	3765	6810	8572	9763	8768	19583	41679
13. Retained profit / Bénéfices mis en réserve	1467	1080	2607	4016	5998	2958	2383	8438	16012	56781
Memoranda / Pour mémoire										
14. Staff costs / Frais de personnel	25625	32376	41811	51695	58343	63957	83952	100241	118929	138279
15. Provisions on loans / Provisions sur prêts	..	..	..	..	..	9491	10760	19350	31240	56171
16. Provisions on securities / Provisions sur titres	..	..	..	..	..	..	..	..	..	..
BALANCE SHEET / BILAN										
Assets / Actif										
17. Cash & balance with Central bank / Caisse & solde auprès de la Banque centrale	259770	268971	468459	509022	512909	737241	851581	787858	937939	1080606
18. Interbank deposits / Dépôts interbancaires	52788	110457	144891	202194	155764	159245	281820	296556	320288	388178
19. Loans / Prêts	664757	747668	902002	1074734	1295144	1410280	1647158	1948042	1996282	2120142
20. Securities / Valeurs mobilières	351841	525453	674909	969482	1210724	1509263	1949543	2527840	2968372	3453143
21. Other assets / Autres actifs	90170	101748	94285	173612	294366	216138	155636	283183	350354	724762
Liabilities / Passif										
22. Capital & reserves / Capital et réserves	62095	64529	67156	71217	77377	81929	149671	167870	247835	351624
23. Borrowing from Central bank / Emprunts auprès de la Banque centrale	65264	90727	137221	194405	186261	136750	41278	5523	12086	5896
24. Interbank deposits / Dépôts interbancaires	22731	31122	29979	44946	34488	37923	47554	59282	65595	129009
25. Non-bank deposits / Dépôts non bancaires	1173352	1459427	1932202	2507426	2998305	3675497	4453687	5395410	6035308	6848311
26. Bonds / Obligations										119125
27. Other liabilities / Autres engagements	95884	108492	117988	111050	172476	100068	193548	215374	212411	312866
Balance sheet total / Total du bilan										
28. End-year total / En fin d'exercice	1419326	1754297	2284546	2929044	3468907	4032167	4885738	5843459	6573235	7766831
29. Average total / Moyen	1254000	1586812	2019422	2606795	3198976	3750537	4458953	5364599	6208347	7170033
Memoranda / Pour mémoire										
30. Short-term securities / Titres à court terme	291843	463493	608586	893488	1073423	1235980	1607086	2133756	2317709	969054
31. Bonds / Obligations	25311	24753	22438	21494	31206	73101	115355	149571	366025	2135623
32. Shares and participations / Actions et participations	34687	37207	43885	54500	106095	200182	227102	244513	284638	348466
33. Claims on non-residents / Créances sur des non résidents	..	..	..	..	..	..	..	..	..	..
34. Liabilities to non-residents / Engagements envers des non résidents	..	..	..	..	..	..	..	..	..	..
SUPPLEMENTARY INFORMATION / RENSEIGNEMENTS COMPLEMENTAIRES										
35. Number of institutions / Nombre d'institutions	4	4	4	4	4	4	4	4	4	4
36. Number of branches / Nombre de succursales	736	748	759	782	795	794	797	799	802	812
37. Number of employees (x 1000) / Nombre de salariés (x 1000)	23.4	24.0	25.1	27.4	28.4	29.0	29.4	29.7	28.7	28.7

GREECE

Large commercial banks

GREECE

Grandes banques commerciales

Per cent / *Pourcentage*

INCOME STATEMENT ANALYSIS / **ANALYSE DU COMPTE DE RESULTATS**

		1982	1983	1984	1985	1986	1987	1988	1989	1990	1991		
% of average balance sheet total												**% du total moyen du bilan**	
38.	Interest income	13.89	13.31	14.04	13.92	13.18	12.53	12.90	13.22	14.35	14.91	38.	Produits financiers
39.	Interest expenses	11.87	11.32	12.31	12.57	11.91	11.85	12.07	12.02	12.86	12.72	39.	Frais financiers
40.	Net interest income	2.02	1.99	1.73	1.35	1.27	0.68	0.83	1.19	1.49	2.19	40.	Produits financiers nets
41.	Non-interest income (net)	1.39	1.30	1.63	1.77	1.78	2.16	2.17	1.93	2.19	2.74	41.	Produits non financiers (nets)
42.	Gross income	3.41	3.29	3.36	3.12	3.05	2.84	2.99	3.12	3.68	4.93	42.	Résultat brut
43.	Operating expenses	2.52	2.52	2.55	2.45	2.29	2.22	2.43	2.39	2.45	2.49	43.	Frais d'exploitation
44.	Net income	0.89	0.77	0.81	0.67	0.76	0.62	0.56	0.73	1.23	2.44	44.	Résultat net
45.	Provisions (net)	0.45	0.36	0.38	0.33	0.32	0.25	0.24	0.36	0.50	0.82	45.	Provisions (nettes)
46.	Profit before tax	0.43	0.41	0.43	0.34	0.44	0.37	0.32	0.37	0.73	1.62	46.	Bénéfices avant impôt
47.	Income tax	0.07	0.06	0.05	0.04	0.04	0.06	0.05	0.05	0.15	0.24	47.	Impôt
48.	Profit after tax	0.36	0.35	0.39	0.30	0.40	0.31	0.27	0.32	0.57	1.37	48.	Bénéfices après impôt
49.	Distributed profit	0.25	0.28	0.26	0.14	0.21	0.23	0.22	0.16	0.32	0.58	49.	Bénéfices distribués
50.	Retained profit	0.12	0.07	0.13	0.15	0.19	0.08	0.05	0.16	0.26	0.79	50.	Bénéfices mis en réserve
51.	Staff costs	2.04	2.04	2.07	1.98	1.82	1.71	1.88	1.87	1.92	1.93	51.	Frais de personnel
52.	Provisions on loans	..	..	..	..	..	0.25	0.24	0.36	0.50	0.78	52.	Provisions sur prêts
53.	Provisions on securities	..	..	..	..	..	..	..	..	..	..	53.	Provisions sur titres
% of gross income												**% du total du résultat brut**	
54.	Net interest income	59.25	60.42	51.51	43.31	41.62	23.97	27.65	38.15	40.53	44.34	54.	Produits financiers nets
55.	Non-interest income (net)	40.75	39.58	48.49	56.69	58.38	76.03	72.35	61.85	59.47	55.66	55.	Produits non financiers (nets)
56.	Operating expenses	74.01	76.54	75.98	78.61	74.98	78.11	81.15	76.57	66.56	50.48	56.	Frais d'exploitation
57.	Net income	25.99	23.46	24.02	21.39	25.02	21.89	18.85	23.43	33.44	49.52	57.	Résultat net
58.	Provisions (net)	13.23	10.89	11.18	10.59	10.61	8.91	8.06	11.54	13.68	16.70	58.	Provisions (nettes)
59.	Profit before tax	12.76	12.57	12.83	10.80	14.41	12.98	10.78	11.88	19.75	32.82	59.	Bénéfices avant impôt
60.	Income tax	2.07	1.86	1.37	1.22	1.27	2.15	1.68	1.62	4.16	4.96	60.	Impôt
61.	Profit after tax	10.69	10.70	11.46	9.58	13.13	10.83	9.10	10.26	15.59	27.85	61.	Bénéfices après impôt
62.	Staff costs	59.95	62.09	61.61	63.65	59.83	60.06	62.92	59.80	52.09	39.12	62.	Frais de personnel
% of net income												**% du total du résultat net**	
63.	Provisions (net)	50.92	46.43	46.57	49.50	42.40	40.72	42.78	49.27	40.93	33.73	63.	Provisions (nettes)
64.	Profit before tax	49.08	53.57	53.43	50.50	57.60	59.28	57.22	50.73	59.07	66.27	64.	Bénéfices avant impôt
65.	Income tax	7.97	7.94	5.72	5.70	5.10	9.82	8.92	6.91	12.44	10.02	65.	Impôt
66.	Profit after tax	41.12	45.63	47.71	44.80	52.50	49.47	48.29	43.81	46.63	56.25	66.	Bénéfices après impôt

GREECE

Large commercial banks

Per cent

BALANCE SHEET ANALYSIS

% of year-end balance sheet total

	1982	1983	1984	1985	1986	1987	1988	1989	1990	1991
Assets										
67. Cash & balance with Central bank	18.30	15.33	20.51	17.38	14.79	18.28	17.43	13.48	14.27	13.91
68. Interbank deposits	3.72	6.30	6.34	6.90	4.49	3.95	5.77	5.07	4.87	5.00
69. Loans	46.84	42.62	39.48	36.69	37.34	34.98	33.71	33.34	30.37	27.30
70. Securities	24.79	29.95	29.54	33.10	34.90	37.43	39.90	43.26	45.16	44.46
71. Other assets	6.35	5.80	4.13	5.93	8.49	5.36	3.19	4.85	5.33	9.33
Liabilities										
72. Capital & reserves	4.37	3.68	2.94	2.43	2.23	2.03	3.06	2.87	3.77	4.53
73. Borrowing from Central bank	4.60	5.17	6.01	6.64	5.37	3.39	0.84	0.09	0.18	0.08
74. Interbank deposits	1.60	1.77	1.31	1.53	0.99	0.94	0.97	1.01	1.00	1.66
75. Non-bank deposits	82.67	83.19	84.58	85.61	86.43	91.15	91.16	92.33	91.82	88.17
76. Bonds	-	-	-	-	-	-	-	-	-	1.53
77. Other liabilities	6.76	6.18	5.16	3.79	4.97	2.48	3.96	3.69	3.23	4.03
Memoranda										
78. Short-term securities	*20.56*	*26.42*	*26.64*	*30.50*	*30.94*	*30.65*	*32.89*	*36.52*	*35.26*	*12.48*
79. Bonds	*1.78*	*1.41*	*0.98*	*0.73*	*0.90*	*1.81*	*2.36*	*2.56*	*5.57*	*27.50*
80. Shares and participations	*2.44*	*2.12*	*1.92*	*1.86*	*3.06*	*4.96*	*4.65*	*4.18*	*4.33*	*4.49*
81. Claims on non-residents	*..*	*..*	*..*	*..*	*..*	*..*	*..*	*..*	*..*	*..*
82. Liabilities to non-residents	*..*	*..*	*..*	*..*	*..*	*..*	*..*	*..*	*..*	*..*

Notes

- Large commercial banks are a sub-group of Commercial banks.

GREECE

Grandes banques commerciales

Pourcentage

ANALYSE DU BILAN

% du total du bilan en fin d'exercice

Actif
67. Caisse & solde auprès de la Banque centrale
68. Dépôts interbancaires
69. Prêts
70. Valeurs mobilières
71. Autres actifs

Passif
72. Capital et réserves
73. Emprunts auprès de la Banque centrale
74. Dépôts interbancaires
75. Dépôts non bancaires
76. Obligations
77. Autres engagements

Pour mémoire
78. Titres à court terme
79. Obligations
80. Actions et participations
81. Créances sur des non résidents
82. Engagements envers des non résidents

Notes

- Les Grandes banques commerciales sont un sous-groupe des Banques commerciales.

91

ITALY / ITALIE

Commercial banks / Banques commerciales

Billion lire / *Milliards de lires*

	1982	1983	1984	1985	1986	1987	1988	1989	1990	1991 (2)	
INCOME STATEMENT											**COMPTE DE RESULTATS**
1. Interest income	49072	53673	60229	63683	60145	57900	61725	71824	79775	86591	1. Produits financiers
2. Interest expenses	36585	39189	44053	45581	38994	35815	36942	43915	48322	51761	2. Frais financiers
3. Net interest income	12487	14484	16176	18102	21151	22085	24783	27909	31453	34830	3. Produits financiers nets
4. Non-interest income (net)	5174	5403	6666	8328	9900	8580	9439	9673	11320	12336	4. Produits non financiers (nets)
5. Gross income	17661	19887	22842	26430	31051	30665	34222	37582	42773	47166	5. Résultat brut
6. Operating expenses	10996	13710	15775	17751	19476	21497	23074	24061	26863	30163	6. Frais d'exploitation
7. Net income	6665	6177	7067	8679	11575	9168	11148	13521	15910	17003	7. Résultat net
8. Provisions (net)	3249	2808	3007	3310	3783	3409	4247	4320	4999	4955	8. Provisions (nettes)
9. Profit before tax	3416	3369	4060	5369	7792	5759	6901	9201	10911	12048	9. Bénéfices avant impôt
10. Income tax	2092	1863	1978	2593	3541	2301	2983	3301	3767	4322	10. Impôt
11. Profit after tax	1324	1506	2082	2776	4251	3458	3918	5900	7144	7726	11. Bénéfices après impôt
12. Distributed profit	..	641	902	1123	1506	1631	1696	1812	2108	2298	12. Bénéfices distribués
13. Retained profit	..	865	1180	1653	2745	1827	2222	4088	5036	5428	13. Bénéfices mis en réserve
Memoranda											*Pour mémoire*
14. Staff costs	7725	10038	11324	12768	13938	15370	16564	17181	18927	21230	14. Frais de personnel
15. Provisions on loans	1697	2421	2640	2361	2796	2564	3329	4183	5084	4934	15. Provisions sur prêts
16. Provisions on securities	458	109	115	81	314	1270	951	1361	840	1104	16. Provisions sur titres
BALANCE SHEET											**BILAN**
Assets											**Actif**
17. Cash & balance with Central bank(1)	2718	3068	50569	59669	65884	71816	79120	85882	95996	98501	17. Caisse & solde auprès de la Banque centrale(1)
18. Interbank deposits (1)	62217	72338	75236	78905	84646	77780	75209	91212	67991	73381	18. Dépôts interbancaires (1)
19. Loans	113312	133051	167469	188828	204929	220573	262148	316595	370512	427161	19. Prêts
20. Securities	102890	117281	128309	135948	146684	148538	137469	129640	120146	130796	20. Valeurs mobilières
21. Other assets	181700	203433	208502	226043	238252	233980	265489	360382	333514	375292	21. Autres actifs
Liabilities											**Passif**
22. Capital & reserves	15932	22447	33298	38858	46275	53052	56194	62474	68246	88526	22. Capital et réserves
23. Borrowing from Central bank	2128	5556	1993	6917	3205	3754	3601	3615	4360	6766	23. Emprunts auprès de la Banque centrale
24. Interbank deposits	55499	66097	76194	77858	85216	79046	72112	90839	63218	65983	24. Dépôts interbancaires
25. Non-bank deposits	232542	265530	292428	322701	352366	376067	404475	444005	486338	539855	25. Dépôts non bancaires
26. Bonds	-	-	-	-	-	-	-	-	-	-	26. Obligations
27. Other liabilities	156736	169541	226172	243058	253334	240767	283054	382779	365998	404001	27. Autres engagements
Balance sheet total											**Total du bilan**
28. End-year total	462837	529171	630085	689392	740396	752687	819435	983711	988159	1105131	28. En fin d'exercice
29. Average total	391180	461612	520940	601149	649765	701002	758922	844587	922348	983084	29. Moyen
Memoranda											*Pour mémoire*
30. Short-term securities	36806	32678	30481	18361	22388	18961	16856	15863	18086	19039	30. Titres à court terme
31. Bonds	69291	89425	97828	117587	124296	129577	120613	113777	102060	111757	31. Obligations
32. Shares and participations	3624	4805	6419	6930	8822	9664	10914	14386	15540	23493	32. Actions et participations
33. Claims on non-residents	40121	50306	69758	76245	73434	67902	72820	92031	90454	90243	33. Créances sur des non résidents
34. Liabilities to non-residents	52975	65530	93910	93115	90391	92651	108960	135678	137106	160537	34. Engagements envers des non résidents
SUPPLEMENTARY INFORMATION											**RENSEIGNEMENTS COMPLEMENTAIRES**
35. Number of institutions	210	205	235	235	232	226	219	198	197	188	35. Nombre d'institutions
36. Number of branches	8894	9025	10304	10388	10427	10540	10556	10564	11328	12071	36. Nombre de succursales
37. Number of employees (x 1000)	220.9	226.3	234.5	235.3	238.2	240.9	241.3	240.3	240.9	245.9	37. Nombre de salariés (x 1000)

ITALY

Commercial banks

Per cent — *Pourcentage*

INCOME STATEMENT ANALYSIS — ANALYSE DU COMPTE DE RESULTATS

	1982	1983	1984	1985	1986	1987	1988	1989	1990	1991 (2)	
% of average balance sheet total											**% du total moyen du bilan**
38. Interest income	12.54	11.63	11.56	10.59	9.26	8.26	8.13	8.50	8.65	8.81	38. Produits financiers
39. Interest expenses	9.35	8.49	8.46	7.58	6.00	5.11	4.87	5.20	5.24	5.27	39. Frais financiers
40. Net interest income	3.19	3.14	3.11	3.01	3.26	3.15	3.27	3.30	3.41	3.54	40. Produits financiers nets
41. Non-interest income (net)	1.32	1.17	1.28	1.39	1.52	1.22	1.24	1.15	1.23	1.25	41. Produits non financiers (nets)
42. Gross income	4.51	4.31	4.38	4.40	4.78	4.37	4.51	4.45	4.64	4.80	42. Résultat brut
43. Operating expenses	2.81	2.97	3.03	2.95	3.00	3.07	3.04	2.85	2.91	3.07	43. Frais d'exploitation
44. Net income	1.70	1.34	1.36	1.44	1.78	1.31	1.47	1.60	1.72	1.73	44. Résultat net
45. Provisions (net)	0.83	0.61	0.58	0.55	0.58	0.49	0.56	0.51	0.54	0.50	45. Provisions (nettes)
46. Profit before tax	0.87	0.73	0.78	0.89	1.20	0.82	0.91	1.09	1.18	1.23	46. Bénéfices avant impôt
47. Income tax	0.53	0.40	0.38	0.43	0.54	0.33	0.39	0.39	0.41	0.44	47. Impôt
48. Profit after tax	0.34	0.33	0.40	0.46	0.65	0.49	0.52	0.70	0.77	0.79	48. Bénéfices après impôt
49. Distributed profit	..	0.14	0.17	0.19	0.23	0.23	0.22	0.21	0.23	0.23	49. Bénéfices distribués
50. Retained profit	..	0.19	0.23	0.27	0.42	0.26	0.29	0.48	0.55	0.55	50. Bénéfices mis en réserve
51. Staff costs	1.97	2.17	2.17	2.12	2.15	2.19	2.18	2.03	2.05	2.16	51. Frais de personnel
52. Provisions on loans	0.43	0.52	0.51	0.39	0.43	0.37	0.44	0.50	0.55	0.50	52. Provisions sur prêts
53. Provisions on securities	0.12	0.02	0.02	0.01	0.05	0.18	0.13	0.16	0.09	0.11	53. Provisions sur titres
% of gross income											**% du total du résultat brut**
54. Net interest income	70.70	72.83	70.82	68.49	68.12	72.02	72.42	74.26	73.53	73.85	54. Produits financiers nets
55. Non-interest income (net)	29.30	27.17	29.18	31.51	31.88	27.98	27.58	25.74	26.47	26.15	55. Produits non financiers (nets)
56. Operating expenses	62.26	68.94	69.06	67.16	62.72	70.10	67.42	64.02	62.80	63.95	56. Frais d'exploitation
57. Net income	37.74	31.06	30.94	32.84	37.28	29.90	32.58	35.98	37.20	36.05	57. Résultat net
58. Provisions (net)	18.40	14.12	13.16	12.52	12.18	11.12	12.41	11.49	11.69	10.51	58. Provisions (nettes)
59. Profit before tax	19.34	16.94	17.77	20.31	25.09	18.78	20.17	24.48	25.51	25.54	59. Bénéfices avant impôt
60. Income tax	11.85	9.37	8.66	9.81	11.40	7.50	8.72	8.78	8.81	9.16	60. Impôt
61. Profit after tax	7.50	7.57	9.11	10.50	13.69	11.28	11.45	15.70	16.70	16.38	61. Bénéfices après impôt
62. Staff costs	43.74	50.48	49.58	48.31	44.89	50.12	48.40	45.72	44.25	45.01	62. Frais de personnel
% of net income											**% du total du résultat net**
63. Provisions (net)	48.75	45.46	42.55	38.14	32.68	37.18	38.10	31.95	31.42	29.14	63. Provisions (nettes)
64. Profit before tax	51.25	54.54	57.45	61.86	67.32	62.82	61.90	68.05	68.58	70.86	64. Bénéfices avant impôt
65. Income tax	31.39	30.16	27.99	29.88	30.59	25.10	26.76	24.41	23.68	25.42	65. Impôt
66. Profit after tax	19.86	24.38	29.46	31.99	36.73	37.72	35.15	43.64	44.90	45.44	66. Bénéfices après impôt

ITALY

Commercial banks

ITALIE

Banques commerciales

Per cent — *Pourcentage*

BALANCE SHEET ANALYSIS — ANALYSE DU BILAN

% of year-end balance sheet total — **% du total du bilan en fin d'exercice**

	1982	1983	1984	1985	1986	1987	1988	1989	1990	1991 (2)	
Assets											**Actif**
67. Cash & balance with Central bank(1)	0.59	0.58	8.03	8.66	8.90	9.54	9.66	8.73	9.71	8.91	67. Caisse & solde auprès de la Banque centrale(1)
68. Interbank deposits (1)	13.44	13.67	11.94	11.45	11.43	10.33	9.18	9.27	6.88	6.64	68. Dépôts interbancaires (1)
69. Loans	24.48	25.14	26.58	27.39	27.68	29.30	31.99	32.18	37.50	38.65	69. Prêts
70. Securities	22.23	22.16	20.36	19.72	19.81	19.73	16.78	13.18	12.16	11.84	70. Valeurs mobilières
71. Other assets	39.26	38.44	33.09	32.79	32.18	31.09	32.40	36.63	33.75	33.96	71. Autres actifs
Liabilities											**Passif**
72. Capital & reserves	3.44	4.24	5.28	5.64	6.25	7.05	6.86	6.35	6.91	8.01	72. Capital et réserves
73. Borrowing from Central bank	0.46	1.05	0.32	1.00	0.43	0.50	0.44	0.37	0.44	0.61	73. Emprunts auprès de la Banque centrale
74. Interbank deposits	11.99	12.49	12.09	11.29	11.51	10.50	8.80	9.23	6.40	5.97	74. Dépôts interbancaires
75. Non-bank deposits	50.24	50.18	46.41	46.81	47.59	49.96	49.36	45.14	49.22	48.85	75. Dépôts non bancaires
76. Bonds	-	-	-	-	-	-	-	-	-	-	76. Obligations
77. Other liabilities	33.86	32.04	35.90	35.26	34.22	31.99	34.54	38.91	37.04	36.56	77. Autres engagements
Memoranda											*Pour mémoire*
78. Short-term securities	*7.95*	*6.18*	*4.84*	*2.66*	*3.02*	*2.52*	*2.06*	*1.61*	*1.83*	*1.72*	*78. Titres à court terme*
79. Bonds	*14.97*	*16.90*	*15.53*	*17.06*	*16.79*	*17.22*	*14.72*	*11.57*	*10.33*	*10.11*	*79. Obligations*
80. Shares and participations	*0.78*	*0.91*	*1.02*	*1.01*	*1.19*	*1.28*	*1.33*	*1.46*	*1.57*	*2.13*	*80. Actions et participations*
81. Claims on non-residents	*8.67*	*9.51*	*11.07*	*11.06*	*9.92*	*9.02*	*8.89*	*9.36*	*9.15*	*8.17*	*81. Créances sur des non résidents*
82. Liabilities to non-residents	*11.45*	*12.38*	*14.90*	*13.51*	*12.21*	*12.31*	*13.30*	*13.79*	*13.87*	*14.53*	*82. Engagements envers des non résidents*

1. Change in methodology.
2. In 1991, break in series due to mergers and acquisitions.

Notes

• Average balance sheet totals (item 29) are based on twelve end-month data.

Change in methodology:

• As from 1984, data relate to a larger number of banks.
• As from 1984, "Cash and balance with Central bank" (item 17 or item 67) also includes required reserves and "Interbank deposits" (item 18 or item 68) includes both domestic and foreign currency deposits.

1. Changement méthodologique.
2. En 1991, rupture de comparabilité dans les séries dûe aux fusions et acquisitions.

Notes

• La moyenne du total des actifs/passifs (poste 29) est basée sur douze données de fin de mois.

Changement méthodologique :

• Depuis 1984, les données se rapportent à un plus grand nombre de banques.
• A partir de 1984 le poste "Caisse et solde auprès de la Banque centrale" (poste 17 ou poste 67) comprend également les réserves obligatoires ; le poste "Dépôts interbancaires" (poste 18 ou poste 68) comprend à la fois les dépôts en monnaie nationale et ceux en devises.

ITALY

Large commercial banks

Billion lire

ITALIE

Grandes banques commerciales

Milliards de lires

	1982	1983	1984	1985	1986	1987	1988	1989	1990	1991
INCOME STATEMENT										
1. Interest income	25813	24150	24110	25687	23792	23308	24883	29897	33116	35245
2. Interest expenses	20248	18178	18080	19055	15811	15040	15495	19325	21192	22435
3. Net interest income	5565	5972	6030	6632	7981	8268	9388	10572	11924	12810
4. Non-interest income (net)	3097	2824	3184	4288	5032	4034	4909	4529	5142	5247
5. Gross income	8662	8796	9214	10920	13013	12302	14297	15101	17066	18057
6. Operating expenses	5880	6832	7149	7803	8628	9480	10028	10226	11241	12381
7. Net income	2782	1964	2065	3117	4385	2822	4269	4875	5825	5676
8. Provisions (net)	1693	1035	1046	1485	1547	1261	1986	1958	2230	1757
9. Profit before tax	1089	929	1019	1632	2838	1561	2283	2917	3595	3919
10. Income tax	365	658	553	862	1143	416	781	778	814	1205
11. Profit after tax	724	271	466	770	1695	1145	1502	2139	2781	2714
12. Distributed profit	..	109	173	188	344	395	412	392	467	524
13. Retained profit	..	162	293	582	1351	750	1090	1747	2314	2190
Memoranda										
14. Staff costs	*1986*	*5257*	*5384*	*5874*	*6460*	*7118*	*7570*	*7677*	*8203*	*9139*
15. Provisions on loans	*367*	*1129*	*1032*	*669*	*965*	*1076*	*1591*	*1844*	*2234*	*1847*
16. Provisions on securities	*12*	*20*	*46*	*73*	*147*	*436*	*367*	*684*	*289*	*466*
BALANCE SHEET										
Assets										
17. Cash & balance with Central bank(1)	694	1186	20292	24131	26633	28769	31095	33268	37171	36727
18. Interbank deposits (1)	8168	29442	24640	32260	31252	25940	29203	38681	21313	25593
19. Loans	25359	59501	68012	75346	80859	86691	102915	128029	151912	170742
20. Securities	50635	54535	54695	53817	59762	65913	55187	54737	47247	47865
21. Other assets	35533	121932	127559	132873	140814	128294	143357	208354	175816	189079
Liabilities										
22. Capital & reserves	2832	8423	11377	13498	16739	20577	21538	25250	27146	36802
23. Borrowing from Central bank	452	1886	849	5561	1877	2313	2348	1759	3028	5059
24. Interbank deposits	12616	33812	36772	35651	42584	40786	32922	52333	25949	27467
25. Non-bank deposits	46738	114052	112770	124480	137106	143589	153261	168383	184964	201227
26. Bonds	-	-	-	-	-	-	-	-	-	-
27. Other liabilities	57751	108423	133429	139237	141013	128341	151687	215345	192372	199452
Balance sheet total										
28. End-year total	120389	266596	295197	318427	339320	335607	361757	463069	433460	470007
29. Average total	98901	236973	234015	272465	289641	310944	338444	381329	410425	414279
Memoranda										
30. Short-term securities	*10705*	*19207*	*18036*	*9608*	*12297*	*8511*	*5321*	*4823*	*6808*	*9781*
31. Bonds	*15570*	*38153*	*36659*	*44208*	*47466*	*57402*	*49866*	*49915*	*40439*	*38084*
32. Shares and participations	*862*	*2826*	*3643*	*3448*	*4702*	*5117*	*5588*	*7788*	*7954*	*14204*
33. Claims on non-residents	*25558*	*36759*	*47071*	*49743*	*48751*	*44345*	*49213*	*65915*	*62337*	*59536*
34. Liabilities to non-residents	*30707*	*48430*	*58689*	*58254*	*54817*	*55731*	*67771*	*88417*	*86087*	*95574*
SUPPLEMENTARY INFORMATION										
35. Number of institutions	3	8	7	7	7	7	7	7	7	7
36. Number of branches	1250	3293	3187	3204	3230	3272	3276	3303	3665	4010
37. Number of employees (x 1000)	58.3	114.9	107.8	107.4	109.3	109.9	108.7	104.0	105.1	105.4

French labels (COMPTE DE RESULTATS / BILAN / RENSEIGNEMENTS COMPLEMENTAIRES):

COMPTE DE RESULTATS
1. Produits financiers
2. Frais financiers
3. Produits financiers nets
4. Produits non financiers (nets)
5. Résultat brut
6. Frais d'exploitation
7. Résultat net
8. Provisions (nettes)
9. Bénéfices avant impôt
10. Impôt
11. Bénéfices après impôt
12. Bénéfices distribués
13. Bénéfices mis en réserve

Pour mémoire
14. Frais de personnel
15. Provisions sur prêts
16. Provisions sur titres

BILAN
Actif
17. Caisse & solde auprès de la Banque centrale(1)
18. Dépôts interbancaires (1)
19. Prêts
20. Valeurs mobilières
21. Autres actifs

Passif
22. Capital et réserves
23. Emprunts auprès de la Banque centrale
24. Dépôts interbancaires
25. Dépôts non bancaires
26. Obligations
27. Autres engagements

Total du bilan
28. En fin d'exercice
29. Moyen

Pour mémoire
30. Titres à court terme
31. Obligations
32. Actions et participations
33. Créances sur des non résidents
34. Engagements envers des non résidents

RENSEIGNEMENTS COMPLEMENTAIRES
35. Nombre d'institutions
36. Nombre de succursales
37. Nombre de salariés (x 1000)

ITALY

Large commercial banks

ITALIE

Grandes banques commerciales

Per cent / *Pourcentage*

INCOME STATEMENT ANALYSIS / **ANALYSE DU COMPTE DE RESULTATS**

		1982	1983	1984	1985	1986	1987	1988	1989	1990	1991		
	% of average balance sheet total												**% du total moyen du bilan**
38.	Interest income	26.10	10.19	10.30	9.43	8.21	7.50	7.35	7.84	8.07	8.51	38.	Produits financiers
39.	Interest expenses	20.47	7.67	7.73	6.99	5.46	4.84	4.58	5.07	5.16	5.42	39.	Frais financiers
40.	Net interest income	5.63	2.52	2.58	2.43	2.76	2.66	2.77	2.77	2.91	3.09	40.	Produits financiers nets
41.	Non-interest income (net)	3.13	1.19	1.36	1.57	1.74	1.30	1.45	1.19	1.25	1.27	41.	Produits non financiers (nets)
42.	Gross income	8.76	3.71	3.94	4.01	4.49	3.96	4.22	3.96	4.16	4.36	42.	Résultat brut
43.	Operating expenses	5.95	2.88	3.05	2.86	2.98	3.05	2.96	2.68	2.74	2.99	43.	Frais d'exploitation
44.	Net income	2.81	0.83	0.88	1.14	1.51	0.91	1.26	1.28	1.42	1.37	44.	Résultat net
45.	Provisions (net)	1.71	0.44	0.45	0.55	0.53	0.41	0.59	0.51	0.54	0.42	45.	Provisions (nettes)
46.	Profit before tax	1.10	0.39	0.44	0.60	0.98	0.50	0.67	0.76	0.88	0.95	46.	Bénéfices avant impôt
47.	Income tax	0.37	0.28	0.24	0.32	0.39	0.13	0.23	0.20	0.20	0.29	47.	Impôt
48.	Profit after tax	0.73	0.11	0.20	0.28	0.59	0.37	0.44	0.56	0.68	0.66	48.	Bénéfices après impôt
49.	Distributed profit	..	0.05	0.07	0.07	0.12	0.13	0.12	0.10	0.11	0.13	49.	Bénéfices distribués
50.	Retained profit	..	0.07	0.13	0.21	0.47	0.24	0.32	0.46	0.56	0.53	50.	Bénéfices mis en réserve
51.	Staff costs	2.01	2.22	2.30	2.16	2.23	2.29	2.24	2.01	2.00	2.21	51.	Frais de personnel
52.	Provisions on loans	0.37	0.48	0.44	0.25	0.33	0.35	0.47	0.48	0.54	0.45	52.	Provisions sur prêts
53.	Provisions on securities	0.01	0.01	0.02	0.03	0.05	0.14	0.11	0.18	0.07	0.11	53.	Provisions sur titres
	% of gross income												**% du total du résultat brut**
54.	Net interest income	64.25	67.89	65.44	60.73	61.33	67.21	65.66	70.01	69.87	70.94	54.	Produits financiers nets
55.	Non-interest income (net)	35.75	32.11	34.56	39.27	38.67	32.79	34.34	29.99	30.13	29.06	55.	Produits non financiers (nets)
56.	Operating expenses	67.88	77.67	77.59	71.46	66.30	77.06	70.14	67.72	65.87	68.57	56.	Frais d'exploitation
57.	Net income	32.12	22.33	22.41	28.54	33.70	22.94	29.86	32.28	34.13	31.43	57.	Résultat net
58.	Provisions (net)	19.55	11.77	11.35	13.60	11.89	10.25	13.89	12.97	13.07	9.73	58.	Provisions (nettes)
59.	Profit before tax	12.57	10.56	11.06	14.95	21.81	12.69	15.97	19.32	21.07	21.70	59.	Bénéfices avant impôt
60.	Income tax	4.21	7.48	6.00	7.89	8.78	3.38	5.46	5.15	4.77	6.67	60.	Impôt
61.	Profit after tax	8.36	3.08	5.06	7.05	13.03	9.31	10.51	14.16	16.30	15.03	61.	Bénéfices après impôt
62.	Staff costs	22.93	59.77	58.43	53.79	49.64	57.86	52.95	50.84	48.07	50.61	62.	Frais de personnel
	% of net income												**% du total du résultat net**
63.	Provisions (net)	60.86	52.70	50.65	47.64	35.28	44.68	46.52	40.16	38.28	30.95	63.	Provisions (nettes)
64.	Profit before tax	39.14	47.30	49.35	52.36	64.72	55.32	53.48	59.84	61.72	69.05	64.	Bénéfices avant impôt
65.	Income tax	13.12	33.50	26.78	27.65	26.07	14.74	18.29	15.96	13.97	21.23	65.	Impôt
66.	Profit after tax	26.02	13.80	22.57	24.70	38.65	40.57	35.18	43.88	47.74	47.82	66.	Bénéfices après impôt

ITALY

Large commercial banks

Per cent

BALANCE SHEET ANALYSIS

% of year-end balance sheet total

	1982	1983	1984	1985	1986	1987	1988	1989	1990	1991
Assets										
67. Cash & balance with Central bank(1)	0.58	0.44	6.87	7.58	7.85	8.57	8.60	7.18	8.58	7.81
68. Interbank deposits (1)	6.78	11.04	8.35	10.13	9.21	7.73	8.07	8.35	4.92	5.45
69. Loans	21.06	22.32	23.04	23.66	23.83	25.83	28.45	27.65	35.05	36.33
70. Securities	42.06	20.46	18.53	16.90	17.61	19.64	15.26	11.82	10.90	10.18
71. Other assets	29.52	45.74	43.21	41.73	41.50	38.23	39.63	44.99	40.56	40.23
Liabilities										
72. Capital & reserves	2.35	3.16	3.85	4.24	4.93	6.13	5.95	5.45	6.26	7.83
73. Borrowing from Central bank	0.38	0.71	0.29	1.75	0.55	0.69	0.65	0.38	0.70	1.08
74. Interbank deposits	10.48	12.68	12.46	11.20	12.55	12.15	9.10	11.30	5.99	5.84
75. Non-bank deposits	38.82	42.78	38.20	39.09	40.41	42.78	42.37	36.36	42.67	42.81
76. Bonds	-	-	-	-	-	-	-	-	-	-
77. Other liabilities	47.97	40.67	45.20	43.73	41.56	38.24	41.93	46.50	44.38	42.44
Memoranda										
78. Short-term securities	*8.89*	*7.20*	*6.11*	*3.02*	*3.62*	*2.54*	*1.47*	*1.04*	*1.57*	*2.08*
79. Bonds	*12.93*	*14.31*	*12.42*	*13.88*	*13.99*	*17.10*	*13.78*	*10.78*	*9.33*	*8.10*
80. Shares and participations	*0.72*	*1.06*	*1.23*	*1.08*	*1.39*	*1.52*	*1.54*	*1.68*	*1.84*	*3.02*
81. Claims on non-residents	*21.23*	*13.79*	*15.95*	*15.62*	*14.37*	*13.21*	*13.60*	*14.23*	*14.38*	*12.67*
82. Liabilities to non-residents	*25.51*	*18.17*	*19.88*	*18.29*	*16.15*	*16.61*	*18.73*	*19.09*	*19.86*	*20.33*

1. Change in methodology.

Notes

- Large commercial banks are a sub-group of Commercial banks.

- Average balance sheet totals (item 29) are based on twelve end-month data.

Change in methodology:

- The number of banks included in the series was increased, in 1983, from three to eight, and lowered to seven as from 1984.

- As from 1984, "Cash and balance with Central bank" (item 17 or item 67) also includes required reserves and "Interbank deposits" (item 18 or item 68) includes both domestic and foreign currency deposits.

ITALIE

Grandes banques commerciales

Pourcentage

ANALYSE DU BILAN

% du total du bilan en fin d'exercice

Actif
67. Caisse & solde auprès de la Banque centrale(1)
68. Dépôts interbancaires (1)
69. Prêts
70. Valeurs mobilières
71. Autres actifs

Passif
72. Capital et réserves
73. Emprunts auprès de la Banque centrale
74. Dépôts interbancaires
75. Dépôts non bancaires
76. Obligations
77. Autres engagements

Pour mémoire
78. Titres à court terme
79. Obligations
80. Actions et participations
81. Créances sur des non résidents
82. Engagements envers des non résidents

1. Changement méthodologique.

Notes

- Les Grandes banques commerciales sont un sous-groupe des Banques commerciales.

- La moyenne du total des actifs/passifs (poste 29) est basée sur douze données de fin de mois.

Changement méthodologique :

- Le nombre de banques reprises dans les données est passé, en 1983, de trois à huit, puis revenu à sept depuis 1984.

- A partir de 1984 le poste "Caisse et solde auprès de la Banque centrale" (poste 17 ou poste 67) comprend également les réserves obligatoires ; le poste "Dépôts interbancaires" (poste 18 ou poste 68) comprend à la fois les dépôts en monnaie nationale et ceux en devises.

ITALY

Savings banks

Billion lire

ITALIE

Caisses d'épargne

Milliards de lires

	1982	1983	1984	1985	1986	1987	1988	1989	1990	1991 (2)	
INCOME STATEMENT											**COMPTE DE RESULTATS**
1. Interest income	15563	18680	20839	22214	21801	20000	22173	25694	28610	29254	1. Produits financiers
2. Interest expenses	11377	13215	14453	15082	13318	11342	12364	14551	16126	16476	2. Frais financiers
3. Net interest income	4186	5465	6386	7132	8483	8658	9809	11143	12484	12778	3. Produits financiers nets
4. Non-interest income (net)	2171	1885	2242	2219	2833	3043	3060	3562	4043	4554	4. Produits non financiers (nets)
5. Gross income	6357	7350	8628	9351	11316	11701	12869	14705	16527	17332	5. Résultat brut
6. Operating expenses	3756	4934	5410	5890	6575	7186	7680	8045	9199	10151	6. Frais d'exploitation
7. Net income	2601	2416	3218	3461	4741	4515	5189	6660	7328	7181	7. Résultat net
8. Provisions (net)	1664	1469	1865	1692	1930	2203	2479	2048	2145	1700	8. Provisions (nettes)
9. Profit before tax	937	947	1353	1769	2811	2312	2710	4612	5183	5481	9. Bénéfices avant impôt
10. Income tax	752	702	946	1109	1644	1430	1685	1956	2123	2008	10. Impôt
11. Profit after tax	185	245	407	660	1167	882	1025	2656	3060	3473	11. Bénéfices après impôt
12. Distributed profit	..	..	-	3	4	5	12	38	52	174	12. Bénéfices distribués
13. Retained profit	..	245	407	657	1163	877	1013	2618	3008	3299	13. Bénéfices mis en réserve
Memoranda											*Pour mémoire*
14. Staff costs	2708	3630	3882	4180	4678	5160	5436	5721	6479	7229	14. Frais de personnel
15. Provisions on loans	639	1193	1296	1298	1174	1420	1493	1838	1843	1830	15. Provisions sur prêts
16. Provisions on securities	395	185	99	54	53	507	464	355	323	125	16. Provisions sur titres
BALANCE SHEET											**BILAN**
Assets											**Actif**
17. Cash & balance with Central bank(1)	870	998	16919	20511	22823	24423	27910	30643	36528	37148	17. Caisse & solde auprès de la Banque centrale(1)
18. Interbank deposits (1)	15687	17137	21144	19796	23044	23251	21810	24767	24378	24621	18. Dépôts interbancaires (1)
19. Loans	35815	41535	51260	59171	65289	69548	82932	101312	117735	133947	19. Prêts
20. Securities	39691	48528	51356	57643	59659	60653	62197	62109	61272	55384	20. Valeurs mobilières
21. Other assets	39953	50906	41540	50972	58367	65862	80170	106053	105763	116706	21. Autres actifs
Liabilities											**Passif**
22. Capital & reserves	3916	6178	9416	11493	13666	16715	19151	22554	25125	35142	22. Capital et réserves
23. Borrowing from Central bank	383	388	466	403	407	1517	1679	2162	2370	1430	23. Emprunts auprès de la Banque centrale
24. Interbank deposits	5089	7626	7988	9889	10374	13427	14260	15708	17488	15469	24. Dépôts interbancaires
25. Non-bank deposits	93246	106452	116877	128411	140308	145804	162219	175583	194949	201689	25. Dépôts non bancaires
26. Bonds	-	-	-	-	-	-	-	-	-	-	26. Obligations
27. Other liabilities	29382	38460	47492	57897	64426	66275	77711	108876	105745	114077	27. Autres engagements
Balance sheet total											**Total du bilan**
28. End-year total	132016	159104	182219	208094	229181	243737	275019	324883	345677	367807	28. En fin d'exercice
29. Average total	118605	142674	165252	190549	209841	228879	260424	289849	320819	322014	29. Moyen
Memoranda											*Pour mémoire*
30. Short-term securities	12571	11141	9544	5605	6502	4842	5004	4442	7366	7668	30. Titres à court terme
31. Bonds	28445	39057	41812	52038	53157	55811	57194	57667	53906	47716	31. Obligations
32. Shares and participations	1333	1678	1943	2217	2565	2903	3365	4767	5421	8091	32. Actions et participations
33. Claims on non-residents	1102	1946	2624	3550	4071	5275	6941	8179	9812	12731	33. Créances sur des non résidents
34. Liabilities to non-residents	3090	4583	5915	6729	8326	10412	13090	16137	18964	24163	34. Engagements envers des non résidents
SUPPLEMENTARY INFORMATION											**RENSEIGNEMENTS COMPLEMENTAIRES**
35. Number of institutions	85	85	83	83	83	79	79	78	78	76	35. Nombre d'institutions
36. Number of branches	4052	4074	4466	4481	4483	4391	4508	4535	4765	4958	36. Nombre de succursales
37. Number of employees (x 1000)	68.2	69.2	70.3	71.0	72.2	70.9	75.1	77.5	80.0	80.5	37. Nombre de salariés (x 1000)

Savings banks

Caisses d'épargne

Per cent / *Pourcentage*

INCOME STATEMENT ANALYSIS / ANALYSE DU COMPTE DE RESULTATS

No.	Item	1982	1983	1984	1985	1986	1987	1988	1989	1990	1991 (2)		Libellé
	% of average balance sheet total												**% du total moyen du bilan**
38.	Interest income	13.12	13.09	12.61	11.66	10.39	8.74	8.51	8.86	8.92	9.08	38.	Produits financiers
39.	Interest expenses	9.59	9.26	8.75	7.92	6.35	4.96	4.75	5.02	5.03	5.12	39.	Frais financiers
40.	Net interest income	3.53	3.83	3.86	3.74	4.04	3.78	3.77	3.84	3.89	3.97	40.	Produits financiers nets
41.	Non-interest income (net)	1.83	1.32	1.36	1.16	1.35	1.33	1.18	1.23	1.26	1.41	41.	Produits non financiers (nets)
42.	Gross income	5.36	5.15	5.22	4.91	5.39	5.11	4.94	5.07	5.15	5.38	42.	Résultat brut
43.	Operating expenses	3.17	3.46	3.27	3.09	3.13	3.14	2.95	2.78	2.87	3.15	43.	Frais d'exploitation
44.	Net income	2.19	1.69	1.95	1.82	2.26	1.97	1.99	2.30	2.28	2.23	44.	Résultat net
45.	Provisions (net)	1.40	1.03	1.13	0.89	0.92	0.96	0.95	0.71	0.67	0.53	45.	Provisions (nettes)
46.	Profit before tax	0.79	0.66	0.82	0.93	1.34	1.01	1.04	1.59	1.62	1.70	46.	Bénéfices avant impôt
47.	Income tax	0.63	0.49	0.57	0.58	0.78	0.62	0.65	0.67	0.66	0.62	47.	Impôt
48.	Profit after tax	0.16	0.17	0.25	0.35	0.56	0.39	0.39	0.92	0.95	1.08	48.	Bénéfices après impôt
49.	Distributed profit	..	..	-	0.00	0.00	0.00	0.00	0.01	0.02	0.05	49.	Bénéfices distribués
50.	Retained profit	..	0.17	0.25	0.34	0.55	0.38	0.39	0.90	0.94	1.02	50.	Bénéfices mis en réserve
51.	Staff costs	2.28	2.54	2.35	2.19	2.23	2.25	2.09	1.97	2.02	2.24	51.	Frais de personnel
52.	Provisions on loans	0.54	0.84	0.78	0.68	0.56	0.62	0.57	0.63	0.57	0.57	52.	Provisions sur prêts
53.	Provisions on securities	0.33	0.13	0.06	0.03	0.03	0.22	0.18	0.12	0.10	0.04	53.	Provisions sur titres
	% of gross income												**% du total du résultat brut**
54.	Net interest income	65.85	74.35	74.01	76.27	74.96	73.99	76.22	75.78	75.54	73.72	54.	Produits financiers nets
55.	Non-interest income (net)	34.15	25.65	25.99	23.73	25.04	26.01	23.78	24.22	24.46	26.28	55.	Produits non financiers (nets)
56.	Operating expenses	59.08	67.13	62.70	62.99	58.10	61.41	59.68	54.71	55.66	58.57	56.	Frais d'exploitation
57.	Net income	40.92	32.87	37.30	37.01	41.90	38.59	40.32	45.29	44.34	41.43	57.	Résultat net
58.	Provisions (net)	26.18	19.99	21.62	18.09	17.06	18.83	19.26	13.93	12.98	9.81	58.	Provisions (nettes)
59.	Profit before tax	14.74	12.88	15.68	18.92	24.84	19.76	21.06	31.36	31.62	31.62	59.	Bénéfices avant impôt
60.	Income tax	11.83	9.55	10.96	11.86	14.53	12.22	13.09	13.30	12.85	11.59	60.	Impôt
61.	Profit after tax	2.91	3.33	4.72	7.06	10.31	7.54	7.96	18.06	18.52	20.04	61.	Bénéfices après impôt
62.	Staff costs	42.60	49.39	44.99	44.70	41.34	44.10	42.24	38.91	39.20	41.71	62.	Frais de personnel
	% of net income												**% du total du résultat net**
63.	Provisions (net)	63.98	60.80	57.96	48.89	40.71	48.79	47.77	30.75	29.27	23.67	63.	Provisions (nettes)
64.	Profit before tax	36.02	39.20	42.04	51.11	59.29	51.21	52.23	69.25	70.73	76.33	64.	Bénéfices avant impôt
65.	Income tax	28.91	29.06	29.40	32.04	34.68	31.67	32.47	29.37	28.97	27.96	65.	Impôt
66.	Profit after tax	7.11	10.14	12.65	19.07	24.62	19.53	19.75	39.88	41.76	48.36	66.	Bénéfices après impôt

ITALY

Savings banks

Per cent

BALANCE SHEET ANALYSIS

% of year-end balance sheet total

	1982	1983	1984	1985	1986	1987	1988	1989	1990	1991 (2)
Assets										
67. Cash & balance with Central bank(1)	0.66	0.63	9.28	9.86	9.96	10.02	10.15	9.43	10.57	10.10
68. Interbank deposits (1)	11.88	10.77	11.60	9.51	10.05	9.54	7.93	7.62	7.05	6.69
69. Loans	27.13	26.11	28.13	28.43	28.49	28.53	30.16	31.18	34.06	36.42
70. Securities	30.07	30.50	28.18	27.70	26.03	24.88	22.62	19.12	17.73	15.06
71. Other assets	30.26	32.00	22.80	24.49	25.47	27.02	29.15	32.64	30.60	31.73
Liabilities										
72. Capital & reserves	2.97	3.88	5.17	5.52	5.96	6.86	6.96	6.94	7.27	9.55
73. Borrowing from Central bank	0.29	0.24	0.26	0.19	0.18	0.62	0.61	0.67	0.69	0.39
74. Interbank deposits	3.85	4.79	4.37	4.75	4.53	5.51	5.19	4.83	5.06	4.21
75. Non-bank deposits	70.63	66.91	64.14	61.71	61.22	59.82	58.98	54.04	56.40	54.84
76. Bonds	-	-	-	-	-	-	-	-	-	-
77. Other liabilities	22.26	24.17	26.06	27.82	28.11	27.19	28.26	33.51	30.59	31.02
Memoranda										
78. *Short-term securities*	*9.52*	*7.00*	*5.24*	*2.69*	*2.84*	*1.99*	*1.82*	*1.37*	*2.13*	*2.08*
79. *Bonds*	*21.55*	*24.55*	*22.95*	*25.01*	*23.19*	*22.90*	*20.80*	*17.75*	*15.59*	*12.97*
80. *Shares and participations*	*1.01*	*1.05*	*1.07*	*1.07*	*1.12*	*1.19*	*1.22*	*1.47*	*1.57*	*2.20*
81. *Claims on non-residents*	*0.83*	*1.22*	*1.44*	*1.71*	*1.78*	*2.16*	*2.52*	*2.52*	*2.84*	*3.46*
82. *Liabilities to non-residents*	*2.34*	*2.88*	*3.25*	*3.23*	*3.63*	*4.27*	*4.76*	*4.97*	*5.49*	*6.57*

1. Change in methodology.
2. In 1991, break in series due to mergers and acquisitions.

Notes

- Average balance sheet totals (item 29) are based on twelve end-month data.

Change in methodology:

- As from 1984, "Cash and balance with Central bank" (item 17 or item 67) also includes required reserves and "Interbank deposits" (item 18 or item 68) includes both domestic and foreign currency deposits.

ITALIE

Caisses d'épargne

Pourcentage

ANALYSE DU BILAN

% du total du bilan en fin d'exercice

Actif
67. Caisse & solde auprès de la Banque centrale(1)
68. Dépôts interbancaires (1)
69. Prêts
70. Valeurs mobilières
71. Autres actifs

Passif
72. Capital et réserves
73. Emprunts auprès de la Banque centrale
74. Dépôts interbancaires
75. Dépôts non bancaires
76. Obligations
77. Autres engagements

Pour mémoire
78. *Titres à court terme*
79. *Obligations*
80. *Actions et participations*
81. *Créances sur des non résidents*
82. *Engagements envers des non résidents*

1. Changement méthodologique.
2. En 1991, rupture de comparabilité dans les séries dûe aux fusions et acquisitions.

Notes

- La moyenne du total des actifs/passifs (poste 29) est basée sur douze données de fin de mois.

Changement méthodologique :

- A partir de 1984 le poste "Caisse et solde auprès de la Banque centrale" (poste 17 ou poste 67) comprend également les réserves obligatoires ; le poste "Dépôts interbancaires" (poste 18 ou poste 68) comprend à la fois les dépôts en monnaie nationale et ceux en devises.

JAPAN — Commercial banks
JAPON — Banques commerciales

100 million Japanese yen / 100 millions de yen japonais

			1982	1983	1984	1985	1986	1987	1988	1989	1990	1991
INCOME STATEMENT	**COMPTE DE RESULTATS**											
1.	Interest income	Produits financiers	194569	191308	226645	212785	205504	225242	281848	388258	481476	462453
2.	Interest expenses	Frais financiers	150656	144755	179559	166626	152514	168596	211888	318008	413323	379443
3.	Net interest income	Produits financiers nets	43913	46553	47086	46159	52990	56646	69960	70250	68153	83010
4.	Non-interest income (net)	Produits non financiers (nets)	7113	8010	10113	12311	12888	18998	24369	21992	21663	10197
5.	Gross income	Résultat brut	51026	54563	57199	58470	65978	75644	94329	92242	89816	93207
6.	Operating expenses	Frais d'exploitation	35263	36804	38943	40353	42516	45629	52811	56619	60639	64193
7.	Net income	Résultat net	15763	17759	18256	18117	23462	30015	41518	35623	29177	29014
8.	Provisions (net)	Provisions (nettes)	1698	1184	1295	723	1596	1631	3147	3101	2125	5335
9.	Profit before tax	Bénéfices avant impôt	14065	16575	16961	17394	21866	28384	38371	32522	27052	23679
10.	Income tax	Impôt	8192	9100	9363	9209	11770	15625	20235	15521	12743	12628
11.	Profit after tax	Bénéfices après impôt	5873	7475	7598	8185	10096	12759	18136	17001	14309	11051
12.	Distributed profit	Bénéfices distribués	1801	1916	2018	2089	2274	2337	1493	1638	1694	1697
13.	Retained profit	Bénéfices mis en réserve	4072	5559	5580	6096	7822	10422	16643	15363	12615	9354
Memoranda	*Pour mémoire*											
14.	Staff costs	Frais de personnel	20927	21583	22421	23032	23600	23774	29558	30796	32255	33713
15.	Provisions on loans	Provisions sur prêts	1614	1064	1182	494	1085	1320	2851	2937	2009	5480
16.	Provisions on securities	Provisions sur titres	84	120	113	229	511	311	296	164	116	-145
BALANCE SHEET	**BILAN**											
Assets	*Actif*											
17.	Cash & balance with Central bank(1)	Caisse & solde auprès de la Banque centrale(1)	487278	541687	635772	594525	724358	820228	994636	1232259	1010134	845110
18.	Interbank deposits	Dépôts interbancaires	378563	401326	447676	474340	581051	648140	835621	1014487	1022177	978035
19.	Loans	Prêts	1595073	1764333	2022864	2175910	2456586	2783332	3537651	4098926	4330109	4484647
20.	Securities	Valeurs mobilières	..	..	..	..	..	..	..	..	..	..
21.	Other assets	Autres actifs	498326	524120	580352	657274	674373	758522	1037496	1287869	1170455	1138940
Liabilities	*Passif*											
22.	Capital & reserves	Capital et réserves	69261	75675	82498	91335	101614	124197	175958	226715	239712	249044
23.	Borrowing from Central bank	Emprunts auprès de la Banque centrale	15735	22922	13588	26192	40878	47166	46336	33141	35555	30535
24.	Interbank deposits (2)	Dépôts interbancaires (2)	2280431	2511214	2865314	2959597	3361047	3797408	4906164	5808225	5736884	5554169
25.	Non-bank deposits	Dépôts non bancaires	18999	21460	22900	30934	33266	44854	57657	58214	55069	56237
26.	Bonds	Obligations	..	..	..	..	..	..	..	..	..	..
27.	Other liabilities	Autres engagements	574814	600195	702364	793991	899563	996597	1219289	1507246	1465655	1556746
Balance sheet total	*Total du bilan*											
28.	End-year total	En fin d'exercice	2959240	3231466	3686664	3902049	4436368	5010222	6405404	7633541	7532875	7446732
29.	Average total	Moyen	2836796	3095353	3459065	3794356	4169208	4723295	5971836	7019472	7583208	7489804
Memoranda	*Pour mémoire*											
30.	Short-term securities	Titres à court terme	..	..	..	..	..	..	..	..	..	..
31.	Bonds	Obligations	..	..	..	..	..	..	..	..	..	..
32.	Shares and participations	Actions et participations	60914	67159	76365	84597	94218	122050	173678	219140	247808	258658
33.	Claims on non-residents	Créances sur des non résidents	..	..	..	..	..	..	..	..	..	..
34.	Liabilities to non-residents	Engagements envers des non résidents	..	..	..	..	..	..	..	..	..	..
SUPPLEMENTARY INFORMATION	**RENSEIGNEMENTS COMPLEMENTAIRES**											
35.	Number of institutions	Nombre d'institutions	76	76	77	77	77	77	145	145	144	143
36.	Number of branches	Nombre de succursales	8399	8550	8899	9037	9251	9355	13727	14045	14325	14632
37.	Number of employees (x 1000)	Nombre de salariés (x 1000)	343	337	333	325	320	314	397	397	399	406

JAPAN

Commercial banks

Per cent

INCOME STATEMENT ANALYSIS

JAPON

Banques commerciales

Pourcentage

ANALYSE DU COMPTE DE RESULTATS

	1982	1983	1984	1985	1986	1987	1988	1989	1990	1991	
% of average balance sheet total											**% du total moyen du bilan**
38. Interest income	6.86	6.18	6.55	5.61	4.93	4.77	4.72	5.53	6.35	6.17	38. Produits financiers
39. Interest expenses	5.31	4.68	5.19	4.39	3.66	3.57	3.55	4.53	5.45	5.07	39. Frais financiers
40. Net interest income	1.55	1.50	1.36	1.22	1.27	1.20	1.17	1.00	0.90	1.11	40. Produits financiers nets
41. Non-interest income (net)	0.25	0.26	0.29	0.32	0.31	0.40	0.41	0.31	0.29	0.14	41. Produits non financiers (nets)
42. Gross income	1.80	1.76	1.65	1.54	1.58	1.60	1.58	1.31	1.18	1.24	42. Résultat brut
43. Operating expenses	1.24	1.19	1.13	1.06	1.02	0.97	0.88	0.81	0.80	0.86	43. Frais d'exploitation
44. Net income	0.56	0.57	0.53	0.48	0.56	0.64	0.70	0.51	0.38	0.39	44. Résultat net
45. Provisions (net)	0.06	0.04	0.04	0.02	0.04	0.03	0.05	0.04	0.03	0.07	45. Provisions (nettes)
46. Profit before tax	0.50	0.54	0.49	0.46	0.52	0.60	0.64	0.46	0.36	0.32	46. Bénéfices avant impôt
47. Income tax	0.29	0.29	0.27	0.24	0.28	0.33	0.34	0.22	0.17	0.17	47. Impôt
48. Profit after tax	0.21	0.24	0.22	0.22	0.24	0.27	0.30	0.24	0.19	0.15	48. Bénéfices après impôt
49. Distributed profit	0.06	0.06	0.06	0.06	0.05	0.05	0.03	0.02	0.02	0.02	49. Bénéfices distribués
50. Retained profit	0.14	0.18	0.16	0.16	0.19	0.22	0.28	0.22	0.17	0.12	50. Bénéfices mis en réserve
51. Staff costs	0.74	0.70	0.65	0.61	0.57	0.50	0.49	0.44	0.43	0.45	51. Frais de personnel
52. Provisions on loans	0.06	0.03	0.03	0.01	0.03	0.03	0.05	0.04	0.03	0.07	52. Provisions sur prêts
53. Provisions on securities	0.00	0.00	0.00	0.01	0.01	0.01	0.00	0.00	0.00	0.00	53. Provisions sur titres
% of gross income											**% du total du résultat brut**
54. Net interest income	86.06	85.32	82.32	78.94	80.31	74.88	74.17	76.16	75.88	89.06	54. Produits financiers nets
55. Non-interest income (net)	13.94	14.68	17.68	21.06	19.69	25.12	25.83	23.84	24.12	10.94	55. Produits non financiers (nets)
56. Operating expenses	69.11	67.45	68.08	69.01	64.44	60.32	55.99	61.38	67.51	68.87	56. Frais d'exploitation
57. Net income	30.89	32.55	31.92	30.99	35.56	39.68	44.01	38.62	32.49	31.13	57. Résultat net
58. Provisions (net)	3.33	2.17	2.26	1.24	2.42	2.16	3.34	3.36	2.37	5.72	58. Provisions (nettes)
59. Profit before tax	27.56	30.38	29.65	29.75	33.14	37.52	40.68	35.26	30.12	25.40	59. Bénéfices avant impôt
60. Income tax	16.05	16.68	16.37	15.75	17.84	20.66	21.45	16.83	14.19	13.55	60. Impôt
61. Profit after tax	11.51	13.70	13.28	14.00	15.30	16.87	19.23	18.43	15.93	11.86	61. Bénéfices après impôt
62. Staff costs	41.01	39.56	39.20	39.39	35.77	31.43	31.34	33.39	35.91	36.17	62. Frais de personnel
% of net income											**% du total du résultat net**
63. Provisions (net)	10.77	6.67	7.09	3.99	6.80	5.43	7.58	8.71	7.28	18.39	63. Provisions (nettes)
64. Profit before tax	89.23	93.33	92.91	96.01	93.20	94.57	92.42	91.29	92.72	81.61	64. Bénéfices avant impôt
65. Income tax	51.97	51.24	51.29	50.83	50.17	52.06	48.74	43.57	43.67	43.52	65. Impôt
66. Profit after tax	37.26	42.09	41.62	45.18	43.03	42.51	43.68	47.72	49.04	38.09	66. Bénéfices après impôt

JAPAN

Commercial banks

Per cent

BALANCE SHEET ANALYSIS

% of year-end balance sheet total

		1982	1983	1984	1985	1986	1987	1988	1989	1990	1991
Assets											
67.	Cash & balance with Central bank (1)	..	..	..	..	..	..	..	..	..	..
68.	Interbank deposits	16.47	16.76	17.25	15.24	16.33	16.37	15.53	16.14	13.41	11.35
69.	Loans	53.90	54.60	54.87	55.76	55.37	55.55	55.23	53.70	57.48	60.22
70.	Securities	12.79	12.42	12.14	12.16	13.10	12.94	13.05	13.29	13.57	13.13
71.	Other assets	16.84	16.22	15.74	16.84	15.20	15.14	16.20	16.87	15.54	15.29
Liabilities											
72.	Capital & reserves	2.34	2.34	2.24	2.34	2.29	2.48	2.75	2.97	3.18	3.34
73.	Borrowing from Central bank	0.53	0.71	0.37	0.67	0.92	0.94	0.72	0.43	0.47	0.41
74.	Interbank deposits (2)	..	..	..	..	..	..	..	..	..	..
75.	Non-bank deposits	77.06	77.71	77.72	75.85	75.76	75.79	76.59	76.09	76.16	74.59
76.	Bonds	0.64	0.66	0.62	0.79	0.75	0.90	0.90	0.76	0.73	0.76
77.	Other liabilities	19.42	18.57	19.05	20.35	20.28	19.89	19.04	19.75	19.46	20.91
Memoranda											
78.	Short-term securities	..	..	..	..	..	..	..	..	..	..
79.	Bonds	..	..	..	..	..	..	..	..	..	..
80.	Shares and participations	2.06	2.08	2.07	2.17	2.12	2.44	2.71	2.87	3.29	3.47
81.	Claims on non-residents	..	..	..	..	..	..	..	..	..	..
82.	Liabilities to non-residents	..	..	..	..	..	..	..	..	..	..

Notes

- Data relate to fiscal years ending 31st March.

Change in methodology

- As from 1988, data also include Sogo banks (banks for medium- and small-size industries).

1. Included under "Interbank deposits" (item 18 or item 68).
2. Included under "Non-bank deposits" (item 25 or item 75).

JAPON

Banques commerciales

Pourcentage

ANALYSE DU BILAN

% du total du bilan en fin d'exercice

Actif
67. Caisse & solde auprès de la Banque centrale(1)
68. Dépôts interbancaires
69. Prêts
70. Valeurs mobilières
71. Autres actifs

Passif
72. Capital et réserves
73. Emprunts auprès de la Banque centrale
74. Dépôts interbancaires (2)
75. Dépôts non bancaires
76. Obligations
77. Autres engagements

Pour mémoire
78. Titres à court terme
79. Obligations
80. Actions et participations
81. Créances sur des non résidents
82. Engagements envers des non résidents

Notes

- Les données portent sur l'exercice financier, qui se termine le 31 mars.

Changement méthodologique

- Depuis 1988, sont aussi reprises dans les données des Sogo Banks (les banques pour les petites et moyennes entreprises).

1. Inclus sous "Dépôts interbancaires" (poste 18 ou poste 68).
2. Inclus sous "Dépôts non bancaires" (poste 25 ou poste 75).

JAPAN / JAPON

Large commercial banks / Grandes banques commerciales

100 million Japanese yen / 100 millions de yen japonais

INCOME STATEMENT / COMPTE DE RESULTATS

No.	Item (EN)	Item (FR)	1982	1983	1984	1985	1986	1987	1988	1989	1990	1991
1.	Interest income	Produits financiers	142794	136601	167142	150656	144688	163562	204088	270559	323647	298368
2.	Interest expenses	Frais financiers	118084	110370	140820	125425	114577	130371	167313	238474	293346	257605
3.	Net interest income	Produits financiers nets	24710	26231	26322	25231	30111	33191	36775	32085	30301	40763
4.	Non-interest income (net)	Produits non financiers (nets)	5838	6132	7759	9140	9787	15787	24566	19003	17000	9026
5.	Gross income	Résultat brut	30548	32363	34081	34371	39898	48978	61341	51088	47301	49789
6.	Operating expenses	Frais d'exploitation	20190	20941	21973	22554	24074	26620	28559	27233	29367	31018
7.	Net income	Résultat net	10358	11422	12108	11817	15824	22358	32782	23855	17934	18771
8.	Provisions (net)	Provisions (nettes)	1445	766	903	368	928	1091	6361	2354	1503	4330
9.	Profit before tax	Bénéfices avant impôt	8913	10656	11205	11449	14896	21267	26421	21501	16431	14441
10.	Income tax	Impôt	5268	5716	6176	5868	7836	12066	13940	10470	7577	7965
11.	Profit after tax	Bénéfices après impôt	3645	4940	5029	5581	7060	9201	12481	11031	8854	6476
12.	Distributed profit	Bénéfices distribués	1211	1308	1371	1417	1581	1624	1838	1069	1115	1113
13.	Retained profit	Bénéfices mis en réserve	2434	3632	3658	4164	5479	7577	10643	9962	7739	5363

Memoranda / Pour mémoire

No.	Item (EN)	Item (FR)	1982	1983	1984	1985	1986	1987	1988	1989	1990	1991
14.	Staff costs	Frais de personnel	11356	11630	11898	12070	12511	12498	12772	13378	14079	14658
15.	Provisions on loans	Provisions sur prêts	1445	753	853	214	576	925	2080	2224	1425	4354
16.	Provisions on securities	Provisions sur titres	-	13	50	154	352	166	4281	130	78	-24

BALANCE SHEET / BILAN

Assets / Actif

No.	Item (EN)	Item (FR)	1982	1983	1984	1985	1986	1987	1988	1989	1990	1991
17.	Cash & balance with Central bank(1)	Caisse & solde auprès de la Banque centrale(1)	..	..	..	..	..	..	..	..	..	..
18.	Interbank deposits	Dépôts interbancaires	435923	483725	573427	527488	648761	723304	883583	1046119	858603	694322
19.	Loans	Prêts	1047347	1162708	1340795	1453591	1672764	1909408	2159315	2520336	2660295	2736541
20.	Securities	Valeurs mobilières	208931	224028	255537	289760	344058	391775	449216	560295	538856	513847
21.	Other assets	Autres actifs	398657	411396	457343	485490	518040	583935	720189	956143	858749	804944

Liabilities / Passif

No.	Item (EN)	Item (FR)	1982	1983	1984	1985	1986	1987	1988	1989	1990	1991
22.	Capital & reserves	Capital et réserves	39197	43394	47196	53621	60837	78740	104939	137039	144097	148493
23.	Borrowing from Central bank	Emprunts auprès de la Banque centrale	14492	21253	11771	24265	38492	44685	43204	27135	28024	26353
24.	Interbank deposits (2)	Dépôts interbancaires (2)	..	..	..	..	..	..	..	..	..	..
25.	Non-bank deposits	Dépôts non bancaires	1535949	1698496	1951891	1991385	2303880	2622945	3045140	3644553	3535869	3292328
26.	Bonds	Obligations	18999	21460	22900	30934	32908	41384	52623	53948	51568	53546
27.	Other liabilities	Autres engagements	482221	497254	593344	656124	747506	820668	966397	1220218	1156945	1228934

Balance sheet total / Total du bilan

No.	Item (EN)	Item (FR)	1982	1983	1984	1985	1986	1987	1988	1989	1990	1991
28.	End-year total	En fin d'exercice	2090858	2281857	2627102	2756329	3183623	3608422	4212303	5082893	4916503	4749654
29.	Average total	Moyen	2000875	2186357	2454479	2691715	2969976	3396022	3910362	4647598	4999698	4833079

Memoranda / Pour mémoire

No.	Item (EN)	Item (FR)	1982	1983	1984	1985	1986	1987	1988	1989	1990	1991
30.	Short-term securities	Titres à court terme	..	..	..	..	..	..	..	..	..	..
31.	Bonds	Obligations	..	..	..	..	..	..	..	..	..	..
32.	Shares and participations	Actions et participations	49037	53796	61152	67468	74847	97885	132497	169114	192011	201849
33.	Claims on non-residents	Créances sur des non résidents	..	..	..	..	..	..	..	..	..	..
34.	Liabilities to non-residents	Engagements envers des non résidents	..	..	..	..	..	..	..	..	..	..

SUPPLEMENTARY INFORMATION / RENSEIGNEMENTS COMPLEMENTAIRES

No.	Item (EN)	Item (FR)	1982	1983	1984	1985	1986	1987	1988	1989	1990	1991
35.	Number of institutions	Nombre d'institutions	13	13	13	13	13	13	13	13	12	11
36.	Number of branches	Nombre de succursales	2823	2859	2883	2904	3032	3050	3099	3182	3249	3280
37.	Number of employees (x 1000)	Nombre de salariés (x 1000)	176	172	166	160	157	154	152	152	152	154

JAPAN

Large commercial banks

JAPON

Grandes banques commerciales

Per cent	1982	1983	1984	1985	1986	1987	1988	1989	1990	1991	Pourcentage	
INCOME STATEMENT ANALYSIS											**ANALYSE DU COMPTE DE RESULTATS**	
% of average balance sheet total											**% du total moyen du bilan**	
38. Interest income	7.14	6.25	6.81	5.60	4.87	4.82	5.22	5.82	6.47	6.17	Produits financiers	38.
39. Interest expenses	5.90	5.05	5.74	4.66	3.86	3.84	4.28	5.13	5.87	5.33	Frais financiers	39.
40. Net interest income	1.23	1.20	1.07	0.94	1.01	0.98	0.94	0.69	0.61	0.84	Produits financiers nets	40.
41. Non-interest income (net)	0.29	0.28	0.32	0.34	0.33	0.46	0.63	0.41	0.34	0.19	Produits non financiers (nets)	41.
42. Gross income	1.53	1.48	1.39	1.28	1.34	1.44	1.57	1.10	0.95	1.03	Résultat brut	42.
43. Operating expenses	1.01	0.96	0.90	0.84	0.81	0.78	0.73	0.59	0.59	0.64	Frais d'exploitation	43.
44. Net income	0.52	0.52	0.49	0.44	0.53	0.66	0.84	0.51	0.36	0.39	Résultat net	44.
45. Provisions (net)	0.07	0.04	0.04	0.01	0.03	0.03	0.16	0.05	0.03	0.09	Provisions (nettes)	45.
46. Profit before tax	0.45	0.49	0.46	0.43	0.50	0.63	0.68	0.46	0.33	0.30	Bénéfices avant impôt	46.
47. Income tax	0.26	0.26	0.25	0.22	0.26	0.36	0.36	0.23	0.15	0.16	Impôt	47.
48. Profit after tax	0.18	0.23	0.20	0.21	0.24	0.27	0.32	0.24	0.18	0.13	Bénéfices après impôt	48.
49. Distributed profit	0.06	0.06	0.06	0.05	0.05	0.05	0.05	0.02	0.02	0.02	Bénéfices distribués	49.
50. Retained profit	0.12	0.17	0.15	0.15	0.18	0.22	0.27	0.21	0.15	0.11	Bénéfices mis en réserve	50.
51. Staff costs	0.57	0.53	0.48	0.45	0.42	0.37	0.33	0.29	0.28	0.30	Frais de personnel	51.
52. Provisions on loans	0.07	0.03	0.03	0.01	0.02	0.03	0.05	0.05	0.03	0.09	Provisions sur prêts	52.
53. Provisions on securities	-	0.00	0.00	0.01	0.01	0.00	0.11	0.00	0.00	0.00	Provisions sur titres	53.
% of gross income											**% du total du résultat brut**	
54. Net interest income	80.89	81.05	77.23	73.41	75.47	67.77	59.95	62.80	64.06	81.87	Produits financiers nets	54.
55. Non-interest income (net)	19.11	18.95	22.77	26.59	24.53	32.23	40.05	37.20	35.94	18.13	Produits non financiers (nets)	55.
56. Operating expenses	66.09	64.71	64.47	65.62	60.34	54.35	46.56	53.31	62.09	62.30	Frais d'exploitation	56.
57. Net income	33.91	35.29	35.53	34.38	39.66	45.65	53.44	46.69	37.91	37.70	Résultat net	57.
58. Provisions (net)	4.73	2.37	2.65	1.07	2.33	2.23	10.37	4.61	3.18	8.70	Provisions (nettes)	58.
59. Profit before tax	29.18	32.93	32.88	33.31	37.34	43.42	43.07	42.09	34.74	29.00	Bénéfices avant impôt	59.
60. Income tax	17.24	17.66	18.12	17.07	19.64	24.64	22.73	20.49	16.02	16.00	Impôt	60.
61. Profit after tax	11.93	15.26	14.76	16.24	17.70	18.79	20.35	21.59	18.72	13.01	Bénéfices après impôt	61.
62. Staff costs	37.17	35.94	34.91	35.12	31.36	25.52	20.82	26.19	29.76	29.44	Frais de personnel	62.
% of net income											**% du total du résultat net**	
63. Provisions (net)	13.95	6.71	7.46	3.11	5.86	4.88	19.40	9.87	8.38	23.07	Provisions (nettes)	63.
64. Profit before tax	86.05	93.29	92.54	96.89	94.14	95.12	80.60	90.13	91.62	76.93	Bénéfices avant impôt	64.
65. Income tax	50.86	50.04	51.01	49.66	49.52	53.97	42.52	43.89	42.25	42.43	Impôt	65.
66. Profit after tax	35.19	43.25	41.53	47.23	44.62	41.15	38.07	46.24	49.37	34.50	Bénéfices après impôt	66.

JAPAN

Large commercial banks

Per cent

BALANCE SHEET ANALYSIS

% of year-end balance sheet total

	1982	1983	1984	1985	1986	1987	1988	1989	1990	1991
Assets										
67. Cash & balance with Central bank (1)	..	..	..	..	..	..	..	..	..	..
68. Interbank deposits	20.85	21.20	21.83	19.14	20.38	20.04	20.98	20.58	17.46	14.62
69. Loans	50.09	50.95	51.04	52.74	52.54	52.92	51.26	49.58	54.11	57.62
70. Securities	9.99	9.82	9.73	10.51	10.81	10.86	10.66	11.02	10.96	10.82
71. Other assets	19.07	18.03	17.41	17.61	16.27	16.18	17.10	18.81	17.47	16.95
Liabilities										
72. Capital & reserves	1.87	1.90	1.80	1.95	1.91	2.18	2.49	2.70	2.93	3.13
73. Borrowing from Central bank	0.69	0.93	0.45	0.88	1.21	1.24	1.03	0.53	0.57	0.55
74. Interbank deposits (2)	..	..	..	..	..	..	..	..	..	..
75. Non-bank deposits	73.46	74.43	74.30	72.25	72.37	72.69	72.29	71.70	71.92	69.32
76. Bonds	0.91	0.94	0.87	1.12	1.03	1.15	1.25	1.06	1.05	1.13
77. Other liabilities	23.06	21.79	22.59	23.80	23.48	22.74	22.94	24.01	23.53	25.87
Memoranda										
78. Short-term securities	..	..	..	..	..	..	..	..	..	..
79. Bonds	..	..	..	..	..	..	..	..	..	..
80. Shares and participations	2.35	2.36	2.33	2.45	2.35	2.71	3.15	3.33	3.91	4.25
81. Claims on non-residents	..	..	..	..	..	..	..	..	..	..
82. Liabilities to non-residents	..	..	..	..	..	..	..	..	..	..

1. Included under "Interbank deposits" (item 18 or item 68).
2. Included under "Non-bank deposits" (item 25 or item 75).

Notes

- Data are based on the annual publication of the Federation of Bankers Associations of Japan "Analysis of Financial Statements of All Banks". The term Large commercial banks corresponds to the term City banks used in Japanese publications.

- Data relate to fiscal years ending 31st March.

JAPON

Grandes banques commerciales

Pourcentage

ANALYSE DU BILAN

% du total du bilan en fin d'exercice

Actif
67. Caisse & solde auprès de la Banque centrale(1)
68. Dépôts interbancaires
69. Prêts
70. Valeurs mobilières
71. Autres actifs

Passif
72. Capital et réserves
73. Emprunts auprès de la Banque centrale
74. Dépôts interbancaires (2)
75. Dépôts non bancaires
76. Obligations
77. Autres engagements

Pour mémoire
78. Titres à court terme
79. Obligations
80. Actions et participations
81. Créances sur des non résidents
82. Engagements envers des non résidents

Notes

- Les données sont extraites d'une publication annuelle de la Fédération des associations de banquiers du Japon "Analysis of Financial Statements of All Banks". Le terme, Grandes banques commerciales correspond au terme City banks utilisé dans les publications japonaises.

- Les données portent sur l'exercice financier, qui se termine le 31 mars.

LUXEMBOURG

Commercial banks

LUXEMBOURG

Banques commerciales

Million Luxembourg francs / *Millions de francs luxembourgeois*

	1982	1983	1984	1985	1986	1987	1988	1989	1990	1991	
INCOME STATEMENT											**COMPTE DE RESULTATS**
1. Interest income	699449	578423	661542	659869	593525	605706	702452	1001719	1185123	1251957	1. Produits financiers
2. Interest expenses	635678	501612	579470	571174	506503	519999	612743	910018	1090911	1143722	2. Frais financiers
3. Net interest income	63771	76811	82072	88695	87022	85707	89709	91701	94212	108235	3. Produits financiers nets
4. Non-interest income (net)	14362	16281	12525	21712	23657	21418	28762	36062	50738	39044	4. Produits non financiers (nets)
5. Gross income	78133	93092	94597	110407	110679	107125	118471	127763	144950	147279	5. Résultat brut
6. Operating expenses	20752	24388	27049	30777	34110	37767	45361	52259	54089	59720	6. Frais d'exploitation
7. Net income	57381	68704	67548	79630	76569	69358	73110	75504	90861	87559	7. Résultat net
8. Provisions (net)	40847	52606	47203	54515	50973	42488	35000	41357	63860	54302	8. Provisions (nettes)
9. Profit before tax	16534	16098	20345	25115	25596	26870	38110	34147	27001	33257	9. Bénéfices avant impôt
10. Income tax	8759	8192	9816	11817	11426	11246	14579	10912	7919	9539	10. Impôt
11. Profit after tax	7775	7906	10529	13298	14170	15624	23531	23235	19082	23718	11. Bénéfices après impôt
12. Distributed profit	2394	2177	5306	5437	5753	7861	8716	NA	NA	NA	12. Bénéfices distribués
13. Retained profit	5381	5729	5223	7861	8417	7763	14815	NA	NA	NA	13. Bénéfices mis en réserve
Memoranda											*Pour mémoire*
14. *Staff costs*	*11606*	*13766*	*15049*	*16751*	*18717*	*20810*	*24038*	*27326*	*28291*	*31205*	14. *Frais de personnel*
15. *Provisions on loans*	..	..	..	..	..	..	..	..	..	..	15. *Provisions sur prêts*
16. *Provisions on securities*	..	..	..	..	..	..	..	..	..	..	16. *Provisions sur titres*
BALANCE SHEET											**BILAN**
Assets											**Actif**
17. Cash & balance with Central bank	8369	7706	12407	15896	17822	14954	22731	22550	21999	23912	17. Caisse & solde auprès de la Banque centrale
18. Interbank deposits	3051563	3325734	3743593	4153414	4493575	5091042	5895411	6827903	7542436	7595436	18. Dépôts interbancaires
19. Loans	2268682	2454326	2680945	2444418	2291377	2239670	2488137	2705253	2991164	3111790	19. Prêts
20. Securities	252918	341257	408332	519801	626933	644846	747022	825196	947786	1030649	20. Valeurs mobilières
21. Other assets	405601	462615	485407	494278	577407	695968	784481	955869	976829	989324	21. Autres actifs
Liabilities											**Passif**
22. Capital & reserves	180850	210619	241075	264572	278847	292956	326944	362536	400727	437490	22. Capital et réserves
23. Borrowing from Central bank	-	-	-	-	-	-	-	-	-	-	23. Emprunts auprès de la Banque centrale
24. Interbank deposits	4295604	4655969	5064551	5087914	5021751	5213590	5456033	5664861	5862019	5781106	24. Dépôts interbancaires
25. Non-bank deposits	1175244	1334310	1580956	1756196	2165763	2567373	3338309	4362287	5018640	5233632	25. Dépôts non bancaires
26. Bonds	63498	96987	125722	110723	108212	133500	291661	361339	557124	643922	26. Obligations
27. Other liabilities	271937	293753	318380	408402	432541	479061	524835	585748	641704	654961	27. Autres engagements
Balance sheet total											**Total du bilan**
28. End-year total	5987133	6591638	7330684	7627807	8007114	8686480	9937782	11336771	12480214	12751111	28. En fin d'exercice
29. Average total	5834190	6244024	6830970	7509547	7669959	8275464	9467853	11126632	12212272	13003686	29. Moyen
Memoranda											*Pour mémoire*
30. *Short-term securities*	*118654*	*151163*	*208068*	*292268*	*310070*	*308259*	*333652*	*324005*	*380893*	*480731*	30. *Titres à court terme*
31. *Bonds*	*29296*	*28440*	*27827*	*31087*	*33769*	*35795*	*49897*	*86293*	*121414*	*86639*	31. *Obligations*
32. *Shares and participations*											32. *Actions et participations*
33. *Claims on non-residents*	*5178799*	*5752587*	*6409467*	*6598617*	*6941873*	*7525666*	*8663424*	*10020284*	*11050104*	*11263515*	33. *Créances sur des non résidents*
34. *Liabilities to non-residents*	*4829036*	*5280549*	*6233881*	*6373914*	*6645544*	*7066412*	*8015812*	*9226691*	*10258514*	*10468546*	34. *Engagements envers des non résidents*
SUPPLEMENTARY INFORMATION											**RENSEIGNEMENTS COMPLEMENTAIRES**
35. Number of institutions	115	114	115	118	122	127	143	166	177	187	35. Nombre d'institutions
36. Number of branches	242	241	237	243	250	258	258	295	297	308	36. Nombre de succursales
37. Number of employees (x 1000)	8.6	9.0	9.4	10.2	11.4	12.7	13.7	15.2	16.3	17.1	37. Nombre de salariés (x 1000)

LUXEMBOURG

Commercial banks

LUXEMBOURG

Banques commerciales

Per cent / *Pourcentage*

INCOME STATEMENT ANALYSIS / ANALYSE DU COMPTE DE RESULTATS

	1982	1983	1984	1985	1986	1987	1988	1989	1990	1991		
% of average balance sheet total												**% du total moyen du bilan**
38. Interest income	11.99	9.26	9.68	8.79	7.74	7.32	7.42	9.00	9.70	9.63	38.	Produits financiers
39. Interest expenses	10.90	8.03	8.48	7.61	6.60	6.28	6.47	8.18	8.93	8.80	39.	Frais financiers
40. Net interest income	1.09	1.23	1.20	1.18	1.13	1.04	0.95	0.82	0.77	0.83	40.	Produits financiers nets
41. Non-interest income (net)	0.25	0.26	0.18	0.29	0.31	0.26	0.30	0.32	0.42	0.30	41.	Produits non financiers (nets)
42. Gross income	1.34	1.49	1.38	1.47	1.44	1.29	1.25	1.15	1.19	1.13	42.	Résultat brut
43. Operating expenses	0.36	0.39	0.40	0.41	0.44	0.46	0.48	0.47	0.44	0.46	43.	Frais d'exploitation
44. Net income	0.98	1.10	0.99	1.06	1.00	0.84	0.77	0.68	0.74	0.67	44.	Résultat net
45. Provisions (net)	0.70	0.84	0.69	0.73	0.66	0.51	0.37	0.52	0.52	0.42	45.	Provisions (nettes)
46. Profit before tax	0.28	0.26	0.30	0.33	0.33	0.32	0.40	0.31	0.22	0.26	46.	Bénéfices avant impôt
47. Income tax	0.15	0.13	0.14	0.16	0.15	0.14	0.15	0.10	0.06	0.07	47.	Impôt
48. Profit after tax	0.13	0.13	0.15	0.18	0.18	0.19	0.25	0.21	0.16	0.18	48.	Bénéfices après impôt
49. Distributed profit	0.04	0.03	0.08	0.07	0.08	0.09	0.09	NA	NA	NA	49.	Bénéfices distribués
50. Retained profit	0.09	0.09	0.08	0.10	0.11	0.09	0.16	NA	NA	NA	50.	Bénéfices mis en réserve
51. Staff costs	0.20	0.22	0.22	0.22	0.24	0.25	0.25	0.25	0.23	0.24	51.	Frais de personnel
52. Provisions on loans	..	..	..	..	..	..	..	..	..	..	52.	Provisions sur prêts
53. Provisions on securities	..	..	..	..	..	..	..	..	..	..	53.	Provisions sur titres
% of gross income												**% du total du résultat brut**
54. Net interest income	81.62	82.51	86.76	80.33	78.63	80.01	75.72	71.77	65.00	73.49	54.	Produits financiers nets
55. Non-interest income (net)	18.38	17.49	13.24	19.67	21.37	19.99	24.28	28.23	35.00	26.51	55.	Produits non financiers (nets)
56. Operating expenses	26.56	26.20	28.59	27.88	30.82	35.26	38.29	40.90	37.32	40.55	56.	Frais d'exploitation
57. Net income	73.44	73.80	71.41	72.12	69.18	64.74	61.71	59.10	62.68	59.45	57.	Résultat net
58. Provisions (net)	52.28	56.51	49.90	49.38	46.05	39.66	29.54	32.37	44.06	36.87	58.	Provisions (nettes)
59. Profit before tax	21.16	17.29	21.51	22.75	23.13	25.08	32.17	26.73	18.63	22.58	59.	Bénéfices avant impôt
60. Income tax	11.21	8.80	10.38	10.70	10.32	10.50	12.31	8.54	5.46	6.48	60.	Impôt
61. Profit after tax	9.95	8.49	11.13	12.04	12.80	14.58	19.86	18.19	13.16	16.10	61.	Bénéfices après impôt
62. Staff costs	14.85	14.79	15.91	15.17	16.91	19.43	20.29	21.39	19.52	21.19	62.	Frais de personnel
% of net income												**% du total du résultat net**
63. Provisions (net)	71.19	76.57	69.88	68.46	66.57	61.26	47.87	54.77	70.28	62.02	63.	Provisions (nettes)
64. Profit before tax	28.81	23.43	30.12	31.54	33.43	38.74	52.13	45.23	29.72	37.98	64.	Bénéfices avant impôt
65. Income tax	15.26	11.92	14.53	14.84	14.92	16.21	19.94	14.45	8.72	10.89	65.	Impôt
66. Profit after tax	13.55	11.51	15.59	16.70	18.51	22.53	32.19	30.77	21.00	27.09	66.	Bénéfices après impôt

LUXEMBOURG

Commercial banks

BALANCE SHEET ANALYSIS

Per cent

% of year-end balance sheet total

	1982	1983	1984	1985	1986	1987	1988	1989	1990	1991
Assets										
67. Cash & balance with Central bank	0.14	0.12	0.17	0.21	0.22	0.17	0.23	0.20	0.18	0.19
68. Interbank deposits	50.97	50.45	51.07	54.45	56.12	58.61	59.32	60.23	60.44	59.57
69. Loans	37.89	37.23	36.57	32.05	28.62	25.78	25.04	23.86	23.97	24.40
70. Securities	4.22	5.18	5.57	6.81	7.83	7.42	7.52	7.28	7.59	8.08
71. Other assets	6.77	7.02	6.62	6.48	7.21	8.01	7.89	8.43	7.83	7.76
Liabilities										
72. Capital & reserves	3.02	3.20	3.29	3.47	3.48	3.37	3.29	3.20	3.21	3.43
73. Borrowing from Central bank	-	-	-	-	-	-	-	-	-	-
74. Interbank deposits	71.75	70.63	69.09	66.70	62.72	60.02	54.90	49.97	46.97	45.34
75. Non-bank deposits	19.63	20.24	21.57	23.02	27.05	29.56	33.59	38.48	40.21	41.04
76. Bonds	1.06	1.47	1.72	1.45	1.35	1.54	2.93	3.19	4.46	5.05
77. Other liabilities	4.54	4.46	4.34	5.35	5.40	5.52	5.28	5.17	5.14	5.14
Memoranda										
78. Short-term securities	*..*	*..*	*..*	*..*	*..*	*..*	*..*	*..*	*..*	*..*
79. Bonds	*1.98*	*2.29*	*2.84*	*3.83*	*3.87*	*3.55*	*3.36*	*2.86*	*3.05*	*3.77*
80. Shares and participations	*0.49*	*0.43*	*0.38*	*0.41*	*0.42*	*0.41*	*0.50*	*0.76*	*0.97*	*0.68*
81. Claims on non-residents	*86.50*	*87.27*	*87.43*	*86.51*	*86.70*	*86.64*	*87.18*	*88.39*	*88.54*	*88.33*
82. Liabilities to non-residents	*80.66*	*80.11*	*85.04*	*83.56*	*83.00*	*81.37*	*80.66*	*81.39*	*82.20*	*82.10*

Notes

- Average balance sheet totals (item 29) are based on thirteen end-month data.

LUXEMBOURG

Banques commerciales

Pourcentage

ANALYSE DU BILAN

% du total du bilan en fin d'exercice

Actif
67. Caisse & solde auprès de la Banque centrale
68. Dépôts interbancaires
69. Prêts
70. Valeurs mobilières
71. Autres actifs

Passif
72. Capital et réserves
73. Emprunts auprès de la Banque centrale
74. Dépôts interbancaires
75. Dépôts non bancaires
76. Obligations
77. Autres engagements

Pour mémoire
78. Titres à court terme
79. Obligations
80. Actions et participations
81. Créances sur des non résidents
82. Engagements envers des non résidents

Notes

- La moyenne du total des actifs/passifs (poste 29) est basée sur treize données de fin de mois.

NETHERLANDS

All banks

PAYS-BAS

Ensemble des banques

Million guilders / *Millions de florins*

#			1983	1984	1985	1986	1987	1988	1989 (2)	1990	1990 (2)	1991
	INCOME STATEMENT	**COMPTE DE RESULTATS**										
1.	Interest income	Produits financiers	..	..	..	..	..	..	..	..	..	..
2.	Interest expenses	Frais financiers	..	..	..	..	..	..	..	..	..	..
3.	Net interest income	Produits financiers nets	10826	10707	11182	13478	14036	15038	16987	17975	18309	20331
4.	Non-interest income (net)	Produits non financiers (nets)	3328	3505	3858	4237	4918	5632	7062	7219	7336	8360
5.	Gross income	Résultat brut	14154	14212	15040	17715	18954	20670	24049	25194	25645	28691
6.	Operating expenses	Frais d'exploitation	8703	8876	9436	11682	13053	13986	15862	17432	17612	19510
7.	Net income	Résultat net	5451	5336	5604	6033	5901	6684	8187	7762	8033	9181
8.	Provisions (net)	Provisions (nettes)	2787	2907	1843	1892	1161	2741	2931	2969	3006	3293
9.	Profit before tax	Bénéfices avant impôt	2664	2429	3761	4141	4740	3943	5256	4793	5027	5888
10.	Income tax	Impôt					1374	1102	1254	1229	1273	1683
11.	Profit after tax	Bénéfices après impôt					3366	2841	4002	3564	3754	4205
12.	Distributed profit	Bénéfices distribués										
13.	Retained profit	Bénéfices mis en réserve										
	Memoranda	*Pour mémoire*										
14.	Staff costs	Frais de personnel	*5729*	*5854*	*6150*	*7085*	*7925*	*8371*	*9162*	*10078*	*10183*	*11242*
15.	Provisions on loans	Provisions sur prêts										
16.	Provisions on securities	Provisions sur titres										
	BALANCE SHEET	**BILAN**										
	Assets	**Actif**										
17.	Cash & bal. with Central bank	Caisse & solde auprès de la Banque centrale	4235	4599	4679	6077	8377	7622	22879	26110	26110	22511
18.	Interbank deposits	Dépôts interbancaires	134042	154422	153339	151908	161571	186233	223004	261984	261984	259165
19.	Loans	Prêts	260636	270342	280217	332268	338626	374264	501308	685356	685356	731174
20.	Securities	Valeurs mobilières	36570	41734	47132	69246	66150	73059	77642	118789	118789	122342
21.	Other assets	Autres actifs	26343	28052	31122	37466	42822	48856	62595	30251	30251	32468
	Liabilities	**Passif**										
22.	Capital & reserves	Capital et réserves	15706	17345	19296	23717	26532	29058	38756	45047	45047	47634
23.	Borrowing from Central bank	Emprunts auprès de la Banque centrale	6675	5527	5610	10701	7351	6093	4891	9328	9328	3045
24.	Interbank deposits	Dépôts interbancaires	147681	154553	150742	154974	164676	179108	197499	265314	265314	285345
25.	Non-bank deposits	Dépôts non bancaires	213133	237901	253320	307565	311773	342967	422644	510650	510650	535246
26.	Bonds	Obligations	37456	39662	42909	49600	54773	67145	138017	167192	167192	167845
27.	Other liabilities	Autres engagements	41175	44161	44612	50408	52441	65663	85621	124959	124959	128545
	Balance sheet total	**Total du bilan**										
28.	End-year total	En fin d'exercice	461826	499149	516489	596965	617546	690034	887428	1122490	1122490	1167660
29.	Average total	Moyen	450660	480488	507819	556727	607256	653790	817041	1004959	1004959	1145075
	Memoranda	*Pour mémoire*										
30.	Short-term securities (1)	Titres à court terme (1)								*27525*	*27525*	*23333*
31.	Bonds	Obligations	*35141*	*40564*	*45863*	*66459*	*63459*	*69532*	*74111*	*86122*	*86122*	*93604*
32.	Shares and participations	Actions et participations	*1429*	*1170*	*1269*	*2787*	*2691*	*3527*	*3531*	*6281*	*6281*	*6708*
33.	Claims on non-residents	Créances sur des non résidents	*178651*	*202017*	*199717*	*199689*	*203974*	*238791*	*280183*	*314206*	*314206*	*321725*
34.	Liabilities to non-residents	Engagements envers des non résidents	*171987*	*187904*	*181741*	*182778*	*192450*	*220035*	*232405*	*259304*	*259304*	*267940*
	SUPPLEMENTARY INFORMATION	**RENSEIGNEMENTS COMPLEMENTAIRES**										
35.	Number of institutions	Nombre d'institutions	92	86	84	83	85	86	170	180	180	173
36.	Number of branches	Nombre de succursales	5406	5475	4786	7388	7352	7233	8006	7992	7992	7827
37.	Number of employees (x 1000)	Nombre de salariés (x 1000)	90.7	91.1	92.4	104.1	106.0	106.4	117.4	122.9	122.9	125.1

NETHERLANDS

All banks

Per cent

INCOME STATEMENT ANALYSIS

		1983	1984	1985	1986	1987	1988	1989 (2)	1990	1990 (2)	1991	
	% of average balance sheet total											**% du total moyen du bilan**
38.	Interest income	:	:	:	:	:	:	:	:	:	:	38. Produits financiers
39.	Interest expenses	:	:	:	:	:	:	:	:	:	0.00	39. Frais financiers
40.	Net interest income	2.40	2.23	2.20	2.42	2.31	2.30	2.08	1.79	1.82	1.78	40. Produits financiers nets
41.	Non-interest income (net)	0.74	0.73	0.76	0.76	0.81	0.86	0.86	0.72	0.73	0.73	41. Produits non financiers (nets)
42.	Gross income	3.14	2.96	2.96	3.18	3.12	3.16	2.94	2.51	2.55	2.51	42. Résultat brut
43.	Operating expenses	1.93	1.85	1.86	2.10	2.15	2.14	1.94	1.73	1.75	1.70	43. Frais d'exploitation
44.	Net income	1.21	1.11	1.10	1.08	0.97	1.02	1.00	0.77	0.80	0.80	44. Résultat net
45.	Provisions (net)	0.62	0.61	0.36	0.34	0.19	0.42	0.36	0.30	0.30	0.29	45. Provisions (nettes)
46.	Profit before tax	0.59	0.51	0.74	0.74	0.78	0.60	0.64	0.48	0.50	0.51	46. Bénéfices avant impôt
47.	Income tax	:	:	:	:	0.23	0.17	0.15	0.12	0.13	0.15	47. Impôt
48.	Profit after tax	:	:	:	:	0.55	0.43	0.49	0.35	0.37	0.37	48. Bénéfices après impôt
49.	Distributed profit	:	:	:	:	:	:	:	:	:	:	49. Bénéfices distribués
50.	Retained profit	:	:	:	:	:	:	:	:	:	:	50. Bénéfices mis en réserve
51.	Staff costs	1.27	1.22	1.21	1.27	1.31	1.28	1.12	1.00	1.01	0.98	51. Frais de personnel
52.	Provisions on loans	:	:	:	:	:	:	:	:	:	:	52. Provisions sur prêts
53.	Provisions on securities	:	:	:	:	:	:	:	:	:	:	53. Provisions sur titres
	% of gross income											**% du total du résultat brut**
54.	Net interest income	76.49	75.34	74.35	76.08	74.05	72.75	70.63	71.35	71.39	70.86	54. Produits financiers nets
55.	Non-interest income (net)	23.51	24.66	25.65	23.92	25.95	27.25	29.37	28.65	28.61	29.14	55. Produits non financiers (nets)
56.	Operating expenses	61.49	62.45	62.74	65.94	68.87	67.66	65.96	69.19	68.68	68.00	56. Frais d'exploitation
57.	Net income	38.51	37.55	37.26	34.06	31.13	32.34	34.04	30.81	31.32	32.00	57. Résultat net
58.	Provisions (net)	19.69	20.45	12.25	10.68	6.13	13.26	12.19	11.78	11.72	11.48	58. Provisions (nettes)
59.	Profit before tax	18.82	17.09	25.01	23.38	25.01	19.08	21.86	19.02	19.60	20.52	59. Bénéfices avant impôt
60.	Income tax	:	:	:	:	7.25	5.33	5.21	4.88	4.96	5.87	60. Impôt
61.	Profit after tax	:	:	:	:	17.76	13.74	16.64	14.15	14.64	14.66	61. Bénéfices après impôt
62.	Staff costs	40.48	41.19	40.89	39.99	41.81	40.50	38.10	40.00	39.71	39.18	62. Frais de personnel
	% of net income											**% du total du résultat net**
63.	Provisions (net)	51.13	54.48	32.89	31.36	19.67	41.01	35.80	38.25	37.42	35.87	63. Provisions (nettes)
64.	Profit before tax	48.87	45.52	67.11	68.64	80.33	58.99	64.20	61.75	62.58	64.13	64. Bénéfices avant impôt
65.	Income tax	:	:	:	:	23.28	16.49	15.32	15.83	15.85	18.33	65. Impôt
66.	Profit after tax	:	:	:	:	57.04	42.50	48.88	45.92	46.73	45.80	66. Bénéfices après impôt

NETHERLANDS

All banks

PAYS-BAS

Ensemble des banques

Per cent / *Pourcentage*

BALANCE SHEET ANALYSIS / **ANALYSE DU BILAN**

% of year-end balance sheet total / **% du total du bilan en fin d'exercice**

	1983	1984	1985	1986	1987	1988	1989 (2)	1990	1990 (2)	1991	
Assets											**Actif**
67. Cash & bal. with Central bank	0.92	0.92	0.91	1.02	1.36	1.10	2.58	2.33	2.33	1.93	67. Caisse & solde auprès de la Banque centrale
68. Interbank deposits	29.02	30.94	29.69	25.45	26.16	26.99	25.13	23.34	23.34	22.20	68. Dépôts interbancaires
69. Loans	56.44	54.16	54.25	55.66	54.83	54.24	56.49	61.06	61.06	62.62	69. Prêts
70. Securities	7.92	8.36	9.13	11.60	10.71	10.59	8.75	10.58	10.58	10.48	70. Valeurs mobilières
71. Other assets	5.70	5.62	6.03	6.28	6.93	7.08	7.05	2.69	2.69	2.78	71. Autres actifs
Liabilities											**Passif**
72. Capital & reserves	3.40	3.47	3.74	3.97	4.30	4.21	4.37	4.01	4.01	4.08	72. Capital et réserves
73. Borrowing from Central bank	1.45	1.11	1.09	1.79	1.19	0.88	0.55	0.83	0.83	0.26	73. Emprunts auprès de la Banque centrale
74. Interbank deposits	31.98	30.96	29.19	25.96	26.67	25.96	22.26	23.64	23.64	24.44	74. Dépôts interbancaires
75. Non-bank deposits	46.15	47.66	49.05	51.52	50.49	49.70	47.63	45.49	45.49	45.84	75. Dépôts non bancaires
76. Bonds	8.11	7.95	8.31	8.31	8.87	9.73	15.55	14.89	14.89	14.37	76. Obligations
77. Other liabilities	8.92	8.85	8.64	8.44	8.49	9.52	9.65	11.13	11.13	11.01	77. Autres engagements
Memoranda											*Pour mémoire*
78. Short-term securities (1)	*7.61*	*8.13*	*8.88*	*11.13*	*10.28*	*10.08*	*8.35*	*2.45*	*2.45*	*2.00*	*78. Titres à court terme (1)*
79. Bonds	*0.31*	*0.23*	*0.25*	*0.47*	*0.44*	*0.51*	*0.40*	*7.67*	*7.67*	*8.02*	*79. Obligations*
80. Shares and participations								*0.56*	*0.56*	*0.57*	*80. Actions et participations*
81. Claims on non-residents	*38.68*	*40.47*	*38.67*	*33.45*	*33.03*	*34.61*	*31.57*	*27.99*	*27.99*	*27.55*	*81. Créances sur des non résidents*
82. Liabilities to non-residents	*37.24*	*37.64*	*35.19*	*30.62*	*31.16*	*31.89*	*26.19*	*23.10*	*23.10*	*22.95*	*82. Engagements envers des non résidents*

1. Up to 1990 (old series), included under "Bonds" (item 31 or item 79).
2. New series. See change in methodology.

1. Jusqu'à 1990 (ancienne série) inclus sous "Obligations" (poste 31 ou poste 79).
2. Nouvelle série. Voir changement méthodologique.

Change in methodology:

• As from 1986, the data include the Postbank.

• As from 1988, Provisions (net) (item 8) consists of "transfers to the provision for general business risks". The addition to the lending/country risk provision out of this "provision for general business risks" in 1991 (1990 new series) amounts to Gld 3 328 million (Gld 2 410 million).

• As from 1989, balance sheet data, in addition to universal banks and banks organised on a co-operative basis (old series), also include savings banks, mortgage banks, capital market institutions and security credit institutions. The income statement data, for the same series (1989 and 1990 old series), include universal banks, banks organised on a credit co-operative basis and savings banks.

• The new series for 1990 cover, both for income statement and balance sheet data, universal banks, banks organised on a co-operative basis, savings banks, mortgage banks, capital market institutions and security credit institutions.

• The old series for 1989 were published in Bank Profitability, Statistical Supplement 1981-1990 (OECD, Paris, 1992).

• Due to the above-mentioned changes, as from this issue, data are published under the title "All banks".

Changement méthodologique :

• A compter de 1986, les données incluent la Banque postale.

• Depuis 1988, les Provisions (nettes) (poste 8), concernent les "dotations aux provisions pour risques généraux". La partie correspondant à la "provision pour risques" dans cette provision générale s'est élevée en 1991 à fl 3 328 millions (fl 2 410 millions en 1990 nouvelle série).

• A partir de 1989, les données de bilan, en plus des banques universelles et des banques organisées en mutuelles (anciennes séries), incluent également les caisses d'épargne, les banques hypothécaires, les institutions du marché financier et les institutions des titres de crédit. Les données du compte de résultat, pour les mêmes séries (1989 et 1990 ancienne série), incluent les banques universelles, les banques organisées en mutuelles et les caisses d'épargne.

• La nouvelle série pour 1990 concerne, aussi bien pour les données du compte de résultat que pour celles du bilan, les banques universelles, les banques organisées en mutuelles, les caisses d'épargne, les banques hypothécaires, les institutions du marché financier et les institutions des titres de crédit.

• L'ancienne série pour 1989 a été publiée dans Rentabilité des banques, Supplément statistique 1981-1990 (OCDE, Paris, 1992).

• Dû aux changements sus-mentionnés les données sont, à partir de ce bulletin, publiées sous le titre "Ensemble des banques".

NORWAY

All banks

NORVEGE

Ensemble des banques

Million Norwegian kroner / *Millions de couronnes norvégiennes*

	1982	1983	1984	1985	1986	1987	1988	1989	1990	1991	
INCOME STATEMENT											**COMPTE DE RESULTATS**
1. Interest income	24996	28272	33966	40872	55270	73541	80265	76422	75021	70070	1. Produits financiers
2. Interest expenses	16906	18413	23060	28976	40490	55847	61632	55286	54808	50888	2. Frais financiers
3. Net interest income	8090	9859	10906	11896	14780	17694	18633	21136	20213	19182	3. Produits financiers nets
4. Non-interest income (net)	2010	2399	3481	4557	5805	3740	6320	7455	5155	3603	4. Produits non financiers (nets)
5. Gross income	10100	12258	14387	16453	20585	21434	24953	28591	25368	22785	5. Résultat brut
6. Operating expenses (1)	6990	8367	9859	11720	13926	16322	17438	17250	17933	20051	6. Frais d'exploitation (1)
7. Net income	3110	3891	4528	4733	6659	5112	7515	11341	7435	2734	7. Résultat net
8. Provisions (net) (1)	936	1732	2251	2745	4049	4444	8882	9891	11655	21630	8. Provisions (nettes) (1)
9. Profit before tax	2174	2159	2277	1988	2610	668	-1367	1450	-4220	-18896	9. Bénéfices avant impôt
10. Income tax	159	399	410	403	468	384	279	570	272	201	10. Impôt
11. Profit after tax	2015	1760	1867	1585	2142	284	-1646	880	-4492	-19097	11. Bénéfices après impôt
12. Distributed profit	317	423	541	651	501	239	167	775	35	25	12. Bénéfices distribués
13. Retained profit	1698	1337	1326	934	1641	45	-1813	105	-4527	-19122	13. Bénéfices mis en réserve
Memoranda											*Pour mémoire*
14. Staff costs	*3968*	*4523*	*5035*	*5787*	*6868*	*7670*	*8436*	*8262*	*8557*	*8416*	14. Frais de personnel
15. Provisions on loans	*641*	*1113*	*1332*	*1432*	*1720*	*4432*	*8769*	*10481*	*10919*	*21370*	15. Provisions sur prêts
16. Provisions on securities	*..*	*..*	*..*	*..*	*..*	*..*	*..*	*..*	*..*	*..*	16. Provisions sur titres
BALANCE SHEET											**BILAN**
Assets											**Actif**
17. Cash & balance with Central bank	1359	3051	2088	2529	2893	3881	3136	3083	3136	3634	17. Caisse & solde auprès de la Banque centrale
18. Interbank deposits	16357	15517	18257	21717	40840	35734	23367	17799	20753	28470	18. Dépôts interbancaires
19. Loans	132246	156582	199689	263201	350155	405581	427506	459632	474753	451560	19. Prêts
20. Securities	63333	69321	83928	86863	83299	117509	96853	91045	84430	65803	20. Valeurs mobilières
21. Other assets	4276	4643	8913	8051	13107	27968	32167	33147	31573	28618	21. Autres actifs
Liabilities											**Passif**
22. Capital & reserves	11259	13397	16162	19450	23168	23461	22831	26204	23768	17724	22. Capital et réserves
23. Borrowing from Central bank	1311	3101	1162	2982	67676	73727	76254	58562	55880	47647	23. Emprunts auprès de la Banque centrale
24. Interbank deposits	27838	30523	42731	58975	69789	97704	80146	77217	76437	64917	24. Dépôts interbancaires
25. Non-bank deposits	165465	186453	227350	262064	268106	312465	326167	354185	370880	374350	25. Dépôts non bancaires
26. Bonds	1858	3456	7121	10147	32310	34569	43738	48038	50602	43858	26. Obligations
27. Other liabilities	9840	12184	18349	28743	29245	48746	33899	40499	37077	29590	27. Autres engagements
Balance sheet total											**Total du bilan**
28. End-year total	217571	249114	312875	382361	490294	590672	583033	604707	614645	578086	28. En fin d'exercice
29. Average total	212574	247763	294024	364215	458355	541430	613904	612183	639192	621560	29. Moyen
Memoranda											*Pour mémoire*
30. Short-term securities	*7659*	*4692*	*22380*	*28935*	*20470*	*33266*	*10354*	*9813*	*13128*	*8549*	30. Titres à court terme
31. Bonds	*52519*	*60534*	*55780*	*49769*	*51655*	*73705*	*75859*	*69770*	*58263*	*47245*	31. Obligations
32. Shares and participations	*3155*	*4095*	*5768*	*8158*	*11174*	*10539*	*10640*	*11462*	*13037*	*10009*	32. Actions et participations
33. Claims on non-residents	*16558*	*19381*	*27593*	*27843*	*49049*	*31792*	*26135*	*31201*	*34083*	*30838*	33. Créances sur des non résidents
34. Liabilities to non-residents	*28168*	*33381*	*50646*	*70471*	*98120*	*132070*	*131271*	*134193*	*129315*	*96144*	34. Engagements envers des non résidents
SUPPLEMENTARY INFORMATION											**RENSEIGNEMENTS COMPLEMENTAIRES**
35. Number of institutions	292	275	248	225	221	201	187	179	164	156	35. Nombre d'institutions
36. Number of branches	1920	1940	1970	2001	1930	2166	2032	1796	1796	1661	36. Nombre de succursales
37. Number of employees (x 1000)	27.0	27.9	29.0	29.9	32.7	34.6	34.4	32.0	31.2	27.8	37. Nombre de salariés (x 1000)

NORWAY

All banks

NORVEGE

Ensemble des banques

Per cent

Pourcentage

INCOME STATEMENT ANALYSIS

ANALYSE DU COMPTE DE RESULTATS

		1982	1983	1984	1985	1986	1987	1988	1989	1990	1991		
% of average balance sheet total													**% du total moyen du bilan**
38.	Interest income	11.76	11.41	11.55	11.22	12.06	13.58	13.07	12.48	11.74	11.27	38.	Produits financiers
39.	Interest expenses	7.95	7.43	7.84	7.96	8.83	10.31	10.04	9.03	8.57	8.19	39.	Frais financiers
40.	Net interest income	3.81	3.98	3.71	3.27	3.22	3.27	3.04	3.45	3.16	3.09	40.	Produits financiers nets
41.	Non-interest income (net)	0.95	0.97	1.18	1.25	1.27	0.69	1.03	1.22	0.81	0.58	41.	Produits non financiers (nets)
42.	Gross income	4.75	4.95	4.89	4.52	4.49	3.96	4.06	4.67	3.97	3.67	42.	Résultat brut
43.	Operating expenses (1)	3.29	3.38	3.35	3.22	3.04	3.01	2.84	2.82	2.81	3.23	43.	Frais d'exploitation (1)
44.	Net income	1.46	1.57	1.54	1.30	1.45	0.94	1.22	1.85	1.16	0.44	44.	Résultat net
45.	Provisions (net) (1)	0.44	0.70	0.77	0.75	0.88	0.82	1.45	1.62	1.82	3.48	45.	Provisions (nettes) (1)
46.	Profit before tax	1.02	0.87	0.77	0.55	0.57	0.12	-0.22	0.24	-0.66	-3.04	46.	Bénéfices avant impôt
47.	Income tax	0.07	0.16	0.14	0.11	0.10	0.07	0.05	0.09	0.04	0.03	47.	Impôt
48.	Profit after tax	0.95	0.71	0.63	0.44	0.47	0.05	-0.27	0.14	-0.70	-3.07	48.	Bénéfices après impôt
49.	Distributed profit	0.15	0.17	0.18	0.18	0.11	0.04	0.03	0.13	0.01	0.00	49.	Bénéfices distribués
50.	Retained profit	0.80	0.54	0.45	0.26	0.36	0.01	-0.30	0.02	-0.71	-3.08	50.	Bénéfices mis en réserve
51.	Staff costs	1.87	1.83	1.71	1.59	1.50	1.42	1.37	1.35	1.34	1.35	51.	Frais de personnel
52.	Provisions on loans	0.30	0.45	0.45	0.39	0.38	0.82	1.43	1.71	1.71	3.44	52.	Provisions sur prêts
53.	Provisions on securities	..	..	..	..	..	..	..	..	..	..	53.	Provisions sur titres
% of gross income													**% du total du résultat brut**
54.	Net interest income	80.10	80.43	75.80	72.30	71.80	82.55	74.67	73.93	79.68	84.19	54.	Produits financiers nets
55.	Non-interest income (net)	19.90	19.57	24.20	27.70	28.20	17.45	25.33	26.07	20.32	15.81	55.	Produits non financiers (nets)
56.	Operating expenses (1)	69.21	68.26	68.53	71.23	67.65	76.15	69.88	60.33	70.69	88.00	56.	Frais d'exploitation (1)
57.	Net income	30.79	31.74	31.47	28.77	32.35	23.85	30.12	39.67	29.31	12.00	57.	Résultat net
58.	Provisions (net) (1)	9.27	14.13	15.65	16.68	19.67	20.73	35.59	34.59	45.94	94.93	58.	Provisions (nettes) (1)
59.	Profit before tax	21.52	17.61	15.83	12.08	12.68	3.12	-5.48	5.07	-16.64	-82.93	59.	Bénéfices avant impôt
60.	Income tax	1.57	3.26	2.85	2.45	2.27	1.79	1.12	1.99	1.07	0.88	60.	Impôt
61.	Profit after tax	19.95	14.36	12.98	9.63	10.41	1.32	-6.60	3.08	-17.71	-83.81	61.	Bénéfices après impôt
62.	Staff costs	39.29	36.90	35.00	35.17	33.36	35.78	33.81	28.90	33.73	36.94	62.	Frais de personnel
% of net income													**% du total du résultat net**
63.	Provisions (net)	30.10	44.51	49.71	58.00	60.80	86.93	118.19	87.21	156.76	..	63.	Provisions (nettes)
64.	Profit before tax	69.90	55.49	50.29	42.00	39.20	13.07	-18.19	12.79	-56.76	..	64.	Bénéfices avant impôt
65.	Income tax	5.11	10.25	9.05	8.51	7.03	7.51	3.71	5.03	3.66	..	65.	Impôt
66.	Profit after tax	64.79	45.23	41.23	33.49	32.17	5.56	-21.90	7.76	-60.42	..	66.	Bénéfices après impôt

NORWAY

All banks

Per cent

BALANCE SHEET ANALYSIS

% of year-end balance sheet total

	1982	1983	1984	1985	1986	1987	1988	1989	1990	1991		
Assets												
67. Cash & balance with Central bank	0.62	1.22	0.67	0.66	0.59	0.66	0.54	0.51	0.51	0.63	67.	Caisse & solde auprès de la Banque centrale
68. Interbank deposits	7.52	6.23	5.84	5.68	8.33	6.05	4.01	2.94	3.38	4.92	68.	Dépôts interbancaires
69. Loans	60.78	62.86	63.82	68.84	71.42	68.66	73.32	76.01	77.24	78.11	69.	Prêts
70. Securities	29.11	27.83	26.82	22.72	16.99	19.89	16.61	15.06	13.74	11.38	70.	Valeurs mobilières
71. Other assets	1.97	1.86	2.85	2.11	2.67	4.73	5.52	5.48	5.14	4.95	71.	Autres actifs
Liabilities												
72. Capital & reserves	5.17	5.38	5.17	5.09	4.73	3.97	3.92	4.33	3.87	3.07	72.	Capital et réserves
73. Borrowing from Central bank	0.60	1.24	0.37	0.78	13.80	12.48	13.08	9.68	9.09	8.24	73.	Emprunts auprès de la Banque centrale
74. Interbank deposits	12.79	12.25	13.66	15.42	14.23	16.54	13.75	12.77	12.44	11.23	74.	Dépôts interbancaires
75. Non-bank deposits	76.05	74.85	72.66	68.54	54.68	52.90	55.94	58.57	60.34	64.76	75.	Dépôts non bancaires
76. Bonds	0.85	1.39	2.28	2.65	6.59	5.85	7.50	7.94	8.23	7.59	76.	Obligations
77. Other liabilities	4.52	4.89	5.86	7.52	5.96	8.25	5.81	6.70	6.03	5.12	77.	Autres engagements
Memoranda												*Pour mémoire*
78. Short-term securities	3.52	1.88	7.15	7.57	4.18	5.63	1.78	1.62	2.14	1.48	78.	Titres à court terme
79. Bonds	24.14	24.30	17.83	13.02	10.54	12.48	13.01	11.54	9.48	8.17	79.	Obligations
80. Shares and participations	1.45	1.64	1.84	2.13	2.28	1.78	1.82	1.90	2.12	1.73	80.	Actions et participations
81. Claims on non-residents	7.61	7.78	8.82	7.28	10.00	5.38	4.48	5.16	5.55	5.33	81.	Créances sur des non résidents
82. Liabilities to non-residents	12.95	13.40	16.19	18.43	20.01	22.36	22.52	22.19	21.04	16.63	82.	Engagements envers des non résidents

1. Change in methodology.

Notes

- Average balance sheet totals (item 29) are based on thirteen end-month data.

- All banks include Commercial banks and Savings banks.

Change in methodology:

- Due to methodological changes, in 1991, value adjustments (NKr 1.1 billion in 1990) are included under "Operating expenses" (item 6 or item 43 or item 56) and not under "Provisions (net)" (item 8 or item 45 or item 58) as in previous years.

NORVEGE

Ensemble des banques

Pourcentage

ANALYSE DU BILAN

% du total du bilan en fin d'exercice

Actif

Passif

1. Changement méthodologique.

Notes

- La moyenne du total des actifs/passifs (poste 29) est basée sur treize données de fin de mois.

- L'Ensemble des banques comprend les Banques commerciales et les Caisses d'épargne.

Changement méthodologique :

- Dû aux changements méthodologiques, pour l'année 1991, les ajustements en valeur (1,1 milliard de KrN en 1990) sont inclus sous la rubrique "Frais d'exploitation" (poste 6 ou poste 43 ou poste 56) et non sous la rubrique "Provisions (nettes)" (poste 8 ou poste 45 ou poste 58) comme dans les années précédentes.

NORWAY
Commercial banks

NORVEGE
Banques commerciales

Million Norwegian kroner — Millions de couronnes norvégiennes

		1982	1983	1984	1985	1986	1987	1988	1989	1990	1991	
INCOME STATEMENT												**COMPTE DE RESULTATS**
1.	Interest income	15020	16421	20130	23179	30974	42243	45572	43709	43631	40234	1. Produits financiers
2.	Interest expenses	10872	11162	14301	16945	23289	33352	36088	33093	33431	30930	2. Frais financiers
3.	Net interest income	4148	5259	5829	6234	7685	8891	9484	10616	10200	9304	3. Produits financiers nets
4.	Non-interest income (net)	1593	1917	2859	3551	4400	2443	4739	5229	3570	2188	4. Produits non financiers (nets)
5.	Gross income	5741	7176	8688	9785	12085	11334	14223	15845	13770	11492	5. Résultat brut
6.	Operating expenses (1)	4214	4843	5789	6676	7857	9358	9681	9522	10151	11742	6. Frais d'exploitation (1)
7.	Net income	1527	2333	2899	3109	4228	1976	4542	6323	3619	-250	7. Résultat net
8.	Provisions (net) (1)	831	996	1391	1684	2500	2734	5712	5710	7593	16780	8. Provisions (nettes) (1)
9.	Profit before tax	696	1337	1508	1425	1728	-758	-1170	613	-3974	-17030	9. Bénéfices avant impôt
10.	Income tax	159	231	264	298	328	151	78	287	61	8	10. Impôt
11.	Profit after tax	537	1106	1244	1127	1400	-909	-1248	326	-4035	-17038	11. Bénéfices après impôt
12.	Distributed profit	317	423	541	651	501	239	157	699	15	13	12. Bénéfices distribués
13.	Retained profit	220	683	703	476	899	-1148	-1405	-373	-4050	-17051	13. Bénéfices mis en réserve
Memoranda												*Pour mémoire*
14.	*Staff costs*	*2359*	*2642*	*2954*	*3250*	*3925*	*4441*	*4833*	*4723*	*4928*	*4751*	14. Frais de personnel
15.	*Provisions on loans*	*475*	*616*	*745*	*736*	*794*	*2688*	*5673*	*5308*	*7051*	*16663*	15. Provisions sur prêts
16.	*Provisions on securities*	..	..	..	..	..	..	..	..	..	..	16. Provisions sur titres
BALANCE SHEET												**BILAN**
Assets												**Actif**
17.	Cash & balance with Central bank	610	1621	893	1001	1136	1756	1512	1404	1283	1797	17. Caisse & solde auprès de la Banque centrale
18.	Interbank deposits	11595	10377	13933	14832	27382	23939	17293	13416	17261	23493	18. Dépôts interbancaires
19.	Loans	76703	91693	119184	152128	203608	237502	245541	272208	281433	258981	19. Prêts
20.	Securities	36784	40546	50149	50296	52925	76414	54137	50082	48439	33969	20. Valeurs mobilières
21.	Other assets	3201	3628	8022	5832	10226	20062	22231	23933	22850	19944	21. Autres actifs
Liabilities												**Passif**
22.	Capital & reserves	5561	7046	9070	11271	14046	13906	13493	15202	13153	8061	22. Capital et réserves
23.	Borrowing from Central bank	997	1601	366	793	41936	41261	39518	27636	32814	33036	23. Emprunts auprès de la Banque centrale
24.	Interbank deposits	24933	26315	36166	44224	52510	72292	58967	60811	62804	48234	24. Dépôts interbancaires
25.	Non-bank deposits	88832	100792	125275	137290	135619	165776	169189	186288	193183	190008	25. Dépôts non bancaires
26.	Bonds	1682	3263	6894	7910	27949	31955	38615	43067	44105	38446	26. Obligations
27.	Other liabilities	6888	8848	14410	22601	23217	34483	20932	28038	25207	20401	27. Autres engagements
Balance sheet total												**Total du bilan**
28.	End-year total	128893	147865	192181	224089	295277	359673	340713	361042	371266	338184	28. En fin d'exercice
29.	Average total	128946	146175	176888	220953	270976	320318	361442	361350	387647	373090	29. Moyen
Memoranda												*Pour mémoire*
30.	*Short-term securities*	*4507*	*2732*	*14690*	*17382*	*14086*	*26421*	*5546*	*6941*	*10318*	*5327*	30. Titres à court terme
31.	*Bonds*	*29687*	*34452*	*30740*	*26420*	*30045*	*42132*	*40352*	*34291*	*28024*	*21172*	31. Obligations
32.	*Shares and participations*	*2590*	*3362*	*4719*	*6493*	*8794*	*7861*	*8238*	*8850*	*10095*	*7470*	32. Actions et participations
33.	*Claims on non-residents*	*14327*	*16789*	*24847*	*22673*	*41215*	*25853*	*20660*	*26830*	*30023*	*27120*	33. Créances sur des non résidents
34.	*Liabilities to non-residents*	*25664*	*30032*	*45012*	*58367*	*85603*	*110579*	*106520*	*114870*	*112266*	*82903*	34. Engagements envers des non résidents
SUPPLEMENTARY INFORMATION												**RENSEIGNEMENTS COMPLEMENTAIRES**
35.	Number of institutions	22	22	21	27	29	28	29	28	22	21	35. Nombre d'institutions
36.	Number of branches	620	640	670	673	702	740	713	602	602	540	36. Nombre de succursales
37.	Number of employees (x 1000)	15.5	15.8	16.2	17.1	17.9	19	18.7	17.0	16.6	14.5	37. Nombre de salariés (x 1000)

NORWAY

Commercial banks

Per cent / *Pourcentage*

		1982	1983	1984	1985	1986	1987	1988	1989	1990	1991		

INCOME STATEMENT ANALYSIS — **ANALYSE DU COMPTE DE RESULTATS**

% of average balance sheet total — **% du total moyen du bilan**

#		1982	1983	1984	1985	1986	1987	1988	1989	1990	1991		
38.	Interest income	11.65	11.23	11.38	10.49	11.43	13.19	12.61	12.10	11.26	10.78	38.	Produits financiers
39.	Interest expenses	8.43	7.64	8.08	7.67	8.59	10.41	9.98	9.16	8.62	8.29	39.	Frais financiers
40.	Net interest income	3.22	3.60	3.30	2.82	2.84	2.78	2.62	2.94	2.63	2.49	40.	Produits financiers nets
41.	Non-interest income (net)	1.24	1.31	1.62	1.61	1.62	0.76	1.31	1.45	0.92	0.59	41.	Produits non financiers (nets)
42.	Gross income	4.45	4.91	4.91	4.43	4.46	3.54	3.94	4.38	3.55	3.08	42.	Résultat brut
43.	Operating expenses (1)	3.27	3.31	3.27	3.02	2.90	2.92	2.68	2.64	2.62	3.15	43.	Frais d'exploitation (1)
44.	Net income	1.18	1.60	1.64	1.41	1.56	0.62	1.26	1.75	0.93	-0.07	44.	Résultat net
45.	Provisions (net) (1)	0.64	0.68	0.79	0.76	0.92	0.85	1.58	1.58	1.96	4.50	45.	Provisions (nettes) (1)
46.	Profit before tax	0.54	0.91	0.85	0.64	0.64	-0.24	-0.32	0.17	-1.03	-4.56	46.	Bénéfices avant impôt
47.	Income tax	0.12	0.16	0.15	0.13	0.12	0.05	0.02	0.08	0.02	0.00	47.	Impôt
48.	Profit after tax	0.42	0.76	0.70	0.51	0.52	-0.28	-0.35	0.09	-1.04	-4.57	48.	Bénéfices après impôt
49.	Distributed profit	0.25	0.29	0.31	0.29	0.18	0.07	0.04	0.19	0.00	0.00	49.	Bénéfices distribués
50.	Retained profit	0.17	0.47	0.40	0.22	0.33	-0.36	-0.39	-0.10	-1.04	-4.57	50.	Bénéfices mis en réserve
51.	Staff costs	1.83	1.81	1.67	1.47	1.45	1.39	1.34	1.31	1.27	1.27	51.	Frais de personnel
52.	Provisions on loans	0.37	0.42	0.42	0.33	0.29	0.84	1.57	1.47	1.82	4.47	52.	Provisions sur prêts
53.	Provisions on securities	:	:	:	:	:	:	:	:	:	:	53.	Provisions sur titres

% of gross income — **% du total du résultat brut**

#		1982	1983	1984	1985	1986	1987	1988	1989	1990	1991		
54.	Net interest income	72.25	73.29	67.09	63.71	63.59	78.45	66.68	67.00	74.07	80.96	54.	Produits financiers nets
55.	Non-interest income (net)	27.75	26.71	32.91	36.29	36.41	21.55	33.32	33.00	25.93	19.04	55.	Produits non financiers (nets)
56.	Operating expenses (1)	73.40	67.49	66.63	68.23	65.01	82.57	68.07	60.09	73.72	102.18	56.	Frais d'exploitation (1)
57.	Net income	26.60	32.51	33.37	31.77	34.99	17.43	31.93	39.91	26.28	-2.18	57.	Résultat net
58.	Provisions (net) (1)	14.47	13.88	16.01	17.21	20.69	24.12	40.16	36.04	55.14	146.01	58.	Provisions (nettes) (1)
59.	Profit before tax	12.12	18.63	17.36	14.56	14.30	-6.69	-8.23	3.87	-28.86	-148.19	59.	Bénéfices avant impôt
60.	Income tax	2.77	3.22	3.04	3.05	2.71	1.33	0.55	1.81	0.44	0.07	60.	Impôt
61.	Profit after tax	9.35	15.41	14.32	11.52	11.58	-8.02	-8.77	2.06	-29.30	-148.26	61.	Bénéfices après impôt
62.	Staff costs	41.09	36.82	34.00	33.21	32.48	39.18	33.98	29.81	35.79	41.34	62.	Frais de personnel

% of net income — **% du total du résultat net**

#		1982	1983	1984	1985	1986	1987	1988	1989	1990	1991		
63.	Provisions (net)	54.42	42.69	47.98	54.17	59.13	138.36	125.76	90.31	209.81	:	63.	Provisions (nettes)
64.	Profit before tax	45.58	57.31	52.02	45.83	40.87	-38.36	-25.76	9.69	-109.81	:	64.	Bénéfices avant impôt
65.	Income tax	10.41	9.90	9.11	9.59	7.76	7.64	1.72	4.54	1.69	:	65.	Impôt
66.	Profit after tax	35.17	47.41	42.91	36.25	33.11	-46.00	-27.48	5.16	-111.49	:	66.	Bénéfices après impôt

117

NORWAY

Commercial banks

Per cent

BALANCE SHEET ANALYSIS

% of year-end balance sheet total

NORVEGE

Banques commerciales

Pourcentage

ANALYSE DU BILAN

% du total du bilan en fin d'exercice

	1982	1983	1984	1985	1986	1987	1988	1989	1990	1991	
Assets											**Actif**
67. Cash & balance with Central bank	0.47	1.10	0.46	0.45	0.38	0.49	0.44	0.39	0.35	0.53	67. Caisse & solde auprès de la Banque centrale
68. Interbank deposits	9.00	7.02	7.25	6.62	9.27	6.66	5.08	3.72	4.65	6.95	68. Dépôts interbancaires
69. Loans	59.51	62.01	62.02	67.89	68.95	66.03	72.07	75.40	75.80	76.58	69. Prêts
70. Securities	28.54	27.42	26.09	22.44	17.92	21.25	15.89	13.87	13.05	10.04	70. Valeurs mobilières
71. Other assets	2.48	2.45	4.17	2.60	3.46	5.58	6.52	6.63	6.15	5.90	71. Autres actifs
Liabilities											**Passif**
72. Capital & reserves	4.31	4.77	4.72	5.03	4.76	3.87	3.96	4.21	3.54	2.38	72. Capital et réserves
73. Borrowing from Central bank	0.77	1.08	0.19	0.35	14.20	11.47	11.60	7.65	8.84	9.77	73. Emprunts auprès de la Banque centrale
74. Interbank deposits	19.34	17.80	18.82	19.74	17.78	20.10	17.31	16.84	16.92	14.26	74. Dépôts interbancaires
75. Non-bank deposits	68.92	68.16	65.19	61.27	45.93	46.09	49.66	51.60	52.03	56.18	75. Dépôts non bancaires
76. Bonds	1.30	2.21	3.59	3.53	9.47	8.88	11.33	11.93	11.88	11.37	76. Obligations
77. Other liabilities	5.34	5.98	7.50	10.09	7.86	9.59	6.14	7.77	6.79	6.03	77. Autres engagements
Memoranda											*Pour mémoire*
78. Short-term securities	*3.50*	*1.85*	*7.64*	*7.76*	*4.77*	*7.35*	*1.63*	*1.92*	*2.78*	*1.58*	*78. Titres à court terme*
79. Bonds	*23.03*	*23.30*	*16.00*	*11.79*	*10.18*	*11.71*	*11.84*	*9.50*	*7.55*	*6.26*	*79. Obligations*
80. Shares and participations	*2.01*	*2.27*	*2.46*	*2.90*	*2.98*	*2.19*	*2.42*	*2.45*	*2.72*	*2.21*	*80. Actions et participations*
81. Claims on non-residents	*11.12*	*11.35*	*12.93*	*10.12*	*13.96*	*7.19*	*6.06*	*7.43*	*8.09*	*8.02*	*81. Créances sur des non résidents*
82. Liabilities to non-residents	*19.91*	*20.31*	*23.42*	*26.05*	*28.99*	*30.74*	*31.26*	*31.82*	*30.24*	*24.51*	*82. Engagements envers des non résidents*

1. Change in methodology.

Notes

- Average balance sheet totals (item 29) are based on thirteen end-month data.

Change in methodology:

- Due to methodological changes, in 1991, value adjustments are included under "Operating expenses" (item 6 or item 43 or item 56) and not under "Provisions (net)" (item 8 or item 45 or item 58) as in previous years.

1. Changement méthodologique.

Notes

- La moyenne du total des actifs/passifs (poste 29) est basée sur treize données de fin de mois.

Changement méthodologique :

- Dû aux changements méthodologiques, pour l'année 1991, les ajustements en valeur sont inclus sous la rubrique "Frais d'exploitation" (poste 6 ou poste 43 ou poste 56) et non sous la rubrique "Provisions (nettes)" (poste 8 ou poste 45 ou poste 58) comme dans les années précédentes.

118

NORWAY
Savings banks

NORVEGE
Caisses d'épargne

Million Norwegian kroner — *Millions de couronnes norvégiennes*

	1982	1983	1984	1985	1986	1987	1988	1989	1990	1991	
INCOME STATEMENT											**COMPTE DE RESULTATS**
1. Interest income	9976	11851	13836	17693	24296	31298	34693	32713	31391	29836	1. Produits financiers
2. Interest expenses	6034	7251	8759	12031	17201	22495	25544	22193	21376	19958	2. Frais financiers
3. Net interest income	3942	4600	5077	5662	7095	8803	9149	10520	10015	9878	3. Produits financiers nets
4. Non-interest income (net)	417	482	622	1006	1405	1297	1581	2226	1585	1415	4. Produits non financiers (nets)
5. Gross income	4359	5082	5699	6668	8500	10100	10730	12746	11600	11293	5. Résultat brut
6. Operating expenses (1)	2776	3524	4070	5044	6069	6964	7757	7728	7782	8309	6. Frais d'exploitation (1)
7. Net income	1583	1558	1629	1624	2431	3136	2973	5018	3818	2984	7. Résultat net
8. Provisions (net) (1)	105	736	860	1061	1549	1710	3170	4181	4062	4850	8. Provisions (nettes) (1)
9. Profit before tax	1478	822	769	563	882	1426	-197	837	-244	-1866	9. Bénéfices avant impôt
10. Income tax	-	168	146	105	140	233	201	283	212	192	10. Impôt
11. Profit after tax	1478	654	623	458	742	1193	-398	554	-456	-2058	11. Bénéfices après impôt
12. Distributed profit	-	-	-	-	-	-	10	76	21	11	12. Bénéfices distribués
13. Retained profit	1478	654	623	458	742	1193	-408	478	-477	-2069	13. Bénéfices mis en réserve
Memoranda											*Pour mémoire*
14. Staff costs	*1609*	*1881*	*2081*	*2537*	*2943*	*3229*	*3603*	*3539*	*3629*	*3665*	*14. Frais de personnel*
15. Provisions on loans	*166*	*497*	*587*	*696*	*926*	*1744*	*3095*	*5173*	*3868*	*4708*	*15. Provisions sur prêts*
16. Provisions on securities	*..*	*..*	*..*	*..*	*..*	*..*	*..*	*..*	*..*	*..*	*16. Provisions sur titres*
BALANCE SHEET											**BILAN**
Assets											**Actif**
17. Cash & balance with Central bank	749	1430	1195	1528	1757	2124	1624	1679	1853	1837	17. Caisse & solde auprès de la Banque centrale
18. Interbank deposits	4762	5140	4324	6885	13458	11794	6074	4383	3492	4977	18. Dépôts interbancaires
19. Loans	55543	64889	80505	111073	146547	168079	181965	187424	193320	192579	19. Prêts
20. Securities	26549	28775	33779	36567	30374	41095	42716	40963	35991	31834	20. Valeurs mobilières
21. Other assets	1075	1015	891	2219	2881	7906	9936	9214	8723	8674	21. Autres actifs
Liabilities											**Passif**
22. Capital & reserves	5698	6351	7092	8179	9122	9555	9338	11002	10615	9663	22. Capital et réserves
23. Borrowing from Central bank	314	1500	796	2189	25740	32466	36736	30926	23066	14611	23. Emprunts auprès de la Banque centrale
24. Interbank deposits	2905	4208	6565	14751	17279	25412	21179	16406	13633	16684	24. Dépôts interbancaires
25. Non-bank deposits	76633	85661	102075	124774	132487	146689	156978	167897	177698	184342	25. Dépôts non bancaires
26. Bonds	176	193	227	2237	4361	2614	5123	4971	6496	5413	26. Obligations
27. Other liabilities	2952	3336	3939	6142	6028	14263	12967	12461	11870	9189	27. Autres engagements
Balance sheet total											**Total du bilan**
28. End-year total	88678	101249	120694	158272	195017	230999	242320	243665	243379	239902	28. En fin d'exercice
29. Average total	83628	101588	117136	143262	187379	221112	252462	250833	251542	248570	29. Moyen
Memoranda											*Pour mémoire*
30. Short-term securities	*3152*	*1960*	*7690*	*11553*	*6384*	*6845*	*4808*	*2872*	*2810*	*3222*	*30. Titres à court terme*
31. Bonds	*22832*	*26082*	*25040*	*23349*	*21610*	*31573*	*35507*	*35479*	*30238*	*26073*	*31. Obligations*
32. Shares and participations	*565*	*733*	*1049*	*1665*	*2380*	*2678*	*2402*	*2612*	*2942*	*2539*	*32. Actions et participations*
33. Claims on non-residents	*2231*	*2692*	*2746*	*5170*	*7834*	*5939*	*5475*	*4371*	*4060*	*3718*	*33. Créances sur des non résidents*
34. Liabilities to non-residents	*2504*	*3349*	*5634*	*12104*	*12517*	*21491*	*24751*	*19323*	*17049*	*13240*	*34. Engagements envers des non résidents*
SUPPLEMENTARY INFORMATION											**RENSEIGNEMENTS COMPLEMENTAIRES**
35. Number of institutions	270	253	227	198	192	173	158	151	142	135	35. Nombre d'institutions
36. Number of branches	1300	1300	1300	1328	1228	1426	1319	1194	1194	1121	36. Nombre de succursales
37. Number of employees (x 1000)	11.5	12.2	12.8	12.8	14.7	15.6	15.7	14.9	14.6	13.3	37. Nombre de salariés (x 1000)

NORWAY
Savings banks

NORVEGE
Caisses d'épargne

Per cent / *Pourcentage*

INCOME STATEMENT ANALYSIS / **ANALYSE DU COMPTE DE RESULTATS**

		1982	1983	1984	1985	1986	1987	1988	1989	1990	1991		
	% of average balance sheet total												**% du total moyen du bilan**
38.	Interest income	11.93	11.67	11.81	12.35	12.97	14.15	13.74	13.04	12.48	12.00	38.	Produits financiers
39.	Interest expenses	7.22	7.14	7.48	8.40	9.18	10.17	10.12	8.85	8.50	8.03	39.	Frais financiers
40.	Net interest income	4.71	4.53	4.33	3.95	3.79	3.98	3.62	4.19	3.98	3.97	40.	Produits financiers nets
41.	Non-interest income (net)	0.50	0.47	0.53	0.70	0.75	0.59	0.63	0.89	0.63	0.57	41.	Produits non financiers (nets)
42.	Gross income	5.21	5.00	4.87	4.65	4.54	4.57	4.25	5.08	4.61	4.54	42.	Résultat brut
43.	Operating expenses (1)	3.32	3.47	3.47	3.52	3.24	3.15	3.07	3.08	3.09	3.34	43.	Frais d'exploitation (1)
44.	Net income	1.89	1.53	1.39	1.13	1.30	1.42	1.18	2.00	1.52	1.20	44.	Résultat net
45.	Provisions (net) (1)	0.13	0.72	0.73	0.74	0.83	0.77	1.26	1.67	1.61	1.95	45.	Provisions (nettes) (1)
46.	Profit before tax	1.77	0.81	0.66	0.39	0.47	0.64	-0.08	0.33	-0.10	-0.75	46.	Bénéfices avant impôt
47.	Income tax	-	0.17	0.12	0.07	0.07	0.11	0.08	0.11	0.08	0.08	47.	Impôt
48.	Profit after tax	1.77	0.64	0.53	0.32	0.40	0.54	-0.16	0.22	-0.18	-0.83	48.	Bénéfices après impôt
49.	Distributed profit	-	-	-	-	-	-	0.00	0.03	0.01	0.00	49.	Bénéfices distribués
50.	Retained profit	1.77	0.64	0.53	0.32	0.40	0.54	-0.16	0.19	-0.19	-0.83	50.	Bénéfices mis en réserve
51.	Staff costs	1.92	1.85	1.78	1.77	1.57	1.46	1.43	1.41	1.44	1.47	51.	Frais de personnel
52.	Provisions on loans	0.20	0.49	0.50	0.49	0.49	0.79	1.23	2.06	1.54	1.89	52.	Provisions sur prêts
53.	Provisions on securities	:	:	:	:	:	:	:	:	:	:	53.	Provisions sur titres
	% of gross income												**% du total du résultat brut**
54.	Net interest income	90.43	90.52	89.09	84.91	83.47	87.16	85.27	82.54	86.34	87.47	54.	Produits financiers nets
55.	Non-interest income (net)	9.57	9.48	10.91	15.09	16.53	12.84	14.73	17.46	13.66	12.53	55.	Produits non financiers (nets)
56.	Operating expenses (1)	63.68	69.34	71.42	75.64	71.40	68.95	72.29	60.63	67.09	73.58	56.	Frais d'exploitation (1)
57.	Net income	36.32	30.66	28.58	24.36	28.60	31.05	27.71	39.37	32.91	26.42	57.	Résultat net
58.	Provisions (net) (1)	2.41	14.48	15.09	15.91	18.22	16.93	29.54	32.80	35.02	42.95	58.	Provisions (nettes) (1)
59.	Profit before tax	33.91	16.17	13.49	8.44	10.38	14.12	-1.84	6.57	-2.10	-16.52	59.	Bénéfices avant impôt
60.	Income tax	-	3.31	2.56	1.57	1.65	2.31	1.87	2.22	1.83	1.70	60.	Impôt
61.	Profit after tax	33.91	12.87	10.93	6.87	8.73	11.81	-3.71	4.35	-3.93	-18.22	61.	Bénéfices après impôt
62.	Staff costs	36.91	37.01	36.52	38.05	34.62	31.97	33.58	27.77	31.28	32.45	62.	Frais de personnel
	% of net income												**% du total du résultat net**
63.	Provisions (net)	6.63	47.24	52.79	65.33	63.72	54.53	106.63	83.32	106.39	162.53	63.	Provisions (nettes)
64.	Profit before tax	93.37	52.76	47.21	34.67	36.28	45.47	-6.63	16.68	-6.39	-62.53	64.	Bénéfices avant impôt
65.	Income tax	-	10.78	8.96	6.47	5.76	7.43	6.76	5.64	5.55	6.43	65.	Impôt
66.	Profit after tax	93.37	41.98	38.24	28.20	30.52	38.04	-13.39	11.04	-11.94	-68.97	66.	Bénéfices après impôt

NORWAY
Savings banks

NORVEGE

Caisses d'épargne

Per cent

Pourcentage

BALANCE SHEET ANALYSIS

% of year-end balance sheet total

ANALYSE DU BILAN

% du total du bilan en fin d'exercice

	1982	1983	1984	1985	1986	1987	1988	1989	1990	1991		
Assets												**Actif**
67. Cash & balance with Central bank	0.84	1.41	0.99	0.97	0.90	0.92	0.67	0.69	0.76	0.77	67.	Caisse & solde auprès de la Banque centrale
68. Interbank deposits	5.37	5.08	3.58	4.35	6.90	5.11	2.51	1.80	1.43	2.07	68.	Dépôts interbancaires
69. Loans	62.63	64.09	66.70	70.18	75.15	72.76	75.09	76.92	79.43	80.27	69.	Prêts
70. Securities	29.94	28.42	27.99	23.10	15.58	17.79	17.63	16.81	14.79	13.27	70.	Valeurs mobilières
71. Other assets	1.21	1.00	0.74	1.40	1.48	3.42	4.10	3.78	3.58	3.62	71.	Autres actifs
Liabilities												**Passif**
72. Capital & reserves	6.43	6.27	5.88	5.17	4.68	4.14	3.85	4.52	4.36	4.03	72.	Capital et réserves
73. Borrowing from Central bank	0.35	1.48	0.66	1.38	13.20	14.05	15.16	12.69	9.48	6.09	73.	Emprunts auprès de la Banque centrale
74. Interbank deposits	3.28	4.16	5.44	9.32	8.86	11.00	8.74	6.73	5.60	6.95	74.	Dépôts interbancaires
75. Non-bank deposits	86.42	84.60	84.57	78.84	67.94	63.50	64.78	68.90	73.01	76.84	75.	Dépôts non bancaires
76. Bonds	0.20	0.19	0.19	1.41	2.24	1.13	2.11	2.04	2.67	2.26	76.	Obligations
77. Other liabilities	3.33	3.29	3.26	3.88	3.09	6.17	5.35	5.11	4.88	3.83	77.	Autres engagements
Memoranda												**Pour mémoire**
78. *Short-term securities*	*3.55*	*1.94*	*6.37*	*7.30*	*3.27*	*2.96*	*1.98*	*1.18*	*1.15*	*1.34*	*78.*	*Titres à court terme*
79. *Bonds*	*25.75*	*25.76*	*20.75*	*14.75*	*11.08*	*13.67*	*14.65*	*14.56*	*12.42*	*10.87*	*79.*	*Obligations*
80. *Shares and participations*	*0.64*	*0.72*	*0.87*	*1.05*	*1.22*	*1.16*	*0.99*	*1.07*	*1.21*	*1.06*	*80.*	*Actions et participations*
81. *Claims on non-residents*	*2.52*	*2.56*	*2.28*	*3.27*	*4.02*	*2.57*	*2.26*	*1.79*	*1.67*	*1.55*	*81.*	*Créances sur des non résidents*
82. *Liabilities to non-residents*	*2.82*	*3.31*	*4.67*	*7.65*	*6.42*	*9.30*	*10.21*	*7.93*	*7.01*	*5.52*	*82.*	*Engagements envers des non résidents*

1. Change in methodology.

1. Changement méthodologique.

Notes

* Average balance sheet totals (item 29) are based on thirteen end-month data.

Change in methodology:

* Due to methodological changes, in 1991, value adjustments are included under "Operating expenses" (item 6 or item 43 or item 56) and not under "Provisions (net)" (item 8 or item 45 or item 58) as in previous years.

Notes

* La moyenne du total des actifs/passifs (poste 29) est basée sur treize données de fin de mois.

Changement méthodologique :

* Dû aux changements méthodologiques, pour l'année 1991, les ajustements en valeur sont inclus sous la rubrique "Frais d'exploitation" (poste 6 ou poste 43 ou poste 56) et non sous la rubrique "Provisions (nettes)" (poste 8 ou poste 45 ou poste 58) comme dans les années précédentes.

Million escudos / *Millions d'escudos*

	1982	1983	1984	1985	1986	1987	1988	1989	1990 (1)	1991	
INCOME STATEMENT											**COMPTE DE RESULTATS**
1. Interest income	366991	511086	737647	933400	880775	848092	944041	1171919	1526170	1853028	1. Produits financiers
2. Interest expenses	305420	452165	663248	821707	718557	614871	649072	780109	980136	1197538	2. Frais financiers
3. Net interest income	61571	58921	74399	117693	162218	233221	294969	391810	546034	655490	3. Produits financiers nets
4. Non-interest income (net)	31079	45375	48327	37271	36132	52303	64212	76182	126968	149699	4. Produits non financiers (nets)
5. Gross income	92650	104296	122726	154964	198350	285524	359181	467992	673002	805189	5. Résultat brut
6. Operating expenses	51348	68077	85495	107744	132113	154510	183213	219080	280859	367504	6. Frais d'exploitation
7. Net income	41302	36219	37231	47220	66237	131014	175968	248912	392143	437685	7. Résultat net
8. Provisions (net)	25255	22667	23623	30831	49399	92362	115176	151446	231747	236298	8. Provisions (nettes)
9. Profit before tax	16047	13552	13608	16389	16838	38652	60792	97466	160396	201387	9. Bénéfices avant impôt
10. Income tax	1759	1103	1227	1622	1668	1846	4053	23304	38814	55937	10. Impôt
11. Profit after tax	14288	12449	12381	14767	15170	36806	56739	74162	121582	145450	11. Bénéfices après impôt
12. Distributed profit	..	..	..	..	..	..	..	..	..	..	12. Bénéfices distribués
13. Retained profit	..	..	..	..	..	..	..	..	..	..	13. Bénéfices mis en réserve
Memoranda											*Pour mémoire*
14. Staff costs	37720	49982	61249	76547	92062	106888	121684	141475	172837	216184	14. Frais de personnel
15. Provisions on loans	..	..	..	..	..	..	..	..	220452	217457	15. Provisions sur prêts
16. Provisions on securities	..	..	..	..	..	..	..	..	11493	19207	16. Provisions sur titres
BALANCE SHEET											**BILAN**
Assets											**Actif**
17. Cash & balance with Central bank	266263	305567	306287	311083	284202	396356	465639	1319298	1424899	1807694	17. Caisse & solde auprès de la Banque centrale
18. Interbank deposits	162670	131568	400402	798040	1072002	1192065	1263484	1244249	2267469	1981227	18. Dépôts interbancaires
19. Loans	1741784	2180816	2642474	2923807	3257965	3384853	3631461	3851876	4692485	5786290	19. Prêts
20. Securities	182756	209588	197661	432504	573087	972915	1407330	1545134	2124880	3795675	20. Valeurs mobilières
21. Other assets	494466	709622	914242	987459	1132528	1432713	1971423	2342169	1257323	1249574	21. Autres actifs
Liabilities											**Passif**
22. Capital & reserves	178009	201099	247872	305897	421556	609487	836160	1063216	1532464	1982141	22. Capital et réserves
23. Borrowing from Central bank	18746	43411	33110	57127	77083	60445	21686	30932	45412	196482	23. Emprunts auprès de la Banque centrale
24. Interbank deposits	94495	77728	60928	86839	106330	245149	333275	505209	1034466	1337458	24. Dépôts interbancaires
25. Non-bank deposits	2167725	2617830	3366521	4203635	4952503	5586231	6465273	7539688	8018707	9686631	25. Dépôts non bancaires
26. Bonds	12430	22717	37779	43152	42025	69277	91676	92159	134255	169405	26. Obligations
27. Other liabilities	376534	574376	714856	756243	720287	808313	991267	1069522	1001752	1248343	27. Autres engagements
Balance sheet total											**Total du bilan**
28. End-year total	2847939	3537161	4461066	5452893	6319784	7378902	8739337	10300726	11767056	14620460	28. En fin d'exercice
29. Average total	2492729	3192550	3999114	4956980	5886339	6849343	8059120	9520032	NA	13193758	29. Moyen
Memoranda											*Pour mémoire*
30. Short-term securities	158034	179707	166259	45711	156355	293109	302597	522655	708908	1375478	30. Titres à court terme
31. Bonds	-	-	-	345710	371191	572003	845926	816299	1096215	1898583	31. Obligations
32. Shares and participations	26829	32210	34361	43628	46503	109391	131635	184629	280616	425311	32. Actions et participations
33. Claims on non-residents	137403	224292	312512	357334	339334	403409	611988	698218	734085	933953	33. Créances sur des non résidents
34. Liabilities to non-residents	121702	221417	298942	257699	221513	229801	301338	466196	637619	935610	34. Engagements envers des non résidents
SUPPLEMENTARY INFORMATION											**RENSEIGNEMENTS COMPLEMENTAIRES**
35. Number of institutions	17	17	18	24	27	27	27	29	33	35	35. Nombre d'institutions
36. Number of branches	1381	1426	1469	1494	1510	1531	1607	1741	1991	2505	36. Nombre de succursales
37. Number of employees (x 1000)	56.4	58.4	58.7	59.1	59.2	59.0	58.4	58.1	59.2	61.1	37. Nombre de salariés (x 1000)

PORTUGAL

Commercial banks

PORTUGAL

Banques commerciales

Per cent / *Pourcentage*

		1982	1983	1984	1985	1986	1987	1988	1989	1990 (1)	1991			
	INCOME STATEMENT ANALYSIS													**ANALYSE DU COMPTE DE RESULTATS**
	% of average balance sheet total													**% du total moyen du bilan**
38.	Interest income	14.72	16.01	18.45	18.95	14.96	12.38	11.71	12.31	NA	14.04	38.	Produits financiers
39.	Interest expenses	12.25	14.16	16.58	16.58	12.21	8.98	8.05	8.19	NA	9.08	39.	Frais financiers
40.	Net interest income	2.47	1.85	1.86	2.37	2.76	3.41	3.66	4.12	NA	4.97	40.	Produits financiers nets
41.	Non-interest income (net)	1.25	1.42	1.21	0.75	0.61	0.76	0.80	0.80	NA	1.13	41.	Produits non financiers (nets)
42.	Gross income	3.72	3.27	3.07	3.13	3.37	4.17	4.46	4.92	NA	6.10	42.	Résultat brut
43.	Operating expenses	2.06	2.13	2.14	2.17	2.24	2.26	2.27	2.30	NA	2.79	43.	Frais d'exploitation
44.	Net income	1.66	1.13	0.93	0.95	1.13	1.91	2.18	2.61	NA	3.32	44.	Résultat net
45.	Provisions (net)	1.01	0.71	0.59	0.62	0.84	1.35	1.43	1.59	NA	1.79	45.	Provisions (nettes)
46.	Profit before tax	0.64	0.42	0.34	0.33	0.29	0.56	0.75	1.02	NA	1.53	46.	Bénéfices avant impôt
47.	Income tax	0.07	0.03	0.03	0.03	0.03	0.03	0.05	0.24	NA	0.42	47.	Impôt
48.	Profit after tax	0.57	0.39	0.31	0.30	0.26	0.54	0.70	0.78	NA	1.10	48.	Bénéfices après impôt
49.	Distributed profit	:	:	:	:	:	:	:	:	:	:	49.	Bénéfices distribués
50.	Retained profit	:	:	:	:	:	:	:	:	:	:	50.	Bénéfices mis en réserve
51.	Staff costs	1.51	1.57	1.53	1.54	1.56	1.56	1.51	1.49	NA	1.64	51.	Frais de personnel
52.	Provisions on loans	:	:	:	:	:	:	:	:	NA	1.65	52.	Provisions sur prêts
53.	Provisions on securities	:	:	:	:	:	:	:	:	NA	0.15	53.	Provisions sur titres
	% of gross income													**% du total du résultat brut**
54.	Net interest income	66.46	56.49	60.62	75.95	81.78	81.68	82.12	83.72	81.13	81.41	54.	Produits financiers nets
55.	Non-interest income (net)	33.54	43.51	39.38	24.05	18.22	18.32	17.88	16.28	18.87	18.59	55.	Produits non financiers (nets)
56.	Operating expenses	55.42	65.27	69.66	69.53	66.61	54.11	51.01	46.81	41.73	45.64	56.	Frais d'exploitation
57.	Net income	44.58	34.73	30.34	30.47	33.39	45.89	48.99	53.19	58.27	54.36	57.	Résultat net
58.	Provisions (net)	27.26	21.73	19.25	19.90	24.90	32.35	32.07	32.36	34.43	29.35	58.	Provisions (nettes)
59.	Profit before tax	17.32	12.99	11.09	10.58	8.49	13.54	16.93	20.83	23.83	25.01	59.	Bénéfices avant impôt
60.	Income tax	1.90	1.06	1.00	1.05	0.84	0.65	1.13	4.98	5.77	6.95	60.	Impôt
61.	Profit after tax	15.42	11.94	10.09	9.53	7.65	12.89	15.80	15.85	18.07	18.06	61.	Bénéfices après impôt
62.	Staff costs	40.71	47.92	49.91	49.40	46.41	37.44	33.88	30.23	25.68	26.85	62.	Frais de personnel
	% of net income													**% du total du résultat net**
63.	Provisions (net)	61.15	62.58	63.45	65.29	74.58	70.50	65.45	60.84	59.10	53.99	63.	Provisions (nettes)
64.	Profit before tax	38.85	37.42	36.55	34.71	25.42	29.50	34.55	39.16	40.90	46.01	64.	Bénéfices avant impôt
65.	Income tax	4.26	3.05	3.30	3.43	2.52	1.41	2.30	9.36	9.90	12.78	65.	Impôt
66.	Profit after tax	34.59	34.37	33.25	31.27	22.90	28.09	32.24	29.79	31.00	33.23	66.	Bénéfices après impôt

PORTUGAL

Commercial banks

Per cent

BALANCE SHEET ANALYSIS

% of year-end balance sheet total

	1982	1983	1984	1985	1986	1987	1988	1989	1990 (1)	1991
Assets										
67. Cash & balance with Central bank	9.35	8.64	6.87	5.70	4.50	5.37	5.33	12.81	12.11	12.36
68. Interbank deposits	5.71	3.72	8.98	14.64	16.96	16.16	14.46	12.06	19.27	13.55
69. Loans	61.16	61.65	59.23	53.62	51.55	45.87	41.55	37.39	39.88	39.58
70. Securities	6.42	5.93	4.43	7.93	9.07	13.19	16.10	15.00	18.06	25.96
71. Other assets	17.36	20.06	20.49	18.11	17.92	19.42	22.56	22.74	10.69	8.55
Liabilities										
72. Capital & reserves	6.25	5.69	5.56	5.61	6.67	8.26	9.57	10.32	13.02	13.56
73. Borrowing from Central bank	0.66	1.23	0.74	1.05	1.22	0.82	0.25	0.30	0.39	1.34
74. Interbank deposits	3.32	2.20	1.37	1.59	1.68	3.32	3.81	4.90	8.79	9.15
75. Non-bank deposits	76.12	74.01	75.46	77.09	78.37	75.71	73.98	73.20	68.15	66.25
76. Bonds	0.44	0.64	0.85	0.79	0.66	0.94	1.05	0.89	1.14	1.16
77. Other liabilities	13.22	16.24	16.02	13.87	11.40	10.95	11.34	10.38	8.51	8.54
Memoranda										
78. *Short-term securities*	5.55	5.08	3.73	0.84	2.47	3.97	3.46	5.07	6.02	9.41
79. *Bonds*	0.94	0.91	0.77	6.34	5.87	7.75	9.68	7.92	9.32	12.99
80. *Shares and participations*	4.82	6.34	7.01	0.80	0.74	1.48	1.51	1.79	2.38	2.91
81. *Claims on non-residents*	4.27	6.26	6.70	6.55	5.37	5.47	7.00	6.78	6.24	6.39
82. *Liabilities to non-residents*				4.73	3.51	3.11	3.45	4.53	5.42	6.40

1. Break in series due to changes in methodology.

Change in methodology:

- Until 1989, time deposits with the Central bank are included under "Interbank deposits" (item 18).

- As from 1990, data are based on the new accounting framework for the Portugese banking sector, introduced in January 1990.

PORTUGAL

Banques commerciales

Pourcentage

ANALYSE DU BILAN

% du total du bilan en fin d'exercice

Actif
67. Caisse & solde auprès de la Banque centrale
68. Dépôts interbancaires
69. Prêts
70. Valeurs mobilières
71. Autres actifs

Passif
72. Capital et réserves
73. Emprunts auprès de la Banque centrale
74. Dépôts interbancaires
75. Dépôts non bancaires
76. Obligations
77. Autres engagements

Pour mémoire
78. *Titres à court terme*
79. *Obligations*
80. *Actions et participations*
81. *Créances sur des non résidents*
82. *Engagements envers des non résidents*

1. Rupture dans les séries consécutive aux changements méthodologiques.

Changement méthodologique :

- Jusqu'en 1989, les dépôts à terme auprès de la Banque centrale sont inclus sous "Dépôts interbancaires" (poste 18).

- A partir de 1990, les données sont établies à l'aide du nouveau cadre comptable pour le secteur bancaire portugais introduit en janvier 1990.

SPAIN
All banks

Billion pesetas

ESPAGNE
Ensemble des banques

Milliards de pesetas

		1982	1983	1984	1985	1986	1987	1988	1989	1990	1991	
	INCOME STATEMENT											**COMPTE DE RESULTATS**
1.	Interest income	2889	3232	3775	4022	4162	4742	5070	6206	7545	8423	Produits financiers
2.	Interest expenses	1895	2018	2396	2518	2445	2753	2845	3711	4792	5442	Frais financiers
3.	Net interest income	994	1214	1379	1504	1717	1989	2225	2495	2753	2981	Produits financiers nets
4.	Non-interest income (net)	166	191	217	278	330	417	505	501	587	744	Produits non financiers (nets)
5.	Gross income	1160	1405	1596	1782	2047	2406	2730	2996	3340	3725	Résultat brut
6.	Operating expenses	805	908	1023	1141	1373	1490	1759	1844	2068	2216	Frais d'exploitation
7.	Net income	355	497	573	641	674	916	971	1152	1272	1509	Résultat net
8.	Provisions (net)	192	310	325	323	309	408	378	336	393	501	Provisions (nettes)
9.	Profit before tax	163	187	248	318	365	508	593	816	879	1008	Bénéfices avant impôt
10.	Income tax	35	43	49	69	85	120	158	231	239	245	Impôt
11.	Profit after tax	128	144	199	249	280	388	435	585	640	763	Bénéfices après impôt
12.	Distributed profit	75	82	84	94	102	136	188	243	256	283	Bénéfices distribués
13.	Retained profit	53	62	115	155	178	252	247	342	384	480	Bénéfices mis en réserve
	Memoranda											*Pour mémoire*
14.	Staff costs	541	605	677	756	954	1016	1228	1236	1337	1392	Frais de personnel
15.	Provisions on loans	150	268	281	236	175	244	299	251	269	428	Provisions sur prêts
16.	Provisions on securities	20	15	2	18	6	27	1	10	55	37	Provisions sur titres
	BALANCE SHEET											**BILAN**
	Assets											**Actif**
17.	Cash & balance with Central bank	2248	3582	3622	3668	3787	5033	5141	5930	5034	5788	Caisse & solde auprès de la Banque centrale
18.	Interbank deposits	2606	2953	3958	5146	5406	5750	6773	8301	9721	11744	Dépôts interbancaires
19.	Loans	13721	15401	15546	16828	18251	20650	23800	28055	31457	37340	Prêts
20.	Securities	3352	3807	7247	8667	10900	11718	13030	14145	15464	14273	Valeurs mobilières
21.	Other assets	3875	4456	5726	5891	5679	5920	6198	7050	8457	9721	Autres actifs
	Liabilities											**Passif**
22.	Capital & reserves	1838	2446	2808	3164	3497	4132	4907	5572	6451	8231	Capital et réserves
23.	Borrowing from Central bank	556	744	1057	980	1426	1384	957	2112	1590	1572	Emprunts auprès de la Banque centrale
24.	Interbank deposits	2851	3388	4252	5496	5584	5562	6250	6804	7563	9863	Dépôts interbancaires
25.	Non-bank deposits	18552	21074	24361	26262	28671	32748	37307	42709	48124	52773	Dépôts non bancaires
26.	Bonds	566	802	1060	1310	1710	1463	1368	1093	1003	1208	Obligations
27.	Other liabilities	1439	1745	2562	2987	3134	3783	4153	5189	5402	5220	Autres engagements
	Balance sheet total											**Total du bilan**
28.	End-year total	25801	30199	36100	40199	44021	49071	54942	63480	70133	78866	En fin d'exercice
29.	Average total	23701	28000	33149	38150	42110	46546	52007	59211	66807	74500	Moyen
	Memoranda											*Pour mémoire*
30.	Short-term securities		172	2705	3831	4484	5412	6204	7237	8142	6064	Titres à court terme
31.	Bonds	2808	2904	3789	4052	5523	5291	5371	5180	5373	5477	Obligations
32.	Shares and participations	507	731	754	784	893	1015	1456	1728	1949	2732	Actions et participations
33.	Claims on non-residents	2181	2495	3039	3089	3152	2804	2800	3019	3792	4511	Créances sur des non résidents
34.	Liabilities to non-residents	2705	3043	3678	3228	3372	3629	4246	4876	6447	7373	Engagements envers des non résidents
	SUPPLEMENTARY INFORMATION											**RENSEIGNEMENTS COMPLEMENTAIRES**
35.	Number of institutions	378	376	369	364	355	346	334	333	327	323	Nombre d'institutions
36.	Number of branches	29810	31053	31615	32462	32616	33049	33542	34519	35084	35811	Nombre de succursales
37.	Number of employees (x 1000)	249.9	248.5	244.7	243.5	240.7	240.0	242.4	248.3	251.6	256.0	Nombre de salariés (x 1000)

SPAIN

All banks

Per cent

INCOME STATEMENT ANALYSIS

ESPAGNE

Ensemble des banques

Pourcentage

ANALYSE DU COMPTE DE RESULTATS

	1982	1983	1984	1985	1986	1987	1988	1989	1990	1991		
% of average balance sheet total												**% du total moyen du bilan**
38. Interest income	12.19	11.54	11.39	10.54	9.88	10.19	9.75	10.48	11.29	11.31	38.	Produits financiers
39. Interest expenses	8.00	7.21	7.23	6.60	5.81	5.91	5.47	6.27	7.17	7.30	39.	Frais financiers
40. Net interest income	4.19	4.34	4.16	3.94	4.08	4.27	4.28	4.21	4.12	4.00	40.	Produits financiers nets
41. Non-interest income (net)	0.70	0.68	0.65	0.73	0.78	0.90	0.97	0.85	0.88	1.00	41.	Produits non financiers (nets)
42. Gross income	4.89	5.02	4.81	4.67	4.86	5.17	5.25	5.06	5.00	5.00	42.	Résultat brut
43. Operating expenses	3.40	3.24	3.09	2.99	3.26	3.20	3.38	3.11	3.10	2.97	43.	Frais d'exploitation
44. Net income	1.50	1.78	1.73	1.68	1.60	1.97	1.87	1.95	1.90	2.03	44.	Résultat net
45. Provisions (net)	0.81	1.11	0.98	0.85	0.73	0.88	0.73	0.57	0.59	0.67	45.	Provisions (nettes)
46. Profit before tax	0.69	0.67	0.75	0.83	0.87	1.09	1.14	1.38	1.32	1.35	46.	Bénéfices avant impôt
47. Income tax	0.15	0.15	0.15	0.18	0.20	0.26	0.30	0.39	0.36	0.33	47.	Impôt
48. Profit after tax	0.54	0.51	0.60	0.65	0.66	0.83	0.84	0.99	0.96	1.02	48.	Bénéfices après impôt
49. Distributed profit	0.32	0.29	0.25	0.25	0.24	0.29	0.36	0.41	0.38	0.38	49.	Bénéfices distribués
50. Retained profit	0.22	0.22	0.35	0.41	0.42	0.54	0.47	0.58	0.57	0.64	50.	Bénéfices mis en réserve
51. Staff costs	2.28	2.16	2.04	1.98	2.27	2.18	2.36	2.09	2.00	1.87	51.	Frais de personnel
52. Provisions on loans	0.63	0.96	0.85	0.62	0.42	0.52	0.57	0.42	0.40	0.57	52.	Provisions sur prêts
53. Provisions on securities	0.08	0.05	0.01	0.05	0.01	0.06	0.00	0.02	0.08	0.05	53.	Provisions sur titres
% of gross income												**% du total du résultat brut**
54. Net interest income	85.69	86.41	86.40	84.40	83.88	82.67	81.50	83.28	82.43	80.03	54.	Produits financiers nets
55. Non-interest income (net)	14.31	13.59	13.60	15.60	16.12	17.33	18.50	16.72	17.57	19.97	55.	Produits non financiers (nets)
56. Operating expenses	69.40	64.63	64.10	64.03	67.07	61.93	64.43	61.55	61.92	59.49	56.	Frais d'exploitation
57. Net income	30.60	35.37	35.90	35.97	32.93	38.07	35.57	38.45	38.08	40.51	57.	Résultat net
58. Provisions (net)	16.55	22.06	20.36	18.13	15.10	16.96	13.85	11.21	11.77	13.45	58.	Provisions (nettes)
59. Profit before tax	14.05	13.31	15.54	17.85	17.83	21.11	21.72	27.24	26.32	27.06	59.	Bénéfices avant impôt
60. Income tax	3.02	3.06	3.07	3.87	4.15	4.99	5.79	7.71	7.16	6.58	60.	Impôt
61. Profit after tax	11.03	10.25	12.47	13.97	13.68	16.13	15.93	19.53	19.16	20.48	61.	Bénéfices après impôt
62. Staff costs	46.64	43.06	42.42	42.42	46.60	42.23	44.98	41.26	40.03	37.37	62.	Frais de personnel
% of net income												**% du total du résultat net**
63. Provisions (net)	54.08	62.37	56.72	50.39	45.85	44.54	38.93	29.17	30.90	33.20	63.	Provisions (nettes)
64. Profit before tax	45.92	37.63	43.28	49.61	54.15	55.46	61.07	70.83	69.10	66.80	64.	Bénéfices avant impôt
65. Income tax	9.86	8.65	8.55	10.76	12.61	13.10	16.27	20.05	18.79	16.24	65.	Impôt
66. Profit after tax	36.06	28.97	34.73	38.85	41.54	42.36	44.80	50.78	50.31	50.56	66.	Bénéfices après impôt

SPAIN

All banks

Per cent

BALANCE SHEET ANALYSIS

ESPAGNE

Ensemble des banques

Pourcentage

ANALYSE DU BILAN

% of year-end balance sheet total / % du total du bilan en fin d'exercice

	1982	1983	1984	1985	1986	1987	1988	1989	1990	1991	
Assets											**Actif**
67. Cash & balance with Central bank	8.71	11.86	10.03	9.12	8.60	10.26	9.36	9.34	7.18	7.34	67. Caisse & solde auprès de la Banque centrale
68. Interbank deposits	10.10	9.78	10.96	12.80	12.28	11.72	12.33	13.08	13.86	14.89	68. Dépôts interbancaires
69. Loans	53.18	51.00	43.06	41.86	41.46	42.08	43.32	44.20	44.85	47.35	69. Prêts
70. Securities	12.99	12.61	20.07	21.56	24.76	23.88	23.72	22.28	22.05	18.10	70. Valeurs mobilières
71. Other assets	15.02	14.76	15.86	14.65	12.90	12.06	11.28	11.11	12.06	12.33	71. Autres actifs
Liabilities											**Passif**
72. Capital & reserves	7.12	8.10	7.78	7.87	7.94	8.42	8.93	8.78	9.20	10.44	72. Capital et réserves
73. Borrowing from Central bank	2.15	2.46	2.93	2.44	3.24	2.82	1.74	3.33	2.27	1.99	73. Emprunts auprès de la Banque centrale
74. Interbank deposits	11.05	11.22	11.78	13.67	12.68	11.33	11.38	10.72	10.78	12.51	74. Dépôts interbancaires
75. Non-bank deposits	71.90	69.78	67.48	65.33	65.13	66.74	67.90	67.28	68.62	66.91	75. Dépôts non bancaires
76. Bonds	2.19	2.66	2.94	3.26	3.88	2.98	2.49	1.72	1.43	1.53	76. Obligations
77. Other liabilities	5.58	5.78	7.10	7.43	7.12	7.71	7.56	8.17	7.70	6.62	77. Autres engagements
Memoranda											***Pour mémoire***
78. Short-term securities	*0.14*	*0.57*	*7.49*	*9.53*	*10.19*	*11.03*	*11.29*	*11.40*	*11.61*	*7.69*	*78. Titres à court terme*
79. Bonds	*10.88*	*9.62*	*10.50*	*10.08*	*12.55*	*10.78*	*9.78*	*8.16*	*7.66*	*6.94*	*79. Obligations*
80. Shares and participations	*1.97*	*2.42*	*2.09*	*1.95*	*2.03*	*2.07*	*2.65*	*2.72*	*2.78*	*3.46*	*80. Actions et participations*
81. Claims on non-residents	*8.45*	*8.26*	*8.42*	*7.68*	*7.16*	*5.71*	*5.10*	*4.76*	*5.41*	*5.72*	*81. Créances sur des non résidents*
82. Liabilities to non-residents	*10.48*	*10.08*	*10.19*	*8.03*	*7.66*	*7.40*	*7.73*	*7.68*	*9.19*	*9.35*	*82. Engagements envers des non résidents*

Notes

- All banks include Commercial banks, Savings banks and Co-operative banks.

Change in methodology:

Revision of the historical series.

- As a consequence of the new legal definition of credit institutions in the Spanish financial system, assets and liabilities of the banking system against bank-like institutions are considered interbank desposits and no longer included in other assets and liabilities.

- According to the new accounting law, bills traded in organized markets are included in the item "Short-term securities".

- In the new sectorization of the information provided by credit institutions, public sector does not include public (state-owned) companies.

Notes

- L'Ensemble des banques comprend les Banques commerciales, les Caisses d'épargne et les Banques mutualistes.

Changement méthodologique :

Révision des séries historiques.

- Comme conséquence des nouvelles définitions juridiques des institutions de crédit dans le système financier espagnol, les créances et dettes du système bancaire envers les institutions quasi-bancaires sont considérées comme dépôts interbancaires et non plus comme autres créances ou dettes.

- Selon la nouvelle loi comptable, les effets négociés sur les marchés organisés sont inclus dans la rubrique "Titres à court terme".

- Dans la nouvelle sectorisation de l'information fournie par les institutions de crédit, le secteur public n'inclut pas les entreprises appartenant à l'état.

SPAIN — Commercial banks

ESPAGNE — Banques commerciales

Billion pesetas / *Milliards de pesetas*

		1982	1983	1984	1985	1986	1987	1988	1989	1990	1991
INCOME STATEMENT	**COMPTE DE RESULTATS**										
1. Interest income	1. Produits financiers	2123	2267	2616	2710	2742	3144	3303	4020	4776	5449
2. Interest expenses	2. Frais financiers	1475	1499	1755	1784	1702	1967	1946	2515	3139	3623
3. Net interest income	3. Produits financiers nets	648	768	861	926	1040	1177	1357	1505	1637	1826
4. Non-interest income (net)	4. Produits non financiers (nets)	145	174	173	211	239	314	375	372	449	595
5. Gross income	5. Résultat brut	793	942	1034	1137	1279	1491	1732	1877	2086	2421
6. Operating expenses	6. Frais d'exploitation	546	599	658	725	833	916	1023	1079	1223	1367
7. Net income	7. Résultat net	247	343	376	412	446	575	709	798	863	1054
8. Provisions (net)	8. Provisions (nettes)	150	217	240	226	220	274	262	223	241	334
9. Profit before tax	9. Bénéfices avant impôt	97	126	136	186	226	301	447	575	622	720
10. Income tax	10. Impôt	29	34	38	48	61	83	134	179	189	185
11. Profit after tax	11. Bénéfices après impôt	68	92	98	138	165	218	313	396	433	535
12. Distributed profit	12. Bénéfices distribués	49	53	52	61	68	91	141	186	207	237
13. Retained profit	13. Bénéfices mis en réserve	19	39	46	77	97	127	172	210	226	298
Memoranda	*Pour mémoire*										
14. Staff costs	14. Frais de personnel	371	403	441	486	582	640	708	722	795	860
15. Provisions on loans	15. Provisions sur prêts	116	189	216	168	131	168	221	196	189	286
16. Provisions on securities	16. Provisions sur titres	13	9	-	15	3	15	5	9	37	31
BALANCE SHEET	**BILAN**										
Assets	*Actif*										
17. Cash & balance with Central bank	17. Caisse & solde auprès de la Banque centrale	1421	2152	2180	1938	1811	2791	2751	2979	2516	3105
18. Interbank deposits	18. Dépôts interbancaires	1683	2029	2843	3418	3481	4000	4585	5504	6384	7636
19. Loans	19. Prêts	10238	11193	11116	11943	12566	13722	15359	17773	19723	23922
20. Securities	20. Valeurs mobilières	1734	2019	4212	5094	6623	6809	7020	7697	8508	8385
21. Other assets	21. Autres actifs	2980	3415	4464	4538	4166	4220	4343	4791	5508	6640
Liabilities	*Passif*										
22. Capital & reserves	22. Capital et réserves	1304	1716	1935	2142	2342	2732	3318	3728	4231	5719
23. Borrowing from Central bank	23. Emprunts auprès de la Banque centrale	542	731	1030	919	1303	1257	919	1553	1296	1243
24. Interbank deposits	24. Dépôts interbancaires	2371	2714	3435	4791	4941	4986	5512	5978	6241	8554
25. Non-bank deposits	25. Dépôts non bancaires	12252	13735	15768	16077	16976	19184	20994	23637	27100	30198
26. Bonds	26. Obligations	486	570	636	712	896	753	689	591	586	720
27. Other liabilities	27. Autres engagements	1100	1343	2011	2290	2190	2631	2627	3255	3186	3254
Balance sheet total	**Total du bilan**										
28. End-year total	28. En fin d'exercice	18056	20809	24815	26930	28648	31542	34059	38743	42639	49688
29. Average total	29. Moyen	16625	19432	22812	25873	27789	30095	32800	36401	40691	46164
Memoranda	*Pour mémoire*										
30. Short-term securities	30. Titres à court terme	31	80	1521	2330	3184	3486	3733	4016	4445	3221
31. Bonds	31. Obligations	1283	1317	2058	2115	2743	2542	2175	2395	2628	2979
32. Shares and participations	32. Actions et participations	420	622	633	650	696	782	1112	1285	1436	2185
33. Claims on non-residents	33. Créances sur des non résidents	2160	2461	2968	3020	3030	2676	2665	2821	3375	3983
34. Liabilities to non-residents	34. Engagements envers des non résidents	2562	2864	3451	2976	3099	3312	3841	4420	5739	6603
SUPPLEMENTARY INFORMATION	**RENSEIGNEMENTS COMPLEMENTAIRES**										
35. Number of institutions	35. Nombre d'institutions	141	140	139	139	138	138	138	145	154	160
36. Number of branches	36. Nombre de succursales	15500	16022	16215	16568	16468	16454	16549	16819	16836	18925
37. Number of employees (x 1000)	37. Nombre de salariés (x 1000)	175.7	170.5	164.3	161.6	157.8	155.3	154.7	155.7	157.0	162.0

SPAIN

Commercial banks

Per cent

ESPAGNE

Banques commerciales

Pourcentage

	1982	1983	1984	1985	1986	1987	1988	1989	1990	1991	
INCOME STATEMENT ANALYSIS											**ANALYSE DU COMPTE DE RESULTATS**
% of average balance sheet total											**% du total moyen du bilan**
38. Interest income	12.77	11.67	11.47	10.47	9.87	10.45	10.07	11.04	11.74	11.80	38. Produits financiers
39. Interest expenses	8.87	7.71	7.69	6.90	6.12	6.54	5.93	6.91	7.71	7.85	39. Frais financiers
40. Net interest income	3.90	3.95	3.77	3.58	3.74	3.91	4.14	4.13	4.02	3.96	40. Produits financiers nets
41. Non-interest income (net)	0.87	0.90	0.76	0.82	0.86	1.04	1.14	1.02	1.10	1.29	41. Produits non financiers (nets)
42. Gross income	4.77	4.85	4.53	4.39	4.60	4.95	5.28	5.16	5.13	5.24	42. Résultat brut
43. Operating expenses	3.28	3.08	2.88	2.80	3.00	3.04	3.12	2.96	3.01	2.96	43. Frais d'exploitation
44. Net income	1.49	1.77	1.65	1.59	1.60	1.91	2.16	2.19	2.12	2.28	44. Résultat net
45. Provisions (net)	0.90	1.12	1.05	0.87	0.79	0.91	0.80	0.61	0.59	0.72	45. Provisions (nettes)
46. Profit before tax	0.58	0.65	0.60	0.72	0.81	1.00	1.36	1.58	1.53	1.56	46. Bénéfices avant impôt
47. Income tax	0.17	0.17	0.17	0.19	0.22	0.28	0.41	0.49	0.46	0.40	47. Impôt
48. Profit after tax	0.41	0.47	0.43	0.53	0.59	0.72	0.95	1.09	1.06	1.16	48. Bénéfices après impôt
49. Distributed profit	0.29	0.27	0.23	0.24	0.24	0.30	0.43	0.51	0.51	0.51	49. Bénéfices distribués
50. Retained profit	0.11	0.20	0.20	0.30	0.35	0.42	0.52	0.58	0.56	0.65	50. Bénéfices mis en réserve
51. Staff costs	2.23	2.07	1.93	1.88	2.09	2.13	2.16	1.98	1.95	1.86	51. Frais de personnel
52. Provisions on loans	0.70	0.97	0.95	0.65	0.47	0.56	0.67	0.54	0.46	0.62	52. Provisions sur prêts
53. Provisions on securities	0.08	0.05	-	0.06	0.01	0.05	0.02	0.02	0.09	0.07	53. Provisions sur titres
% of gross income											**% du total du résultat brut**
54. Net interest income	81.72	81.53	83.27	81.44	81.31	78.94	78.35	80.18	78.48	75.42	54. Produits financiers nets
55. Non-interest income (net)	18.28	18.47	16.73	18.56	18.69	21.06	21.65	19.82	21.52	24.58	55. Produits non financiers (nets)
56. Operating expenses	68.85	63.59	63.64	63.76	65.13	61.44	59.06	57.49	58.63	56.46	56. Frais d'exploitation
57. Net income	31.15	36.41	36.36	36.24	34.87	38.56	40.94	42.51	41.37	43.54	57. Résultat net
58. Provisions (net)	18.92	23.04	23.21	19.88	17.20	18.38	15.13	11.88	11.55	13.80	58. Provisions (nettes)
59. Profit before tax	12.23	13.38	13.15	16.36	17.67	20.19	25.81	30.63	29.82	29.74	59. Bénéfices avant impôt
60. Income tax	3.66	3.61	3.68	4.22	4.77	5.57	7.74	9.54	9.06	7.64	60. Impôt
61. Profit after tax	8.58	9.77	9.48	12.14	12.90	14.62	18.07	21.10	20.76	22.10	61. Bénéfices après impôt
62. Staff costs	46.78	42.78	42.65	42.74	45.50	42.92	40.88	38.47	38.11	35.52	62. Frais de personnel
% of net income											**% du total du résultat net**
63. Provisions (net)	60.73	63.27	63.83	54.85	49.33	47.65	36.95	27.94	27.93	31.69	63. Provisions (nettes)
64. Profit before tax	39.27	36.73	36.17	45.15	50.67	52.35	63.05	72.06	72.07	68.31	64. Bénéfices avant impôt
65. Income tax	11.74	9.91	10.11	11.65	13.68	14.43	18.90	22.43	21.90	17.55	65. Impôt
66. Profit after tax	27.53	26.82	26.06	33.50	37.00	37.91	44.15	49.62	50.17	50.76	66. Bénéfices après impôt

SPAIN

Commercial banks

ESPAGNE

Banques commerciales

Per cent / *Pourcentage*

BALANCE SHEET ANALYSIS / **ANALYSE DU BILAN**

% of year-end balance sheet total / **% du total du bilan en fin d'exercice**

	1982	1983	1984	1985	1986	1987	1988	1989	1990	1991	
Assets											**Actif**
67. Cash & balance with Central bank	7.87	10.34	8.79	7.20	6.32	8.85	8.08	7.69	5.90	6.25	67. Caisse & solde auprès de la Banque centrale
68. Interbank deposits	9.32	9.75	11.46	12.69	12.15	12.68	13.46	14.21	14.97	15.37	68. Dépôts interbancaires
69. Loans	56.70	53.79	44.80	44.35	43.86	43.50	45.10	45.87	46.26	48.14	69. Prêts
70. Securities	9.60	9.70	16.97	18.92	23.12	21.59	20.61	19.87	19.95	16.88	70. Valeurs mobilières
71. Other assets	16.50	16.41	17.99	16.85	14.54	13.38	12.75	12.37	12.92	13.36	71. Autres actifs
Liabilities											**Passif**
72. Capital & reserves	7.22	8.25	7.80	7.95	8.18	8.66	9.74	9.62	9.92	11.51	72. Capital et réserves
73. Borrowing from Central bank	3.00	3.51	4.15	3.41	4.55	3.99	2.70	4.01	3.04	2.50	73. Emprunts auprès de la Banque centrale
74. Interbank deposits	13.13	13.04	13.84	17.79	17.25	15.81	16.18	15.43	14.64	17.22	74. Dépôts interbancaires
75. Non-bank deposits	67.86	66.01	63.54	59.70	59.26	60.82	61.64	61.01	63.56	60.78	75. Dépôts non bancaires
76. Bonds	2.69	2.74	2.56	2.64	3.13	2.39	2.02	1.53	1.37	1.45	76. Obligations
77. Other liabilities	6.09	6.45	8.10	8.50	7.64	8.34	7.71	8.40	7.47	6.55	77. Autres engagements
Memoranda											***Pour mémoire***
78. Short-term securities	*0.17*	*0.38*	*6.13*	*8.65*	*11.11*	*11.05*	*10.96*	*10.37*	*10.42*	*6.48*	*78. Titres à court terme*
79. Bonds	*7.11*	*6.33*	*8.29*	*7.85*	*9.57*	*8.06*	*6.39*	*6.18*	*6.16*	*6.00*	*79. Obligations*
80. Shares and participations	*2.33*	*2.99*	*2.55*	*2.41*	*2.43*	*2.48*	*3.26*	*3.32*	*3.37*	*4.40*	*80. Actions et participations*
81. Claims on non-residents	*11.96*	*11.83*	*11.96*	*11.21*	*10.58*	*8.48*	*7.82*	*7.28*	*7.92*	*8.02*	*81. Créances sur des non résidents*
82. Liabilities to non-residents	*14.19*	*13.76*	*13.91*	*11.05*	*10.82*	*10.50*	*11.28*	*11.41*	*13.46*	*13.29*	*82. Engagements envers des non résidents*

Change in methodology:

Revision of the historical series (see notes under All banks).

Changement méthodologique :

Révision des séries historiques (voir notes sous Ensemble des banques).

SPAIN

Savings banks

Billion pesetas

ESPAGNE

Caisses d'épargne

Milliards de pesetas

		1982	1983	1984	1985	1986	1987	1988	1989	1990	1991	
INCOME STATEMENT												**COMPTE DE RESULTATS**
1.	Interest income	667	856	1046	1182	1278	1434	1600	1999	2548	2718	1. Produits financiers
2.	Interest expenses	361	451	575	660	668	704	811	1099	1531	1675	2. Frais financiers
3.	Net interest income	306	405	471	522	610	730	789	900	1017	1043	3. Produits financiers nets
4.	Non-interest income (net)	21	27	35	57	85	98	125	124	132	144	4. Produits non financiers (nets)
5.	Gross income	327	432	506	579	695	828	914	1024	1149	1187	5. Résultat brut
6.	Operating expenses	231	276	330	377	497	526	685	709	780	776	6. Frais d'exploitation
7.	Net income	96	156	176	202	198	302	229	315	369	411	7. Résultat net
8.	Provisions (net)	34	75	80	86	79	121	106	105	142	157	8. Provisions (nettes)
9.	Profit before tax	62	81	96	116	119	181	123	210	227	254	9. Bénéfices avant impôt
10.	Income tax	5	9	10	20	23	35	22	49	47	59	10. Impôt
11.	Profit after tax	57	72	86	96	96	146	101	161	180	195	11. Bénéfices après impôt
12.	Distributed profit	22	24	27	27	28	38	43	50	41	47	12. Bénéfices distribués
13.	Retained profit	35	48	59	69	68	108	58	111	139	148	13. Bénéfices mis en réserve
	Memoranda											*Pour mémoire*
14.	*Staff costs*	*151*	*180*	*214*	*245*	*345*	*346*	*487*	*479*	*503*	*488*	14. Frais de personnel
15.	*Provisions on loans*	*26*	*61*	*59*	*58*	*35*	*64*	*70*	*49*	*71*	*131*	15. Provisions sur prêts
16.	*Provisions on securities*	*7*	*6*	*3*	*3*	*3*	*12*	*-4*	*1*	*16*	*7*	16. Provisions sur titres
BALANCE SHEET												**BILAN**
Assets												**Actif**
17.	Cash & balance with Central bank	784	1323	1361	1595	1825	2043	2183	2698	2249	2418	17. Caisse & solde auprès de la Banque centrale
18.	Interbank deposits	675	640	840	1402	1592	1428	1800	2412	2827	3494	18. Dépôts interbancaires
19.	Loans	3053	3752	3949	4347	5094	6247	7735	9482	10824	12319	19. Prêts
20.	Securities	1563	1719	2935	3442	4073	4666	5751	6203	6732	5664	20. Valeurs mobilières
21.	Other assets	813	976	1160	1234	1391	1576	1738	2139	2812	2927	21. Autres actifs
Liabilities												**Passif**
22.	Capital & reserves	454	649	783	916	1026	1239	1408	1640	1987	2244	22. Capital et réserves
23.	Borrowing from Central bank	13	12	27	62	123	127	39	559	294	329	23. Emprunts auprès de la Banque centrale
24.	Interbank deposits	340	529	745	627	552	471	640	739	1210	1205	24. Dépôts interbancaires
25.	Non-bank deposits	5694	6626	7756	9182	10619	12359	15004	17641	19409	20686	25. Dépôts non bancaires
26.	Bonds	80	233	422	590	794	693	670	501	417	487	26. Obligations
27.	Other liabilities	307	360	512	642	860	1069	1447	1854	2126	1873	27. Autres engagements
Balance sheet total												**Total du bilan**
28.	End-year total	6888	8409	10245	12019	13975	15959	19208	22934	25444	26823	28. En fin d'exercice
29.	Average total	6288	7649	9327	11132	12997	14967	17583	21071	24189	26134	29. Moyen
	Memoranda											*Pour mémoire*
30.	*Short-term securities*	*6*	*88*	*1173*	*1479*	*1246*	*1813*	*2335*	*3081*	*3556*	*2703*	30. Titres à court terme
31.	*Bonds*	*1475*	*1526*	*1646*	*1834*	*2640*	*2626*	*3080*	*2687*	*2675*	*2429*	31. Obligations
32.	*Shares and participations*	*83*	*105*	*116*	*129*	*188*	*226*	*336*	*435*	*501*	*532*	32. Actions et participations
33.	*Claims on non-residents*	*21*	*34*	*69*	*68*	*122*	*128*	*134*	*196*	*415*	*527*	33. Créances sur des non résidents
34.	*Liabilities to non-residents*	*138*	*172*	*220*	*245*	*266*	*309*	*399*	*450*	*699*	*758*	34. Engagements envers des non résidents
SUPPLEMENTARY INFORMATION												**RENSEIGNEMENTS COMPLEMENTAIRES**
35.	Number of institutions	83	83	81	79	79	79	79	78	66	57	35. Nombre d'institutions
36.	Number of branches	11262	11809	12201	12610	13062	13482	14092	14927	15356	13861	36. Nombre de succursales
37.	Number of employees (x 1000)	63.4	67.1	69.4	71.0	72.7	74.5	78.0	83.0	84.6	83.4	37. Nombre de salariés (x 1000)

SPAIN

Savings banks

ESPAGNE

Caisses d'épargne

Per cent / *Pourcentage*

INCOME STATEMENT ANALYSIS / ANALYSE DU COMPTE DE RESULTATS

	1982	1983	1984	1985	1986	1987	1988	1989	1990	1991		
% of average balance sheet total											**% du total moyen du bilan**	
38. Interest income	10.61	11.19	11.21	10.62	9.83	9.58	9.10	9.49	10.53	10.40	Produits financiers	38.
39. Interest expenses	5.74	5.90	6.16	5.93	5.14	4.70	4.61	5.22	6.33	6.41	Frais financiers	39.
40. Net interest income	4.87	5.29	5.05	4.69	4.69	4.88	4.49	4.27	4.20	3.99	Produits financiers nets	40.
41. Non-interest income (net)	0.33	0.35	0.38	0.51	0.65	0.65	0.71	0.59	0.55	0.55	Produits non financiers (nets)	41.
42. Gross income	5.20	5.65	5.43	5.20	5.35	5.53	5.20	4.86	4.75	4.54	Résultat brut	42.
43. Operating expenses	3.67	3.61	3.54	3.39	3.82	3.51	3.90	3.36	3.22	2.97	Frais d'exploitation	43.
44. Net income	1.53	2.04	1.89	1.81	1.52	2.02	1.30	1.49	1.53	1.57	Résultat net	44.
45. Provisions (net)	0.54	0.98	0.86	0.77	0.61	0.81	0.60	0.50	0.59	0.60	Provisions (nettes)	45.
46. Profit before tax	0.99	1.06	1.03	1.04	0.92	1.21	0.70	1.00	0.94	0.97	Bénéfices avant impôt	46.
47. Income tax	0.08	0.12	0.11	0.18	0.18	0.23	0.13	0.23	0.19	0.23	Impôt	47.
48. Profit after tax	0.91	0.94	0.92	0.86	0.74	0.98	0.57	0.76	0.74	0.75	Bénéfices après impôt	48.
49. Distributed profit	0.35	0.31	0.29	0.24	0.22	0.25	0.24	0.24	0.17	0.18	Bénéfices distribués	49.
50. Retained profit	0.56	0.63	0.63	0.62	0.52	0.72	0.33	0.53	0.57	0.57	Bénéfices mis en réserve	50.
51. Staff costs	2.40	2.35	2.29	2.20	2.65	2.31	2.77	2.27	2.08	1.87	Frais de personnel	51.
52. Provisions on loans	0.41	0.80	0.63	0.52	0.27	0.43	0.40	0.23	0.29	0.50	Provisions sur prêts	52.
53. Provisions on securities	0.11	0.08	0.03	0.03	0.02	0.08	-0.02	0.00	0.07	0.03	Provisions sur titres	53.
% of gross income											**% du total du résultat brut**	
54. Net interest income	93.58	93.75	93.08	90.16	87.77	88.16	86.32	87.89	88.51	87.87	Produits financiers nets	54.
55. Non-interest income (net)	6.42	6.25	6.92	9.84	12.23	11.84	13.68	12.11	11.49	12.13	Produits non financiers (nets)	55.
56. Operating expenses	70.64	63.89	65.22	65.11	71.51	63.53	74.95	69.24	67.89	65.37	Frais d'exploitation	56.
57. Net income	29.36	36.11	34.78	34.89	28.49	36.47	25.05	30.76	32.11	34.63	Résultat net	57.
58. Provisions (net)	10.40	17.36	15.81	14.85	11.37	14.61	11.60	10.25	12.36	13.23	Provisions (nettes)	58.
59. Profit before tax	18.96	18.75	18.97	20.03	17.12	21.86	13.46	20.51	19.76	21.40	Bénéfices avant impôt	59.
60. Income tax	1.53	2.08	1.98	3.45	3.31	4.23	2.41	4.79	4.09	4.97	Impôt	60.
61. Profit after tax	17.43	16.67	17.00	16.58	13.81	17.63	11.05	15.72	15.67	16.43	Bénéfices après impôt	61.
62. Staff costs	46.18	41.67	42.29	42.31	49.64	41.79	53.28	46.78	43.78	41.11	Frais de personnel	62.
% of net income											**% du total du résultat net**	
63. Provisions (net)	35.42	48.08	45.45	42.57	39.90	40.07	46.29	33.33	38.48	38.20	Provisions (nettes)	63.
64. Profit before tax	64.58	51.92	54.55	57.43	60.10	59.93	53.71	66.67	61.52	61.80	Bénéfices avant impôt	64.
65. Income tax	5.21	5.77	5.68	9.90	11.62	11.59	9.61	15.56	12.74	14.36	Impôt	65.
66. Profit after tax	59.38	46.15	48.86	47.52	48.48	48.34	44.10	51.11	48.78	47.45	Bénéfices après impôt	66.

SPAIN

Savings banks

Caisses d'épargne

Per cent / *Pourcentage*

BALANCE SHEET ANALYSIS / **ANALYSE DU BILAN**

% of year-end balance sheet total / *% du total du bilan en fin d'exercice*

	1982	1983	1984	1985	1986	1987	1988	1989	1990	1991	
Assets											**Actif**
67. Cash & balance with Central bank	11.38	15.73	13.28	13.27	13.06	12.80	11.37	11.76	8.84	9.01	67. Caisse & solde auprès de la Banque centrale
68. Interbank deposits	9.80	7.61	8.20	11.66	11.39	8.95	9.37	10.52	11.11	13.03	68. Dépôts interbancaires
69. Loans	44.32	44.62	38.55	36.17	36.45	39.14	40.27	41.34	42.54	45.93	69. Prêts
70. Securities	22.69	20.44	28.65	28.64	29.14	29.24	29.94	27.05	26.46	21.12	70. Valeurs mobilières
71. Other assets	11.80	11.61	11.32	10.27	9.95	9.88	9.05	9.33	11.05	10.91	71. Autres actifs
Liabilities											**Passif**
72. Capital & reserves	6.59	7.72	7.64	7.62	7.34	7.76	7.33	7.15	7.81	8.37	72. Capital et réserves
73. Borrowing from Central bank	0.19	0.14	0.26	0.52	0.88	0.80	0.20	2.44	1.16	1.23	73. Emprunts auprès de la Banque centrale
74. Interbank deposits	4.94	6.29	7.27	5.22	3.95	2.95	3.33	3.22	4.76	4.49	74. Dépôts interbancaires
75. Non-bank deposits	82.67	78.80	75.71	76.40	75.99	77.44	78.11	76.92	76.28	77.12	75. Dépôts non bancaires
76. Bonds	1.16	2.77	4.12	4.91	5.68	4.34	3.49	2.18	1.64	1.82	76. Obligations
77. Other liabilities	4.46	4.28	5.00	5.34	6.15	6.70	7.53	8.08	8.36	6.98	77. Autres engagements
Memoranda											***Pour mémoire***
78. Short-term securities	*0.09*	*1.05*	*11.45*	*12.31*	*8.92*	*11.36*	*12.16*	*13.43*	*13.98*	*10.08*	*78. Titres à court terme*
79. Bonds	*21.41*	*18.15*	*16.07*	*15.26*	*18.89*	*16.45*	*16.03*	*11.72*	*10.51*	*9.06*	*79. Obligations*
80. Shares and participations	*1.20*	*1.25*	*1.13*	*1.07*	*1.35*	*1.42*	*1.75*	*1.90*	*1.97*	*1.98*	*80. Actions et participations*
81. Claims on non-residents	*0.30*	*0.40*	*0.67*	*0.57*	*0.87*	*0.80*	*0.70*	*0.85*	*1.63*	*1.96*	*81. Créances sur des non résidents*
82. Liabilities to non-residents	*2.00*	*2.05*	*2.15*	*2.04*	*1.90*	*1.94*	*2.08*	*1.96*	*2.75*	*2.83*	*82. Engagements envers des non résidents*

Change in methodology:

Revision of the historical series (see notes under All banks).

Changement méthodologique :

Révision des séries historiques (voir notes sous Ensemble des banques).

Co-operative banks

Billion pesetas

Banques mutualistes

Milliards de pesetas

	1982	1983	1984	1985	1986	1987	1988	1989	1990	1991	
INCOME STATEMENT											**COMPTE DE RESULTATS**
1. Interest income	99	109	113	130	142	164	167	186	221	256	1. Produits financiers
2. Interest expenses	60	67	66	74	75	82	88	97	122	143	2. Frais financiers
3. Net interest income	39	42	47	56	67	82	79	89	99	113	3. Produits financiers nets
4. Non-interest income (net)	1	-10	9	9	5	4	5	6	6	6	4. Produits non financiers (nets)
5. Gross income	40	32	56	65	72	86	84	95	105	119	5. Résultat brut
6. Operating expenses	28	33	36	40	42	48	51	57	65	74	6. Frais d'exploitation
7. Net income	12	-1	20	25	30	38	33	38	40	45	7. Résultat net
8. Provisions (net)	8	18	6	11	9	13	9	8	10	10	8. Provisions (nettes)
9. Profit before tax	4	-19	14	14	21	25	24	30	30	35	9. Bénéfices avant impôt
10. Income tax	1	1	1	1	2	2	2	3	3	-	10. Impôt
11. Profit after tax	3	-20	13	13	19	23	22	27	27	35	11. Bénéfices après impôt
12. Distributed profit	4	4	5	5	6	6	5	7	8	-	12. Bénéfices distribués
13. Retained profit	-1	-24	8	8	13	17	17	20	19	35	13. Bénéfices mis en réserve
Memoranda											*Pour mémoire*
14. Staff costs	*19*	*22*	*23*	*26*	*27*	*30*	*33*	*35*	*39*	*44*	*14. Frais de personnel*
15. Provisions on loans	*8*	*18*	*6*	*10*	*9*	*13*	*9*	*7*	*8*	*10*	*15. Provisions sur prêts*
16. Provisions on securities	*-*	*-*	*-*	*-*	*-*	*-*	*-*	*-*	*2*	*-1*	*16. Provisions sur titres*
BALANCE SHEET											**BILAN**
Assets											**Actif**
17. Cash & balance with Central bank	44	107	81	136	151	199	207	253	269	265	17. Caisse & solde auprès de la Banque centrale
18. Interbank deposits	248	284	276	326	332	323	388	385	511	613	18. Dépôts interbancaires
19. Loans	430	456	481	538	591	681	706	800	910	1100	19. Prêts
20. Securities	55	69	100	130	203	243	259	246	224	225	20. Valeurs mobilières
21. Other assets	82	65	102	119	122	124	116	120	137	153	21. Autres actifs
Liabilities											**Passif**
22. Capital & reserves	80	81	89	107	128	160	181	204	234	269	22. Capital et réserves
23. Borrowing from Central bank	1	-	-	-	-	-	-	-	-	-	23. Emprunts auprès de la Banque centrale
24. Interbank deposits	140	145	73	78	91	105	98	87	112	104	24. Dépôts interbancaires
25. Non-bank deposits	607	713	837	1003	1077	1206	1310	1431	1615	1889	25. Dépôts non bancaires
26. Bonds	-	-	2	8	19	17	9	1	1	-	26. Obligations
27. Other liabilities	31	42	39	54	84	83	78	80	89	93	27. Autres engagements
Balance sheet total											**Total du bilan**
28. End-year total	858	981	1040	1250	1399	1571	1676	1804	2050	2355	28. En fin d'exercice
29. Average total	788	920	1010	1145	1324	1485	1623	1740	1927	2203	29. Moyen
Memoranda											*Pour mémoire*
30. Short-term securities	*-*	*5*	*11*	*22*	*54*	*113*	*135*	*140*	*141*	*141*	*30. Titres à court terme*
31. Bonds	*50*	*61*	*85*	*104*	*141*	*123*	*116*	*98*	*70*	*69*	*31. Obligations*
32. Shares and participations	*4*	*4*	*5*	*5*	*8*	*7*	*8*	*8*	*13*	*15*	*32. Actions et participations*
33. Claims on non-residents	*-*	*-*	*2*	*1*	*-*	*-*	*1*	*1*	*1*	*2*	*33. Créances sur des non résidents*
34. Liabilities to non-residents	*6*	*7*	*6*	*7*	*7*	*8*	*5*	*6*	*9*	*12*	*34. Engagements envers des non résidents*
SUPPLEMENTARY INFORMATION											**RENSEIGNEMENTS COMPLEMENTAIRES**
35. Number of institutions	154	153	149	146	138	129	117	110	107	106	35. Nombre d'institutions
36. Number of branches	3048	3222	3199	3284	3086	3113	2901	2773	2892	3025	36. Nombre de succursales
37. Number of employees (x 1000)	10.9	10.9	10.9	10.8	10.2	10.2	9.7	9.6	10.0	10.6	37. Nombre de salariés (x 1000)

SPAIN

Co-operative banks

ESPAGNE

Banques mutualistes

Per cent / *Pourcentage*

INCOME STATEMENT ANALYSIS / ANALYSE DU COMPTE DE RESULTATS

	1982	1983	1984	1985	1986	1987	1988	1989	1990	1991		
% of average balance sheet total												**% du total moyen du bilan**
38. Interest income	12.56	11.85	11.19	11.35	10.73	11.04	10.29	10.69	11.47	11.62	38.	Produits financiers
39. Interest expenses	7.61	7.28	6.53	6.46	5.66	5.52	5.42	5.57	6.33	6.49	39.	Frais financiers
40. Net interest income	4.95	4.57	4.65	4.89	5.06	5.52	4.87	5.11	5.14	5.13	40.	Produits financiers nets
41. Non-interest income (net)	0.13	-1.09	0.89	0.79	0.38	0.27	0.31	0.34	0.31	0.27	41.	Produits non financiers (nets)
42. Gross income	5.08	3.48	5.54	5.68	5.44	5.79	5.18	5.46	5.45	5.40	42.	Résultat brut
43. Operating expenses	3.55	3.59	3.56	3.49	3.17	3.23	3.14	3.28	3.37	3.36	43.	Frais d'exploitation
44. Net income	1.52	-0.11	1.98	2.18	2.27	2.56	2.03	2.18	2.08	2.04	44.	Résultat net
45. Provisions (net)	1.02	1.96	0.59	0.96	0.68	0.88	0.55	0.46	0.52	0.45	45.	Provisions (nettes)
46. Profit before tax	0.51	-2.07	1.39	1.22	1.59	1.68	1.48	1.72	1.56	1.59	46.	Bénéfices avant impôt
47. Income tax	0.13	0.11	0.10	0.09	0.15	0.13	0.12	0.17	0.16	-	47.	Impôt
48. Profit after tax	0.38	-2.17	1.29	1.14	1.44	1.55	1.36	1.55	1.40	1.59	48.	Bénéfices après impôt
49. Distributed profit	0.51	0.43	0.50	0.44	0.45	0.40	0.31	0.40	0.42	-	49.	Bénéfices distribués
50. Retained profit	-0.13	-2.61	0.79	0.70	0.98	1.14	1.05	1.15	0.99	1.59	50.	Bénéfices mis en réserve
51. Staff costs	2.41	2.39	2.28	2.27	2.04	2.02	2.03	2.01	2.02	2.00	51.	Frais de personnel
52. Provisions on loans	1.02	1.96	0.59	0.87	0.68	0.88	0.55	0.40	0.42	0.45	52.	Provisions sur prêts
53. Provisions on securities	-	-	-	-	-	-	-	-	0.10	-0.05	53.	Provisions sur titres
% of gross income												**% du total du résultat brut**
54. Net interest income	97.50	131.25	83.93	86.15	93.06	95.35	94.05	93.68	94.29	94.96	54.	Produits financiers nets
55. Non-interest income (net)	2.50	-31.25	16.07	13.85	6.94	4.65	5.95	6.32	5.71	5.04	55.	Produits non financiers (nets)
56. Operating expenses	70.00	103.13	64.29	61.54	58.33	55.81	60.71	60.00	61.90	62.18	56.	Frais d'exploitation
57. Net income	30.00	-3.13	35.71	38.46	41.67	44.19	39.29	40.00	38.10	37.82	57.	Résultat net
58. Provisions (net)	20.00	56.25	10.71	16.92	12.50	15.12	10.71	8.42	9.52	8.40	58.	Provisions (nettes)
59. Profit before tax	10.00	-59.38	25.00	21.54	29.17	29.07	28.57	31.58	28.57	29.41	59.	Bénéfices avant impôt
60. Income tax	2.50	3.13	1.79	1.54	2.78	2.33	2.38	3.16	2.86	-	60.	Impôt
61. Profit after tax	7.50	-62.50	23.21	20.00	26.39	26.74	26.19	28.42	25.71	29.41	61.	Bénéfices après impôt
62. Staff costs	47.50	68.75	41.07	40.00	37.50	34.88	39.29	36.84	37.14	36.97	62.	Frais de personnel
% of net income												**% du total du résultat net**
63. Provisions (net)	66.67	-1800.00	30.00	44.00	30.00	34.21	27.27	21.05	25.00	22.22	63.	Provisions (nettes)
64. Profit before tax	33.33	1900.00	70.00	56.00	70.00	65.79	72.73	78.95	75.00	77.78	64.	Bénéfices avant impôt
65. Income tax	8.33	-100.00	5.00	4.00	6.67	5.26	6.06	7.89	7.50	-	65.	Impôt
66. Profit after tax	25.00	2000.00	65.00	52.00	63.33	60.53	66.67	71.05	67.50	77.78	66.	Bénéfices après impôt

SPAIN

Co-operative banks

ESPAGNE

Banques mutualistes

Per cent — *Pourcentage*

BALANCE SHEET ANALYSIS — **ANALYSE DU BILAN**

% of year-end balance sheet total — % du total du bilan en fin d'exercice

	1982	1983	1984	1985	1986	1987	1988	1989	1990	1991		
Assets												**Actif**
67. Cash & balance with Central bank	5.13	10.91	7.79	10.88	10.79	12.67	12.35	14.02	13.12	11.25	67.	Caisse & solde auprès de la Banque centrale
68. Interbank deposits	28.90	28.95	26.54	26.08	23.73	20.56	23.15	21.34	24.93	26.03	68.	Dépôts interbancaires
69. Loans	50.12	46.48	46.25	43.04	42.24	43.35	42.12	44.35	44.39	46.71	69.	Prêts
70. Securities	6.41	7.03	9.62	10.40	14.51	15.47	15.45	13.64	10.93	9.55	70.	Valeurs mobilières
71. Other assets	9.56	6.63	9.81	9.52	8.72	7.89	6.92	6.65	6.68	6.50	71.	Autres actifs
Liabilities												**Passif**
72. Capital & reserves	9.32	8.26	8.56	8.56	9.15	10.18	10.80	11.31	11.41	11.42	72.	Capital et réserves
73. Borrowing from Central bank	0.12	-	-	-	-	-	-	-	-	-	73.	Emprunts auprès de la Banque centrale
74. Interbank deposits	16.32	14.78	7.02	6.24	6.50	6.68	5.85	4.82	5.46	4.42	74.	Dépôts interbancaires
75. Non-bank deposits	70.75	72.68	80.48	80.24	76.98	76.77	78.16	79.32	78.78	80.21	75.	Dépôts non bancaires
76. Bonds	-	-	0.19	0.64	1.36	1.08	0.54	0.06	0.05	-	76.	Obligations
77. Other liabilities	3.61	4.28	3.75	4.32	6.00	5.28	4.65	4.43	4.34	3.95	77.	Autres engagements
Memoranda												*Pour mémoire*
78. Short-term securities	-	0.51	1.06	1.76	3.86	7.19	8.05	7.76	6.88	5.99	78.	Titres à court terme
79. Bonds	5.83	6.22	8.17	8.32	10.08	7.83	6.92	5.43	3.41	2.93	79.	Obligations
80. Shares and participations	0.47	0.41	0.48	0.40	0.57	0.45	0.48	0.44	0.63	0.64	80.	Actions et participations
81. Claims on non-residents	-	-	0.19	0.08	-	-	0.06	0.06	0.05	0.08	81.	Créances sur des non résidents
82. Liabilities to non-residents	0.70	0.71	0.58	0.56	0.50	0.51	0.30	0.33	0.44	0.51	82.	Engagements envers des non résidents

Change in methodology:

Revision of the historical series (see notes under All banks).

Changement méthodologique :

Révision des séries historiques (voir notes sous Ensemble des banques).

136

SWEDEN

Commercial banks

SUEDE

Banques commerciales

Million Swedish kroner — *Millions de couronnes suédoises*

	1982	1983	1984	1985	1986	1987	1988	1989	1990	1991	
INCOME STATEMENT											**COMPTE DE RESULTATS**
1. Interest income	46662	48064	53625	58761	53282	58230	70837	97962	130929	131201	1. Produits financiers
2. Interest expenses	38774	37516	42381	47811	38170	41768	51467	76659	105873	104914	2. Frais financiers
3. Net interest income	7888	10548	11244	10950	15112	16462	19370	21403	25056	26287	3. Produits financiers nets
4. Non-interest income (net)	3562	4241	4877	5883	8233	6482	7825	8565	8899	8848	4. Produits non financiers (nets)
5. Gross income	11450	14789	16121	16833	23345	22944	27195	29968	33955	35135	5. Résultat brut
6. Operating expenses	7857	8345	10491	10413	10672	12760	15112	16736	26568	43353	6. Frais d'exploitation
7. Net income	3593	6444	5630	6420	12673	10184	12083	13232	7387	-7218	7. Résultat net
8. Provisions (net)	2185	4423	3853	4526	4888	5380	7397	8582	4786	-42895	8. Provisions (nettes)
9. Profit before tax	1408	2021	1777	1894	5784	4804	4686	4650	2601	35677	9. Bénéfices avant impôt
10. Income tax	541	953	737	636	3797	1638	2507	833	647	10576	10. Impôt
11. Profit after tax	867	1068	1040	1258	1987	3166	2179	3817	1954	25101	11. Bénéfices après impôt
12. Distributed profit	627	784	810	1080	1296	1567	1873	2082	2014	2014	12. Bénéfices distribués
13. Retained profit	240	284	230	178	691	1599	306	1735	-60	23087	13. Bénéfices mis en réserve
Memoranda											*Pour mémoire*
14. Staff costs	*3086*	*3421*	*3924*	*4307*	*4869*	*5718*	*6254*	*7016*	*8308*	*9242*	14. Frais de personnel
15. Provisions on loans	*2201*	*9307*	*1520*	*1566*	*4989*	*5368*	*7602*	*3319*	*5680*	*47814*	15. Provisions sur prêts
16. Provisions on securities	*-102*	*-5444*	*2202*	*3017*	*99*	*42*	*-*	*5482*	*1154*	*9236*	16. Provisions sur titres
BALANCE SHEET (1)											**BILAN (1)**
Assets											**Actif**
17. Cash & balance with Central bank	13768	9422	12450	16407	20156	19514	21016	20754	29467	13756	17. Caisse & solde auprès de la Banque centrale
18. Interbank deposits	60950	61014	66936	67617	100242	134207	179948	189095	237934	194122	18. Dépôts interbancaires
19. Loans	201828	222938	250728	261746	300322	338922	450616	579838	676529	625661	19. Prêts
20. Securities	115830	145004	148651	136173	114419	108167	106185	125842	147546	316226	20. Valeurs mobilières
21. Other assets	29205	38406	48968	58367	59566	65384	77240	104792	173158	57982	21. Autres actifs
Liabilities											**Passif**
22. Capital & reserves	18379	29099	31987	33606	38772	47169	56944	65273	71307	65386	22. Capital et réserves
23. Borrowing from Central bank	186	13066	623	6891	4233	3455	19033	19946	14517	31415	23. Emprunts auprès de la Banque centrale
24. Interbank deposits	140711	151169	169005	158724	173803	235065	314540	399495	526730	408906	24. Dépôts interbancaires
25. Non-bank deposits	212676	224963	250906	261975	294776	292546	325616	372914	440738	503993	25. Dépôts non bancaires
26. Bonds	26067	27562	27673	24734	22546	23905	39335	56383	85724	76723	26. Obligations
27. Other liabilities	23563	30925	47539	54380	60578	64054	79535	106310	125616	121325	27. Autres engagements
Balance sheet total											**Total du bilan**
28. End-year total	421581	476784	527734	540311	594707	666193	835005	1020321	1264632	1207745	28. En fin d'exercice
29. Average total	396908	463799	508851	552021	578578	660427	794416	994864	1202580	1254792	29. Moyen
Memoranda											*Pour mémoire*
30. Short-term securities	*3783*	*6368*	*7319*	*8931*	*6312*	*2122*	*2566*	*3705*	*9720*	*21402*	30. Titres à court terme
31. Bonds	*108026*	*136040*	*136476*	*129920*	*105119*	*98359*	*92876*	*108179*	*112899*	*86868*	31. Obligations
32. Shares and participations	*2737*	*3307*	*4065*	*5113*	*6276*	*8888*	*8386*	*13624*	*25071*	*35877*	32. Actions et participations
33. Claims on non-residents	*8810*	*12321*	*15614*	*14560*	*14395*	*17019*	*35366*	*65010*	*104230*	*303815*	33. Créances sur des non résidents
34. Liabilities to non-residents	*4420*	*7466*	*13080*	*17340*	*24233*	*33592*	*50483*	*68976*	*103509*	*646684*	34. Engagements envers des non résidents
SUPPLEMENTARY INFORMATION											**RENSEIGNEMENTS COMPLEMENTAIRES**
35. Number of institutions	14	14	15	15	14	14	14	14	12	9	35. Nombre d'institutions
36. Number of branches	1454	1450	1442	1436	1424	1403	1394	1376	1345	1288	36. Nombre de succursales
37. Number of employees (x 1000)	20.8	21.4	22.3	22.7	23.5	25.0	25.4	25.4	25.0	25.1	37. Nombre de salariés (x 1000)

Per cent / *Pourcentage*

INCOME STATEMENT ANALYSIS / **ANALYSE DU COMPTE DE RESULTATS**

		1982	1983	1984	1985	1986	1987	1988	1989	1990	1991
% of average balance sheet total	**% du total moyen du bilan**										
38. Interest income	38. Produits financiers	11.76	10.36	10.54	10.64	9.21	8.82	8.92	9.85	10.89	10.46
39. Interest expenses	39. Frais financiers	9.77	8.09	8.33	8.66	6.60	6.32	6.48	7.70	8.80	8.36
40. Net interest income	40. Produits financiers nets	1.99	2.27	2.21	1.98	2.61	2.49	2.44	2.15	2.08	2.09
41. Non-interest income (net)	41. Produits non financiers (nets)	0.90	0.91	0.96	1.07	1.42	0.98	0.99	0.86	0.74	0.71
42. Gross income	42. Résultat brut	2.88	3.19	3.17	3.05	4.03	3.47	3.42	3.01	2.82	2.80
43. Operating expenses	43. Frais d'exploitation	1.98	1.80	2.06	1.89	2.19	1.93	1.90	1.68	2.21	3.38
44. Net income	44. Résultat net	0.91	1.39	1.11	1.16	1.84	1.54	1.52	1.33	0.61	-0.58
45. Provisions (net)	45. Provisions (nettes)	0.55	0.95	0.76	0.82	0.84	0.81	0.93	0.86	0.40	-3.42
46. Profit before tax	46. Bénéfices avant impôt	0.35	0.44	0.35	0.34	1.00	0.73	0.59	0.47	0.22	2.84
47. Income tax	47. Impôt	0.14	0.21	0.14	0.12	0.66	0.25	0.32	0.08	0.05	0.84
48. Profit after tax	48. Bénéfices après impôt	0.22	0.23	0.20	0.23	0.34	0.48	0.27	0.38	0.16	2.00
49. Distributed profit	49. Bénéfices distribués	0.16	0.17	0.16	0.20	0.22	0.24	0.24	0.21	0.17	0.16
50. Retained profit	50. Bénéfices mis en réserve	0.06	0.06	0.05	0.03	0.12	0.24	0.04	0.17	0.00	1.84
51. Staff costs	51. Frais de personnel	0.78	0.74	0.77	0.78	0.84	0.87	0.79	0.71	0.69	0.74
52. Provisions on loans	52. Provisions sur prêts	0.55	2.01	0.30	0.28	0.86	0.81	0.96	0.33	0.47	3.81
53. Provisions on securities	53. Provisions sur titres	-0.03	-1.17	0.43	0.55	0.02	0.01	-	0.55	0.10	0.74
% of gross income	**% du total du résultat brut**										
54. Net interest income	54. Produits financiers nets	68.89	71.32	69.75	65.05	64.73	71.75	71.23	71.42	73.79	74.82
55. Non-interest income (net)	55. Produits non financiers (nets)	31.11	28.68	30.25	34.95	35.27	28.25	28.77	28.58	26.21	25.18
56. Operating expenses	56. Frais d'exploitation	68.62	56.43	65.08	61.86	54.29	55.61	55.57	55.85	78.24	120.54
57. Net income	57. Résultat net	31.38	43.57	34.92	38.14	45.71	44.39	44.43	44.15	21.76	-20.54
58. Provisions (net)	58. Provisions (nettes)	19.08	29.91	23.90	26.89	20.94	23.45	27.20	28.64	14.10	-122.09
59. Profit before tax	59. Bénéfices avant impôt	12.30	13.67	11.02	11.25	24.78	20.94	17.23	15.52	7.66	101.54
60. Income tax	60. Impôt	4.72	6.44	4.57	3.78	16.26	7.14	9.22	2.78	1.91	30.10
61. Profit after tax	61. Bénéfices après impôt	7.57	7.22	6.45	7.47	8.51	13.80	8.01	12.74	5.75	71.44
62. Staff costs	62. Frais de personnel	26.95	23.13	24.34	25.59	20.86	24.92	23.00	23.41	24.47	26.30
% of net income	**% du total du résultat net**										
63. Provisions (net)	63. Provisions (nettes)	60.81	68.64	68.44	70.50	45.80	52.83	61.22	64.86	64.79	..
64. Profit before tax	64. Bénéfices avant impôt	39.19	31.36	31.56	29.50	54.20	47.17	38.78	35.14	35.21	..
65. Income tax	65. Impôt	15.06	14.79	13.09	9.91	35.58	16.08	20.75	6.30	8.76	..
66. Profit after tax	66. Bénéfices après impôt	24.13	16.57	18.47	19.60	18.62	31.09	18.03	28.85	26.45	..

SWEDEN

Commercial banks

SUEDE

Banques commerciales

Per cent / *Pourcentage*

BALANCE SHEET ANALYSIS / ANALYSE DU BILAN

% of year-end balance sheet total / % du total du bilan en fin d'exercice

	1982	1983	1984	1985	1986	1987	1988	1989	1990	1991		
Assets												**Actif**
67. Cash & balance with Central bank	3.27	1.98	2.36	3.04	3.39	2.93	2.52	2.03	2.33	1.14	67.	Caisse & solde auprès de la Banque centrale
68. Interbank deposits	14.46	12.80	12.68	12.51	16.86	20.15	21.55	18.53	18.81	16.07	68.	Dépôts interbancaires
69. Loans	47.87	46.76	47.51	48.44	50.50	50.87	53.97	56.83	53.50	51.80	69.	Prêts
70. Securities	27.48	30.41	28.17	25.20	19.24	16.24	12.72	12.33	11.67	26.18	70.	Valeurs mobilières
71. Other assets	6.93	8.06	9.28	10.80	10.02	9.81	9.25	10.27	13.69	4.80	71.	Autres actifs
Liabilities												**Passif**
72. Capital & reserves	4.36	6.10	6.06	6.22	6.52	7.08	6.82	6.40	5.64	5.41	72.	Capital et réserves
73. Borrowing from Central bank	0.04	2.74	0.12	1.28	0.71	0.52	2.28	1.95	1.15	2.60	73.	Emprunts auprès de la Banque centrale
74. Interbank deposits	33.38	31.71	32.02	29.38	29.22	35.28	37.67	39.15	41.65	33.86	74.	Dépôts interbancaires
75. Non-bank deposits	50.45	47.18	47.54	48.49	49.57	43.91	39.00	36.55	34.85	41.73	75.	Dépôts non bancaires
76. Bonds	6.18	5.78	5.24	4.58	3.79	3.59	4.71	5.53	6.78	6.35	76.	Obligations
77. Other liabilities	5.59	6.49	9.01	10.06	10.19	9.61	9.53	10.42	9.93	10.05	77.	Autres engagements
Memoranda												*Pour mémoire*
78. Short-term securities	*0.90*	*1.34*	*1.39*	*1.65*	*1.06*	*0.32*	*0.31*	*0.36*	*0.77*	*1.77*	*78.*	*Titres à court terme*
79. Bonds	*25.62*	*28.53*	*25.86*	*24.05*	*17.68*	*14.76*	*11.12*	*10.60*	*8.93*	*7.19*	*79.*	*Obligations*
80. Shares and participations	*0.65*	*0.69*	*0.77*	*0.95*	*1.06*	*1.33*	*1.00*	*1.34*	*1.98*	*2.97*	*80.*	*Actions et participations*
81. Claims on non-residents	*2.09*	*2.58*	*2.96*	*2.69*	*2.42*	*2.55*	*4.24*	*6.37*	*8.24*	*25.16*	*81.*	*Créances sur des non résidents*
82. Liabilities to non-residents	*1.05*	*1.57*	*2.48*	*3.21*	*4.07*	*5.04*	*6.05*	*6.76*	*8.18*	*53.54*	*82.*	*Engagements envers des non résidents*

1. Change in methodology.

Notes

• Average balance sheet totals (item 29) are based on thirteen end-month data.

Change in methodology:

• Balance sheet data were recalculated on the basis of banks' annual balance figures. Also, "Capital & reserves" (item 22 or item 72) were revised to include reserves.

• As from 1991, the Föreningsbankernas Bank is included under Co-operative banks and no longer under Commercial banks.

1. Changement méthodologique.

Notes

• La moyenne du total des actifs/passifs (poste 29) est basée sur treize données de fin de mois.

Changement méthodologique :

• Les données du bilan ont été recalculées à partir des soldes annuels des banques. De même les "Capital et réserves" (poste 22 ou poste 72) ont été révisés pour inclure les réserves.

• A partir de 1991, la Föreningsbankernas Bank est comprise dans les Banques mutualistes et non plus dans les Banques commerciales.

SWEDEN

Foreign commercial banks

Million Swedish kroner

SUEDE

Banques commerciales étrangères

Millions de couronnes suédoises

		1986	1987 (1)	1988	1989	1990	1991		
INCOME STATEMENT									**COMPTE DE RESULTATS**
1.	Interest income	417	1592	1591	2708	2959	2440	1.	Produits financiers
2.	Interest expenses	322	1463	1462	2562	2722	2273	2.	Frais financiers
3.	Net interest income	95	129	129	146	237	167	3.	Produits financiers nets
4.	Non-interest income (net)	103	80	80	96	121	231	4.	Produits non financiers (nets)
5.	Gross income	198	209	209	242	358	398	5.	Résultat brut
6.	Operating expenses	213	232	231	319	464	867	6.	Frais d'exploitation
7.	Net income	-15	-23	-22	-77	-106	-469	7.	Résultat net
8.	Provisions (net)	28	-2	4	5	-38	-5	8.	Provisions (nettes)
9.	Profit before tax	-43	-21	-26	-82	-68	-464	9.	Bénéfices avant impôt
10.	Income tax	-	1	1	-	-	1	10.	Impôt
11.	Profit after tax	-43	-22	-27	-82	-68	-465	11.	Bénéfices après impôt
12.	Distributed profit	-	-	4	-	-	5	12.	Bénéfices distribués
13.	Retained profit	-43	-22	-31	-82	-68	-470	13.	Bénéfices mis en réserve
Memoranda									*Pour mémoire*
14.	Staff costs	78	137	136	130	148	161	14.	Frais de personnel
15.	Provisions on loans	4	7	8	3	6171	13	15.	Provisions sur prêts
16.	Provisions on securities	23	3	4	10	600	23	16.	Provisions sur titres
BALANCE SHEET									**BILAN**
Assets									**Actif**
17.	Cash & balance with Central bank	210	64	57	116	209	50	17.	Caisse & solde auprès de la Banque centrale
18.	Interbank deposits	8341	11850	8175	8963	6380	3959	18.	Dépôts interbancaires
19.	Loans	5741	9426	15337	18091	15564	13108	19.	Prêts
20.	Securities	3011	2180	1086	1744	580	3033	20.	Valeurs mobilières
21.	Other assets	784	1973	2834	3633	2252	640	21.	Autres actifs
Liabilities									**Passif**
22.	Capital & reserves	914	887	942	890	835	528	22.	Capital et réserves
23.	Borrowing from Central bank	1129	113	326	603	377	169	23.	Emprunts auprès de la Banque centrale
24.	Interbank deposits	14138	21389	23726	28240	20687	16778	24.	Dépôts interbancaires
25.	Non-bank deposits	364	731	1383	1145	1517	2024	25.	Dépôts non bancaires
26.	Bonds	599	565	361	582	599	443	26.	Obligations
27.	Other liabilities	943	1808	753	1086	970	850	27.	Autres engagements
Balance sheet total									**Total du bilan**
28.	End-year total	18087	25493	27491	32547	24986	20793	28.	En fin d'exercice
29.	Average total	NA	22242	28052	28568	25507	23931	29.	Moyen
Memoranda									*Pour mémoire*
30.	Short-term securities	902	198	230	141	202	1961	30.	Titres à court terme
31.	Bonds	2362	1602	873	1515	140	90	31.	Obligations
32.	Shares and participations	3	4	17	132	117	12	32.	Actions et participations
33.	Claims on non-residents	130	991	1612	3582	2907	5769	33.	Créances sur des non résidents
34.	Liabilities to non-residents	72	108	486	396	524	17898	34.	Engagements envers des non résidents
SUPPLEMENTARY INFORMATION									**RENSEIGNEMENTS COMPLEMENTAIRES**
35.	Number of institutions	12	11	10	9	9	8	35.	Nombre d'institutions
36.	Number of branches	-	-	1	-	-	-	36.	Nombre de succursales
37.	Number of employees (x 1000)	0.3	0.3	0.4	0.3	0.3	0.3	37.	Nombre de salariés (x 1000)

SWEDEN

Foreign commercial banks

Per cent	1986	1987 (1)	1988	1989	1990	1991		*Pourcentage*
INCOME STATEMENT ANALYSIS								**ANALYSE DU COMPTE DE RESULTATS**
% of average balance sheet total								**% du total moyen du bilan**
38. Interest income	NA	7.16	5.67	9.48	11.60	10.20	38.	Produits financiers
39. Interest expenses	NA	6.58	5.21	8.97	10.67	9.50	39.	Frais financiers
40. Net interest income	NA	0.58	0.46	0.51	0.93	0.70	40.	Produits financiers nets
41. Non-interest income (net)	NA	0.36	0.29	0.34	0.47	0.97	41.	Produits non financiers (nets)
42. Gross income	NA	0.94	0.75	0.85	1.40	1.66	42.	Résultat brut
43. Operating expenses	NA	1.04	0.82	1.12	1.82	3.62	43.	Frais d'exploitation
44. Net income	NA	-0.10	-0.08	-0.27	-0.42	-1.96	44.	Résultat net
45. Provisions (net)	NA	-0.01	0.01	0.02	-0.15	-0.02	45.	Provisions (nettes)
46. Profit before tax	NA	-0.09	-0.09	-0.29	-0.27	-1.94	46.	Bénéfices avant impôt
47. Income tax	-	0.00	0.00	-	-	0.00	47.	Impôt
48. Profit after tax	NA	-0.10	-0.10	-0.29	-0.27	-1.94	48.	Bénéfices après impôt
49. Distributed profit	-	-	0.01	-	-	0.02	49.	Bénéfices distribués
50. Retained profit	NA	-0.10	-0.11	-0.29	-0.27	-1.96	50.	Bénéfices mis en réserve
51. Staff costs	NA	0.62	0.48	0.46	0.58	0.67	51.	Frais de personnel
52. Provisions on loans	NA	0.03	0.03	0.01	24.19	0.05	52.	Provisions sur prêts
53. Provisions on securities	NA	0.01	0.01	0.04	2.35	0.10	53.	Provisions sur titres
% of gross income								**% du total du résultat brut**
54. Net interest income	47.98	61.72	61.72	60.33	66.20	41.96	54.	Produits financiers nets
55. Non-interest income (net)	52.02	38.28	38.28	39.67	33.80	58.04	55.	Produits non financiers (nets)
56. Operating expenses	107.58	111.00	110.53	131.82	129.61	217.84	56.	Frais d'exploitation
57. Net income	-7.58	-11.00	-10.53	-31.82	-29.61	-117.84	57.	Résultat net
58. Provisions (net)	14.14	-0.96	1.91	2.07	-10.61	-1.26	58.	Provisions (nettes)
59. Profit before tax	-21.72	-10.05	-12.44	-33.88	-18.99	-116.58	59.	Bénéfices avant impôt
60. Income tax	-	0.48	0.48	-	-	0.25	60.	Impôt
61. Profit after tax	-21.72	-10.53	-12.92	-33.88	-18.99	-116.83	61.	Bénéfices après impôt
62. Staff costs	39.39	65.55	65.07	53.72	41.34	40.45	62.	Frais de personnel
% of net income								**% du total du résultat net**
63. Provisions (net)	-186.67	8.70	-18.18	-6.49	35.85	..	63.	Provisions (nettes)
64. Profit before tax	286.67	91.30	118.18	106.49	64.15	..	64.	Bénéfices avant impôt
65. Income tax	-	-4.35	-4.55	-	-	..	65.	Impôt
66. Profit after tax	286.67	95.65	122.73	106.49	64.15	..	66.	Bénéfices après impôt

SWEDEN

Foreign commercial banks

SUEDE

Banques commerciales étrangères

Per cent / *Pourcentage*

BALANCE SHEET ANALYSIS / ANALYSE DU BILAN

% of year-end balance sheet total / **% du total du bilan en fin d'exercice**

	1986	1987 (1)	1988	1989	1990	1991		
Assets								**Actif**
67. Cash & balance with Central bank	1.16	0.25	0.21	0.36	0.84	0.24	67.	Caisse & solde auprès de la Banque centrale
68. Interbank deposits	46.12	46.48	29.74	27.54	25.53	19.04	68.	Dépôts interbancaires
69. Loans	31.74	36.97	55.79	55.58	62.29	63.04	69.	Prêts
70. Securities	16.65	8.55	3.95	5.36	2.32	14.59	70.	Valeurs mobilières
71. Other assets	4.33	7.74	10.31	11.16	9.01	3.08	71.	Autres actifs
Liabilities								**Passif**
72. Capital & reserves	5.05	3.48	3.43	2.73	3.34	2.54	72.	Capital et réserves
73. Borrowing from Central bank	6.24	0.44	1.19	1.85	1.51	0.81	73.	Emprunts auprès de la Banque centrale
74. Interbank deposits	78.17	83.90	86.30	86.77	82.79	80.69	74.	Dépôts interbancaires
75. Non-bank deposits	2.01	2.87	5.03	3.52	6.07	9.73	75.	Dépôts non bancaires
76. Bonds	3.31	2.22	1.31	1.79	2.40	2.13	76.	Obligations
77. Other liabilities	5.21	7.09	2.74	3.34	3.88	4.09	77.	Autres engagements
Memoranda								*Pour mémoire*
78. Short-term securities	*4.99*	*0.78*	*0.84*	*0.43*	*0.81*	*9.43*	*78.*	*Titres à court terme*
79. Bonds	*13.06*	*6.28*	*3.18*	*4.65*	*0.56*	*0.43*	*79.*	*Obligations*
80. Shares and participations	*0.02*	*0.02*	*0.06*	*0.41*	*0.47*	*0.06*	*80.*	*Actions et participations*
81. Claims on non-residents	*0.72*	*3.89*	*5.86*	*11.01*	*11.63*	*27.74*	*81.*	*Créances sur des non résidents*
82. Liabilities to non-residents	*0.40*	*0.42*	*1.77*	*1.22*	*2.10*	*86.08*	*82.*	*Engagements envers des non résidents*

1. As from 1987, change in methodology.

1. A partir de 1987, changement méthodologique.

Notes

• Average balance sheet totals (item 29) are based on thirteen end-month data.

Change in methodology:

• Balance sheet data were recalculated on the basis of banks' annual balance figures. Also, "Capital & reserves" (item 22 or item 72) were revised to include reserves.

Notes

• La moyenne du total des actifs/passifs (poste 29) est basée sur treize données de fin de mois.

Changement méthodologique :

• Les données du bilan ont été recalculées à partir des soldes annuels des banques. De même les "Capital et réserves" (poste 22 ou poste 72) ont été révisés pour inclure les réserves.

SWEDEN
Savings banks

SUEDE
Caisses d'épargne

Million Swedish kroner / *Millions de couronnes suédoises*

	1982	1983	1984 (1)	1985	1986	1987	1988	1989	1990	1991	
INCOME STATEMENT											**COMPTE DE RESULTATS**
1. Interest income	14167	14370	15536	17868	17053	18109	20328	24461	32005	31956	1. Produits financiers
2. Interest expenses	10604	10010	10851	12508	10765	11356	12593	15744	20871	19994	2. Frais financiers
3. Net interest income	3563	4360	4685	5360	6288	6753	7735	8717	11134	11962	3. Produits financiers nets
4. Non-interest income (net)	918	826	1026	1352	2137	1828	2189	2371	2695	6210	4. Produits non financiers (nets)
5. Gross income	4481	5186	5711	6712	8425	8581	9924	11088	13829	18172	5. Résultat brut
6. Operating expenses	2952	3312	4159	5027	5965	6705	7406	8531	11231	19919	6. Frais d'exploitation
7. Net income	1529	1874	1552	1685	2460	1876	2518	2557	2598	-1747	7. Résultat net
8. Provisions (net)	1357	1672	1349	1457	1334	985	1731	2118	2448	-13356	8. Provisions (nettes)
9. Profit before tax	172	202	203	228	1126	891	787	439	150	11609	9. Bénéfices avant impôt
10. Income tax	91	124	108	121	727	487	544	130	161	3587	10. Impôt
11. Profit after tax	81	78	95	107	399	404	243	309	-11	8022	11. Bénéfices après impôt
12. Distributed profit	..	..	..	1	-	-	-	-	-	-	12. Bénéfices distribués
13. Retained profit	..	..	..	106	399	404	243	309	-11	8022	13. Bénéfices mis en réserve
Memoranda											***Pour mémoire***
14. Staff costs	*1559*	*1769*	*2026*	*2270*	*2440*	*2770*	*2088*	*3651*	*4237*	*4549*	*14. Frais de personnel*
15. Provisions on loans	*980*	*3678*	*679*	*544*	*989*	*980*	*1748*	*1078*	*2035*	*14692*	*15. Provisions sur prêts*
16. Provisions on securities	*218*	*7*	*485*	*807*	*103*	*8*	*5*	*1073*	*644*	*2197*	*16. Provisions sur titres*
BALANCE SHEET											**BILAN**
Assets											**Actif**
17. Cash & balance with Central bank	1043	1098	1556	1764	2291	2766	2822	3225	4230	4592	17. Caisse & solde auprès de la Banque centrale
18. Interbank deposits	13388	13731	16388	13287	13839	15098	19708	20368	26163	17460	18. Dépôts interbancaires
19. Loans	68941	74785	79889	83765	99869	111560	140385	170524	203904	189497	19. Prêts
20. Securities	23603	26323	31310	34717	38488	38437	31320	31368	33334	52710	20. Valeurs mobilières
21. Other assets	14461	14554	4397	5024	5575	5916	6742	8727	9851	9640	21. Autres actifs
Liabilities											**Passif**
22. Capital & reserves	1619	1778	10138	10777	12575	13938	16179	17547	19242	16241	22. Capital et réserves
23. Borrowing from Central bank	-	-	-	-	-	-	-	-	-	88	23. Emprunts auprès de la Banque centrale
24. Interbank deposits	4045	5267	5642	6663	13847	18771	30976	51737	73242	48353	24. Dépôts interbancaires
25. Non-bank deposits	100043	106421	113709	116956	127979	135113	145601	155530	170544	180318	25. Dépôts non bancaires
26. Bonds	283	494	770	895	1190	1735	2946	3826	3544	1139	26. Obligations
27. Other liabilities	15446	16531	3280	3269	4471	4218	5274	5572	10909	27761	27. Autres engagements
Balance sheet total											**Total du bilan**
28. End-year total	121436	130491	133539	138558	160063	173776	200976	234212	277482	273898	28. En fin d'exercice
29. Average total	116189	125964	132015	136049	149311	166920	187376	217594	255847	275689	29. Moyen
Memoranda											***Pour mémoire***
30. Short-term securities	*121*	*-*	*380*	*1742*	*889*	*1369*	*666*	*1426*	*4340*	*6846*	*30. Titres à court terme*
31. Bonds	*25872*	*28783*	*30781*	*33771*	*37412*	*37005*	*29388*	*31027*	*31037*	*24321*	*31. Obligations*
32. Shares and participations	*925*	*1122*	*1360*	*1648*	*1924*	*1686*	*1869*	*1823*	*1890*	*1519*	*32. Actions et participations*
33. Claims on non-residents	*443*	*764*	*124*	*75*	*293*	*467*	*1026*	*3405*	*8186*	*9340*	*33. Créances sur des non résidents*
34. Liabilities to non-residents	*..*	*..*	*49*	*46*	*85*	*52*	*850*	*70*	*442*	*11407*	*34. Engagements envers des non résidents*
SUPPLEMENTARY INFORMATION											**RENSEIGNEMENTS COMPLEMENTAIRES**
35. Number of institutions	160	155	149	139	119	116	110	109	104	101	35. Nombre d'institutions
36. Number of branches	1261	1265	1261	1179	1249	1249	1190	1273	1124	1129	36. Nombre de succursales
37. Number of employees (x 1000)	11.9	12.4	13.1	13.5	14.6	14.6	15.6	15.8	14.9	15.3	37. Nombre de salariés (x 1000)

SWEDEN

Savings banks

SUEDE

Caisses d'épargne

Per cent — *Pourcentage*

INCOME STATEMENT ANALYSIS — ANALYSE DU COMPTE DE RESULTATS

	1982	1983	1984 (1)	1985	1986	1987	1988	1989	1990	1991		
% of average balance sheet total												**% du total moyen du bilan**
38. Interest income	12.19	11.41	11.77	13.13	11.42	10.85	10.85	11.24	12.51	11.59	38.	Produits financiers
39. Interest expenses	9.13	7.95	8.22	9.19	7.21	6.80	6.72	7.24	8.16	7.25	39.	Frais financiers
40. Net interest income	3.07	3.46	3.55	3.94	4.21	4.05	4.13	4.01	4.35	4.34	40.	Produits financiers nets
41. Non-interest income (net)	0.79	0.66	0.78	0.99	1.43	1.10	1.17	1.09	1.05	2.25	41.	Produits non financiers (nets)
42. Gross income	3.86	4.12	4.33	4.93	5.64	5.14	5.30	5.10	5.41	6.59	42.	Résultat brut
43. Operating expenses	2.54	2.63	3.15	3.70	4.00	4.02	3.95	3.92	4.39	7.23	43.	Frais d'exploitation
44. Net income	1.32	1.49	1.18	1.24	1.65	1.12	1.34	1.18	1.02	-0.63	44.	Résultat net
45. Provisions (net)	1.17	1.33	1.07	1.07	0.89	0.59	0.92	0.97	0.96	-4.84	45.	Provisions (nettes)
46. Profit before tax	0.15	0.16	0.15	0.17	0.75	0.53	0.42	0.20	0.06	4.21	46.	Bénéfices avant impôt
47. Income tax	0.08	0.10	0.08	0.09	0.49	0.29	0.29	0.06	0.06	1.30	47.	Impôt
48. Profit after tax	0.07	0.06	0.07	0.08	0.27	0.24	0.13	0.14	0.00	2.91	48.	Bénéfices après impôt
49. Distributed profit	..	..	..	0.00	-	-	-	-	-	-	49.	Bénéfices distribués
50. Retained profit	..	..	..	0.08	0.27	0.24	0.13	0.14	0.00	2.91	50.	Bénéfices mis en réserve
51. Staff costs	1.34	1.40	1.53	1.67	1.63	1.66	1.11	1.68	1.66	1.65	51.	Frais de personnel
52. Provisions on loans	0.84	2.92	0.51	0.40	0.66	0.59	0.93	0.50	0.80	5.33	52.	Provisions sur prêts
53. Provisions on securities	0.19	0.01	0.37	0.59	0.07	0.00	0.00	0.49	0.25	0.80	53.	Provisions sur titres
% of gross income												**% du total du résultat brut**
54. Net interest income	79.51	84.07	82.03	79.86	74.64	78.70	77.94	78.62	80.51	65.83	54.	Produits financiers nets
55. Non-interest income (net)	20.49	15.93	17.97	20.14	25.36	21.30	22.06	21.38	19.49	34.17	55.	Produits non financiers (nets)
56. Operating expenses	65.88	63.86	72.82	74.90	70.80	78.14	74.63	76.94	81.21	109.61	56.	Frais d'exploitation
57. Net income	34.12	36.14	27.18	25.10	29.20	21.86	25.37	23.06	18.79	-9.61	57.	Résultat net
58. Provisions (net)	30.28	32.24	23.62	21.71	15.83	11.48	17.44	19.10	17.70	-73.50	58.	Provisions (nettes)
59. Profit before tax	3.84	3.90	3.55	3.40	13.36	10.38	7.93	3.96	1.08	63.88	59.	Bénéfices avant impôt
60. Income tax	2.03	2.39	1.89	1.80	8.63	5.68	5.48	1.17	1.16	19.74	60.	Impôt
61. Profit after tax	1.81	1.50	1.66	1.59	4.74	4.71	2.45	2.79	-0.08	44.14	61.	Bénéfices après impôt
62. Staff costs	34.79	34.11	35.48	33.82	28.96	32.28	21.04	32.93	30.64	25.03	62.	Frais de personnel
% of net income												**% du total du résultat net**
63. Provisions (net)	88.75	89.22	86.92	86.47	54.23	52.51	68.75	82.83	94.23	..	63.	Provisions (nettes)
64. Profit before tax	11.25	10.78	13.08	13.53	45.77	47.49	31.25	17.17	5.77	..	64.	Bénéfices avant impôt
65. Income tax	5.95	6.62	6.96	7.18	29.55	25.96	21.60	5.08	6.20	..	65.	Impôt
66. Profit after tax	5.30	4.16	6.12	6.35	16.22	21.54	9.65	12.08	-0.42	..	66.	Bénéfices après impôt

SWEDEN

Savings banks

Per cent

BALANCE SHEET ANALYSIS

% of year-end balance sheet total

	1982	1983	1984 (1)	1985	1986	1987	1988	1989	1990	1991
Assets										
67. Cash & balance with Central bank	0.86	0.84	1.17	1.27	1.43	1.59	1.40	1.38	1.52	1.68
68. Interbank deposits	11.02	10.52	12.27	9.59	8.65	8.69	9.81	8.70	9.43	6.37
69. Loans	56.77	57.31	59.82	60.45	62.39	64.20	69.85	72.81	73.48	69.19
70. Securities	19.44	20.17	23.45	25.06	24.05	22.12	15.58	13.39	12.01	19.24
71. Other assets	11.91	11.15	3.29	3.63	3.48	3.40	3.35	3.73	3.55	3.52
Liabilities										
72. Capital & reserves	1.33	1.36	7.59	7.78	7.86	8.02	8.05	7.49	6.93	5.93
73. Borrowing from Central bank	-	-	-	-	-	-	-	-	-	0.03
74. Interbank deposits	3.33	4.04	4.22	4.81	8.65	10.80	15.41	22.09	26.40	17.65
75. Non-bank deposits	82.38	81.55	85.15	84.41	79.96	77.75	72.45	66.41	61.46	65.83
76. Bonds	0.23	0.38	0.58	0.65	0.74	1.00	1.47	1.63	1.28	0.42
77. Other liabilities	12.72	12.67	2.46	2.36	2.79	2.43	2.62	2.38	3.93	10.14
Memoranda										
78. Short-term securities	*0.10*	*-*	*0.28*	*1.26*	*0.56*	*0.79*	*0.33*	*0.61*	*1.56*	*2.50*
79. Bonds	*21.31*	*22.06*	*23.05*	*24.37*	*23.37*	*21.29*	*14.62*	*13.25*	*11.19*	*8.88*
80. Shares and participations	*0.76*	*0.86*	*1.02*	*1.19*	*1.20*	*0.97*	*0.93*	*0.78*	*0.68*	*0.55*
81. Claims on non-residents	*0.36*	*0.59*	*0.09*	*0.05*	*0.18*	*0.27*	*0.51*	*1.45*	*2.95*	*3.41*
82. Liabilities to non-residents	*..*	*..*	*0.04*	*0.03*	*0.05*	*0.03*	*0.42*	*0.03*	*0.16*	*4.16*

1. As from 1984, change in methodology.

Change in methodology:

• Balance sheet data were recalculated on the basis of banks' annual balance figures. Also, "Capital & reserves" (item 22 or item 72) were revised to include reserves.

Pourcentage

ANALYSE DU BILAN

% du total du bilan en fin d'exercice

Actif
67. Caisse & solde auprès de la Banque centrale
68. Dépôts interbancaires
69. Prêts
70. Valeurs mobilières
71. Autres actifs

Passif
72. Capital et réserves
73. Emprunts auprès de la Banque centrale
74. Dépôts interbancaires
75. Dépôts non bancaires
76. Obligations
77. Autres engagements

Pour mémoire
78. Titres à court terme
79. Obligations
80. Actions et participations
81. Créances sur des non résidents
82. Engagements envers des non résidents

1. A partir de 1984, changement méthodologique.

Changement méthodologique :

• Les données du bilan ont été recalculées à partir des soldes annuels des banques. De même les "Capital et réserves" (poste 22 ou poste 72) ont été révisés pour inclure les réserves.

SWEDEN

Co-operative banks

Million Swedish kroner

	1982	1983	1984	1985	1986	1987	1988 (1)	1989	1990	1991
INCOME STATEMENT										
1. Interest income	3268	3369	3728	4433	4314	4556	5323	6340	8249	12157
2. Interest expenses	2415	2330	2581	3086	2687	2751	3200	3857	4942	8427
3. Net interest income	853	1039	1147	1347	1627	1805	2123	2483	3307	3730
4. Non-interest income (net)	152	153	181	287	328	332	391	472	602	1144
5. Gross income	1005	1192	1328	1634	1955	2137	2514	2955	3909	4874
6. Operating expenses	705	816	1003	1208	1390	1625	1838	2159	2981	5717
7. Net income	300	376	325	426	565	512	676	796	928	-843
8. Provisions (net)	269	340	288	328	443	360	497	616	711	-2856
9. Profit before tax	31	36	37	98	122	152	179	180	217	2013
10. Income tax	22	22	25	42	54	79	101	59	67	552
11. Profit after tax	9	14	12	56	68	73	78	121	150	1461
12. Distributed profit	-	-	-	-	-	-	-	-	-	-
13. Retained profit	9	14	12	56	68	73	78	121	150	1461
Memoranda										
14. Staff costs	388	435	502	582	664	776	799	888	1092	1377
15. Provisions on loans	168	604	160	140	177	268	-	366	523	3130
16. Provisions on securities	66	-	87	146	200	3	388	91	47	818
BALANCE SHEET										
Assets										
17. Cash & balance with Central bank	150	152	190	227	274	335	368	443	593	1453
18. Interbank deposits	3393	3964	4534	4488	5986	2398	2572	1067	1515	5548
19. Loans	17112	17986	18898	19851	20850	26500	32805	40411	47201	60019
20. Securities	5300	6170	7300	7977	9666	10647	10009	10874	10828	23689
21. Other assets	4168	4114	4078	5074	5120	5636	1499	1960	2352	3093
Liabilities										
22. Capital & reserves	350	381	421	480	574	718	3407	4174	5035	4627
23. Borrowing from Central bank	-	-	-	-	-	-	-	-	-	982
24. Interbank deposits	662	665	673	652	742	1046	1533	3487	2540	20381
25. Non-bank deposits	24700	26606	28691	30264	33879	36480	41028	45690	52980	58682
26. Bonds	87	96	84	104	152	264	273	332	365	2396
27. Other liabilities	4323	4637	5131	6116	6548	7007	1012	1073	1568	6733
Balance sheet total										
28. End-year total	30123	32385	35000	37616	41895	45516	47253	54756	62488	93803
29. Average total	23759	28854	31097	33152	36266	40232	45259	51406	57278	67395
Memoranda										
30. Short-term securities	-	-	-	-	-	-	381	480	615	2217
31. Bonds	5629	6507	7375	8069	9886	10064	10062	10948	10479	9047
32. Shares and participations	14	14	30	107	108	122	122	122	436	1458
33. Claims on non-residents	-	-	-	-	-	-	-	-	-	1964
34. Liabilities to non-residents	-	-	-	-	-	-	-	-	6	9316
SUPPLEMENTARY INFORMATION										
35. Number of institutions	12	12	12	12	12	12	12	12	12	12
36. Number of branches	387	383	380	377	377	376	288	653	645	630
37. Number of employees (x 1000)	3.0	3.1	3.3	3.5	3.7	3.9	12.5	4.0	4.3	4.7

SUEDE

Banques mutualistes

Millions de couronnes suédoises

COMPTE DE RESULTATS
1. Produits financiers
2. Frais financiers
3. Produits financiers nets
4. Produits non financiers (nets)
5. Résultat brut
6. Frais d'exploitation
7. Résultat net
8. Provisions (nettes)
9. Bénéfices avant impôt
10. Impôt
11. Bénéfices après impôt
12. Bénéfices distribués
13. Bénéfices mis en réserve

Pour mémoire
14. Frais de personnel
15. Provisions sur prêts
16. Provisions sur titres

BILAN

Actif
17. Caisse & solde auprès de la Banque centrale
18. Dépôts interbancaires
19. Prêts
20. Valeurs mobilières
21. Autres actifs

Passif
22. Capital et réserves
23. Emprunts auprès de la Banque centrale
24. Dépôts interbancaires
25. Dépôts non bancaires
26. Obligations
27. Autres engagements

Total du bilan
28. En fin d'exercice
29. Moyen

Pour mémoire
30. Titres à court terme
31. Obligations
32. Actions et participations
33. Créances sur des non résidents
34. Engagements envers des non résidents

RENSEIGNEMENTS COMPLEMENTAIRES
35. Nombre d'institutions
36. Nombre de succursales
37. Nombre de salariés (x 1000)

SWEDEN

Co-operative banks

SUEDE

Banques mutualistes

Per cent / *Pourcentage*

INCOME STATEMENT ANALYSIS / ANALYSE DU COMPTE DE RESULTATS

	1982	1983	1984	1985	1986	1987	1988 (1)	1989	1990	1991		
% of average balance sheet total												**% du total moyen du bilan**
38. Interest income	13.75	11.68	11.99	13.37	11.90	11.32	11.76	12.33	14.40	18.04	38.	Produits financiers
39. Interest expenses	10.16	8.08	8.30	9.31	7.41	6.84	7.07	7.50	8.63	12.50	39.	Frais financiers
40. Net interest income	3.59	3.60	3.69	4.06	4.49	4.49	4.69	4.83	5.77	5.53	40.	Produits financiers nets
41. Non-interest income (net)	0.64	0.53	0.58	0.87	0.90	0.83	0.86	0.92	1.05	1.70	41.	Produits non financiers (nets)
42. Gross income	4.23	4.13	4.27	4.93	5.39	5.31	5.55	5.75	6.82	7.23	42.	Résultat brut
43. Operating expenses	2.97	2.83	3.23	3.64	3.83	4.04	4.06	4.20	5.20	8.48	43.	Frais d'exploitation
44. Net income	1.26	1.30	1.05	1.28	1.56	1.27	1.49	1.55	1.62	-1.25	44.	Résultat net
45. Provisions (net)	1.13	1.18	0.93	0.99	1.22	0.89	1.10	1.20	1.24	-4.24	45.	Provisions (nettes)
46. Profit before tax	0.13	0.12	0.12	0.30	0.34	0.38	0.40	0.35	0.38	2.99	46.	Bénéfices avant impôt
47. Income tax	0.09	0.08	0.08	0.13	0.15	0.20	0.22	0.11	0.12	0.82	47.	Impôt
48. Profit after tax	0.04	0.05	0.04	0.17	0.19	0.18	0.17	0.24	0.26	2.17	48.	Bénéfices après impôt
49. Distributed profit	-	-	-	-	-	-	-	-	-	-	49.	Bénéfices distribués
50. Retained profit	0.04	0.05	0.04	0.17	0.19	0.18	0.17	0.24	0.26	2.17	50.	Bénéfices mis en réserve
51. Staff costs	1.63	1.51	1.61	1.76	1.83	1.93	1.77	1.73	1.91	2.04	51.	Frais de personnel
52. Provisions on loans	0.71	2.09	0.51	0.42	0.49	0.67	-	0.71	0.91	4.64	52.	Provisions sur prêts
53. Provisions on securities	0.28	-	0.28	0.44	0.55	0.01	0.86	0.18	0.08	1.21	53.	Provisions sur titres
% of gross income												**% du total du résultat brut**
54. Net interest income	84.88	87.16	86.37	82.44	83.22	84.46	84.45	84.03	84.60	76.53	54.	Produits financiers nets
55. Non-interest income (net)	15.12	12.84	13.63	17.56	16.78	15.54	15.55	15.97	15.40	23.47	55.	Produits non financiers (nets)
56. Operating expenses	70.15	68.46	75.53	73.93	71.10	76.04	73.11	73.06	76.26	117.30	56.	Frais d'exploitation
57. Net income	29.85	31.54	24.47	26.07	28.90	23.96	26.89	26.94	23.74	-17.30	57.	Résultat net
58. Provisions (net)	26.77	28.52	21.69	20.07	22.66	16.85	19.77	20.85	18.19	-58.60	58.	Provisions (nettes)
59. Profit before tax	3.08	3.02	2.79	6.00	6.24	7.11	7.12	6.09	5.55	41.30	59.	Bénéfices avant impôt
60. Income tax	2.19	1.85	1.88	2.57	2.76	3.70	4.02	2.00	1.71	11.33	60.	Impôt
61. Profit after tax	0.90	1.17	0.90	3.43	3.48	3.42	3.10	4.09	3.84	29.98	61.	Bénéfices après impôt
62. Staff costs	38.61	36.49	37.80	35.62	33.96	36.31	31.78	30.05	27.94	28.25	62.	Frais de personnel
% of net income												**% du total du résultat net**
63. Provisions (net)	89.67	90.43	88.62	77.00	78.41	70.31	73.52	77.39	76.62	..	63.	Provisions (nettes)
64. Profit before tax	10.33	9.57	11.38	23.00	21.59	29.69	26.48	22.61	23.38	..	64.	Bénéfices avant impôt
65. Income tax	7.33	5.85	7.69	9.86	9.56	15.43	14.94	7.41	7.22	..	65.	Impôt
66. Profit after tax	3.00	3.72	3.69	13.15	12.04	14.26	11.54	15.20	16.16	..	66.	Bénéfices après impôt

147

Co-operative banks — Banques mutualistes

Per cent — *Pourcentage*

BALANCE SHEET ANALYSIS — ANALYSE DU BILAN

% of year-end balance sheet total — % du total du bilan en fin d'exercice

	1982	1983	1984	1985	1986	1987	1988 (1)	1989	1990	1991		
Assets												**Actif**
67. Cash & balance with Central bank	0.50	0.47	0.54	0.60	0.65	0.74	0.78	0.81	0.95	1.55	67.	Caisse & solde auprès de la Banque centrale
68. Interbank deposits	11.26	12.24	12.95	11.93	14.29	5.27	5.44	1.95	2.42	5.91	68.	Dépôts interbancaires
69. Loans	56.81	55.54	53.99	52.77	49.77	58.22	69.42	73.80	75.54	63.98	69.	Prêts
70. Securities	17.59	19.05	20.86	21.21	23.07	23.39	21.18	19.86	17.33	25.25	70.	Valeurs mobilières
71. Other assets	13.84	12.70	11.65	13.49	12.22	12.38	3.17	3.58	3.76	3.30	71.	Autres actifs
Liabilities												**Passif**
72. Capital & reserves	1.16	1.18	1.20	1.28	1.37	1.58	7.21	7.62	8.06	4.93	72.	Capital et réserves
73. Borrowing from Central bank	-	-	-	-	-	-	-	-	-	1.05	73.	Emprunts auprès de la Banque centrale
74. Interbank deposits	2.20	2.05	1.92	1.73	1.77	2.30	3.24	6.37	4.06	21.73	74.	Dépôts interbancaires
75. Non-bank deposits	82.00	82.16	81.97	80.46	80.87	80.15	86.83	83.44	84.78	62.56	75.	Dépôts non bancaires
76. Bonds	0.29	0.30	0.24	0.28	0.36	0.58	0.58	0.61	0.58	2.55	76.	Obligations
77. Other liabilities	14.35	14.32	14.66	16.26	15.63	15.39	2.14	1.96	2.51	7.18	77.	Autres engagements
Memoranda												*Pour mémoire*
78. Short-term securities	-	-	-	-	-	-	-	-	-	*2.36*	*78.*	*Titres à court terme*
79. Bonds	*18.69*	*20.09*	*21.07*	*21.45*	*23.60*	*22.11*	*21.29*	*19.99*	*16.77*	*9.64*	*79.*	*Obligations*
80. Shares and participations	*0.05*	*0.04*	*0.09*	*0.28*	*0.26*	*0.27*	*0.26*	*0.22*	*0.70*	*1.55*	*80.*	*Actions et participations*
81. Claims on non-residents	-	-	-	-	-	-	-	-	-	*2.09*	*81.*	*Créances sur des non résidents*
82. Liabilities to non-residents	-	-	-	-	-	-	-	-	*0.01*	*9.93*	*82.*	*Engagements envers des non résidents*

1. As from 1988, change in methodology.

Notes

• Average balance sheet totals (item 29) are based on thirteen end-month data.

Change in methodology:

• Balance sheet data were recalculated on the basis of banks' annual balance figures. Also, "Capital & reserves" (item 22 or item 72) were revised to include reserves.

• As from 1991, the Föreningsbankernas Bank is included under Co-operative banks and no longer under Commercial banks.

1. A partir de 1988, changement méthodologique.

Notes

• La moyenne du total des actifs/passifs (poste 29) est basée sur treize données de fin de mois.

Changement méthodologique :

• Les données du bilan ont été recalculées à partir des soldes annuels des banques. De même les "Capital et réserves" (poste 22 ou poste 72) ont été révisés pour inclure les réserves.

• A partir de 1991, la Föreningsbankernas Bank est comprise dans les Banques mutualistes et non plus dans les Banques commerciales.

Million Swiss francs — Millions de francs suisses

INCOME STATEMENT / COMPTE DE RESULTATS

			1982	1983	1984	1985	1986	1987	1988	1989	1990	1991
1.	Interest income	Produits financiers	38938	34077	39799	40021	39293	41233	45836	59594	70944	75442
2.	Interest expenses	Frais financiers	31270	25998	30800	30025	28705	30474	33563	46326	57257	58970
3.	Net interest income	Produits financiers nets	7669	8080	8999	9996	10588	10759	12273	13268	13687	16472
4.	Non-interest income (net)	Produits non financiers (nets)	6079	7020	7563	9000	10318	11462	10929	13737	13174	16992
5.	Gross income	Résultat brut	13747	15099	16562	18996	20906	22221	23202	27005	26861	33464
6.	Operating expenses	Frais d'exploitation	7787	8321	9067	10084	11302	12370	13386	14934	15939	17349
7.	Net income	Résultat net	5960	6779	7495	8912	9604	9851	9816	12071	10922	16115
8.	Provisions (net)	Provisions (nettes)	2440	2828	3101	3732	3972	4236	4134	5104	5561	10127
9.	Profit before tax	Bénéfices avant impôt	3520	3951	4394	5180	5632	5615	5682	6967	5361	5988
10.	Income tax	Impôt	1042	1184	1251	1474	1528	1531	1476	1535	1313	1382
11.	Profit after tax	Bénéfices après impôt	2478	2767	3143	3706	4104	4084	4206	5432	4048	4606
12.	Distributed profit	Bénéfices distribués	1464	1671	1922	2141	2370	2488	2523	3460	2715	2805
13.	Retained profit	Bénéfices mis en réserve	1014	1095	1222	1565	1734	1596	1683	1972	1333	1801

Memoranda / Pour mémoire

			1982	1983	1984	1985	1986	1987	1988	1989	1990	1991
14.	Staff costs	Frais de personnel	5317	5671	6111	6738	7481	8189	8668	9828	10451	11419
15.	Provisions on loans	Provisions sur prêts	..	..	..	..	..	..	..	..	..	..
16.	Provisions on securities	Provisions sur titres	..	..	..	..	..	..	..	..	..	..

BALANCE SHEET / BILAN

Assets / Actif

			1982	1983	1984	1985	1986	1987	1988	1989	1990	1991
17.	Cash & balance with Central bank	Caisse & solde auprès de la Banque centrale	18530	19920	22054	23832	25140	26375	12360	12332	11876	11715
18.	Interbank deposits	Dépôts interbancaires	139381	146786	166820	180879	207814	213523	226068	197365	196615	187439
19.	Loans	Prêts	315717	336230	373366	402795	431989	473369	540796	621374	670261	711407
20.	Securities	Valeurs mobilières	58204	70033	74190	82079	91261	93583	88245	97684	105054	110906
21.	Other assets	Autres actifs	48237	53069	52676	48555	48878	49634	48342	49591	48973	51855

Liabilities / Passif

			1982	1983	1984	1985	1986	1987	1988	1989	1990	1991
22.	Capital & reserves	Capital et réserves	34729	36619	40094	45107	50349	54177	57993	63371	66743	68676
23.	Borrowing from Central bank	Emprunts auprès de la Banque centrale	5640	5124	8504	7008	10093	7605	4220	1585	1805	1239
24.	Interbank deposits	Dépôts interbancaires	105738	113393	115603	136182	160227	171115	179214	194091	208519	205741
25.	Non-bank deposits	Dépôts non bancaires	310963	342041	380761	387477	406571	432697	467158	494038	510663	534720
26.	Bonds	Obligations	92791	96026	104480	117260	130347	140314	151053	164228	181508	191779
27.	Other liabilities	Autres engagements	30209	32836	39664	45106	47495	50576	56175	61036	63546	71168

Balance sheet total / Total du bilan

			1982	1983	1984	1985	1986	1987	1988	1989	1990	1991
28.	End-year total	En fin d'exercice	580069	626037	689106	738140	805082	856484	915812	978346	1032779	1073321
29.	Average total	Moyen	556672	603053	657572	713623	771611	830783	886148	947079	1005563	1053050

Memoranda / Pour mémoire

			1982	1983	1984	1985	1986	1987	1988	1989	1990	1991
30.	Short-term securities	Titres à court terme	19886	25002	28896	31093	30730	29463	21328	25776	33698	29411
31.	Bonds	Obligations	31102	37744	37628	42389	49316	52547	53313	55961	56826	64916
32.	Shares and participations	Actions et participations	7216	7288	7666	8597	11215	11573	13604	15947	14331	16579
33.	Claims on non-residents	Créances sur des non résidents	208344	229375	264303	279251	305547	317222	337446	339306	354848	372834
34.	Liabilities to non-residents	Engagements envers des non résidents	177744	195477	212128	215294	234092	233768	255951	270950	293525	314501

SUPPLEMENTARY INFORMATION / RENSEIGNEMENTS COMPLEMENTAIRES

			1982	1983	1984	1985	1986	1987	1988	1989	1990	1991
35.	Number of institutions	Nombre d'institutions	435	431	439	441	448	452	454	455	457	445
36.	Number of branches	Nombre de succursales	4986	5005	5179	5293	3948	4005	4082	4130	4191	4190
37.	Number of employees (x 1000)	Nombre de salariés (x 1000)	90.5	91.8	93.7	98.1	105.4	112.5	115.1	119.3	121.4	120.9

SWITZERLAND

All banks

Per cent · *Pourcentage*

INCOME STATEMENT ANALYSIS · ANALYSE DU COMPTE DE RESULTATS

#		1982	1983	1984	1985	1986	1987	1988	1989	1990	1991	
	% of average balance sheet total											**% du total moyen du bilan**
38.	Interest income	6.99	5.65	6.05	5.61	5.09	4.96	5.17	6.29	7.06	7.16	Produits financiers
39.	Interest expenses	5.62	4.31	4.68	4.21	3.72	3.67	3.79	4.89	5.69	5.60	Frais financiers
40.	Net interest income	1.38	1.34	1.37	1.40	1.37	1.30	1.38	1.40	1.36	1.56	Produits financiers nets
41.	Non-interest income (net)	1.09	1.16	1.15	1.26	1.34	1.38	1.23	1.45	1.31	1.61	Produits non financiers (nets)
42.	Gross income	2.47	2.50	2.52	2.66	2.71	2.67	2.62	2.85	2.67	3.18	Résultat brut
43.	Operating expenses	1.40	1.38	1.38	1.41	1.46	1.49	1.51	1.58	1.59	1.65	Frais d'exploitation
44.	Net income	1.07	1.12	1.14	1.25	1.24	1.19	1.11	1.27	1.09	1.53	Résultat net
45.	Provisions (net)	0.44	0.47	0.47	0.52	0.51	0.51	0.47	0.54	0.55	0.96	Provisions (nettes)
46.	Profit before tax	0.63	0.66	0.67	0.73	0.73	0.68	0.64	0.74	0.53	0.57	Bénéfices avant impôt
47.	Income tax	0.19	0.20	0.19	0.21	0.20	0.18	0.17	0.16	0.13	0.13	Impôt
48.	Profit after tax	0.45	0.46	0.48	0.52	0.53	0.49	0.47	0.57	0.40	0.44	Bénéfices après impôt
49.	Distributed profit	0.26	0.28	0.29	0.30	0.31	0.30	0.28	0.37	0.27	0.27	Bénéfices distribués
50.	Retained profit	0.18	0.18	0.19	0.22	0.22	0.19	0.19	0.21	0.13	0.17	Bénéfices mis en réserve
51.	Staff costs	0.96	0.94	0.93	0.94	0.97	0.99	1.00	1.04	1.04	1.08	Frais de personnel
52.	Provisions on loans	..	..	..	..	..	..	..	..	..	..	Provisions sur prêts
53.	Provisions on securities	..	..	..	..	..	..	..	..	..	..	Provisions sur titres
	% of gross income											**% du total du résultat brut**
54.	Net interest income	55.78	53.51	54.33	52.62	50.65	48.42	52.90	49.13	50.95	49.22	Produits financiers nets
55.	Non-interest income (net)	44.22	46.49	45.67	47.38	49.35	51.58	47.10	50.87	49.05	50.78	Produits non financiers (nets)
56.	Operating expenses	56.65	55.11	54.75	53.09	54.06	55.67	57.69	55.30	59.34	51.84	Frais d'exploitation
57.	Net income	43.35	44.89	45.25	46.91	45.94	44.33	42.31	44.70	40.66	48.16	Résultat net
58.	Provisions (net)	17.75	18.73	18.72	19.64	19.00	19.06	17.82	18.90	20.70	30.26	Provisions (nettes)
59.	Profit before tax	25.60	26.16	26.53	27.27	26.94	25.27	24.49	25.80	19.96	17.89	Bénéfices avant impôt
60.	Income tax	7.58	7.84	7.55	7.76	7.31	6.89	6.36	5.68	4.89	4.13	Impôt
61.	Profit after tax	18.03	18.32	18.98	19.51	19.63	18.38	18.13	20.11	15.07	13.76	Bénéfices après impôt
62.	Staff costs	38.68	37.56	36.90	35.47	35.78	36.85	38.22	36.39	38.91	34.12	Frais de personnel
	% of net income											**% du total du résultat net**
63.	Provisions (net)	40.94	41.72	41.37	41.87	41.36	43.00	42.11	42.28	50.92	62.84	Provisions (nettes)
64.	Profit before tax	59.06	58.28	58.63	58.13	58.64	57.00	57.89	57.72	49.08	37.16	Bénéfices avant impôt
65.	Income tax	17.48	17.47	16.69	16.54	15.91	15.54	15.04	12.72	12.02	8.58	Impôt
66.	Profit after tax	41.58	40.81	41.94	41.58	42.73	41.46	42.85	45.00	37.06	28.58	Bénéfices après impôt

SWITZERLAND

All banks

Per cent

BALANCE SHEET ANALYSIS

% of year-end balance sheet total

	1982	1983	1984	1985	1986	1987	1988	1989	1990	1991	
Assets											**Actif**
67. Cash & balance with Central bank	3.19	3.18	3.20	3.23	3.12	3.08	1.35	1.26	1.15	1.09	67. Caisse & solde auprès de la Banque centrale
68. Interbank deposits	24.03	23.45	24.21	24.50	25.81	24.93	24.68	20.17	19.04	17.46	68. Dépôts interbancaires
69. Loans	54.43	53.71	54.18	54.57	53.66	55.27	59.05	63.51	64.90	66.28	69. Prêts
70. Securities	10.03	11.19	10.77	11.12	11.34	10.93	9.64	9.98	10.17	10.33	70. Valeurs mobilières
71. Other assets	8.32	8.48	7.64	6.58	6.07	5.80	5.28	5.07	4.74	4.83	71. Autres actifs
Liabilities											**Passif**
72. Capital & reserves	5.99	5.85	5.82	6.11	6.25	6.33	6.33	6.48	6.46	6.40	72. Capital et réserves
73. Borrowing from Central bank	0.97	0.82	1.23	0.95	1.25	0.89	0.46	0.16	0.17	0.12	73. Emprunts auprès de la Banque centrale
74. Interbank deposits	18.23	18.11	16.78	18.45	19.90	19.98	19.57	19.84	20.19	19.17	74. Dépôts interbancaires
75. Non-bank deposits	53.61	54.64	55.25	52.49	50.50	50.52	51.01	50.50	49.45	49.82	75. Dépôts non bancaires
76. Bonds	16.00	15.34	15.16	15.89	16.19	16.38	16.49	16.79	17.57	17.87	76. Obligations
77. Other liabilities	5.21	5.24	5.76	6.11	5.90	5.91	6.13	6.24	6.15	6.63	77. Autres engagements
Memoranda											***Pour mémoire***
78. Short-term securities	3.43	3.99	4.19	4.21	3.82	3.44	2.33	2.63	3.28	2.74	78. Titres à court terme
79. Bonds	5.36	6.03	5.46	5.74	6.13	6.14	5.82	5.72	5.50	6.05	79. Obligations
80. Shares and participations	1.24	1.16	1.11	1.16	1.39	1.35	1.49	1.63	1.39	1.54	80. Actions et participations
81. Claims on non-residents	35.92	36.64	38.35	37.83	37.95	37.04	36.85	34.68	34.36	34.74	81. Créances sur des non résidents
82. Liabilities to non-residents	30.64	31.22	30.78	29.17	29.08	27.29	27.95	27.69	28.42	29.30	82. Engagements envers des non résidents

SUISSE

Ensemble des banques

Pourcentage

ANALYSE DU BILAN

% du total du bilan en fin d'exercice

Notes

- All banks include Large commercial banks, Cantonal banks, Regional and savings banks, Loan associations and agricultural co-operative banks and Other Swiss and foreign commercial banks.

Notes

- L'Ensemble des banques comprend les Grandes banques commerciales, les Banques cantonales, les Banques régionales et caisses d'épargne, les Caisses de crédit mutuel et les banques mutualistes agricoles, et les Autres banques suisses et étrangères.

SWITZERLAND

Large commercial banks

Million Swiss francs

SUISSE

Grandes banques commerciales

Millions de francs suisses

		1982	1983	1984	1985	1986	1987	1988	1989	1990	1991
INCOME STATEMENT	**COMPTE DE RESULTATS**										
1. Interest income	1. Produits financiers	22032	18578	22496	21995	21157	22449	25335	33228	37805	39353
2. Interest expenses	2. Frais financiers	18200	14440	17800	16737	15530	16796	18894	26427	31374	31220
3. Net interest income	3. Produits financiers nets	3832	4138	4696	5258	5627	5653	6441	6801	6431	8133
4. Non-interest income (net)	4. Produits non financiers (nets)	3437	3806	4107	4885	5571	5965	5800	6879	6676	8544
5. Gross income	5. Résultat brut	7269	7944	8804	10143	11198	11618	12241	13680	13107	16677
6. Operating expenses	6. Frais d'exploitation	4285	4482	4848	5368	5984	6509	7030	7849	8086	9023
7. Net income	7. Résultat net	2984	3461	3955	4776	5214	5109	5211	5831	5021	7654
8. Provisions (net)	8. Provisions (nettes)	1214	1404	1612	1972	2153	2128	2177	2447	2280	4402
9. Profit before tax	9. Bénéfices avant impôt	1770	2057	2344	2804	3061	2981	3034	3384	2741	3252
10. Income tax	10. Impôt	578	674	726	854	872	849	823	827	682	803
11. Profit after tax	11. Bénéfices après impôt	1193	1384	1618	1950	2189	2132	2211	2557	2059	2449
12. Distributed profit	12. Bénéfices distribués	808	923	1056	1257	1366	1423	1432	1623	1576	1585
13. Retained profit	13. Bénéfices mis en réserve	385	461	562	693	823	709	779	934	483	864
Memoranda	*Pour mémoire*										
14. Staff costs	14. Frais de personnel	*2940*	*3076*	*3292*	*3611*	*3982*	*4340*	*4700*	*5242*	*5410*	*6060*
15. Provisions on loans	15. Provisions sur prêts	..	..	..	..	..	..	..	..	..	..
16. Provisions on securities	16. Provisions sur titres	..	..	..	..	..	..	..	..	..	..
BALANCE SHEET	**BILAN**										
Assets	**Actif**										
17. Cash & balance with Central bank	17. Caisse & solde auprès de la Banque centrale	10343	11468	13002	13836	14588	14774	5523	5468	5189	5123
18. Interbank deposits	18. Dépôts interbancaires	85400	87419	101529	112359	132805	135700	142738	117329	110780	100290
19. Loans	19. Prêts	139519	146410	168729	182383	197894	219954	255872	302566	319625	344106
20. Securities	20. Valeurs mobilières	33860	43342	46349	51296	56863	55948	47052	52822	59255	64030
21. Other assets	21. Autres actifs	36626	40018	38620	34753	34675	34377	32313	31528	28678	29637
Liabilities	**Passif**										
22. Capital & reserves	22. Capital et réserves	17072	17890	19807	23290	26260	28051	29619	33143	33196	34148
23. Borrowing from Central bank	23. Emprunts auprès de la Banque centrale	4336	3851	6828	5043	7418	5408	3289	1203	1270	568
24. Interbank deposits	24. Dépôts interbancaires	65747	71362	71010	86610	105967	113804	112882	120732	125757	126306
25. Non-bank deposits	25. Dépôts non bancaires	167319	182657	209528	210121	220935	231597	247005	261719	271651	285212
26. Bonds	26. Obligations	34491	34878	38216	43374	48975	53041	57648	58710	58577	60272
27. Other liabilities	27. Autres engagements	16785	18019	22840	26189	27270	28852	33055	34206	33075	36682
Balance sheet total	**Total du bilan**										
28. End-year total	28. En fin d'exercice	305749	328657	368229	394627	436825	460752	483497	509713	523526	543187
29. Average total	29. Moyen	293987	317203	348443	381428	415726	448788	472125	496605	516620	533357
Memoranda	*Pour mémoire*										
30. Short-term securities	30. Titres à court terme	16264	20596	24873	27284	26777	25097	16756	19541	26556	21777
31. Bonds	31. Obligations	12439	17635	16135	17891	22105	22875	21059	22596	23619	30875
32. Shares and participations	32. Actions et participations	5158	5112	5341	6121	7981	7975	9237	10685	9080	11377
33. Claims on non-residents	33. Créances sur des non résidents	150368	163555	192836	205148	228827	237947	245803	242273	253852	267157
34. Liabilities to non-residents	34. Engagements envers des non résidents	128881	140943	156050	160604	180068	179045	193070	201479	220536	240443
SUPPLEMENTARY INFORMATION	**RENSEIGNEMENTS COMPLEMENTAIRES**										
35. Number of institutions	35. Nombre d'institutions	5	5	5	5	5	5	5	5	4	4
36. Number of branches	36. Nombre de succursales	903	922	1007	1048	876	889	901	933	969	983
37. Number of employees (x 1000)	37. Nombre de salariés (x 1000)	50.6	50.3	50.5	52.7	56.6	59.9	60.8	62.9	62.4	62.5

SWITZERLAND

Large commercial banks

SUISSE

Grandes banques commerciales

Per cent — *Pourcentage*

INCOME STATEMENT ANALYSIS — ANALYSE DU COMPTE DE RESULTATS

	1982	1983	1984	1985	1986	1987	1988	1989	1990	1991		
% of average balance sheet total												**% du total moyen du bilan**
38. Interest income	7.49	5.86	6.46	5.77	5.09	5.00	5.37	6.69	7.32	7.38	38.	Produits financiers
39. Interest expenses	6.19	4.55	5.11	4.39	3.74	3.74	4.00	5.32	6.07	5.85	39.	Frais financiers
40. Net interest income	1.30	1.30	1.35	1.38	1.35	1.26	1.36	1.37	1.24	1.52	40.	Produits financiers nets
41. Non-interest income (net)	1.17	1.20	1.18	1.28	1.34	1.33	1.23	1.39	1.29	1.60	41.	Produits non financiers (nets)
42. Gross income	2.47	2.50	2.53	2.66	2.69	2.59	2.59	2.75	2.54	3.13	42.	Résultat brut
43. Operating expenses	1.46	1.41	1.39	1.41	1.44	1.45	1.49	1.58	1.57	1.69	43.	Frais d'exploitation
44. Net income	1.01	1.09	1.14	1.25	1.25	1.14	1.10	1.17	0.97	1.44	44.	Résultat net
45. Provisions (net)	0.41	0.44	0.46	0.52	0.52	0.47	0.46	0.49	0.44	0.83	45.	Provisions (nettes)
46. Profit before tax	0.60	0.65	0.67	0.74	0.74	0.66	0.64	0.68	0.53	0.61	46.	Bénéfices avant impôt
47. Income tax	0.20	0.21	0.21	0.22	0.21	0.19	0.17	0.17	0.13	0.15	47.	Impôt
48. Profit after tax	0.41	0.44	0.46	0.51	0.53	0.48	0.47	0.51	0.40	0.46	48.	Bénéfices après impôt
49. Distributed profit	0.27	0.29	0.30	0.33	0.33	0.32	0.30	0.33	0.31	0.30	49.	Bénéfices distribués
50. Retained profit	0.13	0.15	0.16	0.18	0.20	0.16	0.16	0.19	0.09	0.16	50.	Bénéfices mis en réserve
51. Staff costs	1.00	0.97	0.94	0.95	0.96	0.97	1.00	1.06	1.05	1.14	51.	Frais de personnel
52. Provisions on loans	..	..	..	..	..	..	..	..	..	..	52.	Provisions sur prêts
53. Provisions on securities	..	..	..	..	..	..	..	..	..	..	53.	Provisions sur titres
% of gross income												**% du total du résultat brut**
54. Net interest income	52.72	52.09	53.35	51.84	50.25	48.66	52.62	49.71	49.07	48.77	54.	Produits financiers nets
55. Non-interest income (net)	47.28	47.91	46.65	48.16	49.75	51.34	47.38	50.29	50.93	51.23	55.	Produits non financiers (nets)
56. Operating expenses	58.95	56.43	55.07	52.92	53.44	56.03	57.43	57.38	61.69	54.10	56.	Frais d'exploitation
57. Net income	41.05	43.57	44.93	47.08	46.56	43.97	42.57	42.62	38.31	45.90	57.	Résultat net
58. Provisions (net)	16.70	17.68	18.31	19.44	19.23	18.32	17.78	17.89	17.40	26.40	58.	Provisions (nettes)
59. Profit before tax	24.35	25.90	26.62	27.64	27.34	25.66	24.79	24.74	20.91	19.50	59.	Bénéfices avant impôt
60. Income tax	7.94	8.48	8.24	8.42	7.79	7.31	6.72	6.05	5.20	4.82	60.	Impôt
61. Profit after tax	16.41	17.42	18.38	19.22	19.55	18.35	18.06	18.69	15.71	14.68	61.	Bénéfices après impôt
62. Staff costs	40.45	38.72	37.40	35.60	35.56	37.36	38.40	38.32	41.28	36.34	62.	Frais de personnel
% of net income												**% du total du résultat net**
63. Provisions (net)	40.68	40.56	40.75	41.30	41.29	41.65	41.78	41.97	45.41	57.51	63.	Provisions (nettes)
64. Profit before tax	59.32	59.44	59.25	58.70	58.71	58.35	58.22	58.03	54.59	42.49	64.	Bénéfices avant impôt
65. Income tax	19.35	19.46	18.35	17.87	16.72	16.62	15.79	14.18	13.58	10.49	65.	Impôt
66. Profit after tax	39.97	39.98	40.91	40.83	41.98	41.73	42.43	43.85	41.01	32.00	66.	Bénéfices après impôt

SWITZERLAND

Large commercial banks

SUISSE

Grandes banques commerciales

Per cent

Pourcentage

BALANCE SHEET ANALYSIS

ANALYSE DU BILAN

% of year-end balance sheet total

% du total du bilan en fin d'exercice

	1982	1983	1984	1985	1986	1987	1988	1989	1990	1991		
Assets												**Actif**
67. Cash & balance with Central bank	3.38	3.49	3.53	3.51	3.34	3.21	1.14	1.07	0.99	0.94	67.	Caisse & solde auprès de la Banque centrale
68. Interbank deposits	27.93	26.60	27.57	28.47	30.40	29.45	29.52	23.02	21.16	18.46	68.	Dépôts interbancaires
69. Loans	45.63	44.55	45.82	46.22	45.30	47.74	52.92	59.36	61.05	63.35	69.	Prêts
70. Securities	11.07	13.19	12.59	13.00	13.02	12.14	9.73	10.36	11.32	11.79	70.	Valeurs mobilières
71. Other assets	11.98	12.18	10.49	8.81	7.94	7.46	6.68	6.19	5.48	5.46	71.	Autres actifs
Liabilities												**Passif**
72. Capital & reserves	5.58	5.44	5.38	5.90	6.01	6.09	6.13	6.50	6.34	6.29	72.	Capital et réserves
73. Borrowing from Central bank	1.42	1.17	1.85	1.28	1.70	1.17	0.68	0.24	0.24	0.10	73.	Emprunts auprès de la Banque centrale
74. Interbank deposits	21.50	21.71	19.28	21.95	24.26	24.70	23.35	23.69	24.02	23.25	74.	Dépôts interbancaires
75. Non-bank deposits	54.72	55.58	56.90	53.25	50.58	50.27	51.09	51.35	51.89	52.51	75.	Dépôts non bancaires
76. Bonds	11.28	10.61	10.38	10.99	11.21	11.51	11.92	11.52	11.19	11.10	76.	Obligations
77. Other liabilities	5.49	5.48	6.20	6.64	6.24	6.26	6.84	6.71	6.32	6.75	77.	Autres engagements
Memoranda												*Pour mémoire*
78. Short-term securities	5.32	6.27	6.75	6.91	6.13	5.45	3.47	3.83	5.07	4.01	78.	Titres à court terme
79. Bonds	4.07	5.37	4.38	4.53	5.06	4.96	4.36	4.43	4.51	5.68	79.	Obligations
80. Shares and participations	1.69	1.56	1.45	1.55	1.83	1.73	1.91	2.10	1.73	2.09	80.	Actions et participations
81. Claims on non-residents	49.18	49.76	52.37	51.99	52.38	51.64	50.84	47.53	48.49	49.18	81.	Créances sur des non résidents
82. Liabilities to non-residents	42.15	42.88	42.38	40.70	41.22	38.86	39.93	39.53	42.13	44.27	82.	Engagements envers des non résidents

Other Swiss and foreign commercial banks

Autres banques commerciales suisses et étrangères

Million Swiss francs / *Millions de francs suisses*

		1982	1983	1984	1985	1986	1987	1988	1989	1990	1991		
INCOME STATEMENT													**COMPTE DE RESULTATS**
1.	Interest income	7212	6055	7247	7139	6542	6725	7791	11134	13187	13228	1.	Produits financiers
2.	Interest expenses	5511	4320	5290	4947	4318	4470	5126	8100	9963	9633	2.	Frais financiers
3.	Net interest income	1701	1735	1957	2192	2224	2255	2665	3034	3224	3595	3.	Produits financiers nets
4.	Non-interest income (net)	1944	2457	2635	3179	3693	4268	4007	5579	5061	6113	4.	Produits non financiers (nets)
5.	Gross income	3645	4192	4593	5371	5917	6523	6672	8613	8285	9708	5.	Résultat brut
6.	Operating expenses	1859	2095	2360	2677	3068	3456	3762	4281	4728	4991	6.	Frais d'exploitation
7.	Net income	1786	2096	2232	2694	2849	3067	2910	4332	3557	4717	7.	Résultat net
8.	Provisions (net)	744	943	964	1155	1158	1355	1236	1794	2034	3003	8.	Provisions (nettes)
9.	Profit before tax	1042	1153	1269	1539	1691	1712	1674	2538	1523	1714	9.	Bénéfices avant impôt
10.	Income tax	334	372	385	468	501	516	487	542	407	410	10.	Impôt
11.	Profit after tax	709	782	884	1071	1190	1196	1187	1996	1116	1304	11.	Bénéfices après impôt
12.	Distributed profit	289	360	448	445	540	573	571	1270	554	654	12.	Bénéfices distribués
13.	Retained profit	420	421	435	626	650	623	616	726	562	650	13.	Bénéfices mis en réserve
Memoranda													***Pour mémoire***
14.	Staff costs	1227	1374	1532	1727	1979	2239	2444	2732	3028	3180	14.	Frais de personnel
15.	Provisions on loans	..	..	..	..	..	..	..	..	..	..	15.	Provisions sur prêts
16.	Provisions on securities	..	..	..	..	..	..	..	..	..	..	16.	Provisions sur titres
BALANCE SHEET													**BILAN**
Assets													**Actif**
17.	Cash & balance with Central bank	4472	4769	5223	5890	6096	6762	3201	3377	3135	2880	17.	Caisse & solde auprès de la Banque centrale
18.	Interbank deposits	31234	34900	40320	42497	44419	44826	51339	50703	57381	58495	18.	Dépôts interbancaires
19.	Loans	36512	40055	43684	46251	47683	49673	59906	67353	74007	76536	19.	Prêts
20.	Securities	9844	11628	12001	13945	16729	18828	20728	24400	24266	25062	20.	Valeurs mobilières
21.	Other assets	5442	6261	6495	5788	6091	6693	6918	7795	8947	9262	21.	Autres actifs
Liabilities													**Passif**
22.	Capital & reserves	9224	9745	10775	11836	13275	14376	15964	17112	19455	19965	22.	Capital et réserves
23.	Borrowing from Central bank	231	67	158	207	486	215	3	40	68	-	23.	Emprunts auprès de la Banque centrale
24.	Interbank deposits	32044	33893	35722	39359	42786	43449	50315	54071	57935	56446	24.	Dépôts interbancaires
25.	Non-bank deposits	35348	42053	47400	47128	46924	49903	55965	59633	63942	67664	25.	Dépôts non bancaires
26.	Bonds	5582	5945	6712	7781	8745	9476	10050	11307	14730	14675	26.	Obligations
27.	Other liabilities	5075	5912	6956	8060	8802	9392	9795	11464	11607	13485	27.	Autres engagements
Balance sheet total													**Total du bilan**
28.	End-year total	87503	97614	107723	114371	121018	126782	142091	153628	167737	172235	28.	En fin d'exercice
29.	Average total	81924	92559	102668	111047	117694	123900	134437	147860	160683	169986	29.	Moyen
Memoranda													***Pour mémoire***
30.	Short-term securities	2489	3180	2706	2559	2765	3245	3471	5328	6501	6875	30.	Titres à court terme
31.	Bonds	6096	7087	7829	9904	11953	13420	14587	15957	15068	15694	31.	Obligations
32.	Shares and participations	1259	1362	1466	1482	2011	2163	2670	3115	2698	2493	32.	Actions et participations
33.	Claims on non-residents	52434	59313	64626	66850	68618	70288	82017	87395	90756	95500	33.	Créances sur des non résidents
34.	Liabilities to non-residents	43991	49235	51707	50228	49455	49847	57374	63889	66742	67487	34.	Engagements envers des non résidents
SUPPLEMENTARY INFORMATION													**RENSEIGNEMENTS COMPLÉMENTAIRES**
35.	Number of institutions	181	178	186	189	197	202	205	209	218	222	35.	Nombre d'institutions
36.	Number of branches	435	436	485	494	480	494	527	549	587	607	36.	Nombre de succursales
37.	Number of employees (x 1000)	17.2	18.0	19.1	20.2	22.4	25.0	25.9	27.0	28.9	28.1	37.	Nombre de salariés (x 1000)

SWITZERLAND

SUISSE

Other Swiss and foreign commercial banks

Autres banques commerciales suisses et étrangères

Per cent — *Pourcentage*

INCOME STATEMENT ANALYSIS — ANALYSE DU COMPTE DE RESULTATS

	1982	1983	1984	1985	1986	1987	1988	1989	1990	1991		
% of average balance sheet total												**% du total moyen du bilan**
38. Interest income	8.80	6.54	7.06	6.43	5.56	5.43	5.80	7.53	8.21	7.78	38.	Produits financiers
39. Interest expenses	6.73	4.67	5.15	4.45	3.67	3.61	3.81	5.48	6.20	5.67	39.	Frais financiers
40. Net interest income	2.08	1.87	1.91	1.97	1.89	1.82	1.98	2.05	2.01	2.11	40.	Produits financiers nets
41. Non-interest income (net)	2.37	2.65	2.57	2.86	3.14	3.44	2.98	3.77	3.15	3.60	41.	Produits non financiers (nets)
42. Gross income	4.45	4.53	4.47	4.84	5.03	5.26	4.96	5.83	5.16	5.71	42.	Résultat brut
43. Operating expenses	2.27	2.26	2.30	2.41	2.61	2.79	2.80	2.90	2.94	2.94	43.	Frais d'exploitation
44. Net income	2.18	2.26	2.17	2.43	2.42	2.48	2.16	2.93	2.21	2.77	44.	Résultat net
45. Provisions (net)	0.91	1.02	0.94	1.04	0.98	1.09	0.92	1.21	1.27	1.77	45.	Provisions (nettes)
46. Profit before tax	1.27	1.25	1.24	1.39	1.44	1.38	1.25	1.72	0.95	1.01	46.	Bénéfices avant impôt
47. Income tax	0.41	0.40	0.37	0.42	0.43	0.42	0.36	0.37	0.25	0.24	47.	Impôt
48. Profit after tax	0.86	0.84	0.86	0.96	1.01	0.97	0.88	1.35	0.69	0.77	48.	Bénéfices après impôt
49. Distributed profit	0.35	0.39	0.44	0.40	0.46	0.46	0.42	0.86	0.34	0.38	49.	Bénéfices distribués
50. Retained profit	0.51	0.46	0.42	0.56	0.55	0.50	0.46	0.49	0.35	0.38	50.	Bénéfices mis en réserve
51. Staff costs	1.50	1.48	1.49	1.56	1.68	1.81	1.82	1.85	1.88	1.87	51.	Frais de personnel
52. Provisions on loans	..	..	..	..	..	..	..	..	..	..	52.	Provisions sur prêts
53. Provisions on securities	..	..	..	..	..	..	..	..	..	..	53.	Provisions sur titres
% of gross income												**% du total du résultat brut**
54. Net interest income	46.67	41.39	42.62	40.82	37.59	34.57	39.94	35.23	38.91	37.03	54.	Produits financiers nets
55. Non-interest income (net)	53.33	58.61	57.38	59.18	62.41	65.43	60.06	64.77	61.09	62.97	55.	Produits non financiers (nets)
56. Operating expenses	50.99	49.99	51.39	49.84	51.85	52.98	56.38	49.70	57.07	51.41	56.	Frais d'exploitation
57. Net income	49.01	50.01	48.61	50.16	48.15	47.02	43.62	50.30	42.93	48.59	57.	Résultat net
58. Provisions (net)	20.41	22.49	20.98	21.50	19.57	20.77	18.53	20.83	24.55	30.93	58.	Provisions (nettes)
59. Profit before tax	28.59	27.52	27.62	28.66	28.58	26.25	25.09	29.47	18.38	17.66	59.	Bénéfices avant impôt
60. Income tax	9.15	8.87	8.38	8.71	8.47	7.91	7.30	6.29	4.91	4.22	60.	Impôt
61. Profit after tax	19.44	18.65	19.24	19.95	20.11	18.34	17.79	23.17	13.47	13.43	61.	Bénéfices après impôt
62. Staff costs	33.67	32.78	33.37	32.15	33.45	34.32	36.63	31.72	36.55	32.76	62.	Frais de personnel
% of net income												**% du total du résultat net**
63. Provisions (net)	41.65	44.98	43.17	42.87	40.65	44.18	42.47	41.41	57.18	63.66	63.	Provisions (nettes)
64. Profit before tax	58.35	55.02	56.83	57.13	59.35	55.82	57.53	58.59	42.82	36.34	64.	Bénéfices avant impôt
65. Income tax	18.68	17.73	17.25	17.37	17.59	16.82	16.74	12.51	11.44	8.69	65.	Impôt
66. Profit after tax	39.67	37.29	39.58	39.76	41.77	39.00	40.79	46.08	31.37	27.64	66.	Bénéfices après impôt

SWITZERLAND

SUISSE

Other Swiss and foreign commercial banks

Autres banques commerciales suisses et étrangères

Per cent — *Pourcentage*

BALANCE SHEET ANALYSIS — ANALYSE DU BILAN

% of year-end balance sheet total — **% du total du bilan en fin d'exercice**

	1982	1983	1984	1985	1986	1987	1988	1989	1990	1991		
Assets											**Actif**	
67. Cash & balance with Central bank	5.11	4.89	4.85	5.15	5.04	5.33	2.25	2.20	1.87	1.67	67.	Caisse & solde auprès de la Banque centrale
68. Interbank deposits	35.69	35.75	37.43	37.16	36.70	35.36	36.13	33.00	34.21	33.96	68.	Dépôts interbancaires
69. Loans	41.73	41.03	40.55	40.44	39.40	39.18	42.16	43.84	44.12	44.44	69.	Prêts
70. Securities	11.25	11.91	11.14	12.19	13.82	14.85	14.59	15.88	14.47	14.55	70.	Valeurs mobilières
71. Other assets	6.22	6.41	6.03	5.06	5.03	5.28	4.87	5.07	5.33	5.38	71.	Autres actifs
Liabilities											**Passif**	
72. Capital & reserves	10.54	9.98	10.00	10.35	10.97	11.34	11.24	11.14	11.60	11.59	72.	Capital et réserves
73. Borrowing from Central bank	0.26	0.07	0.15	0.18	0.40	0.17	0.00	0.03	0.04	-	73.	Emprunts auprès de la Banque centrale
74. Interbank deposits	36.62	34.72	33.16	34.41	35.36	34.25	35.41	35.20	34.54	32.77	74.	Dépôts interbancaires
75. Non-bank deposits	40.40	43.08	44.00	41.21	38.77	39.36	39.39	38.82	38.12	39.29	75.	Dépôts non bancaires
76. Bonds	6.38	6.09	6.23	6.80	7.23	7.47	7.07	7.36	8.78	8.52	76.	Obligations
77. Other liabilities	5.80	6.06	6.46	7.05	7.27	7.41	6.89	7.46	6.92	7.83	77.	Autres engagements
Memoranda											**Pour mémoire**	
78. Short-term securities	2.84	3.26	2.51	2.24	2.28	2.56	2.44	3.47	3.88	3.99	78.	Titres à court terme
79. Bonds	6.97	7.26	7.27	8.66	9.88	10.59	10.27	10.39	8.98	9.11	79.	Obligations
80. Shares and participations	1.44	1.39	1.36	1.30	1.66	1.71	1.88	2.03	1.61	1.45	80.	Actions et participations
81. Claims on non-residents	59.92	60.76	59.99	58.45	56.70	55.44	57.72	56.89	54.11	55.45	81.	Créances sur des non résidents
82. Liabilities to non-residents	50.27	50.44	48.00	43.92	40.87	39.32	40.38	41.59	39.79	39.18	82.	Engagements envers des non résidents

SWITZERLAND
Other Swiss commercial banks

SUISSE
Autres banques commerciales suisses

Million Swiss francs / Millions de francs suisses

		1982	1983	1984	1985	1986	1987	1988	1989	1990	1991
INCOME STATEMENT	**COMPTE DE RESULTATS**										
1. Interest income	Produits financiers	1748	1595	1863	2022	2254	2343	2557	3527	5547	5908
2. Interest expenses	Frais financiers	1108	948	1142	1199	1337	1406	1454	2214	3945	4055
3. Net interest income	Produits financiers nets	640	647	721	823	917	937	1103	1313	1602	1853
4. Non-interest income (net)	Produits non financiers (nets)	745	892	1057	1336	1677	1914	1667	2063	2328	2293
5. Gross income	Résultat brut	1385	1539	1778	2159	2594	2851	2770	3376	3930	4146
6. Operating expenses	Frais d'exploitation	783	860	997	1192	1402	1555	1587	1860	2219	2329
7. Net income	Résultat net	602	680	781	967	1192	1296	1183	1516	1711	1817
8. Provisions (net)	Provisions (nettes)	227	268	317	407	474	537	467	683	957	983
9. Profit before tax	Bénéfices avant impôt	375	411	465	560	718	759	716	833	754	834
10. Income tax	Impôt	137	148	159	191	252	269	249	252	206	190
11. Profit after tax	Bénéfices après impôt	239	264	306	369	466	490	467	581	548	644
12. Distributed profit	Bénéfices distribués	111	127	146	173	213	229	231	270	290	369
13. Retained profit	Bénéfices mis en réserve	127	137	160	196	253	261	236	311	258	275
Memoranda	***Pour mémoire***										
14. Staff costs	Frais de personnel	508	554	638	756	889	979	1000	1162	1407	1469
15. Provisions on loans	Provisions sur prêts	..	..	..	..	..	..	..	..	..	..
16. Provisions on securities	Provisions sur titres	..	..	..	..	..	..	..	..	..	..
BALANCE SHEET	**BILAN**										
Assets	**Actif**										
17. Cash & balance with Central bank	Caisse & solde auprès de la Banque centrale	1765	1838	1995	2348	2591	2959	1351	1261	1296	1128
18. Interbank deposits	Dépôts interbancaires	6545	6845	7867	8558	12144	13064	12107	12697	20466	21116
19. Loans	Prêts	13928	15563	18247	20506	22518	24130	28866	32209	39791	42316
20. Securities	Valeurs mobilières	2519	2813	3206	3826	4657	5002	5663	6629	11232	10817
21. Other assets	Autres actifs	2184	2552	2594	2292	2549	2737	2777	3076	4518	4585
Liabilities	**Passif**										
22. Capital & reserves	Capital et réserves	2861	3003	3436	3913	4665	5285	5469	6070	8125	7893
23. Borrowing from Central bank	Emprunts auprès de la Banque centrale	28	6	69	78	118	113	-	40	68	-
24. Interbank deposits	Dépôts interbancaires	4596	4749	5876	6846	8829	8844	10180	11126	16780	16001
25. Non-bank deposits	Dépôts non bancaires	14386	16316	18148	19231	22139	24172	24975	26768	36031	38948
26. Bonds	Obligations	3406	3553	3918	4557	5280	5709	6244	7654	11218	11433
27. Other liabilities	Autres engagements	1663	1984	2462	2905	3428	3766	3695	4215	5082	5688
Balance sheet total	**Total du bilan**										
28. End-year total	En fin d'exercice	26940	29611	33909	37530	44459	47891	50564	55872	77304	79963
29. Average total	Moyen	25401	28275	31760	35720	40994	46175	49228	53218	66588	78634
Memoranda	***Pour mémoire***										
30. Short-term securities	Titres à court terme	472	524	573	665	724	940	1254	1711	4667	4596
31. Bonds	Obligations	1643	1882	1978	2487	2995	3086	3297	3403	5288	4955
32. Shares and participations	Actions et participations	403	408	655	674	948	977	1111	1514	1277	1267
33. Claims on non-residents	Créances sur des non résidents	8501	9224	10874	11879	14957	15425	17047	19024	30140	32653
34. Liabilities to non-residents	Engagements envers des non résidents	7839	8453	9188	9164	11834	12210	12759	14484	21644	25164
SUPPLEMENTARY INFORMATION	**RENSEIGNEMENTS COMPLEMENTAIRES**										
35. Number of institutions	Nombre d'institutions	86	82	82	85	88	91	89	91	92	92
36. Number of branches	Nombre de succursales	244	242	264	277	266	273	287	301	327	333
37. Number of employees (x 1000)	Nombre de salariés (x 1000)	7.1	7.3	8.0	8.8	10.1	11.2	11.2	11.8	13.9	13.6

SWITZERLAND

Other Swiss commercial banks

SUISSE

Autres banques commerciales suisses

Per cent / *Pourcentage*

INCOME STATEMENT ANALYSIS / ANALYSE DU COMPTE DE RESULTATS

	1982	1983	1984	1985	1986	1987	1988	1989	1990	1991	
% of average balance sheet total											**% du total moyen du bilan**
38. Interest income	6.88	5.64	5.87	5.66	5.50	5.07	5.19	6.63	8.33	7.51	38. Produits financiers
39. Interest expenses	4.36	3.35	3.60	3.36	3.26	3.04	2.95	4.16	5.92	5.16	39. Frais financiers
40. Net interest income	2.52	2.29	2.27	2.30	2.24	2.03	2.24	2.47	2.41	2.36	40. Produits financiers nets
41. Non-interest income (net)	2.93	3.16	3.33	3.74	4.09	4.15	3.39	3.88	3.50	2.92	41. Produits non financiers (nets)
42. Gross income	5.45	5.44	5.60	6.04	6.33	6.17	5.63	6.34	5.90	5.27	42. Résultat brut
43. Operating expenses	3.08	3.04	3.14	3.34	3.42	3.37	3.22	3.50	3.33	2.96	43. Frais d'exploitation
44. Net income	2.37	2.40	2.46	2.71	2.91	2.81	2.40	2.85	2.57	2.31	44. Résultat net
45. Provisions (net)	0.89	0.95	1.00	1.14	1.16	1.16	0.95	1.28	1.44	1.25	45. Provisions (nettes)
46. Profit before tax	1.48	1.45	1.46	1.57	1.75	1.64	1.45	1.57	1.13	1.06	46. Bénéfices avant impôt
47. Income tax	0.54	0.52	0.50	0.53	0.61	0.58	0.51	0.47	0.31	0.24	47. Impôt
48. Profit after tax	0.94	0.93	0.96	1.03	1.14	1.06	0.95	1.09	0.82	0.82	48. Bénéfices après impôt
49. Distributed profit	0.44	0.45	0.46	0.48	0.52	0.50	0.47	0.51	0.44	0.47	49. Bénéfices distribués
50. Retained profit	0.50	0.48	0.50	0.55	0.62	0.57	0.48	0.58	0.39	0.35	50. Bénéfices mis en réserve
51. Staff costs	2.00	1.96	2.01	2.12	2.17	2.12	2.03	2.18	2.11	1.87	51. Frais de personnel
52. Provisions on loans	..	..	..	..	..	..	..	..	..	..	52. Provisions sur prêts
53. Provisions on securities	..	..	..	..	..	..	..	..	..	..	53. Provisions sur titres
% of gross income											**% du total du résultat brut**
54. Net interest income	46.22	42.05	40.57	38.12	35.35	32.87	39.82	38.89	40.76	44.69	54. Produits financiers nets
55. Non-interest income (net)	53.78	57.95	59.43	61.88	64.65	67.13	60.18	61.11	59.24	55.31	55. Produits non financiers (nets)
56. Operating expenses	56.53	55.86	56.06	55.21	54.05	54.54	57.29	55.09	56.46	56.17	56. Frais d'exploitation
57. Net income	43.47	44.14	43.94	44.79	45.95	45.46	42.71	44.91	43.54	43.83	57. Résultat net
58. Provisions (net)	16.38	17.43	17.82	18.85	18.27	18.84	16.86	20.23	24.35	23.71	58. Provisions (nettes)
59. Profit before tax	27.08	26.71	26.12	25.94	27.68	26.62	25.85	24.67	19.19	20.12	59. Bénéfices avant impôt
60. Income tax	9.86	9.58	8.92	8.85	9.71	9.44	8.99	7.46	5.24	4.58	60. Impôt
61. Profit after tax	17.23	17.13	17.20	17.09	17.96	17.19	16.86	17.21	13.94	15.53	61. Bénéfices après impôt
62. Staff costs	36.68	35.96	35.88	35.02	34.27	34.34	36.10	34.42	35.80	35.43	62. Frais de personnel
% of net income											**% du total du résultat net**
63. Provisions (net)	37.69	39.48	40.56	42.09	39.77	41.44	39.48	45.05	55.93	54.10	63. Provisions (nettes)
64. Profit before tax	62.31	60.52	59.44	57.91	60.23	58.56	60.52	54.95	44.07	45.90	64. Bénéfices avant impôt
65. Income tax	22.67	21.71	20.30	19.75	21.14	20.76	21.05	16.62	12.04	10.46	65. Impôt
66. Profit after tax	39.63	38.81	39.15	38.16	39.09	37.81	39.48	38.32	32.03	35.44	66. Bénéfices après impôt

SWITZERLAND
Other Swiss commercial banks

SUISSE
Autres banques commerciales suisses

Per cent	1982	1983	1984	1985	1986	1987	1988	1989	1990	1991	Pourcentage
BALANCE SHEET ANALYSIS											**ANALYSE DU BILAN**
% of year-end balance sheet total											**% du total du bilan en fin d'exercice**
Assets											**Actif**
67. Cash & balance with Central bank	6.55	6.21	5.88	6.26	5.83	6.18	2.67	2.26	1.68	1.41	67. Caisse & solde auprès de la Banque centrale
68. Interbank deposits	24.29	23.12	23.20	22.80	27.32	27.28	23.94	22.73	26.47	26.41	68. Dépôts interbancaires
69. Loans	51.70	52.56	53.81	54.64	50.65	50.39	56.69	57.65	51.47	52.92	69. Prêts
70. Securities	9.35	9.50	9.45	10.19	10.47	10.44	11.20	11.86	14.53	13.53	70. Valeurs mobilières
71. Other assets	8.11	8.62	7.65	6.11	5.73	5.72	5.49	5.51	5.84	5.73	71. Autres actifs
Liabilities											**Passif**
72. Capital & reserves	10.62	10.14	10.13	10.43	10.49	11.04	10.82	10.86	10.51	9.87	72. Capital et réserves
73. Borrowing from Central bank	0.10	0.02	0.20	0.21	0.27	0.24	-	0.07	0.09	-	73. Emprunts auprès de la Banque centrale
74. Interbank deposits	17.06	16.04	17.33	18.24	19.86	18.47	20.13	19.91	21.71	20.01	74. Dépôts interbancaires
75. Non-bank deposits	53.40	55.10	53.52	51.24	49.80	50.47	49.39	47.91	46.61	48.71	75. Dépôts non bancaires
76. Bonds	12.64	12.00	11.55	12.14	11.88	11.92	12.35	13.70	14.51	14.30	76. Obligations
77. Other liabilities	6.17	6.70	7.26	7.74	7.71	7.86	7.31	7.54	6.57	7.11	77. Autres engagements
Memoranda											**Pour mémoire**
78. Short-term securities	1.75	1.77	1.69	1.77	1.63	1.96	2.48	3.06	6.04	5.75	78. Titres à court terme
79. Bonds	6.10	6.35	5.83	6.63	6.71	6.44	6.52	6.09	6.84	6.20	79. Obligations
80. Shares and participations	1.50	1.38	1.93	1.80	2.13	2.04	2.20	2.71	1.65	1.58	80. Actions et participations
81. Claims on non-residents	31.55	31.15	32.07	31.65	33.64	32.21	33.71	34.05	38.99	40.84	81. Créances sur des non résidents
82. Liabilities to non-residents	29.10	28.55	27.10	24.42	26.62	25.50	25.23	25.92	28.00	31.47	82. Engagements envers des non résidents

Notes

- Other Swiss commercial banks are a sub-group of Other Swiss and foreign commercial banks.

Notes

- Les Autres banques commerciales suisses sont un sous-groupe des Autres banques commerciales suisses et étrangères.

SWITZERLAND
Foreign commercial banks

SUISSE
Banques commerciales étrangères

Million Swiss francs — *Millions de francs suisses*

	1982	1983	1984	1985	1986	1987	1988	1989	1990	1991	COMPTE DE RESULTATS
INCOME STATEMENT											
1. Interest income	5464	4460	5384	5117	4288	4382	5235	7607	7640	7320	1. Produits financiers
2. Interest expenses	4403	3373	4148	3748	2981	3064	3672	5886	6017	5578	2. Frais financiers
3. Net interest income	1061	1088	1236	1369	1307	1318	1563	1721	1623	1742	3. Produits financiers nets
4. Non-interest income (net)	1199	1565	1578	1843	2016	2354	2340	3516	2734	3820	4. Produits non financiers (nets)
5. Gross income	2260	2652	2814	3212	3323	3672	3903	5237	4357	5562	5. Résultat brut
6. Operating expenses	1076	1236	1363	1485	1666	1901	2175	2421	2509	2662	6. Frais d'exploitation
7. Net income	1184	1417	1451	1727	1657	1771	1728	2816	1848	2900	7. Résultat net
8. Provisions (net)	517	675	647	748	684	818	769	1112	1077	2021	8. Provisions (nettes)
9. Profit before tax	667	742	804	979	973	953	959	1704	771	879	9. Bénéfices avant impôt
10. Income tax	197	224	226	277	249	247	238	290	201	220	10. Impôt
11. Profit after tax	470	518	578	702	724	706	721	1414	570	659	11. Bénéfices après impôt
12. Distributed profit	177	233	303	272	327	344	340	1000	264	285	12. Bénéfices distribués
13. Retained profit	293	285	275	430	397	362	381	414	306	374	13. Bénéfices mis en réserve
Memoranda											*Pour mémoire*
14. Staff costs	719	820	894	971	1090	1260	1444	1569	1621	1712	14. Frais de personnel
15. Provisions on loans	..	..	..	..	..	..	..	..	..	..	15. Provisions sur prêts
16. Provisions on securities	..	..	..	..	..	..	..	..	..	..	16. Provisions sur titres
BALANCE SHEET											**BILAN**
Assets											*Actif*
17. Cash & balance with Central bank	2707	2932	3228	3542	3505	3805	1850	2116	1839	1753	17. Caisse & solde auprès de la Banque centrale
18. Interbank deposits	24689	28055	32453	33939	32275	31762	39232	38006	36915	37379	18. Dépôts interbancaires
19. Loans	22584	24492	25437	25745	25165	25543	31239	35144	34215	34220	19. Prêts
20. Securities	7325	8815	8795	10119	12072	13826	15065	17771	13034	14244	20. Valeurs mobilières
21. Other assets	3259	3709	3901	3496	3542	3956	4141	4719	4429	4677	21. Autres actifs
Liabilities											*Passif*
22. Capital & reserves	6363	6742	7339	7923	8610	9091	10494	11042	11329	12072	22. Capital et réserves
23. Borrowing from Central bank	-	-	89	129	368	102	3	-	-	-	23. Emprunts auprès de la Banque centrale
24. Interbank deposits	27651	29205	29846	32513	33957	34575	40134	42946	41156	40444	24. Dépôts interbancaires
25. Non-bank deposits	20961	25736	29252	27897	24785	25731	30990	32865	27910	28716	25. Dépôts non bancaires
26. Bonds	2176	2392	2794	3224	3465	3767	3806	3653	3512	3243	26. Obligations
27. Other liabilities	3412	3927	4494	5155	5374	5626	6099	7249	6525	7797	27. Autres engagements
Balance sheet total											**Total du bilan**
28. End-year total	60564	68003	73814	76841	76559	78891	91527	97756	90433	92272	28. En fin d'exercice
29. Average total	56523	64283	70908	75328	76700	77725	85209	94642	94095	91353	29. Moyen
Memoranda											*Pour mémoire*
30. Short-term securities	2017	2656	2133	1894	2041	2305	2217	3617	1834	2280	30. Titres à court terme
31. Bonds	4453	5205	5851	7417	8968	10334	11289	12554	9780	10739	31. Obligations
32. Shares and participations	856	954	811	808	1063	1186	1559	1601	1421	1226	32. Actions et participations
33. Claims on non-residents	43933	50088	53752	54971	53661	54863	64970	68371	60616	62847	33. Créances sur des non résidents
34. Liabilities to non-residents	36151	40782	42519	41064	37621	37637	44614	49405	45098	42323	34. Engagements envers des non résidents
SUPPLEMENTARY INFORMATION											**RENSEIGNEMENTS COMPLEMENTAIRES**
35. Number of institutions	95	96	104	104	109	111	116	118	126	130	35. Nombre d'institutions
36. Number of branches	191	194	221	217	214	221	240	248	260	274	36. Nombre de succursales
37. Number of employees (x 1000)	10.1	10.6	11.1	11.5	12.3	13.9	14.7	15.2	15.0	14.5	37. Nombre de salariés (x 1000)

SWITZERLAND

Foreign commercial banks

Per cent

INCOME STATEMENT ANALYSIS

SUISSE

Banques commerciales étrangères

Pourcentage

ANALYSE DU COMPTE DE RESULTATS

		1982	1983	1984	1985	1986	1987	1988	1989	1990	1991		
	% of average balance sheet total												**% du total moyen du bilan**
38.	Interest income	9.67	6.94	7.59	6.79	5.59	5.64	6.14	8.04	8.12	8.01	38.	Produits financiers
39.	Interest expenses	7.79	5.25	5.85	4.98	3.89	3.94	4.31	6.22	6.39	6.11	39.	Frais financiers
40.	Net interest income	1.88	1.69	1.74	1.82	1.70	1.70	1.83	1.82	1.72	1.91	40.	Produits financiers nets
41.	Non-interest income (net)	2.12	2.43	2.23	2.45	2.63	3.03	2.75	3.72	2.91	4.18	41.	Produits non financiers (nets)
42.	Gross income	4.00	4.13	3.97	4.26	4.33	4.72	4.58	5.53	4.63	6.09	42.	Résultat brut
43.	Operating expenses	1.90	1.92	1.92	1.97	2.17	2.45	2.55	2.56	2.67	2.91	43.	Frais d'exploitation
44.	Net income	2.10	2.20	2.05	2.29	2.16	2.28	2.03	2.98	1.96	3.17	44.	Résultat net
45.	Provisions (net)	0.92	1.05	0.91	0.99	0.89	1.05	0.90	1.17	1.14	2.21	45.	Provisions (nettes)
46.	Profit before tax	1.18	1.15	1.13	1.30	1.27	1.23	1.13	1.80	0.82	0.96	46.	Bénéfices avant impôt
47.	Income tax	0.35	0.35	0.32	0.37	0.32	0.32	0.28	0.31	0.21	0.24	47.	Impôt
48.	Profit after tax	0.83	0.81	0.81	0.93	0.94	0.91	0.85	1.49	0.61	0.72	48.	Bénéfices après impôt
49.	Distributed profit	0.31	0.36	0.43	0.36	0.43	0.44	0.40	1.06	0.28	0.31	49.	Bénéfices distribués
50.	Retained profit	0.52	0.44	0.39	0.57	0.52	0.47	0.45	0.44	0.33	0.41	50.	Bénéfices mis en réserve
51.	Staff costs	1.27	1.28	1.26	1.29	1.42	1.62	1.69	1.66	1.72	1.87	51.	Frais de personnel
52.	Provisions on loans	..	..	..	..	..	..	..	..	..	..	52.	Provisions sur prêts
53.	Provisions on securities	..	..	..	..	..	..	..	..	..	..	53.	Provisions sur titres
	% of gross income												**% du total du résultat brut**
54.	Net interest income	46.95	41.01	43.92	42.63	39.33	35.89	40.05	32.86	37.25	31.32	54.	Produits financiers nets
55.	Non-interest income (net)	53.05	58.99	56.08	57.37	60.67	64.11	59.95	67.14	62.75	68.68	55.	Produits non financiers (nets)
56.	Operating expenses	47.60	46.59	48.45	46.24	50.14	51.77	55.73	46.23	57.59	47.86	56.	Frais d'exploitation
57.	Net income	52.40	53.41	51.55	53.76	49.86	48.23	44.27	53.77	42.41	52.14	57.	Résultat net
58.	Provisions (net)	22.88	25.43	22.98	23.29	20.58	22.28	19.70	21.23	24.72	36.34	58.	Provisions (nettes)
59.	Profit before tax	29.52	27.98	28.57	30.47	29.28	25.95	24.57	32.54	17.70	15.80	59.	Bénéfices avant impôt
60.	Income tax	8.73	8.45	8.04	8.62	7.49	6.73	6.10	5.54	4.61	3.96	60.	Impôt
61.	Profit after tax	20.80	19.53	20.53	21.85	21.79	19.23	18.47	27.00	13.08	11.85	61.	Bénéfices après impôt
62.	Staff costs	31.83	30.93	31.78	30.22	32.80	34.31	37.00	29.96	37.20	30.78	62.	Frais de personnel
	% of net income												**% du total du résultat net**
63.	Provisions (net)	43.67	47.62	44.58	43.32	41.28	46.19	44.50	39.49	58.28	69.69	63.	Provisions (nettes)
64.	Profit before tax	56.33	52.38	55.42	56.68	58.72	53.81	55.50	60.51	41.72	30.31	64.	Bénéfices avant impôt
65.	Income tax	16.65	15.82	15.60	16.03	15.03	13.95	13.77	10.30	10.88	7.59	65.	Impôt
66.	Profit after tax	39.68	36.56	39.82	40.64	43.69	39.86	41.72	50.21	30.84	22.72	66.	Bénéfices après impôt

Foreign commercial banks

Banques commerciales étrangères

Per cent — *Pourcentage*

BALANCE SHEET ANALYSIS / ANALYSE DU BILAN

% of year-end balance sheet total / % du total du bilan en fin d'exercice

	1982	1983	1984	1985	1986	1987	1988	1989	1990	1991		
Assets											**Actif**	
67. Cash & balance with Central bank	4.47	4.31	4.37	4.61	4.58	4.82	2.02	2.16	2.03	1.90	67.	Caisse & solde auprès de la Banque centrale
68. Interbank deposits	40.77	41.26	43.97	44.17	42.16	40.26	42.86	38.88	40.82	40.51	68.	Dépôts interbancaires
69. Loans	37.29	36.02	34.46	33.50	32.87	32.38	34.13	35.95	37.83	37.09	69.	Prêts
70. Securities	12.09	12.96	11.92	13.17	15.77	17.53	16.46	18.18	14.41	15.44	70.	Valeurs mobilières
71. Other assets	5.38	5.45	5.28	4.55	4.63	5.01	4.52	4.83	4.90	5.07	71.	Autres actifs
Liabilities											**Passif**	
72. Capital & reserves	10.51	9.91	9.94	10.31	11.25	11.52	11.47	11.30	12.53	13.08	72.	Capital et réserves
73. Borrowing from Central bank	-	-	0.12	0.17	0.48	0.13	0.00	-	-	-	73.	Emprunts auprès de la Banque centrale
74. Interbank deposits	45.66	42.95	40.43	42.31	44.35	43.83	43.85	43.93	45.51	43.83	74.	Dépôts interbancaires
75. Non-bank deposits	34.61	37.85	39.63	36.30	32.37	32.62	33.86	33.62	30.86	31.12	75.	Dépôts non bancaires
76. Bonds	3.59	3.52	3.79	4.20	4.53	4.77	4.16	3.74	3.88	3.51	76.	Obligations
77. Other liabilities	5.63	5.78	6.09	6.71	7.02	7.13	6.66	7.42	7.22	8.45	77.	Autres engagements
Memoranda											*Pour mémoire*	
78. Short-term securities	*3.33*	*3.91*	*2.89*	*2.46*	*2.67*	*2.92*	*2.42*	*3.70*	*2.03*	*2.47*	*78.*	*Titres à court terme*
79. Bonds	*7.35*	*7.65*	*7.93*	*9.65*	*11.71*	*13.10*	*12.33*	*12.84*	*10.81*	*11.64*	*79.*	*Obligations*
80. Shares and participations	*1.41*	*1.40*	*1.10*	*1.05*	*1.39*	*1.50*	*1.70*	*1.64*	*1.57*	*1.33*	*80.*	*Actions et participations*
81. Claims on non-residents	*72.54*	*73.66*	*72.82*	*71.54*	*70.09*	*69.54*	*70.98*	*69.94*	*67.03*	*68.11*	*81.*	*Créances sur des non résidents*
82. Liabilities to non-residents	*59.69*	*59.97*	*57.60*	*53.44*	*49.14*	*47.71*	*48.74*	*50.54*	*49.87*	*45.87*	*82.*	*Engagements envers des non résidents*

Notes

- Foreign commercial banks are a sub-group of Other Swiss and foreign commercial banks.

Notes

- Les Banques commerciales étrangères sont un sous-groupe des Autres banques commerciales suisses et étrangères.

163

SWITZERLAND

Cantonal banks

Million Swiss francs

		1982	1983	1984	1985	1986	1987	1988	1989	1990	1991
INCOME STATEMENT											
1.	Interest income	6131	5902	6297	6825	7216	7470	7834	9504	12441	14496
2.	Interest expenses	4815	4547	4850	5246	5519	5704	5879	7387	9950	11531
3.	Net interest income	1316	1355	1447	1579	1697	1766	1955	2117	2491	2965
4.	Non-interest income (net)	478	517	544	625	707	794	740	845	937	1794
5.	Gross income	1794	1872	1991	2204	2404	2560	2695	2962	3428	4759
6.	Operating expenses	1054	1113	1183	1297	1422	1523	1636	1771	2006	2173
7.	Net income	740	759	808	907	982	1037	1059	1191	1422	2586
8.	Provisions (net)	330	336	357	417	458	482	468	546	732	1980
9.	Profit before tax	409	423	451	490	524	555	591	645	690	606
10.	Income tax	47	43	42	49	52	60	60	60	114	64
11.	Profit after tax	362	380	409	441	472	495	531	585	576	542
12.	Distributed profit	267	283	305	321	338	360	379	413	427	406
13.	Retained profit	96	97	105	120	134	135	152	172	149	136
Memoranda											
14.	Staff costs	761	808	846	921	994	1053	1124	1210	1320	1455
15.	Provisions on loans	..	..	..	..	..	..	..	..	..	..
16.	Provisions on securities	..	..	..	..	..	..	..	..	..	..
BALANCE SHEET											
Assets											
17.	Cash & balance with Central bank	2172	2137	2249	2439	2688	2942	2146	2024	2080	2203
18.	Interbank deposits	16792	17918	18552	19155	22901	24626	23943	20976	19885	20112
19.	Loans	86998	92779	98702	106569	112661	122697	134904	152419	170371	182581
20.	Securities	9184	9568	10023	10774	11251	12011	13218	13513	14639	15121
21.	Other assets	3869	4303	4811	5070	5069	5205	5490	6241	6904	8265
Liabilities											
22.	Capital & reserves	5089	5480	5798	6094	6582	7214	7603	8078	8838	9182
23.	Borrowing from Central bank	867	930	1137	1303	1573	1396	691	199	338	213
24.	Interbank deposits	6230	6314	6542	7160	7491	8854	9819	11736	15500	15821
25.	Non-bank deposits	67447	72744	76428	80065	85217	92911	100577	106657	109647	115245
26.	Bonds	33522	34986	37432	41656	45500	48334	51554	57677	66223	72846
27.	Other liabilities	5860	6252	7000	7729	8207	8772	9457	10831	13337	14978
Balance sheet total											
28.	End-year total	119015	126705	134337	144007	154570	167481	179701	195173	213879	228282
29.	Average total	115005	122860	130521	139172	149289	161025	173591	187437	204526	221081
Memoranda											
30.	Short-term securities	891	1004	1058	1002	974	941	932	712	660	588
31.	Bonds	7854	8123	8500	9240	9574	10215	11224	11396	12167	12653
32.	Shares and participations	440	441	465	532	703	855	1062	1405	1812	1880
33.	Claims on non-residents	4849	5740	6020	6251	7051	7938	8632	8620	9208	9342
34.	Liabilities to non-residents	4188	4539	3588	3600	3684	3905	4475	4569	5283	5679
SUPPLEMENTARY INFORMATION											
35.	Number of institutions	29	29	29	29	29	29	29	29	29	28
36.	Number of branches	1308	1316	1330	1359	709	722	741	755	768	771
37.	Number of employees (x 1000)	14.0	14.4	14.7	15.3	16.1	16.9	17.3	18.0	18.8	19.5

SUISSE

Banques cantonales

Millions de francs suisses

COMPTE DE RESULTATS
1. Produits financiers
2. Frais financiers
3. Produits financiers nets
4. Produits non financiers (nets)
5. Résultat brut
6. Frais d'exploitation
7. Résultat net
8. Provisions (nettes)
9. Bénéfices avant impôt
10. Impôt
11. Bénéfices après impôt
12. Bénéfices distribués
13. Bénéfices mis en réserve

Pour mémoire
14. Frais de personnel
15. Provisions sur prêts
16. Provisions sur titres

BILAN

Actif
17. Caisse & solde auprès de la Banque centrale
18. Dépôts interbancaires
19. Prêts
20. Valeurs mobilières
21. Autres actifs

Passif
22. Capital et réserves
23. Emprunts auprès de la Banque centrale
24. Dépôts interbancaires
25. Dépôts non bancaires
26. Obligations
27. Autres engagements

Total du bilan
28. En fin d'exercice
29. Moyen

Pour mémoire
30. Titres à court terme
31. Obligations
32. Actions et participations
33. Créances sur des non résidents
34. Engagements envers des non résidents

RENSEIGNEMENTS COMPLEMENTAIRES
35. Nombre d'institutions
36. Nombre de succursales
37. Nombre de salariés (x 1000)

SWITZERLAND

Cantonal banks

SUISSE

Banques cantonales

Per cent	1982	1983	1984	1985	1986	1987	1988	1989	1990	1991	Pourcentage
INCOME STATEMENT ANALYSIS											**ANALYSE DU COMPTE DE RESULTATS**
% of average balance sheet total											**% du total moyen du bilan**
38. Interest income	5.33	4.80	4.82	4.90	4.83	4.64	4.51	5.07	6.08	6.56	38. Produits financiers
39. Interest expenses	4.19	3.70	3.72	3.77	3.70	3.54	3.39	3.94	4.86	5.22	39. Frais financiers
40. Net interest income	1.14	1.10	1.11	1.13	1.14	1.10	1.13	1.13	1.22	1.34	40. Produits financiers nets
41. Non-interest income (net)	0.42	0.42	0.42	0.45	0.47	0.49	0.43	0.45	0.46	0.81	41. Produits non financiers (nets)
42. Gross income	1.56	1.52	1.53	1.58	1.61	1.59	1.55	1.58	1.68	2.15	42. Résultat brut
43. Operating expenses	0.92	0.91	0.91	0.93	0.95	0.95	0.94	0.94	0.98	0.98	43. Frais d'exploitation
44. Net income	0.64	0.62	0.62	0.65	0.66	0.64	0.61	0.64	0.70	1.17	44. Résultat net
45. Provisions (net)	0.29	0.27	0.27	0.30	0.31	0.30	0.27	0.29	0.36	0.90	45. Provisions (nettes)
46. Profit before tax	0.36	0.34	0.35	0.35	0.35	0.34	0.34	0.34	0.34	0.27	46. Bénéfices avant impôt
47. Income tax	0.04	0.03	0.03	0.04	0.03	0.04	0.03	0.03	0.06	0.03	47. Impôt
48. Profit after tax	0.32	0.31	0.31	0.32	0.32	0.31	0.31	0.31	0.28	0.25	48. Bénéfices après impôt
49. Distributed profit	0.23	0.23	0.23	0.23	0.23	0.22	0.22	0.22	0.21	0.18	49. Bénéfices distribués
50. Retained profit	0.08	0.08	0.08	0.09	0.09	0.08	0.09	0.09	0.07	0.06	50. Bénéfices mis en réserve
51. Staff costs	0.66	0.66	0.65	0.66	0.67	0.65	0.65	0.65	0.65	0.66	51. Frais de personnel
52. Provisions on loans	..	..	..	..	..	..	..	..	..	..	52. Provisions sur prêts
53. Provisions on securities	..	..	..	..	..	..	..	..	..	..	53. Provisions sur titres
% of gross income											**% du total du résultat brut**
54. Net interest income	73.38	72.39	72.67	71.64	70.59	68.98	72.54	71.47	72.67	62.30	54. Produits financiers nets
55. Non-interest income (net)	26.62	27.61	27.33	28.36	29.41	31.02	27.46	28.53	27.33	37.70	55. Produits non financiers (nets)
56. Operating expenses	58.75	59.47	59.39	58.85	59.15	59.49	60.71	59.79	58.52	45.66	56. Frais d'exploitation
57. Net income	41.25	40.53	40.61	41.15	40.85	40.51	39.29	40.21	41.48	54.34	57. Résultat net
58. Provisions (net)	18.42	17.95	17.95	18.92	19.05	18.83	17.37	18.43	21.35	41.61	58. Provisions (nettes)
59. Profit before tax	22.83	22.58	22.66	22.23	21.80	21.68	21.93	21.78	20.13	12.73	59. Bénéfices avant impôt
60. Income tax	2.62	2.29	2.10	2.21	2.16	2.34	2.23	2.03	3.33	1.34	60. Impôt
61. Profit after tax	20.21	20.29	20.56	20.02	19.63	19.34	19.70	19.75	16.80	11.39	61. Bénéfices après impôt
62. Staff costs	42.45	43.15	42.50	41.79	41.35	41.13	41.71	40.85	38.51	30.57	62. Frais de personnel
% of net income											**% du total du résultat net**
63. Provisions (net)	44.66	44.29	44.19	45.98	46.64	46.48	44.19	45.84	51.48	76.57	63. Provisions (nettes)
64. Profit before tax	55.34	55.71	55.81	54.02	53.36	53.52	55.81	54.16	48.52	23.43	64. Bénéfices avant impôt
65. Income tax	6.35	5.64	5.18	5.38	5.30	5.79	5.67	5.04	8.02	2.47	65. Impôt
66. Profit after tax	48.99	50.07	50.62	48.65	48.07	47.73	50.14	49.12	40.51	20.96	66. Bénéfices après impôt

SWITZERLAND

Cantonal banks

SUISSE

Banques cantonales

Per cent / *Pourcentage*

BALANCE SHEET ANALYSIS / **ANALYSE DU BILAN**

% of year-end balance sheet total / **% du total du bilan en fin d'exercice**

	1982	1983	1984	1985	1986	1987	1988	1989	1990	1991	
Assets											**Actif**
67. Cash & balance with Central bank	1.82	1.69	1.67	1.69	1.74	1.76	1.19	1.04	0.97	0.97	67. Caisse & solde auprès de la Banque centrale
68. Interbank deposits	14.11	14.14	13.81	13.30	14.82	14.70	13.32	10.75	9.30	8.81	68. Dépôts interbancaires
69. Loans	73.10	73.22	73.47	74.00	72.89	73.26	75.07	78.09	79.66	79.98	69. Prêts
70. Securities	7.72	7.55	7.46	7.48	7.28	7.17	7.36	6.92	6.84	6.62	70. Valeurs mobilières
71. Other assets	3.25	3.40	3.58	3.52	3.28	3.11	3.06	3.20	3.23	3.62	71. Autres actifs
Liabilities											**Passif**
72. Capital & reserves	4.28	4.32	4.32	4.23	4.26	4.31	4.23	4.14	4.13	4.02	72. Capital et réserves
73. Borrowing from Central bank	0.73	0.73	0.85	0.90	1.02	0.83	0.38	0.10	0.16	0.09	73. Emprunts auprès de la Banque centrale
74. Interbank deposits	5.23	4.98	4.87	4.97	4.85	5.29	5.46	6.01	7.25	6.93	74. Dépôts interbancaires
75. Non-bank deposits	56.67	57.41	56.89	55.60	55.13	55.48	55.97	54.65	51.27	50.48	75. Dépôts non bancaires
76. Bonds	28.17	27.61	27.86	28.93	29.44	28.86	28.69	29.55	30.96	31.91	76. Obligations
77. Other liabilities	4.92	4.93	5.21	5.37	5.31	5.24	5.26	5.55	6.24	6.56	77. Autres engagements
Memoranda											*Pour mémoire*
78. Short-term securities	*0.75*	*0.79*	*0.79*	*0.70*	*0.63*	*0.56*	*0.52*	*0.36*	*0.31*	*0.26*	*78. Titres à court terme*
79. Bonds	*6.60*	*6.41*	*6.33*	*6.42*	*6.19*	*6.10*	*6.25*	*5.84*	*5.69*	*5.54*	*79. Obligations*
80. Shares and participations	*0.37*	*0.35*	*0.35*	*0.37*	*0.45*	*0.51*	*0.59*	*0.72*	*0.85*	*0.82*	*80. Actions et participations*
81. Claims on non-residents	*4.07*	*4.53*	*4.48*	*4.34*	*4.56*	*4.74*	*4.80*	*4.42*	*4.31*	*4.09*	*81. Créances sur des non résidents*
82. Liabilities to non-residents	*3.52*	*3.58*	*2.67*	*2.50*	*2.38*	*2.33*	*2.49*	*2.34*	*2.47*	*2.49*	*82. Engagements envers des non résidents*

SWITZERLAND / SUISSE

Regional and savings banks / Banques régionales et caisses d'épargne

Million Swiss francs / Millions de francs suisses

	1982	1983	1984	1985	1986	1987	1988	1989	1990	1991	
INCOME STATEMENT											**COMPTE DE RESULTATS**
1. Interest income	2770	2737	2886	3102	3319	3460	3666	4306	5606	6085	1. Produits financiers
2. Interest expenses	2109	2050	2168	2334	2494	2603	2708	3276	4402	4707	2. Frais financiers
3. Net interest income	661	687	718	768	825	857	958	1030	1204	1378	3. Produits financiers nets
4. Non-interest income (net)	196	213	242	272	303	386	327	370	418	446	4. Produits non financiers (nets)
5. Gross income	857	900	960	1040	1128	1243	1285	1400	1622	1824	5. Résultat brut
6. Operating expenses	488	517	548	596	662	700	755	803	859	873	6. Frais d'exploitation
7. Net income	370	384	412	444	466	543	530	597	763	951	7. Résultat net
8. Provisions (net)	129	121	138	152	163	230	201	252	411	596	8. Provisions (nettes)
9. Profit before tax	241	263	274	292	303	313	329	345	352	355	9. Bénéfices avant impôt
10. Income tax	67	81	82	87	87	90	90	91	92	87	10. Impôt
11. Profit after tax	174	182	192	205	216	223	239	254	260	268	11. Bénéfices après impôt
12. Distributed profit	98	102	109	114	122	128	137	149	153	155	12. Bénéfices distribués
13. Retained profit	76	80	83	91	94	95	102	105	107	113	13. Bénéfices mis en réserve
Memoranda											*Pour mémoire*
14. Staff costs	334	351	370	399	435	456	489	519	553	566	14. Frais de personnel
15. Provisions on loans	..	..	..	..	..	..	..	..	..	..	15. Provisions sur prêts
16. Provisions on securities	..	..	..	..	..	..	..	..	..	..	16. Provisions sur titres
BALANCE SHEET											**BILAN**
Assets											**Actif**
17. Cash & balance with Central bank	1295	1277	1306	1370	1452	1543	1143	1108	1112	1119	17. Caisse & solde auprès de la Banque centrale
18. Interbank deposits	3281	3734	3531	3896	4384	4625	4141	4382	4303	3841	18. Dépôts interbancaires
19. Loans	40560	43557	47279	50924	55236	60738	67342	73364	78230	77898	19. Prêts
20. Securities	5189	5368	5682	5921	6252	6628	7045	6725	6665	6464	20. Valeurs mobilières
21. Other assets	1856	1979	2156	2277	2297	2548	2743	3028	3284	3418	21. Autres actifs
Liabilities											**Passif**
22. Capital & reserves	2767	2888	3059	3192	3499	3767	4000	4193	4369	4456	22. Capital et réserves
23. Borrowing from Central bank	204	275	381	455	616	586	236	143	111	439	23. Emprunts auprès de la Banque centrale
24. Interbank deposits	1488	1494	1864	2350	2830	3622	4572	5376	6975	4868	24. Dépôts interbancaires
25. Non-bank deposits	29952	32411	34164	35909	38035	41198	44577	46076	45037	44756	25. Dépôts non bancaires
26. Bonds	15707	16644	18110	19903	22006	23963	25833	29091	32677	33547	26. Obligations
27. Other liabilities	2063	2202	2376	2579	2635	2946	3195	3727	4425	4675	27. Autres engagements
Balance sheet total											**Total du bilan**
28. End-year total	52181	55914	59954	64388	69621	76082	82414	88607	93595	92741	28. En fin d'exercice
29. Average total	50699	54048	57934	62171	67004	72851	79248	85511	91101	93168	29. Moyen
Memoranda											*Pour mémoire*
30. Short-term securities	242	222	254	241	203	167	152	172	152	142	30. Titres à court terme
31. Bonds	4702	4887	5149	5333	5664	6016	6425	5994	5953	5676	31. Obligations
32. Shares and participations	245	259	279	347	385	446	468	559	560	646	32. Actions et participations
33. Claims on non-residents	693	767	821	1002	1051	1049	994	1018	1032	834	33. Créances sur des non résidents
34. Liabilities to non-residents	685	760	783	862	885	971	1032	1013	963	892	34. Engagements envers des non résidents
SUPPLEMENTARY INFORMATION											**RENSEIGNEMENTS COMPLEMENTAIRES**
35. Number of institutions	218	217	217	216	215	214	213	210	204	189	35. Nombre d'institutions
36. Number of branches	1096	1086	1106	1111	640	658	672	664	654	637	36. Nombre de succursales
37. Number of employees (x 1000)	6.7	6.9	7.1	7.4	7.7	8.0	8.2	8.4	8.5	8.2	37. Nombre de salariés (x 1000)

SWITZERLAND

Regional and savings banks

SUISSE

Banques régionales et caisses d'épargne

Per cent — *Pourcentage*

INCOME STATEMENT ANALYSIS — **ANALYSE DU COMPTE DE RESULTATS**

	1982	1983	1984	1985	1986	1987	1988	1989	1990	1991		
% of average balance sheet total												**% du total moyen du bilan**
38. Interest income	5.46	5.06	4.98	4.99	4.95	4.75	4.63	5.04	6.15	6.53	38.	Produits financiers
39. Interest expenses	4.16	3.79	3.74	3.75	3.72	3.57	3.42	3.83	4.83	5.05	39.	Frais financiers
40. Net interest income	1.30	1.27	1.24	1.24	1.23	1.18	1.21	1.20	1.32	1.48	40.	Produits financiers nets
41. Non-interest income (net)	0.39	0.39	0.42	0.44	0.45	0.53	0.41	0.43	0.46	0.48	41.	Produits non financiers (nets)
42. Gross income	1.69	1.67	1.66	1.67	1.68	1.71	1.62	1.64	1.78	1.96	42.	Résultat brut
43. Operating expenses	0.96	0.96	0.95	0.96	0.99	0.96	0.95	0.94	0.94	0.94	43.	Frais d'exploitation
44. Net income	0.73	0.71	0.71	0.71	0.70	0.75	0.67	0.70	0.84	1.02	44.	Résultat net
45. Provisions (net)	0.25	0.22	0.24	0.24	0.24	0.32	0.25	0.29	0.45	0.64	45.	Provisions (nettes)
46. Profit before tax	0.47	0.49	0.47	0.47	0.45	0.43	0.42	0.40	0.39	0.38	46.	Bénéfices avant impôt
47. Income tax	0.13	0.15	0.14	0.14	0.13	0.12	0.11	0.11	0.10	0.09	47.	Impôt
48. Profit after tax	0.34	0.34	0.33	0.33	0.32	0.31	0.30	0.30	0.29	0.29	48.	Bénéfices après impôt
49. Distributed profit	0.19	0.19	0.19	0.18	0.18	0.18	0.17	0.17	0.17	0.17	49.	Bénéfices distribués
50. Retained profit	0.15	0.15	0.14	0.15	0.14	0.13	0.13	0.12	0.12	0.12	50.	Bénéfices mis en réserve
51. Staff costs	0.66	0.65	0.64	0.64	0.65	0.63	0.62	0.61	0.61	0.61	51.	Frais de personnel
52. Provisions on loans	:	:	:	:	:	:	:	:	:	:	52.	Provisions sur prêts
53. Provisions on securities	:	:	:	:	:	:	:	:	:	:	53.	Provisions sur titres
% of gross income												**% du total du résultat brut**
54. Net interest income	77.12	76.33	74.79	73.84	73.14	68.95	74.55	73.57	74.23	75.55	54.	Produits financiers nets
55. Non-interest income (net)	22.88	23.67	25.21	26.16	26.86	31.05	25.45	26.43	25.77	24.45	55.	Produits non financiers (nets)
56. Operating expenses	56.87	57.37	57.08	57.28	58.69	56.32	58.75	57.36	52.96	47.86	56.	Frais d'exploitation
57. Net income	43.13	42.63	42.92	42.72	41.31	43.68	41.25	42.64	47.04	52.14	57.	Résultat net
58. Provisions (net)	15.04	13.45	14.33	14.62	14.45	18.50	15.64	18.00	25.34	32.68	58.	Provisions (nettes)
59. Profit before tax	28.09	29.18	28.58	28.09	26.86	25.18	25.60	24.64	21.70	19.46	59.	Bénéfices avant impôt
60. Income tax	7.80	8.97	8.55	8.37	7.71	7.24	7.00	6.50	5.67	4.77	60.	Impôt
61. Profit after tax	20.29	20.20	20.03	19.72	19.15	17.94	18.60	18.14	16.03	14.69	61.	Bénéfices après impôt
62. Staff costs	38.95	39.00	38.54	38.32	38.56	36.69	38.05	37.07	34.09	31.03	62.	Frais de personnel
% of net income												**% du total du résultat net**
63. Provisions (net)	34.87	31.55	33.40	34.24	34.98	42.36	37.92	42.21	53.87	62.67	63.	Provisions (nettes)
64. Profit before tax	65.13	68.45	66.60	65.76	65.02	57.64	62.08	57.79	46.13	37.33	64.	Bénéfices avant impôt
65. Income tax	18.10	21.05	19.93	19.59	18.67	16.57	16.98	15.24	12.06	9.15	65.	Impôt
66. Profit after tax	47.04	47.39	46.67	46.17	46.35	41.07	45.09	42.55	34.08	28.18	66.	Bénéfices après impôt

SWITZERLAND

Regional and savings banks

SUISSE

Banques régionales et caisses d'épargne

	1982	1983	1984	1985	1986	1987	1988	1989	1990	1991	
Per cent											*Pourcentage*
BALANCE SHEET ANALYSIS											**ANALYSE DU BILAN**
% of year-end balance sheet total											**% du total du bilan en fin d'exercice**
Assets											**Actif**
67. Cash & balance with Central bank	2.48	2.28	2.18	2.13	2.09	2.03	1.39	1.25	1.19	1.21	67. Caisse & solde auprès de la Banque centrale
68. Interbank deposits	6.29	6.68	5.89	6.05	6.30	6.08	5.02	4.95	4.60	4.14	68. Dépôts interbancaires
69. Loans	77.73	77.90	78.86	79.09	79.34	79.83	81.71	82.80	83.58	84.00	69. Prêts
70. Securities	9.94	9.60	9.48	9.20	8.98	8.71	8.55	7.59	7.12	6.97	70. Valeurs mobilières
71. Other assets	3.56	3.54	3.60	3.54	3.30	3.35	3.33	3.42	3.51	3.69	71. Autres actifs
Liabilities											**Passif**
72. Capital & reserves	5.30	5.16	5.10	4.96	5.03	4.95	4.85	4.73	4.67	4.80	72. Capital et réserves
73. Borrowing from Central bank	0.39	0.49	0.64	0.71	0.88	0.77	0.29	0.16	0.12	0.47	73. Emprunts auprès de la Banque centrale
74. Interbank deposits	2.85	2.67	3.11	3.65	4.06	4.76	5.55	6.07	7.45	5.25	74. Dépôts interbancaires
75. Non-bank deposits	57.40	57.97	56.98	55.77	54.63	54.15	54.09	52.00	48.12	48.26	75. Dépôts non bancaires
76. Bonds	30.10	29.77	30.21	30.91	31.61	31.50	31.35	32.83	34.91	36.17	76. Obligations
77. Other liabilities	3.95	3.94	3.96	4.01	3.78	3.87	3.88	4.21	4.73	5.04	77. Autres engagements
Memoranda											***Pour mémoire***
78. Short-term securities	*0.46*	*0.40*	*0.42*	*0.37*	*0.29*	*0.22*	*0.18*	*0.19*	*0.16*	*0.15*	*78. Titres à court terme*
79. Bonds	*9.01*	*8.74*	*8.59*	*8.28*	*8.14*	*7.91*	*7.80*	*6.76*	*6.36*	*6.12*	*79. Obligations*
80. Shares and participations	*0.47*	*0.46*	*0.47*	*0.54*	*0.55*	*0.59*	*0.57*	*0.63*	*0.60*	*0.70*	*80. Actions et participations*
81. Claims on non-residents	*1.33*	*1.37*	*1.37*	*1.56*	*1.51*	*1.38*	*1.21*	*1.15*	*1.10*	*0.90*	*81. Créances sur des non résidents*
82. Liabilities to non-residents	*1.31*	*1.36*	*1.31*	*1.34*	*1.27*	*1.28*	*1.25*	*1.14*	*1.03*	*0.96*	*82. Engagements envers des non résidents*

SWITZERLAND

Loan associations and agricultural co-operative banks

SUISSE

Caisses de crédit mutuel et banques mutualistes agricoles

Million Swiss francs / *Millions de francs suisses*

		1982	1983	1984	1985	1986	1987	1988	1989	1990	1991
INCOME STATEMENT	**COMPTE DE RESULTATS**										
1. Interest income	1. Produits financiers	793	804	873	960	1059	1129	1209	1422	1906	2280
2. Interest expenses	2. Frais financiers	635	640	692	761	844	901	955	1137	1567	1878
3. Net interest income	3. Produits financiers nets	158	164	180	199	215	228	254	285	339	402
4. Non-interest income (net)	4. Produits non financiers (nets)	24	28	34	39	44	49	55	63	81	96
5. Gross income	5. Résultat brut	182	192	215	238	259	277	309	348	420	498
6. Operating expenses	6. Frais d'exploitation	102	113	128	146	166	183	203	230	259	291
7. Net income	7. Résultat net	80	79	87	92	93	94	106	118	161	207
8. Provisions (net)	8. Provisions (nettes)	23	24	30	36	40	42	53	64	106	146
9. Profit before tax	9. Bénéfices avant impôt	57	55	56	56	53	52	53	54	55	61
10. Income tax	10. Impôt	17	15	16	16	16	15	16	15	18	18
11. Profit after tax	11. Bénéfices après impôt	40	40	40	40	37	37	37	39	37	43
12. Distributed profit	12. Bénéfices distribués	3	3	4	4	4	4	4	5	5	5
13. Retained profit	13. Bénéfices mis en réserve	37	36	36	36	33	33	33	34	32	38
Memoranda	*Pour mémoire*										
14. *Staff costs*	14. *Frais de personnel*	*55*	*62*	*70*	*80*	*91*	*101*	*111*	*125*	*139*	*158*
15. *Provisions on loans*	15. *Provisions sur prêts*	..	..	..	..	..	..	..	..	..	..
16. *Provisions on securities*	16. *Provisions sur titres*	..	..	..	..	..	..	..	..	..	..
BALANCE SHEET	**BILAN**										
Assets	**Actif**										
17. Cash & balance with Central bank	17. Caisse & solde auprès de la Banque centrale	247	270	274	297	316	353	347	355	360	389
18. Interbank deposits	18. Dépôts interbancaires	2674	2814	2888	2972	3305	3747	3907	3975	4266	4700
19. Loans	19. Prêts	12130	13429	14972	16668	18515	20310	22773	25672	28028	30286
20. Securities	20. Valeurs mobilières	126	127	135	143	166	168	204	223	229	229
21. Other assets	21. Autres actifs	443	508	594	667	746	809	878	999	1159	1273
Liabilities	**Passif**										
22. Capital & reserves	22. Capital et réserves	577	616	655	695	733	770	807	845	885	926
23. Borrowing from Central bank	23. Emprunts auprès de la Banque centrale	-	-	-	-	-	-	-	-	18	20
24. Interbank deposits	24. Dépôts interbancaires	231	331	465	703	1153	1414	1627	2176	2352	2301
25. Non-bank deposits	25. Dépôts non bancaires	10898	12177	13241	14254	15460	17089	19034	19953	20386	21844
26. Bonds	26. Obligations	3489	3573	4010	4546	5121	5501	5968	7443	9301	10439
27. Other liabilities	27. Autres engagements	426	451	492	549	581	612	674	808	1101	1347
Balance sheet total	**Total du bilan**										
28. End-year total	28. En fin d'exercice	15621	17148	18863	20747	23048	25387	28109	31225	34042	36876
29. Average total	29. Moyen	15057	16385	18006	19805	21898	24217	26748	29667	32634	35459
Memoranda	*Pour mémoire*										
30. *Short-term securities*	30. *Titres à court terme*	..	..	*5*	*7*	*11*	*12*	*18*	*24*	*28*	*29*
31. *Bonds*	31. *Obligations*	*12*	*13*	*15*	*21*	*20*	*21*	*18*	*18*	*20*	*17*
32. *Shares and participations*	32. *Actions et participations*	*115*	*115*	*115*	*115*	*135*	*135*	*167*	*181*	*181*	*183*
33. *Claims on non-residents*	33. *Créances sur des non résidents*	..	..	..	..	..	..	..	..	..	..
34. *Liabilities to non-residents*	34. *Engagements envers des non résidents*	..	..	..	..	..	..	..	..	..	..
SUPPLEMENTARY INFORMATION	**RENSEIGNEMENTS COMPLEMENTAIRES**										
35. Number of institutions	35. Nombre d'institutions	2	2	2	2	2	2	2	2	2	2
36. Number of branches	36. Nombre de succursales	1244	1245	1251	1281	1243	1242	1241	1229	1213	1192
37. Number of employees (x 1000)	37. Nombre de salariés (x 1000)	2.1	2.2	2.3	2.4	2.6	2.7	2.8	3.0	2.7	2.6

SWITZERLAND

Loan associations and agricultural co-operative banks

SUISSE

Caisses de crédit mutuel et banques mutualistes agricoles

Per cent / *Pourcentage*

INCOME STATEMENT ANALYSIS / **ANALYSE DU COMPTE DE RESULTATS**

	1982	1983	1984	1985	1986	1987	1988	1989	1990	1991		
% of average balance sheet total												**% du total moyen du bilan**
38. Interest income	5.27	4.91	4.85	4.85	4.84	4.66	4.52	4.79	5.84	6.43	38.	Produits financiers
39. Interest expenses	4.22	3.91	3.85	3.84	3.85	3.72	3.57	3.83	4.80	5.30	39.	Frais financiers
40. Net interest income	1.05	1.00	1.00	1.00	0.98	0.94	0.95	0.96	1.04	1.13	40.	Produits financiers nets
41. Non-interest income (net)	0.16	0.17	0.19	0.20	0.20	0.20	0.21	0.21	0.25	0.27	41.	Produits non financiers (nets)
42. Gross income	1.21	1.17	1.19	1.20	1.18	1.14	1.16	1.17	1.29	1.40	42.	Résultat brut
43. Operating expenses	0.68	0.69	0.71	0.74	0.76	0.76	0.76	0.78	0.79	0.82	43.	Frais d'exploitation
44. Net income	0.53	0.48	0.48	0.46	0.42	0.39	0.40	0.40	0.49	0.58	44.	Résultat net
45. Provisions (net)	0.15	0.15	0.17	0.18	0.18	0.17	0.20	0.22	0.32	0.41	45.	Provisions (nettes)
46. Profit before tax	0.38	0.34	0.31	0.28	0.24	0.21	0.20	0.18	0.17	0.17	46.	Bénéfices avant impôt
47. Income tax	0.11	0.09	0.09	0.08	0.07	0.06	0.06	0.05	0.06	0.05	47.	Impôt
48. Profit after tax	0.27	0.24	0.22	0.20	0.17	0.15	0.14	0.13	0.11	0.12	48.	Bénéfices après impôt
49. Distributed profit	0.02	0.02	0.02	0.02	0.02	0.02	0.01	0.02	0.02	0.01	49.	Bénéfices distribués
50. Retained profit	0.25	0.22	0.20	0.18	0.15	0.14	0.12	0.11	0.10	0.11	50.	Bénéfices mis en réserve
51. Staff costs	0.36	0.38	0.39	0.40	0.42	0.42	0.41	0.42	0.43	0.45	51.	Frais de personnel
52. Provisions on loans	..	..	..	..	..	..	..	..	..	..	52.	Provisions sur prêts
53. Provisions on securities	..	..	..	..	..	..	..	..	..	..	53.	Provisions sur titres
% of gross income												**% du total du résultat brut**
54. Net interest income	86.72	85.56	83.96	83.61	83.01	82.31	82.20	81.90	80.71	80.72	54.	Produits financiers nets
55. Non-interest income (net)	13.28	14.44	16.04	16.39	16.99	17.69	17.80	18.10	19.29	19.28	55.	Produits non financiers (nets)
56. Operating expenses	56.15	58.81	59.63	61.34	64.09	66.06	65.70	66.09	61.67	58.43	56.	Frais d'exploitation
57. Net income	43.85	41.19	40.37	38.66	35.91	33.94	34.30	33.91	38.33	41.57	57.	Résultat net
58. Provisions (net)	12.46	12.57	14.17	15.13	15.44	15.16	17.15	18.39	25.24	29.32	58.	Provisions (nettes)
59. Profit before tax	31.39	28.62	26.20	23.53	20.46	18.77	17.15	15.52	13.10	12.25	59.	Bénéfices avant impôt
60. Income tax	9.22	7.98	7.60	6.72	6.18	5.42	5.18	4.31	4.29	3.61	60.	Impôt
61. Profit after tax	22.17	20.65	18.60	16.81	14.29	13.36	11.97	11.21	8.81	8.63	61.	Bénéfices après impôt
62. Staff costs	29.97	32.38	32.68	33.65	35.14	36.46	35.92	35.92	33.10	31.73	62.	Frais de personnel
% of net income												**% du total du résultat net**
63. Provisions (net)	28.41	30.51	35.10	39.13	43.01	44.68	50.00	54.24	65.84	70.53	63.	Provisions (nettes)
64. Profit before tax	71.59	69.49	64.90	60.87	56.99	55.32	50.00	45.76	34.16	29.47	64.	Bénéfices avant impôt
65. Income tax	21.03	19.37	18.82	17.39	17.20	15.96	15.09	12.71	11.18	8.70	65.	Impôt
66. Profit after tax	50.56	50.13	46.07	43.48	39.78	39.36	34.91	33.05	22.98	20.77	66.	Bénéfices après impôt

SWITZERLAND

Loan associations and agricultural co-operative banks

SUISSE

Caisses de crédit mutuel et banques mutualistes agricoles

Per cent / *Pourcentage*

BALANCE SHEET ANALYSIS / **ANALYSE DU BILAN**

% of year-end balance sheet total / **% du total du bilan en fin d'exercice**

	1982	1983	1984	1985	1986	1987	1988	1989	1990	1991	
Assets											**Actif**
67. Cash & balance with Central bank	1.58	1.58	1.45	1.43	1.37	1.39	1.23	1.14	1.06	1.05	67. Caisse & solde auprès de la Banque centrale
68. Interbank deposits	17.12	16.41	15.31	14.32	14.34	14.76	13.90	12.73	12.53	12.75	68. Dépôts interbancaires
69. Loans	77.65	78.31	79.37	80.34	80.33	80.00	81.02	82.22	82.33	82.13	69. Prêts
70. Securities	0.81	0.74	0.72	0.69	0.72	0.66	0.73	0.71	0.67	0.62	70. Valeurs mobilières
71. Other assets	2.84	2.96	3.15	3.21	3.24	3.19	3.12	3.20	3.40	3.45	71. Autres actifs
Liabilities											**Passif**
72. Capital & reserves	3.69	3.59	3.47	3.35	3.18	3.03	2.87	2.71	2.60	2.51	72. Capital et réserves
73. Borrowing from Central bank	-	-	-	-	-	-	-	-	0.05	0.05	73. Emprunts auprès de la Banque centrale
74. Interbank deposits	1.48	1.93	2.47	3.39	5.00	5.57	5.79	6.97	6.91	6.24	74. Dépôts interbancaires
75. Non-bank deposits	69.77	71.01	70.20	68.70	67.08	67.31	67.71	63.90	59.88	59.24	75. Dépôts non bancaires
76. Bonds	22.33	20.84	21.26	21.91	22.22	21.67	21.23	23.84	27.32	28.31	76. Obligations
77. Other liabilities	2.73	2.63	2.61	2.65	2.52	2.41	2.40	2.59	3.23	3.65	77. Autres engagements
Memoranda											***Pour mémoire***
78. Short-term securities	*0.08*	*..*	*0.03*	*0.03*	*0.05*	*0.05*	*0.06*	*0.08*	*0.08*	*0.08*	*78. Titres à court terme*
79. Bonds	*..*	*0.07*	*0.08*	*0.10*	*0.09*	*0.08*	*0.06*	*0.06*	*0.06*	*0.05*	*79. Obligations*
80. Shares and participations	*0.73*	*0.67*	*0.61*	*0.55*	*0.59*	*0.53*	*0.59*	*0.58*	*0.53*	*0.50*	*80. Actions et participations*
81. Claims on non-residents	*..*	*..*	*..*	*..*	*..*	*..*	*..*	*..*	*..*	*..*	*81. Créances sur des non résidents*
82. Liabilities to non-residents	*..*	*..*	*..*	*..*	*..*	*..*	*..*	*..*	*..*	*..*	*82. Engagements envers des non résidents*

TURKEY
Commercial banks

TURQUE
Banques commerciales

Billion Turkish liras — *Milliards de livres turques*

		1982	1983	1984	1985	1986	1987	1988	1989	1990	1991	
INCOME STATEMENT												**COMPTE DE RESULTATS**
1.	Interest income	NA	859	1567	2609	4317	6314	12165	20232	33243	63597	Produits financiers
2.	Interest expenses	NA	727	1325	2386	3437	4482	9177	17250	23803	42282	Frais financiers
3.	Net interest income	NA	132	242	224	880	1832	2988	2982	9440	21315	Produits financiers nets
4.	Non-interest income (net)	NA	115	180	229	185	417	1098	2854	1963	-1956	Produits non financiers (nets)
5.	Gross income	NA	248	422	453	1065	2249	4086	5836	11403	19359	Résultat brut
6.	Operating expenses	NA	180	243	346	534	855	1658	3014	5943	10896	Frais d'exploitation
7.	Net income	NA	67	179	107	531	1394	2428	2822	5460	8463	Résultat net
8.	Provisions (net)	NA	16	36	39	128	498	841	947	1341	2430	Provisions (nettes)
9.	Profit before tax	NA	52	143	68	403	896	1587	1875	4119	6033	Bénéfices avant impôt
10.	Income tax	NA	9	25	24	50	81	185	406	637	804	Impôt
11.	Profit after tax	NA	43	118	44	353	815	1402	1469	3482	5229	Bénéfices après impôt
12.	Distributed profit	NA	17	43	54	163	321	695	762	1788	2399	Bénéfices distribués
13.	Retained profit	NA	26	75	-11	190	494	707	707	1694	2830	Bénéfices mis en réserve
Memoranda												*Pour mémoire*
14.	*Staff costs*	*NA*	*144*	*202*	*286*	*433*	*684*	*1313*	*2420*	*4820*	*8353*	*Frais de personnel*
15.	*Provisions on loans*	*NA*	*-*	*-*	*-*	*119*	*438*	*654*	*671*	*861*	*1772*	*Provisions sur prêts*
16.	*Provisions on securities*	*NA*	*-*	*-*	*-*	*-*	*-*	*-*	*-*	*7*	*148*	*Provisions sur titres*
BALANCE SHEET												**BILAN**
Assets												**Actif**
17.	Cash & balance with Central bank	354	492	736	1317	2143	3984	5331	7340	10349	16911	Caisse & solde auprès de la Banque centrale
18.	Interbank deposits	350	501	1154	1615	2415	3375	8037	9733	14701	32039	Dépôts interbancaires
19.	Loans	1900	2630	3479	6080	10378	16989	24496	38904	68887	111813	Prêts
20.	Securities	183	195	663	1458	2279	4180	6987	12476	17111	34283	Valeurs mobilières
21.	Other assets	1314	2051	2998	4395	6042	9702	16701	28229	41544	74912	Autres actifs
Liabilities												**Passif**
22.	Capital & reserves	164	288	454	677	726	1407	2793	4517	6999	13635	Capital et réserves
23.	Borrowing from Central bank	321	524	284	450	657	2033	2538	3088	3129	4013	Emprunts auprès de la Banque centrale
24.	Interbank deposits	50	103	232	244	1375	1984	3222	4262	6837	8259	Dépôts interbancaires
25.	Non-bank deposits	2593	3336	5256	8627	14452	22128	35111	58141	88726	160595	Dépôts non bancaires
26.	Bonds	7	12	9	7	7	7	54	389	413	704	Obligations
27.	Other liabilities	966	1606	2794	4859	6040	10671	17834	26285	46488	82752	Autres engagements
Balance sheet total												**Total du bilan**
28.	End-year total	4101	5868	9029	14865	23257	38230	61552	96682	152592	269958	En fin d'exercice
29.	Average total	3414	4985	7449	11947	19061	30744	49891	79117	124637	211275	Moyen
Memoranda												*Pour mémoire*
30.	*Short-term securities*	*..*	*..*	*482*	*1073*	*1627*	*2611*	*3961*	*9417*	*12579*	*19296*	*Titres à court terme*
31.	*Bonds*	*72*	*185*	*161*	*257*	*355*	*706*	*1305*	*2666*	*4081*	*6370*	*Obligations*
32.	*Shares and participations*	*77*	*117*	*160*	*26*	*1635*	*2351*	*6848*	*9208*	*13931*	*36108*	*Actions et participations*
33.	*Claims on non-residents*	*16*	*51*	*177*	*36*	*1015*	*2192*	*3578*	*5040*	*12821*	*22428*	*Créances sur des non résidents*
34.	*Liabilities to non-residents*	*13*	*45*									*Engagements envers des non résidents*
SUPPLEMENTARY INFORMATION												**RENSEIGNEMENTS COMPLEMENTAIRES**
35.	Number of institutions	43	44	44	48	50	51	53	53	56	56	Nombre d'institutions
36.	Number of branches	6344	6272	6193	6259	6338	6407	6517	6579	6543	6463	Nombre de succursales
37.	Number of employees (x 1000)	129.3	131.0	133.4	136.3	141.8	147.3	149.4	151.1	152.0	150.8	Nombre de salariés (x 1000)

173

TURKEY

Commercial banks

Per cent

INCOME STATEMENT ANALYSIS

		1982	1983	1984	1985	1986	1987	1988	1989	1990	1991
	% of average balance sheet total										
38.	Interest income	NA	17.24	21.03	21.84	22.65	20.54	24.38	25.57	26.67	30.10
39.	Interest expenses	NA	14.59	17.79	19.97	18.03	14.58	18.39	21.80	19.10	20.01
40.	Net interest income	NA	2.65	3.25	1.87	4.62	5.96	5.99	3.77	7.57	10.09
41.	Non-interest income (net)	NA	2.32	2.42	1.92	0.97	1.36	2.20	3.61	1.57	-0.93
42.	Gross income	NA	4.97	5.66	3.79	5.59	7.32	8.19	7.38	9.15	9.16
43.	Operating expenses	NA	3.61	3.26	2.89	2.80	2.78	3.32	3.81	4.77	5.16
44.	Net income	NA	1.35	2.41	0.90	2.79	4.53	4.87	3.57	4.38	4.01
45.	Provisions (net)	NA	0.31	0.48	0.33	0.67	1.62	1.69	1.20	1.08	1.15
46.	Profit before tax	NA	1.04	1.92	0.57	2.11	2.91	3.18	2.37	3.30	2.86
47.	Income tax	NA	0.17	0.34	0.20	0.26	0.26	0.37	0.51	0.51	0.38
48.	Profit after tax	NA	0.87	1.58	0.37	1.85	2.65	2.81	1.86	2.79	2.47
49.	Distributed profit	NA	0.34	0.58	0.45	0.86	1.04	1.39	0.96	1.43	1.14
50.	Retained profit	NA	0.53	1.00	-0.09	1.00	1.61	1.42	0.89	1.36	1.34
51.	Staff costs	NA	2.89	2.71	2.39	2.27	2.22	2.63	3.06	3.87	3.95
52.	Provisions on loans	NA	-	-	-	0.62	1.42	1.31	0.85	0.69	0.84
53.	Provisions on securities	NA	-	-	-	-	-	-	-	0.01	0.07
	% of gross income										
54.	Net interest income	NA	53.35	57.33	49.44	82.63	81.46	73.13	51.10	82.79	110.10
55.	Non-interest income (net)	NA	46.65	42.67	50.56	17.37	18.54	26.87	48.90	17.21	-10.10
56.	Operating expenses	NA	72.78	57.52	76.36	50.14	38.02	40.58	51.64	52.12	56.28
57.	Net income	NA	27.22	42.48	23.64	49.86	61.98	59.42	48.36	47.88	43.72
58.	Provisions (net)	NA	6.30	8.55	8.69	12.02	22.14	20.58	16.23	11.76	12.55
59.	Profit before tax	NA	20.92	33.93	14.95	37.84	39.84	38.84	32.13	36.12	31.16
60.	Income tax	NA	3.47	6.00	5.32	4.69	3.60	4.53	6.96	5.59	4.15
61.	Profit after tax	NA	17.44	27.93	9.63	33.15	36.24	34.31	25.17	30.54	27.01
62.	Staff costs	NA	58.24	47.81	63.17	40.66	30.41	32.13	41.47	42.27	43.15
	% of net income										
63.	Provisions (net)	NA	23.15	20.13	36.76	24.11	35.72	34.64	33.56	24.56	28.71
64.	Profit before tax	NA	76.85	79.87	63.24	75.89	64.28	65.36	66.44	75.44	71.29
65.	Income tax	NA	12.76	14.12	22.49	9.42	5.81	7.62	14.39	11.67	9.50
66.	Profit after tax	NA	64.09	65.76	40.75	66.48	58.46	57.74	52.06	63.77	61.79

TURQUE

Banques commerciales

Pourcentage

ANALYSE DU COMPTE DE RESULTATS

% du total moyen du bilan
38. Produits financiers
39. Frais financiers
40. Produits financiers nets
41. Produits non financiers (nets)
42. Résultat brut
43. Frais d'exploitation
44. Résultat net
45. Provisions (nettes)
46. Bénéfices avant impôt
47. Impôt
48. Bénéfices après impôt
49. Bénéfices distribués
50. Bénéfices mis en réserve
51. Frais de personnel
52. Provisions sur prêts
53. Provisions sur titres

% du total du résultat brut
54. Produits financiers nets
55. Produits non financiers (nets)
56. Frais d'exploitation
57. Résultat net
58. Provisions (nettes)
59. Bénéfices avant impôt
60. Impôt
61. Bénéfices après impôt
62. Frais de personnel

% du total du résultat net
63. Provisions (nettes)
64. Bénéfices avant impôt
65. Impôt
66. Bénéfices après impôt

TURKEY
Commercial banks

TURQUIE
Banques commerciales

Per cent — *Pourcentage*

BALANCE SHEET ANALYSIS — **ANALYSE DU BILAN**

% of year-end balance sheet total — **% du total du bilan en fin d'exercice**

	1982	1983	1984	1985	1986	1987	1988	1989	1990	1991		
Assets												**Actif**
67. Cash & balance with Central bank	8.62	8.38	8.15	8.86	9.21	10.42	8.66	7.59	6.78	6.26	67.	Caisse & solde auprès de la Banque centrale
68. Interbank deposits	8.53	8.53	12.78	10.86	10.38	8.83	13.06	10.07	9.63	11.87	68.	Dépôts interbancaires
69. Loans	46.34	44.82	38.53	40.90	44.62	44.44	39.80	40.24	45.14	41.42	69.	Prêts
70. Securities	4.46	3.31	7.34	9.81	9.80	10.93	11.35	12.90	11.21	12.70	70.	Valeurs mobilières
71. Other assets	32.05	34.96	33.20	29.57	25.98	25.38	27.13	29.20	27.23	27.75	71.	Autres actifs
Liabilities												**Passif**
72. Capital & reserves	4.00	4.91	5.03	4.55	3.12	3.68	4.54	4.67	4.59	5.05	72.	Capital et réserves
73. Borrowing from Central bank	7.83	8.93	3.15	3.03	2.82	5.32	4.12	3.19	2.05	1.49	73.	Emprunts auprès de la Banque centrale
74. Interbank deposits	1.22	1.76	2.57	1.64	5.91	5.19	5.23	4.41	4.48	3.06	74.	Dépôts interbancaires
75. Non-bank deposits	63.23	56.85	58.21	58.04	62.14	57.88	57.04	60.14	58.15	59.49	75.	Dépôts non bancaires
76. Bonds	0.17	0.20	0.10	0.05	0.03	0.02	0.09	0.40	0.27	0.26	76.	Obligations
77. Other liabilities	23.56	27.37	30.94	32.69	25.97	27.91	28.97	27.19	30.47	30.65	77.	Autres engagements
Memoranda												*Pour mémoire*
78. Short-term securities	*1.76*	*3.15*	*5.34*	*7.22*	*7.00*	*6.83*	*6.44*	*9.74*	*8.24*	*7.15*	*78.*	*Titres à court terme*
79. Bonds	*1.88*	*1.99*	*1.78*	*1.73*	*1.53*	*1.85*	*2.12*	*2.76*	*2.67*	*2.36*	*79.*	*Obligations*
80. Shares and participations	*0.39*	*0.87*	*1.77*	*0.17*	*7.03*	*6.15*	*11.13*	*9.52*	*9.13*	*13.38*	*80.*	*Actions et participations*
81. Claims on non-residents	*0.32*	*0.77*	*1.96*	*0.24*	*4.36*	*5.73*	*5.81*	*5.21*	*8.40*	*8.31*	*81.*	*Créances sur des non résidents*
82. Liabilities to non-residents											*82.*	*Engagements envers des non résidents*

Change in methodology

• Iller Bankasi, although not being a full commercial bank, is included in the data until end-1988.

• Until 1986, "Interest income" (item 1) includes interest paid by the Central bank on required reserves for Turkish lira denominated deposits.

• "Operating expenses" (item 6) do not include rents for the period 1981-85.

• Data were revised to include, as from 1986, the foreign branches of domestic banks.

Changement méthodologique :

• Jusqu'en fin 1988, Iller Bankasi, bien que celle-ci ne soit pas à tous égards une banque commerciale, est incluse dans les données.

• Jusqu'en 1986 les "Produits financiers" (poste 1) couvrent la rémunération par la Banque centrale des réserves obligatoires assises sur les dépôts en livres turques.

• Les "Frais d'exploitation" (poste 6) ne comprennent pas les loyers pour la période 1981-85.

• A compter de 1986 les données ont été révisées afin d'inclure les filiales étrangères des banques domestiques.

UNITED KINGDOM
Commercial banks

ROYAUME-UNI
Banques commerciales

Million pounds sterling — Millions de livres sterling

	EN	FR	1984	1985	1986	1987	1988	1989	1990	1991
	INCOME STATEMENT	**COMPTE DE RESULTATS**								
1.	Interest income	Produits financiers	31359	31941	31684	34363	39998	56101	63140	57765
2.	Interest expenses	Frais financiers	22665	22544	21607	23124	27121	41736	48286	42200
3.	Net interest income	Produits financiers nets	8694	9397	10077	11239	12877	14365	14854	15565
4.	Non-interest income (net)	Produits non financiers (nets)	4807	4951	5750	6710	7502	8906	9530	10654
5.	Gross income	Résultat brut	13501	14348	15827	17949	20379	23271	24384	26219
6.	Operating expenses	Frais d'exploitation	9025	9378	10319	11583	13159	14977	16021	17189
7.	Net income	Résultat net	4476	4970	5508	6366	7220	8294	8363	9030
8.	Provisions (net)	Provisions (nettes)	1956	1676	1733	5382	1228	969	4766	6901
9.	Profit before tax	Bénéfices avant impôt	2520	3294	3775	984	5992	7325	3597	2129
10.	Income tax	Impôt	1356	1488	1345	763	2113	593	1630	872
11.	Profit after tax	Bénéfices après impôt	1164	1806	2430	221	3879	376	1967	1257
12.	Distributed profit	Bénéfices distribués	369	450	576	710	949	1201	1262	1272
13.	Retained profit	Bénéfices mis en réserve	795	1356	1854	-489	2930	-825	705	-15
	Memoranda	*Pour mémoire*								
14.	Staff costs	Frais de personnel	5397	5612	6167	6749	7719	8658	9114	9526
15.	Provisions on loans	Provisions sur prêts	..	..	..	..	..	..	..	..
16.	Provisions on securities	Provisions sur titres	..	..	..	..	..	..	..	..
	BALANCE SHEET	**BILAN**								
	Assets	*Actif*								
17.	Cash & balance with Central bank	Caisse & solde auprès de la Banque centrale	5984	5879	6091	5864	6107	7433	7249	7057
18.	Interbank deposits	Dépôts interbancaires	66411	62873	70466	72308	77191	79191	80039	81916
19.	Loans	Prêts	181924	179618	191201	219420	257865	306456	319817	322240
20.	Securities	Valeurs mobilières	17281	20347	23878	28987	27986	34189	38401	46009
21.	Other assets	Autres actifs	31016	33133	42994	43463	52112	65416	69913	75129
	Liabilities	*Passif*								
22.	Capital & reserves	Capital et réserves	12099	13632	17506	19791	23833	24728	24614	24440
23.	Borrowing from Central bank	Emprunts auprès de la Banque centrale	-	-	-	-	-	-	-	-
24.	Interbank deposits (1)	Dépôts interbancaires (1)	275619	269036	290594	326047	366372	429820	453145	465404
25.	Non-bank deposits	Dépôts non bancaires	8364	10495	12677	11230	13941	16778	15077	16616
26.	Bonds	Obligations	6534	8687	13853	12974	17115	21359	22583	25891
27.	Other liabilities	Autres engagements								
	Balance sheet total	*Total du bilan*								
28.	End-year total	En fin d'exercice	302616	301850	334630	370042	421261	492685	515419	532351
29.	Average total	Moyen	286369	302233	318240	352336	395652	456973	504052	523885
	Memoranda	*Pour mémoire*								
30.	Short-term securities	Titres à court terme	4237	5639	5993	8709	10718	15405	16403	18019
31.	Bonds	Obligations	..	..	..	..	..	..	..	..
32.	Shares and participations	Actions et participations	..	..	..	..	..	..	..	..
33.	Claims on non-residents	Créances sur des non résidents	..	..	..	..	..	..	..	..
34.	Liabilities to non-residents	Engagements envers des non résidents	..	..	..	..	..	..	..	..
	SUPPLEMENTARY INFORMATION	**RENSEIGNEMENTS COMPLEMENTAIRES**								
35.	Number of institutions	Nombre d'institutions	48	54	53	53	52	49	47	41
36.	Number of branches	Nombre de succursales	13683	13615	13332	13813	13702	13467	12994	12325
37.	Number of employees (x 1000)	Nombre de salariés (x 1000)	335.9	340.0	350.0	374.6	402.6	414.2	411.5	399.9

Per cent

Pourcentage

INCOME STATEMENT ANALYSIS

ANALYSE DU COMPTE DE RESULTATS

		1984	1985	1986	1987	1988	1989	1990	1991		
	% of average balance sheet total										**% du total moyen du bilan**
38.	Interest income	10.95	10.57	9.96	9.75	10.11	12.28	12.53	11.03	38.	Produits financiers
39.	Interest expenses	7.91	7.46	6.79	6.56	6.85	9.13	9.58	8.06	39.	Frais financiers
40.	Net interest income	3.04	3.11	3.17	3.19	3.25	3.14	2.95	2.97	40.	Produits financiers nets
41.	Non-interest income (net)	1.68	1.64	1.81	1.90	1.90	1.95	1.89	2.03	41.	Produits non financiers (nets)
42.	Gross income	4.71	4.75	4.97	5.09	5.15	5.09	4.84	5.00	42.	Résultat brut
43.	Operating expenses	3.15	3.10	3.24	3.29	3.33	3.28	3.18	3.28	43.	Frais d'exploitation
44.	Net income	1.56	1.64	1.73	1.81	1.82	1.81	1.66	1.72	44.	Résultat net
45.	Provisions (net)	0.68	0.55	0.54	1.53	0.31	1.60	0.95	1.32	45.	Provisions (nettes)
46.	Profit before tax	0.88	1.09	1.19	0.28	1.51	0.21	0.71	0.41	46.	Bénéfices avant impôt
47.	Income tax	0.47	0.49	0.42	0.22	0.53	0.13	0.32	0.17	47.	Impôt
48.	Profit after tax	0.41	0.60	0.76	0.06	0.98	0.08	0.39	0.24	48.	Bénéfices après impôt
49.	Distributed profit	0.13	0.15	0.18	0.20	0.24	0.26	0.25	0.24	49.	Bénéfices distribués
50.	Retained profit	0.28	0.45	0.58	-0.14	0.74	-0.18	0.14	0.00	50.	Bénéfices mis en réserve
51.	Staff costs	1.88	1.86	1.94	1.92	1.95	1.89	1.81	1.82	51.	Frais de personnel
52.	Provisions on loans	..	..	..	..	..	..	..	..	52.	Provisions sur prêts
53.	Provisions on securities	..	..	..	..	..	..	..	..	53.	Provisions sur titres
	% of gross income										**% du total du résultat brut**
54.	Net interest income	64.40	65.49	63.67	62.62	63.19	61.73	60.92	59.37	54.	Produits financiers nets
55.	Non-interest income (net)	35.60	34.51	36.33	37.38	36.81	38.27	39.08	40.63	55.	Produits non financiers (nets)
56.	Operating expenses	66.85	65.36	65.20	64.53	64.57	64.36	65.70	65.56	56.	Frais d'exploitation
57.	Net income	33.15	34.64	34.80	35.47	35.43	35.64	34.30	34.44	57.	Résultat net
58.	Provisions (net)	14.49	11.68	10.95	29.98	6.03	31.48	19.55	26.32	58.	Provisions (nettes)
59.	Profit before tax	18.67	22.96	23.85	5.48	29.40	4.16	14.75	8.12	59.	Bénéfices avant impôt
60.	Income tax	10.04	10.37	8.50	4.25	10.37	2.55	6.68	3.33	60.	Impôt
61.	Profit after tax	8.62	12.59	15.35	1.23	19.03	1.62	8.07	4.79	61.	Bénéfices après impôt
62.	Staff costs	39.97	39.11	38.97	37.60	37.88	37.21	37.38	36.33	62.	Frais de personnel
	% of net income										**% du total du résultat net**
63.	Provisions (net)	43.70	33.72	31.46	84.54	17.01	88.32	56.99	76.42	63.	Provisions (nettes)
64.	Profit before tax	56.30	66.28	68.54	15.46	82.99	11.68	43.01	23.58	64.	Bénéfices avant impôt
65.	Income tax	30.29	29.94	24.42	11.99	29.27	7.15	19.49	9.66	65.	Impôt
66.	Profit after tax	26.01	36.34	44.12	3.47	53.73	4.53	23.52	13.92	66.	Bénéfices après impôt

UNITED KINGDOM
Commercial banks

ROYAUME-UNI
Banques commerciales

Per cent / *Pourcentage*

BALANCE SHEET ANALYSIS / **ANALYSE DU BILAN**

% of year-end balance sheet total / % du total du bilan en fin d'exercice

	1984	1985	1986	1987	1988	1989	1990	1991		
Assets										**Actif**
67. Cash & balance with Central bank	1.98	1.95	1.82	1.58	1.45	1.51	1.41	1.33	67.	Caisse & solde auprès de la Banque centrale
68. Interbank deposits	21.95	20.83	21.06	19.54	18.32	16.07	15.53	15.39	68.	Dépôts interbancaires
69. Loans	60.12	59.51	57.14	59.30	61.21	62.20	62.05	60.53	69.	Prêts
70. Securities	5.71	6.74	7.14	7.83	6.64	6.94	7.45	8.64	70.	Valeurs mobilières
71. Other assets	10.25	10.98	12.85	11.75	12.37	13.28	13.56	14.11	71.	Autres actifs
Liabilities										**Passif**
72. Capital & reserves	4.00	4.52	5.23	5.35	5.66	5.02	4.78	4.59	72.	Capital et réserves
73. Borrowing from Central bank	..	..	..	..	..	..	..	..	73.	Emprunts auprès de la Banque centrale
74. Interbank deposits (1)	..	..	..	..	..	..	..	..	74.	Dépôts interbancaires (1)
75. Non-bank deposits	91.08	89.13	86.84	88.11	86.97	87.24	87.92	87.42	75.	Dépôts non bancaires
76. Bonds	2.76	3.48	3.79	3.03	3.31	3.41	2.93	3.12	76.	Obligations
77. Other liabilities	2.16	2.88	4.14	3.51	4.06	4.34	4.38	4.86	77.	Autres engagements
Memoranda										*Pour mémoire*
78. Short-term securities	*1.40*	*1.87*	*1.79*	*2.35*	*2.54*	*3.13*	*3.18*	*3.38*	*78.*	*Titres à court terme*
79. Bonds	..	..	..	..	..	..	..	..	*79.*	*Obligations*
80. Shares and participations	..	..	..	..	..	..	..	..	*80.*	*Actions et participations*
81. Claims on non-residents	..	..	..	..	..	..	..	..	*81.*	*Créances sur des non résidents*
82. Liabilities to non-residents	..	..	..	..	..	..	..	..	*82.*	*Engagements envers des non résidents*

1. Included under "Non-bank deposits" (item 25 or item 75).

1. Inclus sous "Dépôts non bancaires" (poste 25 ou poste 75).

Notes

- Data on London clearing banks' groups (consolidated worldwide) for the years 1980-84 are included in "Bank Profitability, Statistical Supplement, Financial Statements of Banks 1982-86" (OECD,Paris, 1988). Series for this banking group have been discontinued.

Change in methodology:

- Data were revised as from 1987 to include Abbey National Plc.

Notes

- Les chiffres relatifs aux "Grandes banques de Londres (consolidées à l'échelle mondiale)" pour les années 1980 à 1984 figurent dans "Rentabilité des banques, Supplément statistique, Comptes des banques 1982-86" (OCDE, Paris, 1988). Cette série de données a été interrompue.

Changement méthodologique :

- A compter de 1987 les données ont été révisées afin d'inclure Abbey National Plc.

UNITED STATES
Commercial banks

ETATS-UNIS
Banques commerciales

Million US dollars / *Millions de dollars des EU*

	1982	1983	1984	1985	1986	1987	1988	1989	1990	1991		
INCOME STATEMENT												**COMPTE DE RESULTATS**
1. Interest income	235615	214182	249348	247047	236290	243740	270954	315724	318787	287653	1.	Produits financiers
2. Interest expenses	168978	143421	168470	156650	142024	144352	164254	204134	203932	166465	2.	Frais financiers
3. Net interest income	66637	70761	80878	90397	94266	99388	106700	111590	114855	121188	3.	Produits financiers nets
4. Non-interest income (net)	21755	25563	26548	32701	39937	43003	45893	51968	55996	63094	4.	Produits non financiers (nets)
5. Gross income	88392	96324	107426	123098	134203	142391	152593	163558	170851	184282	5.	Résultat brut
6. Operating expenses	61481	66603	73487	81898	89628	96784	100810	107555	114994	124026	6.	Frais d'exploitation
7. Net income	26911	29721	33939	41200	44575	45607	51783	56003	55857	60256	7.	Résultat net
8. Provisions (net)	8461	10656	13753	17601	21929	37452	16998	30920	31734	34098	8.	Provisions (nettes)
9. Profit before tax	18450	19065	20186	23599	22646	8155	34785	25083	24123	26158	9.	Bénéfices avant impôt
10. Income tax	3610	4098	4717	5588	5265	5387	9964	9611	7785	8290	10.	Impôt
11. Profit after tax	14840	14967	15469	18011	17381	2768	24821	15472	16338	17868	11.	Bénéfices après impôt
12. Distributed profit	6549	7338	7606	8497	9183	10634	13190	14046	13842	14264	12.	Bénéfices distribués
13. Retained profit	8291	7629	7863	9514	8198	-7866	11631	1426	2496	3604	13.	Bénéfices mis en réserve
Memoranda												***Pour mémoire***
14. Staff costs	*31383*	*33719*	*36706*	*39765*	*42617*	*44948*	*46316*	*48891*	*51442*	*52787*	*14.*	*Frais de personnel*
15. Provisions on loans	*8461*	*10649*	*13716*	*17535*	*21879*	*37376*	*16833*	*30811*	*31738*	*34069*	*15.*	*Provisions sur prêts*
16. Provisions on securities	*..*	*..*	*..*	*..*	*..*	*..*	*..*	*..*	*..*	*..*	*16.*	*Provisions sur titres*
BALANCE SHEET												**BILAN**
Assets												**Actif**
17. Cash & balance with Central bank	116017	130632	129618	146601	168246	145135	158039	165772	167049	154003	17.	Caisse & solde auprès de la Banque centrale
18. Interbank deposits	212657	203959	151162	153425	165107	172428	160223	151887	121267	124135	18.	Dépôts interbancaires
19. Loans	1313235	1391275	1596117	1734729	1857726	1901949	2004151	2141682	2187635	2135482	19.	Prêts
20. Securities	385381	439378	412298	477817	524840	550941	569013	598113	648749	753875	20.	Valeurs mobilières
21. Other assets	161865	167769	209569	205941	208638	215392	224276	225818	243258	244343	21.	Autres actifs
Liabilities												**Passif**
22. Capital & reserves	128439	140036	153506	168464	181097	179815	195704	203764	217501	230268	22.	Capital et réserves
23. Borrowing from Central bank											23.	Emprunts auprès de la Banque centrale
24. Interbank deposits	196423	183064	163926	163460	163398	165018	144602	144132	122878	136273	24.	Dépôts interbancaires
25. Non-bank deposits	1505995	1652230	1790797	1944314	2106379	2158471	2274436	2390972	2508565	2535516	25.	Dépôts non bancaires
26. Bonds	10043	9798	13100	17528	19668	20203	20042	22083	25897	26766	26.	Obligations
27. Other liabilities	348255	347885	377435	424747	454015	462238	480917	522321	493116	483015	27.	Autres engagements
Balance sheet total												**Total du bilan**
28. End-year total	2189155	2333013	2498764	2718513	2924557	2985845	3115701	3283271	3367958	3411838	28.	En fin d'exercice
29. Average total	2106998	2261084	2415889	2608639	2821535	2955201	3050773	3199486	3325615	3389898	29.	Moyen
Memoranda												***Pour mémoire***
30. Short-term securities	*..*	*..*	*..*	*..*	*..*	*..*	*..*	*..*	*..*	*..*	*30.*	*Titres à court terme*
31. Bonds	*..*	*..*	*..*	*..*	*..*	*..*	*..*	*..*	*..*	*..*	*31.*	*Obligations*
32. Shares and participations	*..*	*..*	*..*	*..*	*..*	*..*	*..*	*..*	*..*	*..*	*32.*	*Actions et participations*
33. Claims on non-residents	*..*	*..*	*..*	*..*	*..*	*..*	*..*	*..*	*..*	*..*	*33.*	*Créances sur des non résidents*
34. Liabilities to non-residents	*..*	*..*	*..*	*..*	*..*	*..*	*..*	*..*	*..*	*..*	*34.*	*Engagements envers des non résidents*
SUPPLEMENTARY INFORMATION												**RENSEIGNEMENTS COMPLEMENTAIRES**
35. Number of institutions	14437	14454	14460	14357	14130	13669	13094	12689	12319	11899	35.	Nombre d'institutions
36. Number of branches	NA	NA	NA	NA	NA	NA	NA	NA	NA	NA	36.	Nombre de succursales
37. Number of employees (x 1000)	NA	NA	NA	NA	NA	NA	NA	NA	NA	NA	37.	Nombre de salariés (x 1000)

UNITED STATES
Commercial banks

ETATS-UNIS
Banques commerciales

Per cent — *Pourcentage*

INCOME STATEMENT ANALYSIS — ANALYSE DU COMPTE DE RESULTATS

	1982	1983	1984	1985	1986	1987	1988	1989	1990	1991	
% of average balance sheet total											**% du total moyen du bilan**
38. Interest income	11.18	9.47	10.32	9.47	8.37	8.25	8.88	9.87	9.59	8.49	38. Produits financiers
39. Interest expenses	8.02	6.34	6.97	6.01	5.03	4.88	5.38	6.38	6.13	4.91	39. Frais financiers
40. Net interest income	3.16	3.13	3.35	3.47	3.34	3.36	3.50	3.49	3.45	3.57	40. Produits financiers nets
41. Non-interest income (net)	1.03	1.13	1.10	1.25	1.42	1.46	1.50	1.62	1.68	1.86	41. Produits non financiers (nets)
42. Gross income	4.20	4.26	4.45	4.72	4.76	4.82	5.00	5.11	5.14	5.44	42. Résultat brut
43. Operating expenses	2.92	2.95	3.04	3.14	3.18	3.28	3.30	3.36	3.46	3.66	43. Frais d'exploitation
44. Net income	1.28	1.31	1.40	1.58	1.58	1.54	1.70	1.75	1.68	1.78	44. Résultat net
45. Provisions (net)	0.40	0.47	0.57	0.67	0.78	1.27	0.56	0.97	0.95	1.01	45. Provisions (nettes)
46. Profit before tax	0.88	0.84	0.84	0.90	0.80	0.28	1.14	0.78	0.73	0.77	46. Bénéfices avant impôt
47. Income tax	0.17	0.18	0.20	0.21	0.19	0.18	0.33	0.30	0.23	0.24	47. Impôt
48. Profit after tax	0.70	0.66	0.64	0.69	0.62	0.09	0.81	0.48	0.49	0.53	48. Bénéfices après impôt
49. Distributed profit	0.31	0.32	0.31	0.33	0.33	0.36	0.43	0.44	0.42	0.42	49. Bénéfices distribués
50. Retained profit	0.39	0.34	0.33	0.36	0.29	-0.27	0.38	0.04	0.08	0.11	50. Bénéfices mis en réserve
51. Staff costs	1.49	1.49	1.52	1.52	1.51	1.52	1.52	1.53	1.55	1.56	51. Frais de personnel
52. Provisions on loans	0.40	0.47	0.57	0.67	0.78	1.26	0.55	0.96	0.95	1.01	52. Provisions sur prêts
53. Provisions on securities	:	:	:	:	:	:	:	:	:	:	53. Provisions sur titres
% of gross income											**% du total du résultat brut**
54. Net interest income	75.39	73.46	75.29	73.43	70.24	69.80	69.92	68.23	67.23	65.76	54. Produits financiers nets
55. Non-interest income (net)	24.61	26.54	24.71	26.57	29.76	30.20	30.08	31.77	32.77	34.24	55. Produits non financiers (nets)
56. Operating expenses	69.55	69.14	68.41	66.53	66.79	67.97	66.06	65.76	67.31	67.30	56. Frais d'exploitation
57. Net income	30.45	30.86	31.59	33.47	33.21	32.03	33.94	34.24	32.69	32.70	57. Résultat net
58. Provisions (net)	9.57	11.06	12.80	14.30	16.34	26.30	11.14	18.90	18.57	18.50	58. Provisions (nettes)
59. Profit before tax	20.87	19.79	18.79	19.17	16.87	5.73	22.80	15.34	14.12	14.19	59. Bénéfices avant impôt
60. Income tax	4.08	4.25	4.39	4.54	3.92	3.78	6.53	5.88	4.56	4.50	60. Impôt
61. Profit after tax	16.79	15.54	14.40	14.63	12.95	1.94	16.27	9.46	9.56	9.70	61. Bénéfices après impôt
62. Staff costs	35.50	35.01	34.17	32.30	31.76	31.57	30.35	29.89	30.11	28.64	62. Frais de personnel
% of net income											**% du total du résultat net**
63. Provisions (net)	31.44	35.85	40.52	42.72	49.20	82.12	32.83	55.21	56.81	56.59	63. Provisions (nettes)
64. Profit before tax	68.56	64.15	59.48	57.28	50.80	17.88	67.17	44.79	43.19	43.41	64. Bénéfices avant impôt
65. Income tax	13.41	13.79	13.90	13.56	11.81	11.81	19.24	17.16	13.94	13.76	65. Impôt
66. Profit after tax	55.14	50.36	45.58	43.72	38.99	6.07	47.93	27.63	29.25	29.65	66. Bénéfices après impôt

UNITED STATES

Commercial banks

Per cent

BALANCE SHEET ANALYSIS

% of year-end balance sheet total

	1982	1983	1984	1985	1986	1987	1988	1989	1990	1991
Assets										
67. Cash & balance with Central bank	5.30	5.60	5.19	5.39	5.75	4.86	5.07	5.05	4.96	4.51
68. Interbank deposits	9.71	8.74	6.05	5.64	5.65	5.77	5.14	4.63	3.60	3.64
69. Loans	59.99	59.63	63.88	63.81	63.52	63.70	64.32	65.23	64.95	62.59
70. Securities	17.60	18.83	16.50	17.58	17.95	18.45	18.26	18.22	19.26	22.10
71. Other assets	7.39	7.19	8.39	7.58	7.13	7.21	7.20	6.88	7.22	7.16
Liabilities										
72. Capital & reserves	5.87	6.00	6.14	6.20	6.19	6.02	6.28	6.21	6.46	6.75
73. Borrowing from Central bank	..	..	..	..	..	..	..	..	..	..
74. Interbank deposits	8.97	7.85	6.56	6.01	5.59	5.53	4.64	4.39	3.65	3.99
75. Non-bank deposits	68.79	70.82	71.67	71.52	72.02	72.29	73.00	72.82	74.48	74.32
76. Bonds	0.46	0.42	0.52	0.64	0.67	0.68	0.64	0.67	0.77	0.78
77. Other liabilities	15.91	14.91	15.10	15.62	15.52	15.48	15.44	15.91	14.64	14.16
Memoranda										
78. Short-term securities	..	..	..	..	..	..	..	..	..	..
79. Bonds	..	..	..	..	..	..	..	..	..	..
80. Shares and participations	..	..	..	..	..	..	..	..	..	..
81. Claims on non-residents	..	..	..	..	..	..	..	..	..	..
82. Liabilities to non-residents	..	..	..	..	..	..	..	..	..	..

Notes

- The term Commercial banks corresponds to the term Insured commercial banks used in United States publications.

ETATS-UNIS

Banques commerciales

Pourcentage

ANALYSE DU BILAN

% du total du bilan en fin d'exercice

Actif
67. Caisse & solde auprès de la Banque centrale
68. Dépôts interbancaires
69. Prêts
70. Valeurs mobilières
71. Autres actifs

Passif
72. Capital et réserves
73. Emprunts auprès de la Banque centrale
74. Dépôts interbancaires
75. Dépôts non bancaires
76. Obligations
77. Autres engagements

Pour mémoire
78. Titres à court terme
79. Obligations
80. Actions et participations
81. Créances sur des non résidents
82. Engagements envers des non résidents

Notes

- Le terme Banques commerciales correspond à la rubrique Banques commerciales assurées des publications américaines.

UNITED STATES
Large commercial banks

ETATS-UNIS
Grandes banques commerciales

Million US dollars / *Millions de dollars des EU*

		1982	1983	1984	1985	1986	1987	1988	1989	1990	1991
INCOME STATEMENT	**COMPTE DE RESULTATS**										
1. Interest income	Produits financiers	147198	130099	156427	156651	151729	163337	188200	224285	226559	199937
2. Interest expenses	Frais financiers	112663	92578	110687	103389	94174	100856	118630	151652	151151	119134
3. Net interest income	Produits financiers nets	34535	37521	45740	53262	57555	62481	69570	72633	75408	80803
4. Non-interest income (net)	Produits non financiers (nets)	15507	18449	18869	23852	29817	33839	37049	42296	46157	51719
5. Gross income	Résultat brut	50042	55970	64609	77114	87372	96320	106619	114929	121565	132522
6. Operating expenses	Frais d'exploitation	35126	38908	44460	51185	57892	65094	69338	75349	81976	89117
7. Net income	Résultat net	14916	17062	20149	25929	29480	31226	37281	39580	39589	43405
8. Provisions (net)	Provisions (nettes)	5187	6806	9055	10888	13784	31117	11742	25871	25994	28151
9. Profit before tax	Bénéfices avant impôt	9729	10256	11094	15041	15696	109	25539	13709	13595	15254
10. Income tax	Impôt	2188	2614	2993	3838	3784	3067	7220	6249	4669	4951
11. Profit after tax	Bénéfices après impôt	7541	7642	8101	11203	11912	-2958	18319	7460	8926	10303
12. Distributed profit	Bénéfices distribués	3469	4013	3994	4593	5387	6734	8830	9172	8851	9485
13. Retained profit	Bénéfices mis en réserve	4072	3629	4107	6610	6525	-9692	9489	-1712	75	818
Memoranda	*Pour mémoire*										
14. Staff costs	Frais de personnel	18208	20089	22460	25111	27867	30288	31790	33868	36182	37118
15. Provisions on loans	Provisions sur prêts	5187	6799	9019	10824	13736	31041	11587	25769	25998	28121
16. Provisions on securities	Provisions sur titres	..	..	..	..	..	..	..	..	..	..
BALANCE SHEET	**BILAN**										
Assets	**Actif**										
17. Cash & balance with Central bank	Caisse & solde auprès de la Banque centrale	86642	97653	106301	122800	141487	122822	134678	142180	144020	131216
18. Interbank deposits	Dépôts interbancaires	153667	145829	125671	128446	137490	147859	137214	131386	102223	106357
19. Loans	Prêts	843563	898966	1043432	1154006	1255740	1304663	1405018	1513367	1554404	1516894
20. Securities	Valeurs mobilières	161945	185860	177599	237792	283584	305231	321587	352720	383338	458504
21. Other assets	Autres actifs	126149	129654	130037	127943	125595	138083	150078	154726	173680	175764
Liabilities	**Passif**										
22. Capital & reserves	Capital et réserves	64801	72509	82895	94767	107057	104631	119991	124617	135155	146026
23. Borrowing from Central bank	Emprunts auprès de la Banque centrale	..	..	..	..	..	..	..	..	..	..
24. Interbank deposits	Dépôts interbancaires	187714	175239	155072	155001	155444	158033	137956	137503	116972	130189
25. Non-bank deposits	Dépôts non bancaires	814500	901880	1004695	1128235	1254687	1322324	1438049	1537914	1636025	1648085
26. Bonds	Obligations	6987	6888	10439	15203	17357	17825	18279	19851	24472	25551
27. Other liabilities	Autres engagements	297964	301446	329939	377781	409351	415845	434299	474493	445041	438884
Balance sheet total	**Total du bilan**										
28. End-year total	En fin d'exercice	1371966	1457962	1583040	1770987	1943896	2018658	2148574	2294379	2357665	2388736
29. Average total	Moyen	1312392	1414964	1520501	1677014	1857442	1981277	2083616	2221477	2326022	2373201
Memoranda	*Pour mémoire*										
30. Short-term securities	Titres à court terme	..	..	..	..	..	..	..	..	..	..
31. Bonds	Obligations	..	..	..	..	..	..	..	..	..	..
32. Shares and participations	Actions et participations	..	..	..	..	..	..	..	..	..	..
33. Claims on non-residents	Créances sur des non résidents	..	..	..	..	..	..	..	..	..	..
34. Liabilities to non-residents	Engagements envers des non résidents	..	..	..	..	..	..	..	..	..	..
SUPPLEMENTARY INFORMATION	**RENSEIGNEMENTS COMPLEMENTAIRES**										
35. Number of institutions	Nombre d'institutions	230	253	274	311	335	348	360	373	370	365
36. Number of branches	Nombre de succursales	NA	NA	NA	NA	NA	NA	NA	NA	NA	NA
37. Number of employees (x 1000)	Nombre de salariés (x 1000)	NA	NA	NA	NA	NA	NA	NA	NA	NA	NA

UNITED STATES

Large commercial banks

ETATS-UNIS

Grandes banques commerciales

Per cent / *Pourcentage*

	1982	1983	1984	1985	1986	1987	1988	1989	1990	1991		
INCOME STATEMENT ANALYSIS												**ANALYSE DU COMPTE DE RESULTATS**
% of average balance sheet total												**% du total moyen du bilan**
38. Interest income	11.22	9.19	10.29	9.34	8.17	8.24	9.03	10.10	9.74	8.42	38.	Produits financiers
39. Interest expenses	8.58	6.54	7.28	6.17	5.07	5.09	5.69	6.83	6.50	5.02	39.	Frais financiers
40. Net interest income	2.63	2.65	3.01	3.18	3.10	3.15	3.34	3.27	3.24	3.40	40.	Produits financiers nets
41. Non-interest income (net)	1.18	1.30	1.24	1.42	1.61	1.71	1.78	1.90	1.98	2.18	41.	Produits non financiers (nets)
42. Gross income	3.81	3.96	4.25	4.60	4.70	4.86	5.12	5.17	5.23	5.58	42.	Résultat brut
43. Operating expenses	2.68	2.75	2.92	3.05	3.12	3.29	3.33	3.39	3.52	3.76	43.	Frais d'exploitation
44. Net income	1.14	1.21	1.33	1.55	1.59	1.58	1.79	1.78	1.70	1.83	44.	Résultat net
45. Provisions (net)	0.40	0.48	0.60	0.65	0.74	1.57	0.56	1.16	1.12	1.19	45.	Provisions (nettes)
46. Profit before tax	0.74	0.72	0.73	0.90	0.85	0.01	1.23	0.62	0.58	0.64	46.	Bénéfices avant impôt
47. Income tax	0.17	0.18	0.20	0.23	0.20	0.15	0.35	0.28	0.20	0.21	47.	Impôt
48. Profit after tax	0.57	0.54	0.53	0.67	0.64	-0.15	0.88	0.34	0.38	0.43	48.	Bénéfices après impôt
49. Distributed profit	0.26	0.28	0.26	0.27	0.29	0.34	0.42	0.41	0.38	0.40	49.	Bénéfices distribués
50. Retained profit	0.31	0.26	0.27	0.39	0.35	-0.49	0.46	-0.08	0.00	0.03	50.	Bénéfices mis en réserve
51. Staff costs	1.39	1.42	1.48	1.50	1.50	1.53	1.53	1.52	1.56	1.56	51.	Frais de personnel
52. Provisions on loans	0.40	0.48	0.59	0.65	0.74	1.57	0.56	1.16	1.12	1.18	52.	Provisions sur prêts
53. Provisions on securities	..	..	..	..	..	..	..	..	..	..	53.	Provisions sur titres
% of gross income												**% du total du résultat brut**
54. Net interest income	69.01	67.04	70.80	69.07	65.87	64.87	65.25	63.20	62.03	60.97	54.	Produits financiers nets
55. Non-interest income (net)	30.99	32.96	29.20	30.93	34.13	35.13	34.75	36.80	37.97	39.03	55.	Produits non financiers (nets)
56. Operating expenses	70.19	69.52	68.81	66.38	66.26	67.58	65.03	65.56	67.43	67.25	56.	Frais d'exploitation
57. Net income	29.81	30.48	31.19	33.62	33.74	32.42	34.97	34.44	32.57	32.75	57.	Résultat net
58. Provisions (net)	10.37	12.16	14.02	14.12	15.78	32.31	11.01	22.51	21.38	21.24	58.	Provisions (nettes)
59. Profit before tax	19.44	18.32	17.17	19.50	17.96	0.11	23.95	11.93	11.18	11.51	59.	Bénéfices avant impôt
60. Income tax	4.37	4.67	4.63	4.98	4.33	3.18	6.77	5.44	3.84	3.74	60.	Impôt
61. Profit after tax	15.07	13.65	12.54	14.53	13.63	-3.07	17.18	6.49	7.34	7.77	61.	Bénéfices après impôt
62. Staff costs	36.39	35.89	34.76	32.56	31.89	31.45	29.82	29.47	29.76	28.01	62.	Frais de personnel
% of net income												**% du total du résultat net**
63. Provisions (net)	34.77	39.89	44.94	41.99	46.76	99.65	31.50	65.36	65.66	64.86	63.	Provisions (nettes)
64. Profit before tax	65.23	60.11	55.06	58.01	53.24	0.35	68.50	34.64	34.34	35.14	64.	Bénéfices avant impôt
65. Income tax	14.67	15.32	14.85	14.80	12.84	9.82	19.37	15.79	11.79	11.41	65.	Impôt
66. Profit after tax	50.56	44.79	40.21	43.21	40.41	-9.47	49.14	18.85	22.55	23.74	66.	Bénéfices après impôt

UNITED STATES

Large commercial banks

ETATS-UNIS

Grandes banques commerciales

Per cent / *Pourcentage*

BALANCE SHEET ANALYSIS / ANALYSE DU BILAN

% of year-end balance sheet total / **% du total du bilan en fin d'exercice**

		1982	1983	1984	1985	1986	1987	1988	1989	1990	1991	
	Assets											**Actif**
67.	Cash & balance with Central bank	6.32	6.70	6.71	6.93	7.28	6.08	6.27	6.20	6.11	5.49	Caisse & solde auprès de la Banque centrale
68.	Interbank deposits	11.20	10.00	7.94	7.25	7.07	7.32	6.39	5.73	4.34	4.45	Dépôts interbancaires
69.	Loans	61.49	61.66	65.91	65.16	64.60	64.63	65.39	65.96	65.93	63.50	Prêts
70.	Securities	11.80	12.75	11.22	13.43	14.59	15.12	14.97	15.37	16.26	19.19	Valeurs mobilières
71.	Other assets	9.19	8.89	8.21	7.22	6.46	6.84	6.99	6.74	7.37	7.36	Autres actifs
	Liabilities											**Passif**
72.	Capital & reserves	4.72	4.97	5.24	5.35	5.51	5.18	5.58	5.43	5.73	6.11	Capital et réserves
73.	Borrowing from Central bank	..	..	..	..	..	..	..	..	..	..	Emprunts auprès de la Banque centrale
74.	Interbank deposits	13.68	12.02	9.80	8.75	8.00	7.83	6.42	5.99	4.96	5.45	Dépôts interbancaires
75.	Non-bank deposits	59.37	61.86	63.47	63.71	64.54	65.51	66.93	67.03	69.39	68.99	Dépôts non bancaires
76.	Bonds	0.51	0.47	0.66	0.86	0.89	0.88	0.85	0.87	1.04	1.07	Obligations
77.	Other liabilities	21.72	20.68	20.84	21.33	21.06	20.60	20.21	20.68	18.88	18.37	Autres engagements
	Memoranda											***Pour mémoire***
78.	Short-term securities	..	..	..	..	..	..	..	..	..	..	Titres à court terme
79.	Bonds	..	..	..	..	..	..	..	..	..	..	Obligations
80.	Shares and participations	..	..	..	..	..	..	..	..	..	..	Actions et participations
81.	Claims on non-residents	..	..	..	..	..	..	..	..	..	..	Créances sur des non résidents
82.	Liabilities to non-residents	..	..	..	..	..	..	..	..	..	..	Engagements envers des non résidents

Notes

- The term Large commercial banks corresponds to the term Large insured commercial banks used in United States publications.
- Large commercial banks are a sub-group of Commercial banks and include institutions with total assets of US$ 1000 million or more.

Notes

- Le terme Grandes banques commerciales correspond à la rubrique Grandes banques commerciales assurées des publications américaines.
- Les Grandes banques commerciales, qui sont un sous-groupe des Banques commerciales, sont les banques dont le total du bilan atteint ou dépasse $US 1000 million.

UNITED STATES

Mutual savings banks

Million US dollars

	1982	1983	1984	1985	1986	1987	1988	1989	1990	1991
INCOME STATEMENT										
1. Interest income	13563	14586	12619	14220	15910	18005	20056	22085	21014	17426
2. Interest expenses	14198	13399	11129	11118	11007	12118	14018	16168	15265	11737
3. Net interest income	-635	1187	1490	3102	4903	5887	6038	5917	5749	5689
4. Non-interest income (net)	1766	1458	1025	1374	1545	1280	1288	1450	1200	1425
5. Gross income	1131	2645	2515	4476	6448	7167	7326	7367	6949	7114
6. Operating expenses	2352	2522	2172	2630	3432	4195	4768	5222	5574	5239
7. Net income	-1221	123	343	1846	3016	2972	2558	2145	1375	1875
8. Provisions (net)	39	51	68	180	265	361	624	1925	2787	1985
9. Profit before tax	-1260	72	275	1666	2751	2611	1934	220	-1412	-110
10. Income tax	-25	120	134	457	1025	1054	903	450	189	424
11. Profit after tax	-1235	-48	141	1209	1726	1557	1031	-230	-1601	-534
12. Distributed profit	NA	NA	NA	NA	50	211	339	494	353	307
13. Retained profit (1)	NA	NA	NA	NA	1676	1346	692	-724	-1954	-841
Memoranda										
14. Staff costs	*1032*	*1145*	*1001*	*1231*	*1539*	*1885*	*2081*	*2171*	*2193*	*1983*
15. Provisions on loans	*39*	*51*	*68*	*180*	*265*	*361*	*624*	*1925*	*2787*	*1985*
16. Provisions on securities	*..*	*..*	*..*	*..*	*..*	*..*	*..*	*..*	*..*	*..*
BALANCE SHEET										
Assets										
17. Cash & balance with Central bank	6000	5634	4089	4665	6666	6334	7537	5939	5418	5330
18. Interbank deposits	..	..	..	..	..	..	..	..	..	..
19. Loans	99283	103564	84966	101041	116017	140616	161359	166242	154429	138274
20. Securities	42722	53515	40403	42469	47310	53488	50048	48967	46982	48181
21. Other assets	7323	8069	6043	7588	8019	10157	11518	12455	14349	12882
Liabilities										
22. Capital & reserves	7430	8244	7004	9378	13871	16339	17489	17200	15275	14564
23. Borrowing from Central bank	..	..	..	..	..	..	..	..	..	..
24. Interbank deposits	..	..	..	..	..	..	..	..	..	..
25. Non-bank deposits	139463	153785	121559	137317	148251	168329	182795	188592	182191	173557
26. Bonds	576	593	476	647	844	906	927	668	627	420
27. Other liabilities	7859	8160	6462	8421	15046	25021	29251	27143	23086	16127
Balance sheet total										
28. End-year total	155328	170782	135501	155763	178012	210595	230462	233603	221179	204667
29. Average total	155476	163055	153142	145632	166888	194304	220529	232033	227391	212923
Memoranda										
30. Short-term securities	*3681*	*5104*	*5403*	*7004*	*..*	*..*	*..*	*..*	*..*	*..*
31. Bonds	*..*	*..*	*..*	*..*	*..*	*..*	*..*	*..*	*..*	*..*
32. Shares and participations	*..*	*..*	*..*	*..*	*..*	*..*	*..*	*..*	*..*	*..*
33. Claims on non-residents	*..*	*..*	*..*	*..*	*..*	*..*	*..*	*..*	*..*	*..*
34. Liabilities to non-residents	*..*	*..*	*..*	*..*	*..*	*..*	*..*	*..*	*..*	*..*
SUPPLEMENTARY INFORMATION										
35. Number of institutions	315	294	267	343	359	371	375	374	356	338
36. Number of branches	NA	NA	NA	NA	NA	NA	NA	NA	NA	NA
37. Number of employees (x 1000)	NA	NA	NA	NA	NA	NA	NA	NA	NA	NA

ETATS-UNIS

Caisses d'épargne mutuelles

Millions de dollars des EU

COMPTE DE RESULTATS
1. Produits financiers
2. Frais financiers
3. Produits financiers nets
4. Produits non financiers (nets)
5. Résultat brut
6. Frais d'exploitation
7. Résultat net
8. Provisions (nettes)
9. Bénéfices avant impôt
10. Impôt
11. Bénéfices après impôt
12. Bénéfices distribués
13. Bénéfices mis en réserve (1)

Pour mémoire
14. Frais de personnel
15. Provisions sur prêts
16. Provisions sur titres

BILAN

Actif
17. Caisse & solde auprès de la Banque centrale
18. Dépôts interbancaires
19. Prêts
20. Valeurs mobilières
21. Autres actifs

Passif
22. Capital et réserves
23. Emprunts auprès de la Banque centrale
24. Dépôts interbancaires
25. Dépôts non bancaires
26. Obligations
27. Autres engagements

Total du bilan
28. En fin d'exercice
29. Moyen

Pour mémoire
30. Titres à court terme
31. Obligations
32. Actions et participations
33. Créances sur des non résidents
34. Engagements envers des non résidents

RENSEIGNEMENTS COMPLEMENTAIRES
35. Nombre d'institutions
36. Nombre de succursales
37. Nombre de salariés (x 1000)

UNITED STATES
Mutual savings banks

ETATS-UNIS
Caisses d'épargne mutuelles

Per cent — *Pourcentage*

	1982	1983	1984	1985	1986	1987	1988	1989	1990	1991		
INCOME STATEMENT ANALYSIS												**ANALYSE DU COMPTE DE RESULTATS**
% of average balance sheet total												**% du total moyen du bilan**
38. Interest income	8.72	8.95	8.24	9.76	9.53	9.27	9.09	9.52	9.24	8.18	38.	Produits financiers
39. Interest expenses	9.13	8.22	7.27	7.63	6.60	6.24	6.36	6.97	6.71	5.51	39.	Frais financiers
40. Net interest income	-0.41	0.73	0.97	2.13	2.94	3.03	2.74	2.55	2.53	2.67	40.	Produits financiers nets
41. Non-interest income (net)	1.14	0.89	0.67	0.94	0.93	0.66	0.58	0.62	0.53	0.67	41.	Produits non financiers (nets)
42. Gross income	0.73	1.62	1.64	3.07	3.86	3.69	3.32	3.17	3.06	3.34	42.	Résultat brut
43. Operating expenses	1.51	1.55	1.42	1.81	2.06	2.16	2.16	2.25	2.45	2.46	43.	Frais d'exploitation
44. Net income	-0.79	0.08	0.22	1.27	1.81	1.53	1.16	0.92	0.60	0.88	44.	Résultat net
45. Provisions (net)	0.03	0.03	0.04	0.12	0.16	0.19	0.28	0.83	1.23	0.93	45.	Provisions (nettes)
46. Profit before tax	-0.81	0.04	0.18	1.14	1.65	1.34	0.88	0.09	-0.62	-0.05	46.	Bénéfices avant impôt
47. Income tax	-0.02	0.07	0.09	0.31	0.61	0.54	0.41	0.19	0.08	0.20	47.	Impôt
48. Profit after tax	-0.79	-0.03	0.09	0.83	1.03	0.80	0.47	-0.10	-0.70	-0.25	48.	Bénéfices après impôt
49. Distributed profit	NA	NA	NA	NA	0.03	0.11	0.15	0.21	0.16	0.14	49.	Bénéfices distribués
50. Retained profit (1)	NA	NA	NA	NA	1.00	0.69	0.31	-0.31	-0.86	-0.39	50.	Bénéfices mis en réserve (1)
51. Staff costs	0.66	0.70	0.65	0.85	0.92	0.97	0.94	0.94	0.96	0.93	51.	Frais de personnel
52. Provisions on loans	0.03	0.03	0.04	0.12	0.16	0.19	0.28	0.83	1.23	0.93	52.	Provisions sur prêts
53. Provisions on securities	:	:	:	:	:	:	:	:	:	:	53.	Provisions sur titres
% of gross income												**% du total du résultat brut**
54. Net interest income	-56.15	44.88	59.24	69.30	76.04	82.14	82.42	80.32	82.73	79.97	54.	Produits financiers nets
55. Non-interest income (net)	156.15	55.12	40.76	30.70	23.96	17.86	17.58	19.68	17.27	20.03	55.	Produits non financiers (nets)
56. Operating expenses	207.96	95.35	86.36	58.76	53.23	58.53	65.08	70.88	80.21	73.64	56.	Frais d'exploitation
57. Net income	-107.96	4.65	13.64	41.24	46.77	41.47	34.92	29.12	19.79	26.36	57.	Résultat net
58. Provisions (net)	3.45	1.93	2.70	4.02	4.11	5.04	8.52	26.13	40.11	27.90	58.	Provisions (nettes)
59. Profit before tax	-111.41	2.72	10.93	37.22	42.66	36.43	26.40	2.99	-20.32	-1.55	59.	Bénéfices avant impôt
60. Income tax	-2.21	4.54	5.33	10.21	15.90	14.71	12.33	6.11	2.72	5.96	60.	Impôt
61. Profit after tax	-109.20	-1.81	5.61	27.01	26.77	21.72	14.07	-3.12	-23.04	-7.51	61.	Bénéfices après impôt
62. Staff costs	91.25	43.29	39.80	27.50	23.87	26.30	28.41	29.47	31.56	27.87	62.	Frais de personnel
% of net income												**% du total du résultat net**
63. Provisions (net)	-3.19	41.46	19.83	9.75	8.79	12.15	24.39	89.74	202.69	105.87	63.	Provisions (nettes)
64. Profit before tax	103.19	58.54	80.17	90.25	91.21	87.85	75.61	10.26	-102.69	-5.87	64.	Bénéfices avant impôt
65. Income tax	2.05	97.56	39.07	24.76	33.99	35.46	35.30	20.98	13.75	22.61	65.	Impôt
66. Profit after tax	101.15	-39.02	41.11	65.49	57.23	52.39	40.30	-10.72	-116.44	-28.48	66.	Bénéfices après impôt

UNITED STATES
Mutual savings banks

Per cent

BALANCE SHEET ANALYSIS

% of year-end balance sheet total

	1982	1983	1984	1985	1986	1987	1988	1989	1990	1991
Assets										
67. Cash & balance with Central bank	..	..	..	..	..	..	..	..	..	..
68. Interbank deposits	3.86	3.30	3.02	2.99	3.74	3.01	3.27	2.54	2.45	2.60
69. Loans	63.92	60.64	62.71	64.87	65.17	66.77	70.02	71.16	69.82	67.56
70. Securities	27.50	31.34	29.82	27.27	26.58	25.40	21.72	20.96	21.24	23.54
71. Other assets	4.71	4.72	4.46	4.87	4.50	4.82	5.00	5.33	6.49	6.29
Liabilities										
72. Capital & reserves	4.78	4.83	5.17	6.02	7.79	7.76	7.59	7.36	6.91	7.12
73. Borrowing from Central bank	..	..	..	..	..	..	..	..	..	..
74. Interbank deposits	..	..	..	..	..	..	..	..	..	..
75. Non-bank deposits	89.79	90.05	89.71	88.16	83.28	79.93	79.32	80.73	82.37	84.80
76. Bonds	0.37	0.35	0.35	0.42	0.47	0.43	0.40	0.29	0.28	0.21
77. Other liabilities	5.06	4.78	4.77	5.41	8.45	11.88	12.69	11.62	10.44	7.88
Memoranda										
78. Short-term securities	2.37	2.99	3.99	4.50	..	..	..	..	..	..
79. Bonds	..	..	..	..	..	..	..	..	..	..
80. Shares and participations	..	..	..	..	..	..	..	..	..	..
81. Claims on non-residents	..	..	..	..	..	..	..	..	..	..
82. Liabilities to non-residents	..	..	..	..	..	..	..	..	..	..

1. Exclusive of dividend payouts.

ETATS-UNIS
Caisses d'épargne mutuelles

Pourcentage

ANALYSE DU BILAN

% du total du bilan en fin d'exercice

Actif
67. Caisse & solde auprès de la Banque centrale
68. Dépôts interbancaires
69. Prêts
70. Valeurs mobilières
71. Autres actifs

Passif
72. Capital et réserves
73. Emprunts auprès de la Banque centrale
74. Dépôts interbancaires
75. Dépôts non bancaires
76. Obligations
77. Autres engagements

Pour mémoire
78. Titres à court terme
79. Obligations
80. Actions et participations
81. Créances sur des non résidents
82. Engagements envers des non résidents

1. A l'exclusion des dividendes payés.

MAIN SALES OUTLETS OF OECD PUBLICATIONS
PRINCIPAUX POINTS DE VENTE DES PUBLICATIONS DE L'OCDE

ARGENTINA – ARGENTINE
Carlos Hirsch S.R.L.
Galería Güemes, Florida 165, 4° Piso
1333 Buenos Aires   Tel. (1) 331.1787 y 331.2391
Telefax: (1) 331.1787

AUSTRALIA – AUSTRALIE
D.A. Information Services
648 Whitehorse Road, P.O.B 163
Mitcham, Victoria 3132   Tel. (03) 873.4411
Telefax: (03) 873.5679

AUSTRIA – AUTRICHE
Gerold & Co.
Graben 31
Wien I   Tel. (0222) 533.50.14

BELGIUM – BELGIQUE
Jean De Lannoy
Avenue du Roi 202
B-1060 Bruxelles   Tel. (02) 538.51.69/538.08.41
Telefax: (02) 538.08.41

CANADA
Renouf Publishing Company Ltd.
1294 Algoma Road
Ottawa, ON K1B 3W8   Tel. (613) 741.4333
Telefax: (613) 741.5439
Stores:
61 Sparks Street
Ottawa, ON K1P 5R1   Tel. (613) 238.8985
211 Yonge Street
Toronto, ON M5B 1M4   Tel. (416) 363.3171

Les Éditions La Liberté Inc.
3020 Chemin Sainte-Foy
Sainte-Foy, PQ G1X 3V6   Tel. (418) 658.3763
Telefax: (418) 658.3763

Federal Publications
165 University Avenue
Toronto, ON M5H 3B8   Tel. (416) 581.1552
Telefax: (416) 581.1743

Les Publications Fédérales
1185 Avenue de l'Université
Montréal, PQ H3B 3A7   Tel. (514) 954.1633
Telefax : (514) 954.1633

CHINA – CHINE
China National Publications Import
Export Corporation (CNPIEC)
16 Gongti E. Road, Chaoyang District
P.O. Box 88 or 50
Beijing 100704 PR   Tel. (01) 506.6688
Telefax: (01) 506.3101

DENMARK – DANEMARK
Munksgaard Export and Subscription Service
35, Nørre Søgade, P.O. Box 2148
DK-1016 København K   Tel. (33) 12.85.70
Telefax: (33) 12.93.87

FINLAND – FINLANDE
Akateeminen Kirjakauppa
Keskuskatu 1, P.O. Box 128
00100 Helsinki   Tel. (358 0) 12141
Telefax: (358 0) 121.4441

FRANCE
OECD/OCDE
Mail Orders/Commandes par correspondance:
2, rue André-Pascal
75775 Paris Cedex 16   Tel. (33-1) 45.24.82.00
Telefax: (33-1) 45.24.81.76   or (33-1) 45.24.85.00
Telex: 640048 OCDE

OECD Bookshop/Librairie de l'OCDE :
33, rue Octave-Feuillet
75016 Paris   Tel. (33-1) 45.24.81.67
(33-1) 45.24.81.81

Documentation Française
29, quai Voltaire
75007 Paris   Tel. 40.15.70.00
Gibert Jeune (Droit-Économie)
6, place Saint-Michel
75006 Paris   Tel. 43.25.91.19
Librairie du Commerce International
10, avenue d'Iéna
75016 Paris   Tel. 40.73.34.60
Librairie Dunod
Université Paris-Dauphine
Place du Maréchal de Lattre de Tassigny
75016 Paris   Tel. 47.27.18.56
Librairie Lavoisier
11, rue Lavoisier
75008 Paris   Tel. 42.65.39.95
Librairie L.G.D.J. - Montchrestien
20, rue Soufflot
75005 Paris   Tel. 46.33.89.85
Librairie des Sciences Politiques
30, rue Saint-Guillaume
75007 Paris   Tel. 45.48.36.02
P.U.F.
49, boulevard Saint-Michel
75005 Paris   Tel. 43.25.83.40
Librairie de l'Université
12a, rue Nazareth
13100 Aix-en-Provence   Tel. (16) 42.26.18.08
Documentation Française
165, rue Garibaldi
69003 Lyon   Tel. (16) 78.63.32.23
Librairie Decitre
29, place Bellecour
69002 Lyon   Tel. (16) 72.40.54.54

GERMANY – ALLEMAGNE
OECD Publications and Information Centre
August-Bebel-Allee 6
D-W 5300 Bonn 2   Tel. (0228) 959.120
Telefax: (0228) 959.12.17

GREECE – GRÈCE
Librairie Kauffmann
Mavrokordatou 9
106 78 Athens   Tel. 322.21.60
Telefax: 363.39.67

HONG-KONG
Swindon Book Co. Ltd.
13–15 Lock Road
Kowloon, Hong Kong   Tel. 366.80.31
Telefax: 739.49.75

HUNGARY – HONGRIE
Euro Info Service
kázmér u.45
1121 Budapest   Tel. (1) 182.00.44
Telefax : (1) 182.00.44

ICELAND – ISLANDE
Mál Mog Menning
Laugavegi 18, Pósthólf 392
121 Reykjavik   Tel. 162.35.23

INDIA – INDE
Oxford Book and Stationery Co.
Scindia House
New Delhi 110001   Tel.(11) 331.5896/5308
Telefax: (11) 332.5993
17 Park Street
Calcutta 700016   Tel. 240832

INDONESIA – INDONÉSIE
Pdii-Lipi
P.O. Box 269/JKSMG/88
Jakarta 12790   Tel. 583467
Telex: 62 875

IRELAND – IRLANDE
TDC Publishers – Library Suppliers
12 North Frederick Street
Dublin 1   Tel. 74.48.35/74.96.77
Telefax: 74.84.16

ISRAEL
Electronic Publications only
Publications électroniques seulement
Sophist Systems Ltd.
71 Allenby Street
Tel-Aviv 65134   Tel. 3-29.00.21
Telefax: 3-29.92.39

ITALY – ITALIE
Libreria Commissionaria Sansoni
Via Duca di Calabria 1/1
50125 Firenze   Tel. (055) 64.54.15
Telefax: (055) 64.12.57
Via Bartolini 29
20155 Milano   Tel. (02) 36.50.83
Editrice e Libreria Herder
Piazza Montecitorio 120
00186 Roma   Tel. 679.46.28
Telefax: 678.47.51
Libreria Hoepli
Via Hoepli 5
20121 Milano   Tel. (02) 86.54.46
Telefax: (02) 805.28.86
Libreria Scientifica
Dott. Lucio de Biasio 'Aeiou'
Via Coronelli, 6
20146 Milano   Tel. (02) 48.95.45.52
Telefax: (02) 48.95.45.48

JAPAN – JAPON
OECD Publications and Information Centre
Landic Akasaka Building
2-3-4 Akasaka, Minato-ku
Tokyo 107   Tel. (81.3) 3586.2016
Telefax: (81.3) 3584.7929

KOREA – CORÉE
Kyobo Book Centre Co. Ltd.
P.O. Box 1658, Kwang Hwa Moon
Seoul   Tel. 730.78.91
Telefax: 735.00.30

MALAYSIA – MALAISIE
Co-operative Bookshop Ltd.
University of Malaya
P.O. Box 1127, Jalan Pantai Baru
59700 Kuala Lumpur
Malaysia   Tel. 756.5000/756.5425
Telefax: 757.3661

MEXICO – MEXIQUE
Revistas y Periodicos Internacionales S.A. de C.V.
Florencia 57 - 1004
Mexico, D.F. 06600   Tel. 207.81.00
Telefax : 208.39.79

NETHERLANDS – PAYS-BAS
SDU Uitgeverij
Christoffel Plantijnstraat 2
Postbus 20014
2500 EA's-Gravenhage   Tel. (070 3) 78.99.11
Voor bestellingen: Tel. (070 3) 78.98.80
Telefax: (070 3) 47.63.51

NEW ZEALAND
NOUVELLE-ZÉLANDE
Legislation Services
P.O. Box 12418
Thorndon, Wellington   Tel. (04) 496.5652
Telefax: (04) 496.5698

OECD PUBLICATIONS, 2 rue André-Pascal, 75775 PARIS CEDEX 16
PRINTED IN FRANCE
(21 93 01 3) ISBN 92-64-03719-5 - No. 46498 1993